# JUST
## A MOMENT

# GARRY FRICKER

JUST A MOMENT: A DAILY DEVOTIONAL
By Garry Fricker

© 2006 by Garry Fricker
All rights reserved

ISBN # 1-894928-69-5

Printed by Word Alive Press

WORD ALIVE PRESS

# FOREWORD

We are living in an age of constant technical advancements. Each new discovery is intended to give us more "free" time to relax and "smell the roses." However, we are finding it increasingly more difficult to do the things that we really want to do. *Just A Moment* is intended to give us all a few minutes of Biblical preparation for each day as well as to present a challenge to grow in our confidence and trust in an Awesome God.

*Just A Moment* is a compilation of editorial portions that were used for my church bulletin over a number of years. They were designed to coincide with the sermon of the day to put into writing some of the things that were being said from the pulpit. I trust that you will discover these to be a life-strengthening resource for your daily experience. Some of the articles also summarize experiences that many Pastors encounter in the course of ministry in a needy world. I have had the opportunity to be a part of what God has been doing in the wonderful country of Argentina as well as serving in Pastoral ministry in Canada. Forty-three years of serving the Lord has unquestionably left a great impression upon my own life. I trust that this is obvious through many of the daily readings. God has been good to us in providing for our needs, in granting us guidance and wisdom for a variety of experiences, in providing health and strength and in giving us the privilege of being His representatives in various parts of the World. No question about it... God is good!

Thanks to all who had a part in supporting our ministry and at times "enduring" these sermons that were designed to teach, encourage, sometimes reprove and always to be what the Lord wanted to say.

Let your heart be blessed as you peruse the passages and the themes each day. May you also find the spiritual food that the Word of God was designed to give to those who would hunger and thirst after righteousness.

~**Rev. Garry Fricker**

# CONTENTS

▌ **HAPPY NEW YEAR**

*"The prayer of a righteous man is powerful and effective."*

~James 5:16b

Although time flows continuously like a river, our calendars indicate breaks that suggest new periods in time. We have entered a New Year. What lies behind us, with all the lessons we have learned by experience, we call history. What lies before us, with all the potential and possibilities of our greatest dreams, we call opportunity and that is one of the good things about a New Year.

We distinguish the line clearly between the Old and the New. We can't change the past with its failures and disappointments or its victories and successes, and so we must leave it behind and press on to a brand new day that has never been used before. God's grace will cover our weak points when we ask Him, and we should be grateful for the blessings that He has shared with us already.

I believe that God has great things in store for each New Year. There are many promises that He has made that fit our changing times. One that I receive today, I pass on to you. "...I have placed before you an open door that no one can shut" (Revelation 3:8a). God is the door opener. The old Television program, "Let's Make A Deal" used to offer contestants three doors of opportunity. They could choose whichever they thought was best. Some found riches and others a wheelbarrow with a shovel. But God chooses the door for our lives. To each of us He has promised to be near and to guide us under His blessing as we trust in Him. We need to be confident that He does all things well and that He will be there, whatever the situation may be.

We want God's best in the coming year for every challenge and opportunity. But there is a very important principle that we need to remember. "If my people, who are called by my name, will humble themselves and pray and seek my face and turn from their wicked ways, then will I hear from heaven and will forgive their sin and will heal their land" (2 Chronicles 7:14). You can make a personal investment in the spiritual welfare of your family, your church and your nation from knee level. We have a brand new year to enjoy God's promises, but we will only be rewarded for what we put into it and the best way to begin with God is through prayer. We want His direction and blessing for our lives. We are getting close to the end of all things and I believe that it is really important that we be involved in seeking the Lord, together. Many churches have a special prayer focus at the beginning of a New Year. Be a part of the prayer emphasis to seek the Lord's blessing upon yourself, the Church and the Nation. God bless you.

"The prayer of a righteous man is powerful and effective" (James 5:16b).

Prayer changes things.

1

▌ **YEAR END/BEGINNING**

*"Finally, be strong in the Lord and in His mighty power."*

~Ephesians 6:10

It's a brand new page; a brand new calendar; a brand New Year! When everything else seems to be the same, it is refreshing to enter into a New Year with a sense of newness that comes with the celebrations of family and friends. It's like sitting in a brand new car. The aroma and cleanness of it all leads to visions of potential and possibility that new opportunities will bring.

Consider the Children of Israel as they stood on the banks of the Jordan River and viewed, before them, the Promised Land. Behind them lay the Wilderness and the desert wanderings. Behind them were the conflicts and miracles that led a fledgling nation into becoming a dynamic force for God. Before them, like the New Year before us, lay the promises of God. This was the Promised Land. It belonged to the Children of God. No question, there would be problems and difficulties ahead just like in the past. The enemy would do His best to hinder and destroy the advance of God's people into His will, but God has promised that, "No one will be able to stand up against you, all the days of your life. As I was with Moses, so I will be with you; I will never leave you nor forsake you." (Joshua 1:5b)

Let this be your motto in the coming days. It is time that the family of God arose to the reality of the victory that is ours because of His promises. The past has become history but it is not intended to be an anchor that holds us back from advancing in our spiritual growth with God and the fulfillment of His plan for our lives. We are called to be more that conquerors through Jesus Christ. There is a battle to be waged. Please don't think that because you are His that all the problems will go away. Let me suggest a couple of things that will help 'us' for what lies ahead:

1. *Be prayerful!* There is nothing more important in your Christian walk than that you communicate with your Leader. He needs to know that you are prepared to take time to hear what He has to say about your life and what He has in store for you. He wants to hear you express, personally, your needs for each day.

2. *Keep yourself clean!* I mean, on the inside. Don't allow the enemy any opportunity to plug into things we do that are not pleasing to God. Examine yourself from time to time and allow the Holy Spirit to show you things that need repair or forgiveness.

3. *Get involved in areas that you can serve the Lord.* Check out the opportunities that God brings your way and volunteer. If you need help in this area, talk to your Pastor or another mature Christian for guidance.

There is so much to do for the advancement of His Kingdom on earth. Every person is important because He has given each of us special talents to serve Him in a special way.

Happy New Year!

2

▮ **THE END OF ANOTHER YEAR**

*"When I am afraid, I will trust in you."*

~Psalm 56:3

We've come to the end of another year. We have cultivated experiences, habits and memories, throughout the last year that didn't disappear at the sound of the midnight bells and whistles. We've discovered that not everything that happens in life makes us feel good. We, along with some of our family and friends, have gone through some absolutely horrible things this past year that we hope we will never have to repeat. To some, the advantage of seeing with hindsight allows us to rejoice that God was there all the time and that we made it through the deep waters. Now we can laugh. To others, the problems have just not gone away. Let me assure you of two very important things that every Christian needs to know.

1. *God cares!* I can say this with absolute confidence born out of experience and founded in the Word of God. The promise of His Word is plain: "Cast all your anxiety on Him because He cares for you" (1 Peter 5:7). It is true that the problems may not go away immediately but the fact remains that God will never leave you nor forsake you as long as you trust in Him. Be patient. Be persistent in prayer. Be joyful. But in everything, do not lose your confidence that God will see you through. He is Faithful. He is able to give you a calm assurance that you are not alone. The fact of the cross of Calvary should serve to remind us that 'Someone' went through a tremendously frightful and forsaken experience to demonstrate the length of His willingness to carry upon Himself the things that cause us distress. He has promised to be with you.

2. *God's Church cares!* Those that worship with you are a part of your spiritual family. They may not understand exactly how you are feeling under the pressures that you are experiencing, but they are there to support you. Find someone you can relate to and sit down with them and bare your heart. You'll find that most people are willing to be a listening ear and a helping hand. Some may even give you more advice than you want to hear, but listen; there are people who care. If we only believed that, we would not feel like we were intruding on the privacy of anyone else. At the same time we need to be available to share in some of the tragedies of life that aren't necessarily of our own making. There are people that need to know what it means to be a part of the Church, the greatest project of the plan of God.

In another 360+ days we'll come to another time of review and we'll laugh together. Until then, keep trusting in the wisdom of God.

| **HUMILITY**

*"Blessed are the meek, for they will inherit the earth."*

~Matthew 5:5

Jesus often used illustrations to give impact to the truths He was teaching. There were lilies of the field, birds of the air, foxes of the fields, yeast in the kitchen, sunsets, mustard seeds, weeds in the grain, a lost sheep, marauding wolves, rain, rock and sand. Each reference drove home the teaching that Jesus was giving. I think it's interesting that when Jesus wanted to teach on the dynamics of humility His example was a little child:

"Therefore, whoever humbles himself like this child is the greatest in the kingdom of heaven" (Matthew 18:4).

As far as Jesus was concerned, the humble attitude of the child put him or her in the same category as Moses: "Now Moses was a very humble man, more humble than anyone else on the face of the earth" (Numbers 12:3).

In the illustration of Jesus it was the little child who would have a sure heavenly reward. In the story of Moses, God demonstrated that He would judge anyone who stood against His humble servant. God would be the Mediator and the Judge. Meekness is not weakness. "In honour preferring one another..." is a good way to please God, because in the 'giving in' process God always adds more to us in return. As far as God is concerned, being meek and humble is an attribute that pleases Him.

One of the reasons that the Children of Israel were kept wandering in the wilderness was to learn the lessons of humility. "Remember how the Lord your God led you all the way in the desert these forty years, to humble you and to test you..." (Deuteronomy 8:2) It took them forty years to learn their lessons. That's more time than it takes to get a doctoral degree! But then again, maybe it was like the little boy who spent three years in grade three before he was allowed to move on to grade four. He had a hard time learning his lessons so it was back to the old stuff again and again.

Learning how to surrender when you know you're right has got to be one of the hardest lessons in the world. To let someone else be first when you've been waiting so long is tough, but patience and a longsuffering attitude are attributes of a humble heart that are pleasing to the Lord. We all want to excel but God wants us to learn to be submissive and sensitive to the needs of others.

4

▍ **WATER BAPTISM**

*"If we have been united with Him like this in his death,*
*we will certainly also be united with Him in His resurrection."*

~Romans 6:5

Water Baptism was practiced in Old Testament times as an act of Dedication and Commitment to the Lord. It came to special prominence throughout the ministry of the prophet, John the Baptist. He was a preacher of righteousness who called the people to repentance in preparation for the coming of the Messiah. His ministry grew in popularity, not because he did any miracles, nor because of the way he dressed, nor because of his classy diet, but because he called people back to God. The act of Baptism, to him, was the outward sign of the sincere rejection of sin and a commitment of the heart to serving God in a brand new way. He didn't mince words when he addressed his wandering congregation. It was always a clear message of condemnation against the things that drew people away from God. He was not content with a show of hands for those who wanted to repent. He instructed about the necessity of letting others know about their decision by taking a step of faith into the waters of baptism. The process signified death to the old way of life and rising to serve God in a new beginning that the Lord extends to all people who come to Him.

Jesus was one of his baptismal candidates. John understood the fact that the One who stood before Him to be baptized was far greater than he was, and that he was not worthy to serve the Lord this way. Jesus made a statement that down through the ages has reminded us that, "...it is proper for us to do this to fulfill all righteousness" (Matthew 3:15). In my own translation, Jesus was saying, "Let's do things right." Although Jesus had no sin to repent of, His act demonstrated what every person who ever wants to serve the Lord ought to do. So much so, that before He ascended into heaven He instructed His disciples to, "...go and make disciples of all nations, *baptizing* them in the name of the Father and of the Son and of the Holy Spirit" (Matthew 28:19). Rather than doing away with an Old Testament ceremony, He insisted that all believers who sincerely commit themselves to the Lord should continue it. Is there another option?

As far as I can understand in scripture the procedure should always be:

1. Repent of your sins by trusting in Jesus Christ as your Saviour.

2. Follow the Lord's example by being baptized as an outward testimony of your inward experience.

Jesus always called people to take steps of faith as a witness of their trust and confidence in Him. "Come," "Arise," "Go," "Do," "Stretch out your hand," etc. were statements that Jesus often made to people who wanted something from Him or had received something from Him. Water Baptism is one of those requirements that Jesus makes of all those who believe in Him. If you have not been baptized in water, it's time that you gave serious consideration to obeying the Lord's command.

5

▌ **SIGNS OF THE TIMES**

*"There will be terrible (exceeding fierce) times in the last days."*

~2 Timothy 3:1b

I think that every mother and father who took their little boys and girls to school on Wednesday April 21, 1999 was thinking of the holocaust of Littleton, Colorado. The tragedy of the events threw a nation into shock. The thoughtless brutality that launched so much pain into the world is almost unbelievable. Our hearts go out to those who lived through those terrible events and especially to the parents of the young people who lost their lives.

Then we look across the sea to other continents where warring nations and uncivilized tribal warfare shed innocent blood in selfish aggression. In a recent African war zone 100,000 young men disappeared, simply taken from their homes and workplaces. Their crime? They *could have become* soldiers that would fight in the opposing army. Mothers, wives and girlfriends mourn together as they await final notice of their loved ones.

There is despair everywhere. It's like the devil knows that his time is short and he's getting one last kick at the can. He is described as 'a roaring lion seeking whom he may devour.' He is revealed as a wolf out to destroy the flock. There is nothing nice about him. Even the things inspired by him that bring us excitement and pleasure have very serious consequences. His greatest joy is to rob, kill and destroy. Don't be fooled into thinking that it's fun to toy around with anything related to the kingdom of darkness. He's an eternal terrorist. He's not hanging around for any other reason than to lash out in violent anger at God's creation. He may try to disguise himself in ways that hide his intentions, but don't be deceived—there is nothing good about him. He is violence, hatred, lust and murder all wrapped together in his wicked nature.

But remember this, "Greater is He (Jesus) that is in you, than he (Satan) that is in the world" (1 John 4:4 KJV). The power of the name of Jesus and the Word of God are still available for every child of God. Perhaps the most dreaded weapon that the devil fears is to see a humble believer on his knees, for God hears the cry of our hearts. Our Lord has stopped the mouths of lions before and has made the enemy giants fall. And He will do it again. He is our protection in times of trouble. He cares and answers prayer.

The Bible reminds us that when we see these things coming to pass that we should lift up our heads because our Redeemer is coming back again. These are signs of the times. That does not relieve us of our responsibility to intercede on the behalf of those who struggle, while at the same time taking a strong stand of commitment to serve God in these days when people are expecting a compromise of standards. It's time to seek the Lord.

█ **NEVER FORSAKEN**

*"Last night an angel of the God whose I am and whom I serve
stood beside me and said, 'Do not be afraid...'"*

~Acts 27:23

David was caught. The enemy was all around him and he had no way to escape. It was a sure death situation and no one was there to show him any compassion. His own people had turned on him after years of committed service to the king and his nation. David was in the hometown of Goliath and his brothers. Although he thought people wouldn't recognize him, the message was soon taken to the king of Gath that David was visiting their city. (1 Samuel 21:10) With the sword of Goliath strapped to his waist, he should have realized that it was a give-away. He thought he could get away from his friends by hiding with his enemies. Some chance!

But then, where do you go when no one seems to care or understand and everyone is quick to judge and condemn? Your friends are unfriendly and your enemies hate you. Well, to make a long story short, David played the fool as though he was some insane impersonator of the famed Warrior of Israel and he got himself out of a life-threatening situation. When he escaped and found a place to meditate over the happenings of the day, he wrote a psalm. Knowing where he was coming from, I can appreciate his emotions as he penned the words:

"I will extol the LORD at all times; his praise will always be on my lips." (Psalm 34:1)

What a guy! He remembered that the Lord had placed His hand upon him for some very important purposes. From the deepest point of his despair and utter loneliness he lifted his voice in praise to God who never fails; who is always there; who is mindful of our deepest distresses; who is available as our Helper, strength and protection.

Maybe you've never been in a jam that bad or rather, maybe you have. What an awesome peace the Lord can give you when you have only Him to fall back on. He has proven himself through the ages as the God who can resolve the impossible or give us the grace to see our way through the problems. Even when we don't gain the victory the way we think we should, He moves in to turn things around and make them work out right. "...and we know that in all things God works for the good of those who love him..." (Romans 8:28)

One thing that is very clear in the Bible is the fact that when we think we are alone, we are not alone. He has promised: "...Never will I leave you; never will I forsake you." (Hebrews 13:5) There may come times that you'll need to reach into the depths of your soul to believe this and then praise the Lord. Even though the circumstances don't change, God is still in control. The truth is, we will understand it better by and by. Meanwhile, *trust* God.

▌ **LIKE A LITTLE CHILD**

*"Some trust in chariots and some in horses,
but we trust in the name of the Lord our God."*

~Psalm 20:7

Jesus used many things as object lessons for His sermons. He spoke of yeast and its infiltrating powers; of the tiny mustard seed that grows to be a large tree. A coin became a lesson on the difference in values between the kingdom of heaven and Caesar's dominion on earth. He taught about laying good foundations on solid rock rather than shifting sand. He used salt, candles, foxes, birds, lilies, and sunsets each to convey a special message to the people He taught. But one day, He took a little child and with the attention of every mother, father, brother and sister focused on Him, He said: "I tell you the truth, unless you change and become like little children, you will never enter the kingdom of heaven" (Matthew 18:3).

Do I hear you say that you were "once" a child but you've passed that stage of life? After all, we argue, we have become mature adults and have put away all childish things. Maybe that's the reason for the major problems of our world. We've lost a basic trust and confidence in people. We believe that people have ulterior motives in their actions. We have become independent and self-sufficient and somehow we've lost the simplicity of trusting our heavenly Father for His supply for our need. We are educated and capable of working through our own problems; just give us time. We are strong enough to defend our rights. We've arrived at where we are by the sweat of our brow and our own ingenuity and we don't need anyone else to help us.

Hey, that's what Jesus wanted us to see—how far we have fallen from a total dependence on Him. We've lost sight of the Father and our need of His resources for the burdens and cares of life. Worse, we have arrived at "maturity" and don't need God. Society is the proof; most people believe they can make it to heaven on their own. But Jesus said that we needed to become like little children. Have you noticed the innocence and the trusting beauty of little children as they work and play, sing and talk? What simplicity!

Children teach us lessons like:

1. We need to humble ourselves and acknowledge that we need the help of our heavenly Father. He's waiting for us to call.

2. We can't get to heaven unless we come to the Father as trusting little children and commit our ways to Him.

3. There are times when we need to drop our guard and let those around us have access to what is happening in our lives.

4. But most importantly of all, we need to exercise simple faith and trust in our Heavenly Father who loves each of us as His own children.

Jesus said, "Let the little children come to me, and do not hinder them, for the kingdom of God belongs to such as these" (Matthew 19:14).

▌ **GOOD AND FAITHFUL STEWARD**

*"For by him all things were created: things in heaven and on earth,
visible and invisible, whether thrones or powers or rulers or authorities;
all things were created by him and for him."*

~Colossians 1:16

Who's running this world, anyway? I know that there is someone who is called "the god of this world" (2 Corinthians 4:4), who seems to have a lot of influence over the hearts and lives of people who live on planet earth, however, is he really considered the final authority on God's creation?

We are reminded, again and again, that he played a terrible trick on Adam and Eve in the garden of Eden that appears to have opened the door for him to continue his deception and to undermine our influence in creation. Let me advise you that Jesus Christ came into the world to set things straight. He came to demonstrate that Satan's power is a lot of bluff and blow. That he speaks with the 'noise' of a roaring lion and that he's dressed as an angel of light are facts that are confirmed by scripture. But he has no authority whatsoever over our lives because of Calvary, except in the areas that we surrender to him. So...*let's take control.*

It's time that we used the things of this world to glorify our Father in heaven. After all, the Lord has called us to serve Him by being wise stewards over His goods. Any time we have something in our control or influence that we do not convert to bringing glory to the Lord, that stuff remains under the control of the god of this world.

I need to recognize the areas of responsibility that God has committed to me to serve Him as a wise husband, father, neighbour and friend. I need to be godly and wise in my deeds and my example. What I consider as "my" time, "my" things, "my" business, "my" money—if it is not under the obedience and submission of His standards, it remains a part of "the kingdom of this world."

The truth is that Satan doesn't mind how much I prosper or possess, as long as I don't give any of it to God. That's what bugs him the most. He does not want any earthly thing to be used for the glory of God. He doesn't want to hear any credit for blessings given to God. He wants us to think that we have accomplished our own goals, and have beautiful homes and cars and other possessions simply by our own investments. He wants us to think that it makes God happy to see how well we've done without His help. So let me lay out a challenge. I call us to obedience of God's Word, to search for times of prayer, to give back to Him a tithe of all we receive, and to speak the witness of our faith to others who do not know Jesus Christ as we do. Satan is the god of this world only as long as he has subjects that choose to not obey the Lord, and the moment you submit to God's authority you upset the devils plans. Let's be people who live to please God with all our hearts.

9

█ **POWER IN PRAYER**

*"Then you call on the name of your god, and I will call on the name of the LORD. The god who answers by fire—he is God."*

~1 Kings 18:24

There's power in prayer. We don't see its action as in an atomic explosion. We may not even feel its benefit at the moment of prayer. (I enjoy it when I do.) It's more like a seed that is sown in the ground that immediately changes from inert potential into an active, though unseen, life force. That's what prayer was designed to do as our hearts and thoughts are lifted to God. To many, the possibilities of what our prayers can accomplish lie latent in the packages of our hearts because they have not been released, by faith, to God.

Prayer is both a privilege and a responsibility.

The *privilege* is that we have freedom at any time, any place and under any circumstance to come into the presence of the Most High God to express our needs and our worship. As a matter of fact, God wants us to relate to Him as a loving child relates to a loving father. Think of it, the God of all creation and the upholder of all things wants me to talk to Him. What an honour!

The *responsibility* is that God has called us to 'work together with Him' in matters related to His purposes on earth. Our greatest work is the work of faith that brings us to Him with our view of matters and the sense of burden to have His will accomplished. That's what prayer is all about.

That's why we are told that we should pray for our leaders "...that we might live peaceful and quiet lives..." (1 Timothy 2:2).

We are called to pray for the Lord of harvest to send forth reapers into the harvest fields. That's a call to intercede for those without Christ that the Holy Spirit would work on their hearts. (Matthew 9:38)

We are instructed to pray in spiritual warfare because our enemy 'like a roaring lion' is seeking to destroy and devour those that the Lord loves. We are told to put on the whole armour of God and then to "...pray in the Spirit on all occasions with all kinds of prayers and requests" (Ephesians 6:18).

We are to pray for our enemies. Now that may be a very hard task because it's easier to surrender to thoughts of vengeance and reprisal than wishing blessing upon those who have offended us. Jesus said, "...pray for those who persecute you" (Matthew 5:44).

We are taught that *we* should pray for the sick that they might be healed. (James 5:16) That's me and you called to be a part of God's miracle-working power to remove discomfort and to restore health and strength.

There's a lot more involved in prayer that we learn about as we pray. Let's be a people who are known for our prayers.

**THE EXAMPLE**

*"Be completely humble and gentle; be patient
bearing with one another in love."*

~Ephesians 4:2

He stood up from His kneeling position, placed the washbasin aside, put on His clothes and sat again with the rest of the men. "Do you understand what I have done for you?" They had just been humbled by the actions of their Lord. In silence they reviewed the scene as Jesus bowed in lowly service before each of the disciples and did the task, normally relegated to slaves, of washing feet. Jesus said, "I have set you an example."

Some churches continue with a regular foot washing ceremony to this day. It serves as a personal humbling process as well as a reminder that believers are called to be servants. The truth is that most of us often feel we have progressed beyond that stage to higher purposes of service. Humbling oneself is viewed as part of the slave/master relationship of times past and is no longer a part of our world today. It is more common to hear people proclaiming their 'rights' than it is to see them surrendering their 'rights.' We know that there are classes that teach self-awareness, self-assertion and self-esteem, but I have never heard of a class on learning how to humble oneself. Perhaps that is the reason there is so much aggression and anger in our world today. Instead of turning the other cheek it has become, 'you asked for it!' and then *pow, pow.*

But Jesus set us an example. Equal with God, He made Himself nothing and took the nature of a servant, made like us. He came to serve His Father's interests and He came to serve the greatest needs of men. Only He and the angels in Heaven could understand what a gigantic step that was. What an example! He gave His all. If He had stood on His rights as the Son of God and King of kings this would be a world without hope of pleasing God. He surrendered His position to come to our world and live His life in the ordinary routines of our lives. He brought no angelic servants to wait on Him. Nor did He wear His Royal crown and robes to impress us.

He said, "I have set you an example." An example is only an example if it is duplicated; otherwise it is just an ornament or monument. It's a sample to be imitated. Jesus fully intends that we should do the things that He has done. It may be difficult for our human nature to comprehend, but it must become a part of our life of faith. The Word reminds us that "your attitude should be the same as that of Christ Jesus." There aren't a lot of people scrambling to be servants these days, but that is one of the most important personnel positions in the body of Christ today. We're called to serve. Let's serve with loving patience. One day you'll find that the rewards are tremendous!

| **ARGENTINE REVIVAL**

*"Humble yourselves before the Lord, and He will lift you up."*

~James 4:10

Argentina is a country that has been touched with great sorrow. It is a nation of people who are very sensitive, industrious and scholarly. They have faced years of economic struggles through poor administration, yet because of their abundant resources and the ingenuity of the people they have surmounted tremendous obstacles. Through the last seventy years, the Evangelical message was shared through missionaries from various parts of the world but was not always welcomed. Early missionaries often had their faith tested by the persecution and opposition of both political and religious leaders of the country, but seed was sown! Labours of love made an investment in the nation through the missionary servants that the Lord sent to that land. Small congregations met together, prayed and believed that God would break through upon them.

During the '70s and the early '80s, the nation was bruised and torn by the "Dirty War" where urban guerrillas robbed banks, kidnapped the wealthy and murdered anyone connected with the government. They were like an invisible enemy who reacted with impunity in the secret places of the night. A military government came to power and began to purge the nation of 'reactionaries.' Many young people disappeared from college and university campuses as the military sought out any who had potential leanings toward an anti-government doctrine. Thousands of young people disappeared during those years and the hearts of mothers and of the nation was broken. A military government sought for a way to regain the confidence of the people and launched into the war with Britain over the Falkland Islands. Again, hundreds of young Argentine boys were sacrificed for an impossible cause and the nation was in mourning. It was a kind of mourning that God could not allow to continue.

To this wonderful, humble people, God sent a mighty revival. Tens of thousands of brokenhearted God-seekers began flocking to places where the gospel was being preached. Miracles of healing and deliverance swept across congregations as the Spirit of God did a faithful work of healing. God began to do things that were beyond the expectation and the imagination of the people. From the ashes of sorrow was born a Mighty visitation of the power of God as the sick were healed, relationships were restored and strengthened and repentance swept across the land.

The Key? God was at work in the lives of many in spite of the tragedies of their history. When they learned the value of humbling themselves God appeared and revival swept into their homes, churches and communities. God made Himself known to a people who began to seek the Lord.

**TIMES OF PRAYER**

*"You will seek me and find me when you seek me with all your heart."*

~Jeremiah 29:13

We make prayer complicated! God has always wanted it to be plain and simple, easier than conversing with your neighbour over the back fence. From the beginnings in the Garden of Eden it was obvious that the Lord had a desire to be with the people that He had made. There is no question that He wanted to demonstrate His eternal love in ways that He had not done before. The angels in heaven must have been amazed at the fact that He would design mankind in such a way that they could have a mutual appreciation of each other. That God would consider man as being worthy of such great attention ought to make us appreciate, more than ever before, the magnitude of His Grace and Mercy. I'm sure He had a lot of other things He could have done with His timelessness, but it was His choice to meet with Adam and Eve in the cool of the day. Look into the heavens on a cloudless night and measure the expanse of all the things that He had created and yet He purposed to a regular schedule of meeting in the Garden of Eden. He was always there on time although we know that Adam was not that committed. I believe it's still in the heart of God, with great desire, to meet with you and me.

We ought to learn the importance of prayer. We need to practice prayer by ourselves, each day, in humble gratitude for His faithfulness and abundant blessings. We ought to be gathering together with others of like faith to focus our attention upon Him. He is worthy to be worshipped and adored beyond anything we have done in the past. We confess that we want His blessings and guidance upon the things that happen in our homes and in the places of our occupations. In this country, we have been gifted with ample church facilities, wonderful congregations and a potential in our community that both challenges and excites the heart of faith. But most of all, we want Jesus to be honoured through our lives. That doesn't just happen by itself! The Lord has promised that those who seek Him will find Him when they search for Him with all our hearts. That means that we need to make the effort or make the time to be in His presence. We become concerned, too often, about the things that we have or do not have, but there is a simple promise that Jesus made that we need to take to heart. Listen, we need to, "...seek first his kingdom and his righteousness, and [then] all these things will be added to [us]" (Matthew 6:33).

Please don't take it for granted! Let's rise to each prayer meeting opportunity to be together to call upon the Lord. He has promised to draw near to us when we draw near to Him. He has promised that those who hunger and thirst after righteousness shall be filled. Let's follow the Biblical pattern to humble ourselves, to pray and to seek His face. We can be the generation used to bring revival to our land.

▌ **BE CONTENT**

*"I have learned to be content whatever the circumstances."*

~Philippians 4:11b


Learning the art of being content is definitely a walk of faith. Paul wrote, "Godliness with contentment is great gain" (1 Timothy 6:6).

There are two parts to this statement:

1.*Godline s* is something that God works in us as we walk by faith and trust Him. This requires the humble cooperation of each of us with the prompting and leading of the Holy Spirit. Being godly is the expression of our desire to do things that please God in spite of the direction of the world or our peers. There is a measure of effort implied as we learn to discern between the things that please Him and the things that don't. Godliness – looking like God.

2.*Contentment* is learning to be satisfied with the plan and purpose of God. That means that we may not always have our way and we may not see our desires fulfilled the way we expect. However, we demonstrate by our submissive attitude that we understand that God is still in control of all the details and, somehow, He lovingly is supplying our true needs with His bountiful provisions of peace and joy. We learn not to lament the fact that we don't have what others may possess. We do not allow envy to drive us beyond the purposes of God for what we think we deserve. We can be at peace about that.

She was 96 years old; a little hard of hearing, but very sharp. As I sat beside her in her room in the seniors' residence she told me about Mary, down the hall, who was always complaining. Mary was 94 years old and obviously was considered her junior. "Yesterday," she said, "I told Mary, 'Listen here little girl, you'll get nowhere in this world by always complaining.'"

I laughed with her as I pictured the scene. The truth is, we all have things that displease us in life. Trials, tests and hardships come to all believers at some time and they are real trials, tests and hardships. God allows them for reasons that are best known to Him. Trusting God for answers and victories in spite of the pain is what contentment is all about. No one likes a constant complainer. We need to look at the bright side of the promises of God as in: "all things work together for good to them who love God," and "I am with you always," and "The steps of a good man are ordered by the Lord." Paul set an example. "I have learned, in whatsoever state I am, therewith to be content." (Philippians 4:11b KJV)

As God works His wonderful blessings in us and sustains us through every trial and test, we ought to express our trust in Him with contentment. After all, He's still in control, whether we recognize it or not.

▌ **CLEANSING POWER**

*"In fact, the law requires that nearly everything be cleansed with blood,*
*and without the shedding of blood there is no forgiveness."*

~Hebrews 9:22

It was the blood. Everything else that was important in the ceremony and ritual was secondary to the shedding of the blood. The sacrifice met stringent requirements and must necessarily be healthy, whole and natural. When the Israelite priests brought the lamb to the altar, it must have passed the scrutiny of many eyes in order to qualify, and 'good enough' wasn't acceptable. It had to be a perfect lamb in the completeness of what a lamb was expected to be. Impediments, frailties, sickness or scars were sufficient reason to reject a lamb. But when all was said and done it was the blood that was to be the covering for the sins and offences of the people. It was imperative that the regulations be strictly followed.

In the ceremony the important ingredient was the blood that was carried in a small basin, sprinkled before the Priest as he made his way into the place of worship in the tabernacle, and finally sprinkled on the Ark of the Covenant inside the Holy of Holies. It was through the blood that the Priest gained access to the throne of God. Only through the blood could the people expect that they would be accepted before God as His specially chosen ones. Only through the blood was there forgiveness of sin and a welcome into a living relationship with God. There was no other provision established that would give them those kinds of privileges.

And finally, it was His blood, shed on Calvary, which became the only sufficient covering for all the sins of the world, for all time. Jesus went through the same kind of examination as the lamb for the requirements of the law. People listened to Him; watched Him critically. They discovered that He was a flawless man, without sin. Even Pilate made that discovery after a few moments of interrogation. "I find no fault in Him," he said. Pilate's wife warned him as well, "Don't have anything to do with this innocent man, for I have suffered a great deal in a dream because of Him" (Matthew 27:19b).

It was Jesus' blood that was accepted before God as the sufficient price for the sins of all men. The writer of the book of Hebrews in Chapter 9 reminds us that Jesus, "... entered the Most Holy Place once for all by His own blood." It pleased the Father that His own Son would provide the perfect covering for the sins of the sinner and give us freedom of access into His presence.

The devil may remind us that we are unworthy of such a price for our Salvation. However, we don't need to be concerned about the scrutiny and condemnation that he may bring against us because we come to the Father, by faith, through the blood of the perfect Lamb of God. That is the guarantee that He will pardon our transgressions and make us welcome as His children into the family of God.

15

█ # REJOICE!

*"May the nations be glad and sing for joy, for you rule the peoples justly and guide the nations of the earth."*

~Psalm 67:4

The Psalmist David had his share of problems. He was appointed and anointed to serve God in an exceptional fashion, but his life was no bed of roses. In spite of the delays and setbacks to the fulfillment of God's call on his life David was able to keep focused on the fact that his God is Almighty and able to resolve all situations. He maintained that confidence because He believed that God had a bigger plan than he could comprehend in the moment. In Psalm 5, he begins by expressing reality in the fact that things sometimes press hard and heavy upon him just like they do upon us, but he ends that Psalm with a note of victory. "...let all who take refuge in you be glad; let them ever sing for joy."

I've discovered that in most of our trials, the first thing to go is joy. Our faith may not be moved; our confidence in God does not change, but somehow we lose our joy.

Sometimes good advice is like the proverbial pill; it's hard to swallow. Let me give it to you anyway.

1. "Don't let your heart be troubled," Jesus said.
2. "Rejoice in the Lord always and again I say rejoice," wrote the apostle Paul.

Keep your eyes on the fact that God is still on His throne and that He loves you through every situation. That may not take away the pain, discomfort or urgent need right away but it will be the foundation of faith that believes that God is still God and that He cares for His children. We sometimes need to subject ourselves to an attitude check–up. We might need a "fill-up" of trust in the Lord that will sustain us through emergency moments. A secular song was made famous through a simple tune and an equally simple message, "Don't worry, be happy."

Check your joy level. The Word reminds us, "In your presence is fullness of joy and at your right hand there are pleasures for evermore." There's not a lot of joy in the world but the Lord is the One who can give us peace in the midst of the storm and satisfaction when there's nothing around to encourage us. Jesus said that one of the reasons that He came was to "give us life and that to the full." There's no question that He is not honoured by droopy-mouthed followers. When people see that we react differently than those who don't know the Lord it can make an impact on them. We do serve an awesome God who has promised to be with us through all circumstances, so lift up your smile and rejoice in the Lord. Let's keep close to the Lord where we receive the kind of pleasure that lasts and lasts.

"With joy you will draw water from the wells of salvation." (Isaiah 12:3)

| **LOVING THE WORLD**

*"Come to me, all you who are weary and burdened,*
*and I will give you rest."*

~Matthew 11:28

"For God so loved the world that He gave His one and only Son, that whoever believes in Him should not perish but have everlasting life" (John 3:16). We call it Missions. God calls it, "loving the world," that is, loving the lost.

We are warned that we should not love worldly pleasures or the worldly system but that we should love people who were made in God's likeness.

There is no thing that has ever been made that means so much to the Lord as does the soul of every living human being. We sometimes find it difficult to relate to some people as part of the consequences of the choices they have made. We view the results of alcohol, tobacco, immoral living, and the abuses of mankind with each other. There is no question that what we see and hear can cause us much concern and sometimes pain, but God sees them too and He loves the people apart from their actions. That is one of the great differences between God and people. He is able to see what each one could be through a changed heart, lifestyle and in a right relationship with Himself. That is why we need to look by FAITH at people who do not know the Lord as their personal Saviour. There is a potential in each one that is far beyond the visible. The very fact that through the Cross of Calvary we receive the privilege of being called the "sons of God," that we receive eternal life, and that we are given liberty to come into the very presence of God with "boldness and confidence," demonstrates what the love of God can do. If it works for you and me, I believe it can work for anyone.

We need to see beyond the exterior of an individual and see what God is able to do on the inside of a person's life when He is given the opportunity to work in their hearts. It comes down to the basic pattern that God, Himself, established. God "...sent His one and only Son."

God needs messengers. That's where you and I enter the picture. Our world needs to know that God still loves the lost; but how shall they hear unless someone tells them? You and I hold in our possession, by experience, the wonderful story that God cares greatly for every one of us, no matter our status in life or our geographical location. Now we need to think with the mind of Christ and share this marvellous experience with others. That's what Missions and Evangelism are all about. We are all called to be people with a Mission. Don't be sidetracked by any of the tricks that the devil might put in your pathway to deter you from the project that is closest to the heart of God. The enemy uses fear and busy-ness as tools to keep us from doing God's will. Let us be people who pray, give and go to obey His command to, "... go into all the world."

17

| **INVESTING IN THE KINGDOM**

*"But store up for yourselves treasures in heaven, where moth and rust
do not destroy, and where thieves do not break in and steal."*

~Matthew 6:20

"What good is it for a man to gain the whole world and yet lose or forfeit his very self?" (Luke 9:25). Our society believes the myth "he who has the most toys when he dies, wins." That's the materialistic generation we're living in. There's a striving for possessions, for security and the things that will make our lives more comfortable. It seems that our comfort level depends on our accessibility to finances or things that give us immediate pleasure. We are prepared to do almost anything to assure that we will be in control of our destiny by the way we prepare for our earthly future.

At a time when his nation was under the authority of a foreign power, Jesus was warning his generation that there are more important things in life than material things. As far as Jesus is concerned anything that takes away from the development of the soul or the reaching of the lost doesn't rate with God. When we stand before Him at the judgment throne, He's not going to be impressed with how much money we have in the bank or the amount of stocks and bonds we were able to invest in prospering businesses. He will ask us all, "What did you do with my Son, Jesus?" As far as God is concerned "the sole issue is the issue of the soul."

That is a progressive process. It begins within ourselves by building a relationship with the Lord in committed obedience and prayer. Then it reaches to others to help them into the same experience that we have. These are the things that are more valuable than the whole world. Jesus told the story of a wealthy farmer who planned a period of time in his life where he would set aside his spiritual development and be committed to his farm and the profit that he could gain. The story concludes with a simple principle; it is far better to commit ourselves to loving and serving God than spending our energies for things that will not last.

Someone said to a very busy man, "You must take time to smell the roses." Imagine, after working your heart out to grow a rose plant you never had time to enjoy the fragrance of your efforts.

Laying up treasure in heaven (doing God's will), provides an opportunity to enjoy the dividends of our labours for eternity. Somehow, we need to get our priorities in line with the purposes of God. Don't let anything bend you to compromise your commitment to serving and honouring the Lord. You're giving away a chunk of yourself if you do. We need to be keenly aware that God gives us many opportunities during our days to invest in His heavenly kingdom. It's time to work for the Lord, wherever we are.

**IMITATORS OF JESUS**

*"Follow my example, as I follow the example of Christ."*

~1 Corinthians 11:1

It was a natural result of their Faith lived in everyday situations and especially in the way they served the Lord that, "The disciples were called Christians first at Antioch" (Acts 11:26). It was not the decision of some important committee or conference that made the choice for the name. It was the consequence of their conversation and their actions. When people heard them speak and the compassion they had for the real needs of mankind, it made them think of Jesus Christ. It was as though they were seeing an absolute proof of the resurrection of the Lord because He was alive before their eyes. By their own observation, Jesus was living through each of the believers. It was as though Jesus had been cloned, many times over, and they were seeing a community who acted and reacted just like their Master. It was natural that they should be identified by calling them, *the Christ like ones.* (That's what being a Christian is all about.) It's a chosen lifestyle.

I wonder what the world sees in us. I've heard testimony of some in our congregation who are respected for their Christian witness because they are believers who are lovingly living their example of faith in their place of employment. We may be far from perfect but our goal is to be like Jesus as much and as often as we possibly can. We are careful to be loving and patient, generous and diligent so that our example will be a clear witness of what a Christian ought to be.

For our own personal assessment, does the world even know that we are different? You have heard the saying, "How does a lion eat an elephant? One bite at a time." It may not be by dramatic things that the world sees Jesus in us but through the small details of each day. How can we change the world, to bring about a transformation in the attitude of the hearts and minds of men who are far from Him? One person at a time. Small as it may seem that's all that Jesus asks of us. Each soul needs a witness. God has placed us in certain areas of our world and delegated a great responsibility to be like Him in that area.

When we touch the lives of others in the normal routine of our activities, let's be aware that we can leave behind a sense of the presence of Jesus. We don't need to be obnoxious by pushing a brash witness upon others, but rather, through the gentle, kind and courteous things we say and do, we can make a deposit of the Kingdom of God in their lives.

19

▌ **GETTING THUMPED?**

*"But he knows the way that I take; when he has tested me,*
*I will come forth as gold."*

~Job 23:10

It has been said that when a Potter takes his vessel out of the fiery kiln that he performs a simple test to see if it has been burned enough. He thumps the side of the vase. If it is done, it gives a firm ring that he recognizes. If it is not done and needs to be returned to the fire, it gives a sound like a dull clunk.

Have you been thumped lately? It is part of the testing process that the Master Potter uses to see if you are well on your way to being the finished product. It is interesting how different people respond to the different tests of life. Try this test on yourself. How did you respond the last time you were thumped by a tough situation? What was your reaction? Most often we retaliate against people or we become groaners, looking for the sympathies of others who, we are sure, have never had a problem as severe as this one. While it may be true, the fact of the matter is that it is important to pass the test first, by our attitude, or it will be back into the fire until we become the kind of people we ought to be. This may not be the kind of message that will make us jump up and down with great excitement but it is a fact that once the lesson is learned, it is easy to pass the test. Let me tell you a few things that we all need to learn before we get into the fire:

1. *We need to learn how to endure.* "Endure hardship with us like a good soldier of Jesus Christ" (2 Timothy 2:3). It is important that we be prepared to put up with some things that we may not particularly enjoy. We all have to learn early in our childhood that not everything we like is good for us nor is everything that is good for us what we like.

2. *We need to learn to stand fast.* "Be on your guard; stand firm in your faith..." (1 Corinthians 16:13). Don't run from your family, your church, your marriage or your job, just because things don't happen the way you want. We need more "stick-to-it-ive-ness" in all aspects of our generation. The accepted process of our times is... just get out.

3. *Keep your eyes on Jesus.* "I press on toward the goal to win the prize for which God has called me heavenward in Christ Jesus" (Philippians 3:14). Situations and circumstances may or may not change, but Jesus is still Lord of all and is able to change the whole scene if He wants to. If he doesn't, I know that He will sustain me.

Let me advise you that if you're getting thumped, it really means there is some checking up going on. I want to see you passing the test with flying colours.

| **SETTING KIDS FREE**

*"...being confident of this, that he who began a good work in you will carry it on to completion until the day of Christ Jesus."*

~Philippians 1:6

When the Father embraced his son after the prodigal journey it was obvious that, in spite of the selfish wanderings of a thrill-seeking young man, the Father still loved his son. The boy remains nameless although I've heard speak of him in times of prayer when parents, reaching out to God on the behalf of their loved ones, have mentioned a name.

It is always interesting that love is willing to hold on and persistently wait. Listen to what the Bible says: "Let us not become weary in doing good, for at the proper time we will reap a harvest if we do not give up" (*at the proper time or in the right moment*) (Galatians 6:9). It is important to keep our eyes fixed firmly upon the gracious kindness of a loving God who will never fail. Our families are one of the most valuable treasures that we may ever hold. They are important to us and absolutely important to God.

Even though it is difficult, there does come a time when we need to let go of our kids, physically, and allow them to make their own choices. However, we never let them go spiritually! We must maintain a guard for their spiritual welfare all the days of our lives. It would be easy to let them go completely with the thought that they have to grow up and make their own choices, but I am confident that true love will hold them always close to the throne of God. It is difficult to measure the value of our contribution into the lives of our children. We would probably be the first to question whether we have done a good enough job or not. We want to see the evidences of their understanding and trusting in their commitment to serve and honour a loving, heavenly Father.

Though some may not express the growth in their spiritual lives that we, as parents, would like to see, we ought to remember, "After I've done my best, I let God do the rest." But don't let go, completely. Your love, through prayer, can span any distance to wherever your loved one may be. God may allow some to walk a distant highway to learn some awful experiences before He brings them back to your waiting love. His watchful eye will not let them get too far before He will send a person, a circumstance, a memory that will be the instrument to bring him back home.

Patience and prayer seem to go hand in hand in many Bible situations. The praying part is difficult, but it is the easiest; the waiting is most difficult. However, God is God and He has promised to hear in heaven and answer prayer. Don't give up when things seem to be impossible, because that's where God shines best. I think it's fair to say someone waited for you at one time in your life. Let's learn to pray and trust God to work out the means to bring the answer. But don't stop praying. God is still on the throne.

▌ **THE ONE AND ONLY WAY**

*"Salvation is found in no one else, for there is no other name under heaven given to men by which we must be saved."*

~Acts 4:12

We may be called "narrow- minded" and insensitive to the beliefs of others, but we stand on what Jesus said: "I am THE way, THE truth and THE life." I can't offer any other solution for those who are on their quest for eternal life. Jesus is the answer. He is the *only* answer. There is "no other name under heaven given to men by which we must be saved." (Acts 4:12) That's a specific absolute. It is not a matter to debate. We don't need to apologize for believing what the Word of God teaches. The Bible makes it clear that works will not get us there, nor will any other gods or prophets. We acknowledge that there are a lot of good people who serve other gods who think that they're doing what is right. I believe that there are others who are sincere in their efforts to worship in ways that are different from my ways and who guard themselves on moral issues, but Jesus is still the only door that will open to heaven. I know that it sometimes is difficult to explain to others who think they have the truth in religions that do not acknowledge that Jesus is the Saviour of the whole world, but the truth is still the truth.

I hope that Christians will not think themselves superior because we hold that principle. We are a very privileged people who have experienced the Grace of God apart from personal efforts; but the gospel message is for everyone in the whole world and they need to be told. How do we get that message out to them? We are an exclusive group of people because we hold to the principle that there is only one way to get to heaven, but we also believe that everyone can come. That's not exclusive. That's as wide open as the heavens. The Bible says, "Everyone who calls on the name of the Lord will be saved" (Romans 10:13). Jesus' answer to the reality of hell and the judgment of sin is to offer heaven as a free gift to all who would believe. The whole purpose of His coming was to make a way for us to come to the Father and to live in His presence for all of eternity. It doesn't happen automatically. We each must make a decision. What would you choose? As sure as hell is the destiny of everyone who dies without Jesus Christ, so heaven is the sure destiny of all those who believe that Jesus Christ is the ONLY answer to our eternal future.

I think we need to deal with two major problems that people must resolve in order to make the right decision:

1. There are those who think they are too good to go to hell and that God already knows that so He will receive them just as they are.

2. There are those who think they are too bad for heaven and that God would never accept them just as they are.

Both reasonings are wrong. No one is good enough to go to heaven apart from faith in Jesus Christ and no one is too bad that the Lord won't forgive them if they will only call on His name. The world needs to know this.

▌ **THE VALUE OF ONE**

*"You also **go** and work in my vineyard."*

~Matthew 20:7

He stood on the highest arm of the Hydro tower at the farthest point of the cross bar. One full step more would be fatal. The crowd gathered below in anticipation of the impending tragedy. Emotions stirred in the crowd as some wept and prayed while others shouted, "Jump." This was real life! The police negotiators began their gentle persuasive conversations as Hydro crews rushed to shut down the power lines, locate a crane that would reach the top and standby for whatever reason. Ambulance crews were at the ready. A man's life was at risk. No expense was spared to halt the tragedy and rescue the life of one man. The value of one human life was demonstrated. He was a stranger to everyone but for nearly 5 hours he stood as the focus of attention in our community. Something must be done to halt this terrible waste of a human life. That's Missions! The example is of a secular society involved at great sacrifice and expense in the plan to rescue a hurting man. Millions each day walk the road to tragedy, oblivious of the concern and compassion that the Church should have for lost souls. Let's learn the lesson and stand in the gap with prayerful interest. Souls without Christ are lost! Scripture reminds us that, from the side of eternity, there is weeping and wailing and gnashing of teeth. Some may even be our own loved ones. I guess the real tragedy of this is that we don't take it seriously. The truth of the matter is, if we don't show some heartfelt concern, who will care? Jesus said, "Go! He said, "The harvest is great... pray the Lord of harvest that he will send labourers into the harvest fields." His word says, "How can they hear without someone preaching to them."

## THE HEART OF GOD

Missions expresses the heart of God. The lost must be found while the opportunity avails. The broken and bruised must be healed. The rebellious prodigals need to hear that there is forgiveness for everyone who returns to the Father. The Father knows the terrible consequences that will come upon mankind for their bad choices and He, too, grieves for the lost. Those who have never had an opportunity to hear the message of God's love need to be told that they are loved. Every man, woman and child should be given the choice of accepting or rejecting the most wonderful story ever told. That's the project of Missions and the call for service to carry the message goes out to everyone who calls on the name of Jesus. Someone has said, "If you aren't involved in Missions, you are a Mission field." Your faithful giving and committed praying and, if necessary, your willingness to go are ways that God has designed for each of us to be involved in the matter that is the closest to His heart. It's a love story and His focus is upon every person from the deepest jungle forests of Africa to the highest Himalayas. That's the heart of God and it's Missions.

23

▌ **FOLLOWING FOR FUN**

*"Jesus answered, 'If I want him to remain alive until I return,
what is that to you? You must follow me.'"*

~John 21:22

Walking with Jesus wasn't always fun. There were those special occasions when He reached out to the sick and infirm and brought complete health into their bodies. They could laugh as they remembered the looks on the faces of those who didn't know what to expect when this stranger touched them. And there were those moments when the sound of His voice stilled the restless crowds as He taught the principles of the Kingdom of God. Then there were the many quiet walks through the countryside as they traveled from village to village on the meandering paths following the Master to His next destination. No question, these were moments to treasure.

Then there were the other times, moments when you could almost cut the atmosphere with a knife. Many of the old teachers of the law came to hear His message with a critical ear. They had their minds made up and were not prepared to exchange the traditions of the fathers for any message from God or man. But it wasn't just a matter of argument; it was a matter of life and death. Anyone who disagreed with the religious leaders in those days was taking his life in his hands. I mean, this was serious stuff. Remember His first sermon in His hometown. Somehow, He was able to escape through the angry mass and make His get-a-way. It was probably after that experience that He moved to Capernaum in the province of Galilee. But that kind of situation was not uncommon. His words were often challenged by men who had murder in their hearts, and early in His ministry He became a marked man because His teachings were upsetting the status quo. On one occasion, He told His disciples that He wanted to go to Jerusalem. Their quick response was, "But Rabbi, a short while ago the Jews tried to stone you, and yet you are going back there?" (John 11:8). There was serious stress and tension among the disciples. They didn't feel the liberty of going wherever they wanted. They soon discovered that a price had been placed on Jesus' head and anyone connected to Him would be condemned as well. You can imagine the pressure that they all felt when they recognized the Jewish leaders were also in the congregation. I'd probably find a seat close to the door, wouldn't you?

On one occasion, Jesus told His disciples, "When you are persecuted in one place, flee to another." (Matthew 10:23a) Does that sound like fun to you? As much as some may think that living with Jesus was a glamorous and exciting thing, there were the many times that they had serious concerns about the length of their lives. But things haven't changed a lot.

There will always be wonderful times as we serve the Lord and fellowship with others who believe in Him, but we also face an enemy that isn't happy with our message. He uses subtle methods to enter our thoughts and bring depression upon us, but Jesus provided a way that we could defeat Him. In spite of the 'down' times, lift up your heart in gratitude and worship the One who has overcome the wicked one. Be strong in the Lord! Be not afraid!

24

**THE CALL TO WORSHIP**

*"Give thanks to the LORD, call on his name;*
*make known among the nations what he has done."*

~1 Chronicles 16:8

The message that Moses had to convey to Pharaoh was plain and simple. "Let my people go, so that they may worship." The children of Israel had lived 400 years under the leadership of the Pharaohs. Many of those years they lived as slaves to the Egyptian people. It didn't begin that way. They were once regarded as a people of great spiritual influence under the direction and wisdom of Joseph. But something happened during those 400 years that took away the godly inspiration of the sons of Jacob and left them as slaves in a foreign land. How they lost their freedom is not told to us. We do know that the godly authority of Joseph was soon forgotten and that a new generation came to rule on Egypt's throne that was unaware of the deliverance that God had brought to Egypt through Joseph. What God did through the sons of Jacob and especially through Joseph was not remembered. Egyptian children were not told the fascinating story. Mothers and Father's didn't think it was an important part of history that was worth repeating. The sons of Jacob stopped telling their friends and neighbours that God had delivered this nation through a miraculous experience.

It appears that the lesson we need to learn is that when we neglect or forget to give credit to the Lord for His wonderful works, people will soon forget what God has done. Even the specially chosen lost their freedom because they were not faithfully giving honour to the Lord. The message of Moses was God's call to return to worship. "Let my people go, that they may worship!" True freedom is all about worship. It's all about giving honour to the Lord and proclaiming His goodness and greatness faithfully. It is more than a weekly service at an altar. It's a call to come out of the things that hold us back from serving God. He becomes the centre of the plans and purposes of men.

We should want to learn how to live each day of our lives in such a way that the Lord feels that we are honouring Him and that people around us will know that we serve a wonderful God. Perhaps now, as never before in the history of mankind, it is so important to get our focus on the Lord and away from the things that would hold us down so that we do not feel free to worship. All kinds of pressures and stresses are cast along the pathway but let's keep our eyes on Jesus. Let's worship Him with all our hearts. Let me remind you that not everything that we need to leave behind is painful. There are some of the comforts of life, too, that aren't bad, but they occupy our time and thoughts so that there is no room for the Lord to speak to us. Let's be free of the petty and the pleasurable things and come back to worshiping the Lord. He is worthy to be praised. We need to be the judge in our own lives. God is calling, once again: "Let my people go, that they may worship."

▌ **GOD STILL LOVES SINNERS**

*"Everyone who calls on the name of the Lord will be saved."*

~Romans 10:13

The sign was clear, to be read by national and international television viewers: "God hates fags." I took exception to that because it is not true; God does not hate fags. Never, ever, does the Bible speak that way about homosexuals. I confess that I have trouble with their lifestyle and some of the gross things that they propagate. And I am aware that it appears that one of the principle reasons for the destruction of Sodom and Gomorra was because of the persistence of the people of those cities to permit homosexuality within their borders.

But I am still persuaded that God doesn't hate fags. Yes, what they do is an offence against God like every other sin that we could list. God does hate sin, but He loves people in spite of their sin. For that reason the Gospel message of His love and forgiveness reaches out to all who have done anything to displease Him. This may be a concept that is hard for us to comprehend but it is what His Grace and Mercy are all about. He gives us all an invitation and opportunity to turn from our wicked ways and to do the things that please Him. But He doesn't come to us in hate; never, ever. It is obvious that He cares very much about all of us. Again and again, He extends a summons for us to draw near to Him and He will draw near to us; to seek His face and He would be found; to call upon Him and He would hear.

It is very unfortunate that we cannot grasp the depth of God's marvellous love. We are very quick to expect God's judgment to fall on everyone who does things that offend God. I, for one, am very grateful that God is patient and merciful to all who have failed Him or else there would be no one in heaven. Let me show you something.

Manasseh of 2 Chronicles 33 is noted as being the most vile, wicked, perverse, brutal king of Judah. The things that he did in his lifetime are listed as a living indictment against him. His crimes knew no boundary. But, he repented, (33:12-13) and God forgave him and restored him to his throne as king in Judah, because he humbled himself.

To get back to the beginning, I believe there is hope for every sinner. Our Lord is a God of love and is able to save, "completely those who come to God through him, (Jesus) because he always lives to intercede for them" (Hebrews 7:25).

Although God loves us just as we are He is not prepared to leave us just as we are. He has higher purposes for us than to remain in things that will destroy us or cause us distress. His plan is to change us and to deal with the issues that displease Him. The Bible does list a number of sins that we need to avoid because they have consequences, but God always speaks to us in LOVE.

▌ **GETTING THINGS INTO FOCUS**

*"Finally, be strong in the Lord and in his mighty power."*

~Ephesians 6:10

When the news of the death of John the Baptist was brought to Jesus, the story tells us that He "...withdrew by boat privately to a solitary place..." (Matthew 14:13). We all need quiet times in peaceful places occasionally in our lives. I'm sure that the sorrow for the loss of a very powerful voice for the kingdom of God on earth was heavy upon His heart. The fact that another terrible injustice had touched the life of a wonderful servant of God whose sole desire was to be no more than a steady, consistent voice in our world, made that loss so much greater.

Hey, listen, bad things sometimes happen to good people. I guess you've discovered that already. How we handle our hurts and disappointments demonstrates the measure of trust and confidence we have in God. In some cases, it would be so much easier to take things into our own hands and do something about it as we judge the situation. That is one way to work towards a solution. Another way is the process that Jesus used: He just stepped back for a season of solitude and then came right back to do what He was sent to do. Things may never change around us to our satisfaction, but we need to get it clear in our hearts and minds that God wants to use our lives in spite of everything else, and then get back to doing what we know He wants us to do.

The passage we quoted above goes on to say that Jesus saw a great multitude, "and was moved with compassion." To Him, it was time to get back to work. There were people out there who were looking for someone to care for them. It wasn't time to bemoan that He, too, was hurting—that He, too, could not reconcile the injustices around Him with the will of God. His focus turned out and away from Himself to the needs of others.

I think that He established a pattern for the Church. The fact that there will always be problems in the Church is based on the fact that the Church is made up of people (human and ordinary). But it's when we look out at the needs of those around us and get involved in reaching out to those that need the Lord that the problems inside the Church fade into insignificance. If we resist the prompting of the Holy Spirit to be a caring people, we'll become introverted and possessed by the problems around us.

That's what kept Jesus' ministry so alive and vibrant; He didn't let persecution and problems hinder the direction of His life. He was prepared to do the Father's will and do what He had to do whether He was acclaimed as a wonderful teacher or otherwise. The souls of the multitude are too precious to be sidetracked by feelings and emotions. The lost must be found. The bruised must have their wounds bound up. Those in bondage must be set free. That's our world too.

27

**A REAL TREASURE**

*"For in Christ all the fullness of the Deity dwells in bodily form."*

~Colossians 2:9

Family treasures are very precious. They are things that hold special memories or extraordinary values such as hard-won medals, jewellery, crystal, gold or silver. Generally they hang on walls, sit on shelves behind glass doors or hidden from view in a storage trunk or secret safe; but they are not to be used lest they be damaged, lost or stolen.

Generations ago, the Father shared the greatest treasure of heaven to our world. He did not come to be put on public display but to become a part of our everyday living. The wealth of heaven was wrapped up in Jesus, God's gift. In comparison, there is not enough earthly treasure to measure up to the price of God's one and only Son. There is infinite value in who He is and what He does. The marvellous mystery of God's grace is in the fact that Jesus was given to be received by all men, regardless of their status in life and regardless of their willingness to receive. This gift was not meant to be hidden in some cloistered hall nor in the shadowy niche of private devotion. He has been shared with us to be publicly displayed through our daily lives and in the streets of our cities. He will never lose His value; He can't wear out; He cannot be stolen nor damaged any longer. He is enduring and as beautiful as the day He first came to dwell among us. His friendship and love continue to inspire our devotion and to strengthen our faith as we journey toward His home. His Presence changes the sorrows of life into moments of hope and peace in anticipation of what will yet be a part of our lives.

It was His precious blood that ransomed us from the slavery of sin. It was His precious blood that pardoned us from the condemnation and guilt that gave the enemy the power to have dominion over us. It is His precious blood that gives us access to the Father's presence where our communion is not blemished by our weaknesses or failures of the past.. It was His blood that brought us into the adopted membership of the family of God with all the saints throughout the ages who have come to Him by faith and who together will inherit the rich promises of the Father.

It was the stripes on His back, dispensed in an unjust judgment hall, that still provide healing for our mortal bodies for all the sicknesses and diseases of all time. And it was the teasing and the torment by His captors that became the means of our sanity and peace in heart. (Isaiah 53:5)

These are the kind of treasures that we can pass on to this generation. They're the kind of things that don't wear out and can be shared, freely, with everyone. His words were, "I came not to be ministered unto but to minister and to give my life a ransom for many" (Matthew 20:28, author's paraphrase).

28

**WAITING**

*"Let a little water be brought, and then you may all wash your feet and rest under this tree."*

~Genesis 18:4

Waiting is always difficult; that is, the kind of waiting where you don't know what is going to happen next. It is difficult to shift the mind into neutral and idle for a while. It is especially more difficult in our "instant" generation where waiting must be for only brief moments. Our world is geared for speed and hurry. We want all of our activities to happen with "Rush" signs on them. In any day you can have a full meal prepared for you in less than five minutes or your car's oil changed with a lube job in less than seven minutes. We have our choice of instant coffee, cereal, pizza, pastry—you name it—coming either in "microwavable" packages or appearing by means of a drive-through window. Our methods and speeds of transportation have converted the continents into a "small, small world." Time to accomplish our routine tasks has almost become insignificant compared to that of a couple of generations previous. Waiting has become a waste of time.

I want to call us back to a very important principle, one that is tremendously important to the growing and maturing of our faith. We need to retrain ourselves to be more patient in spiritual matters. I know it goes against the grain of our worldly system, but we need to pause and reflect on the goodness of God and His many promises. "*Be still*, and know that I am God" (Psalm 46:10). Hush yourself and wait on Him.

The Psalmist adds, "*Wait* for the Lord; be strong and take heart and *wait* for the Lord." (Psalm 27:14) Isn't that a hard thing to do? Waiting seems to be against our nature when we have so many other things that capture our attention. Catch yourself and believe it when the Bible tells us that it is for our good. "*Be still* before the Lord and *wait patiently* for him; do not fret when men succeed in their ways..." (Psalm 37:7) The truth is that as fast, efficient and innovative as our society may be, it is running low on spiritual energy. The depressed and discouraged are looking for people who have a strong faith. Let me advise you that we need to make time for a walk in the park or to do some other thing that will help to slow us down. It is important for our mental and spiritual health to eliminate a lot of the pressures around us and to spend time in prayerful meditation and thoughtful quiet conversation with the Lord. I wouldn't want you to think that all of your problems will go away if you develop this kind of routine, but I can assure you that you'll be better equipped to face difficult situations after waiting on the Lord.

The Wonderful Gift of the Holy Spirit came on a Pentecost Sunday after a waiting process. We need to be refreshed again but we must take the initiative and pause to wait on the Lord.

▍ **PARTING SORROW**

*"Do you not say, 'Four months more and then the harvest'? I tell you,
open your eyes and look at the fields! They are ripe for harvest."*

~John 4:35

Jesus said He would come back again. The News Hour of television reported that a group in Quebec had announced, some time ago, the date they had determined for His return to earth. So, if you are one of them and you're here to read this article today, something went wrong.

But listen carefully, the Bible says that we will not know the day nor the hour of His arrival to this world. The errors of man's guessing only proves that point. The fact remains that the Lord has given us enough warning for us to be prepared for that very important date. Most of us receive that news with mixed feelings. I am delighted at the prospect that our Saviour has promised to come and receive us to Himself and that we will spend the rest of timeless eternity in His presence and in His heavenly Kingdom. The other part of my mixed feelings comes from recognizing that there are still so very many who have not received Jesus Christ as Lord and Saviour and haven't yet a hope, under heaven, of being a part of that exciting voyage. They aren't going anywhere when He comes back for us. The sad thing about this is that some of those people are very important to us. I can imagine that some wives will be separated from their husbands, some parents from their children, and some of our good friends will not make the trip, either. It is going to be a very sad day for each of them.

My recommendation is that we should do one of two things every day.

*Firstly*, seek every opportunity to talk to them about the Lord and His love for each of us, because the hour is late and He is coming soon. Let it be known that the invitation to be a part of that exciting moment has always been open to any that will put their trust in Jesus Christ. Then, let's follow that up with concerted prayer. The Holy Spirit can do a work in the lives of those we love.

Or, *secondly*, we should say good-bye.

You see, there is a real finality to all our earthly relationships when it comes to the day of separation. We need to have a restoration of the seriousness of that moment. The devil would have us think that the Lord's delaying of His coming is proof that He isn't coming. Don't forget that the prophecies from Old Testament times concerning His coming to Bethlehem were fulfilled in every detail, yet missed by so many. Some of us sit in our comfort zones today with great plans for some other day, soon, to do what God wants us to do. However, we may not have until midnight tonight before the trumpet call of God and the voice of the archangel summons us into His presence (1 Thessalonians 4:16). Jesus is coming again.

So, it's either now or good-bye.

| # SIGNS IN THE HEAVENS

*"Therefore keep watch, because you do not know*
*on what day your Lord will come."*

~Matthew 24:42

Can you remember a time such as this when the weather was the main news of the evening? We see pictures of the awesome floods in China that leave families and communities in devastation. We all watched the news broadcasts as the 'Tsunami' wave hit the coastal villages of Sri Lanka, Indonesia and India. We followed the winding pathway of Hurricane Bonnie as she approached the American East coast to vent her power upon a fleeing and hiding population. We've heard of El Nino and its universal effects on the weather patterns and understand that La Nina, to follow, may cast opposite results upon the world. We hear of the Heat Wave that has swept across the Equatorial countries with temperatures that have broken records. India and Indonesia face famines as their crops sizzle in the searing sun.

The Prophet Joel spoke about these kinds of things to happen in the last days almost 2500 years ago, and the Apostle Peter repeated that prophecy on the day of Pentecost:

Acts 2:19 "I will show wonders in the heaven above and signs on the earth below..."

Let me remind you of two things from this passage:

1. WONDERS does not refer to 'wonderful' in the sense of 'excitement.' It's one of those words that has changed through the years and more literally means 'strange; different to the point of frightening.' That's what happens when God bares His mighty arm. We need to tremble at the recognition of His power. Some call it Mother Nature but I call it Father God. These things don't just happen by themselves. It was Elihu in the book of Job who painted this Awesome picture of God to his friend Job. "Do you know how God controls the clouds and makes his lightning flash? Do you know how the clouds hang poised, those wonders of him who is perfect in knowledge? You who swelter in your clothes when the land lies hushed under the south wind...The Almighty is beyond our reach and exalted in power..."(Job 37:15-17, 23).

2. The things that are happening in our world today are no surprise to God, but they are SIGNS to us. They speak about the direction of the plan of God and His interest in letting us know that He is actively involved in our world, although we do not honour Him as we should. The Signs tell us that He is coming soon; that there is a judgement day coming and that life, as we see it today, will not continue. Signs are important and speak valuable messages to us. Let's read them carefully.

▋ MISSIONS

*"The harvest is plentiful, but workers are few. Ask the Lord of the harvest, therefore, to send out workers into His harvest field."*

~Luke 10:2

The Pentecostal Assemblies of Canada was birthed out of the desire of a group of pastors to combine their efforts for a foreign missions outreach. The purpose of the coming together was to share in the common vision of the Great Commission to seek the lost at any cost in other parts of the world. God blessed the common desire and raised up this organization to make an impact in many nations around the world. The principle is still the same today: "The lost must be found." It was necessary that someone should go to the regions across the seas where multitudes were dying without the hope of the gospel message. A number of assemblies united their resources and sent out the first pioneer missionaries. The small beginnings were very difficult but necessary. The sowing of the seed of the Word of God in the lives of the nationals was done with much sacrifice. Some of the pioneer missionaries literally gave their lives under unhealthy and austere conditions. But it was a beginning.

Today, many mission fields have outgrown their founding organizations in size and number of Churches. However, there are still, "untold millions yet untold" in other parts of the world. They are people ignorant of the most wonderful story that could ever be told to them. Their gods are gods of wood, stone and jewels. They continue a lengthy heritage of spiritual darkness in fear of the anger of their created gods. Into this tremendous need the Lord of the Harvest would send out labourers to the harvest fields. "How then, can they call on the one they have not believed in? And how can they believe in the one of whom they have not heard? And how can they hear without someone preaching to them? And how can they preach unless they are sent?" (Romans 10:14-15a).

Somewhere along this line of God's plea to mission-minded people, there is a place for you. But before we are quick to point the finger at others who should go, it's important to understand that the word "sent" means more than pushing people out the door. Somehow, we must see the bigger picture—that when they go out the door they are holding on to our hand. Although they may be physically thousands of kilometres away from us, they don't let go of the hands of those who stand in the comfort and shelter of the homeland. Our concern for the lost will be demonstrated by how much we care for those who are ministering directly on the frontlines where the gospel is reaching out to the needs of men.

We, as Christians, should at least commit to the partial support of a number of people who represent the Lord and our local churches in various parts of the world. That's the reason for Missions giving on a regular basis. Plan to give to Missions.

| ## WE SERVE AN AWESOME GOD

*"How precious to me are Your thoughts, O God!*
*How vast is the sum of them!*
*Were I to count them, they would outnumber the grains of sand.*
*When I awake I am still with You."*

~Psalm 139:17-18

We serve a Big God. He is Great in size, in power, in love, in wisdom and in time. There are no limits to the immensity of His majesty and influence. He is a Great, Big, Awesome God.

He is the God of the impossible. The God of the miraculous. There is nothing that He cannot do. There are no mysteries that He does not understand, nor any secrets in all of creation that He does not know. There are no enemies that He fears, because He is greater than them all, nor are there any surprises that catch Him off guard, because He is aware of every microscopic detail in His vast creation. To Him, every miniscule fragment of the future—minutes, seconds and milliseconds—are all as clear to Him as the happenings of yesterday. There is nothing throughout His entire handiwork that does not function to fulfill His purposes. Even the deepest and darkest of life's difficult experiences serve to accomplish His goals.

There is no room for despair for the child of God, no matter how deep our sorrow and distress, because God is in control. He rules and over-rules. He makes the painful things to work together for good, so that His will be seen in the dark places of life as well as in the happy times. Only He can do that. He is the Master of the Rescue Plan of the Ages. The Author of every unfinished chapter of our lives. The Master Builder of broken dreams. The Giver of Life to dying hopes. The Satisfier of our hearts' desires. He is the Lover of the unlovable, the lonely and the lost. He is the Creator of purpose for those who are seeking for a reason in life. He never forgets us, never leaves us, never stops loving us.

We serve an Awesome God. He watches over us as a loving Father watching over his little children. He's available as our Protector, Provider, Counsellor and Friend. He's our midnight Watchman and daytime Guide, the Supplier of our daily bread and our spiritual needs. He makes no mistakes and He forgives and repairs ours. He's Gentle and Kind to us but Powerful and Dramatic in Who He is.

He is the best companion anyone could ever have. He does not force Himself on anyone but freely makes Himself available to us all. If you have never met the Lord I'm talking about, I ask, today, that you invite Him to take control of your life and trust Him. You'll find that in surrendering to Him you lose nothing but your heartache, guilt and despair. He is a Wonderful Friend.

▎**PATIENCE AND PRAYER**

*"Until now you have not asked for anything in my name.*
*Ask and you will receive, and your joy will be complete."*

~John 16:24

James chapter 5 brings to light two parallel themes that are connected throughout scripture. We don't always see them so pronounced in their relationship but they are interwoven in the practical aspects of the Christian life as inseparable entities. I wish to remind us of the importance of PATIENCE and PRAYER. They go hand in hand. We need to acknowledge that our God is Awesome in His works and His ways are marvellous. However, let's not forget that He is Sovereign to do as He wills. We must not attempt to rob Him of His prerogatives and demand that He conform to our will. His ways are higher than our ways and His thoughts above our thoughts. (Isaiah 55:9) He remains the Master of every situation. He knows the end from the beginning and His plan will prove to be absolutely perfect. That does not mean that everything will be 'peaches and cream' in our lives, but it should give us the assurance that, based on His love, He will never allow anything to come our way that is not for our benefit, ultimately.

Patience in prayer is understanding that God's love remains true in spite of the fact that we may not get our answers in an instant. He still hears and answers prayer. He cares about the things that cause us distress and discomfort, but sometimes the delays of His answers are tuned specifically to our needs to develop His higher purposes. Our impatience may rob us of the joy of seeing the greater gain that we receive because His designs for us are more important than what we could ever imagine. Perhaps we need to possess the patience of the caterpillar, who, for a period of time, awaits his personal transformation into the beauty of the Creator's ingenuity, and eventually comes forth from his cocoon in rainbow radiance.

Prayers must be made for all men and for all kinds of needs. It is not sufficient to think good thoughts and dream nice dreams. We need to purpose within ourselves that this world, indeed, would be a far better place if we learned the real value and practice of prayer. Who knows what would happen in our generation if every child of God was prepared to give a portion of each day to solicit Divine intervention in our families and in our society? Let God be God and let us be subject to Him in humble recognition that His plans are spectacular. He has promised to hear from heaven and give us the desires of our hearts in leading us into the joy of what He has reserved for us at just the right time.

Let us learn to pray and continue to be people of prayer.

▌ **CHILDREN**

*"Train a child in the way he should go and when he is old*
*he will not turn from it."*

~Proverbs 22:6

It's easier to place your initials in soft clay than in a fire-hardened brick. As the saying goes, "You can't teach old dogs new tricks." It's children that are most receptive to the gospel message, and it's their young lives that can be moulded to form lifelong godly characteristics and wholesome attitudes. To neglect the children and youth of our generation is to allow the weeds of the enemy to take over where the good seed should have been planted. It's true that no one is beyond repair and the Gospel message is powerful to transform even the vilest life and redirect it into service for God. Nevertheless, Jesus often used the little children as His examples of faith because of the trust and confidence that is so natural to a little child. He took them up in His arms and blessed them. Scripture describes children in very loving terms:

"Sons are an heritage from the Lord, children a reward from him. Like arrows in the hands of a warrior are sons born in one's youth. Blessed is the man whose quiver is full of them" (Psalm 127:3-5a).

Of course, there are great responsibilities that all parents need to accept. Children are entrusted to us as a treasure from God. We need to feed, educate, care for and protect their young lives. But most of all, we need to give them examples of our commitment to serve and honour the Lord. This doesn't happen all by itself. We must make a plan to train our children in the ways of the Lord and by example and word lead them into a personal experience with Jesus Christ. Let me share with you a few things that may help you in this project.

1. *Teach your children to pray* (...for meals; before bed time; for healing from the bumps and bruises they get; for the problems they face with their friends and schooling, etc.).

2. *Be thankful.* Watch for opportunities to let your children know how wonderful the Lord really is throughout the normal activities of each day. Let it be known that God does good things for us all the time, not just on Sunday.

3. *Get involved in some area of ministry in the Church.* Your children will follow your example in their commitment to the House of the Lord.

4. *Be careful not to speak bad things about anyone in the Church.* This includes the Pastors, Board members, Department executives and Teachers. We all have our flaws and weaknesses, but the kids don't need to hear about them. It undermines the authority of the leadership and is seen as a lack of respect.

5. *Read to your children.* "I said, read to your children." There are lots of Bible storybooks that will help you to spend a few minutes each day reading and telling them about the things that God has done.

**| REJOICE WITH REAL JOY**

*"This is the Lord, we trusted in Him;*
*let us rejoice and be glad in His salvation."*

~Isaiah 25:9b

Jesus came into the world to make a difference. The truth is that, for too long, the enemy of our souls has been robbing God's creation of the joy and peace that we were designed to possess. Selfishness and sin has taken its toll upon mankind and burdened all of us with needless cares and countless struggles because we are not living in the victory planned for humanity.

Jesus said, "I have come that they may  have life, and have it to the full." (John 10:10b) Jesus was not at all interested in half-way joy. His offer is fullness of joy; living life to the full. Let's not be content with anything less than what God wants for us.

But let's be real! There is a joy and a pleasure that the world knows. It's the kind of stuff that the people demonstrated nearly 2000 years ago when they welcomed Jesus into Jerusalem with great cries of rejoicing and acts of celebration. It was done in His honour and Jesus was worthy of all that. But less than a week down the road the same voices that were lifted in jubilation were changed to angry tones, and "crucify Him" filled the dusty air of that early Friday morning. What on earth happened?

Emotion can be a wonderful thing, but when it is based on selfish desires or the "bless me now" attitude, it stands on an insecure foundation. The lasting joy that Jesus offers us does not depend upon what we get out of Him but rather, what we give to Him. It becomes a day-by-day experience as we surrender ourselves to Him. You see, Jesus is honoured more by our lifestyle than by our vocabulary. If we stop praising Him when we don't get what we expect, we become embittered, prune-faced, lemon-lipped, spoiled brats. However, when we learn to praise Him through every circumstance, then the "joy of the Lord will be our strength." And that's the kind of life He wants us to have all the time.

Our source of special joy as we approach the Easter season is based on the fact that, just like Jesus, for the Christian, every valley of the shadow has a resurrection experience, some day, that will liberate us from the encumbrances of our present experiences. This is true of every trial and test of these days of our lives. We ought to rejoice in the truth that God lovingly cares for us and His promises are sure. "Let us rejoice and be glad." Our God is good. He is a Faithful friend.

"Do not let your hearts be troubled. Trust in God; ...if I go and prepare a place for you, I will come back and take you to be with me" (John 14:1, 3).

▌ **WHY GO TO CHURCH?**

*"What then shall we say, brothers? When you come together,*
*everyone has a hymn, or a word of instruction, a revelation,*
*a tongue or an interpretation. All of these must be done*
*for the strengthening of the church."*

~1 Corinthians 14:26

There's an interesting phrase found in Acts 19 concerning the report of the riot in Ephesus, which made me think about the purpose of our assembling together. Listen to this. "Most of the people did not even know why they were there" (Acts 19:32b). Maybe you can relate to that feeling, occasionally, as you sit in Church. It is possible that some would be thinking that they should be out on the golf course or at some secret lake where the fishing is really good, or _____, (well, you could probably fill in the blanks!). But, in this example, they were at the meeting place and they didn't know why.

In case the question is floating in your mind, let me give you a few reasons why we go to Church:

1. We are exhorted, "Let us not give up on meeting together as some are in the habit of doing, but let us encourage one another..." (Hebrews 10:25). It is a fact that we are encouraged when we come together in a large group and focus, unitedly, on our worship and service to the Lord. Jesus is coming soon.

2. The Lord has promised to be "Where two or three are gathered together in my name..." (Matthew 18:20).

3. We come together to learn through the teaching, exhorting, and reproving ministries of the Church.

4. We place ourselves within the security of body ministry where each one comes with a contribution of talents and abilities to share with the rest, while at the same time, giving correction and guidance so that we grow into maturity together.

5. We affirm a positive testimony, to the world, that we are Christians. We're people of like faith. Our priorities are different from those of the world. We unite on a regular basis to let them know where we stand.

6. We gather together to offer a place of refuge to a world that is hurting. Our meeting place serves as a hospital to offer tender and loving care for people who are bruised and abused by the enemy of our souls. The fact is that we need more willing workers to be involved in the outreach of concern for those who come in and are looking for a God to answer their prayers and a people who will be a friend and help them in their search for peace and wholeness.

By the way, do you know why you are on this earth? We should be involved in a Mission to honour the Lord. One of the ways we accomplish this is meeting together to worship Him. That should send a clear message to the world that we are on the Lord's side.

▍ ## WE'RE PART OF THE MISSION TEAM

*"Ask the Lord of the harvest, therefore, to send out
workers into his harvest field."*

~Matthew 9:38

Psalm 126:6 is a verse that we often designate specifically for our Missionaries: "He who goes out weeping, carrying seed to sow, will return with songs of joy, carrying sheaves with him." The question that comes to mind is, are the reapers supposed to be the weepers too? If I understand the work of Missions—to reach the lost—and that it is not a task given only to certain individuals but to all of us, I think it follows true that if we are going to see souls saved we need to get serious about it and learn to be concerned enough that we will be moved to tears at the thought of those without Christ. Why should our missionaries be delegated such depth of emotion and the rest of us be exempt? We are a part of the same team as they. The only difference is that they are front-line warriors in foreign situations while we have the comforts of home and family.

We should be participating directly in financial support of missionaries and projects all around the world. There are many other places that we can be personally involved as well. Some of the lost and the needy live right next door to us. The "weeping of the sower" ought to touch us as we see the distress that is happening in the homes of our own neighbourhoods. There are hurting people everywhere that are looking for some kind of solution to the things that cause them grief. We need to learn what it means to weep for the lost. And then, how about our own families where our own loved ones are 'existing' without any hope of heaven and the Love of Christ? Could it be that our vision of service for the Lord is in the 'long distance' while we miss the ones nearby who are looking for solutions, too? Perhaps we need to be stirred to weep for our own families in concerted intercession for a transformation in their lives because Jesus is their only answer.

We are not doing ourselves any favours by thinking that the task of sowing seed for the harvest depends on others. We need to learn the principle that if the world is going to be won for Christ it is going to take every one of us doing our part. Some need to fight for the lost in battles of prayerful intercession, where weeping before the Throne brings great victories to other members of the team on Mission fields at home and abroad. We need to be concerned for the lost wherever they may be. Jesus loves them as much as He loves you and me.

Let's be committed to doing what we can.

▌ **THE KEY TO REVIVAL**

> *"They will call on my name and I will answer them;*
> *I will say, 'They are my people...'"*

> ~Zechariah 13:9

What is the key that brings revival? What keeps revival growing? What strengthens new believers and old ones too? What makes the preaching of the gospel most effective? What helps us to understand God in a more clear way? What helps to prepare the heart of the unbeliever to be more receptive to the gospel? What makes the stony heart soft? What makes the shadows of a discouraging day turn a heart to peaceful understanding? What lifts the burdens of depression and weariness? What brings comfort to a sorrowing heart? What eases the pain of separation and loneliness? What makes the presence of the Living God more real? What gives us hope when the future doesn't look so bright? What helps us to resist temptations that press us to surrender? What is it that helps influence the lives of wayward children to return to Jesus Christ? What causes the powers of darkness to tremble? What causes joy to rise in the heart of the believer each day and gives us the confidence that God is still on His throne and in full control of all the details of our lives?

Do you know the one answer to all those questions? Prayer. We all need to realize that God has given us the most wonderful privilege of prayer, and that there is a great need for people to pray. We can't offer you a monitory paycheque nor can we extend any particular credits of prestige and popularity, but God has other ways of rewarding those who apply effort to calling on Him and waiting in His presence. We have all wondered, at some time, why the world is in such a sad condition. We have all been concerned about the emphases of violence and sex that are subtly destroying the lives of this generation. The question is, are we concerned enough to make it a matter of prayerful intercession that God would intervene in these matters and in the lengthy list of questions above? It's not going to go away all by itself. Someone has to be willing to pay the price to get some answers. The truth is, we think that somebody else will do it and we'll be able to share in the benefits. It just doesn't work that way.

God answers prayer. That means that we've got to pray if we want answers. If we don't want to pray, why should we expect answers? I think it's interesting that when Jesus described the Temple, he didn't call it the House of preaching. He didn't even call it the House of music. Excuse me, one more time; He didn't even call it the House of worship. He said, "...My house will be called a house of prayer..." (Matthew 21:13).

I want to call us all to being people of prayer. Let's begin at home. Then let's be people of prayer at the pre-service prayer time. Let's pray by ourselves and with our families, and let's seek for opportunities to pray with our Church family as well.

**CALL TO WORSHIP**

*"Come, let us bow down in worship,*
*let us kneel before the Lord our Maker."*

~Psalm 95:6

Only folk who know what worship is all about can get excited at this kind of invitation. This is a call to humble ourselves in the presence of the Creator of all things. It's an acknowledgement of His Majesty. The writers of many of the Psalms often broke out in expressions of praise as they put their thoughts to song. The great issues of the Old Testament were almost always related to worship. For example, the very first murder recorded in the history of the world was committed following a worship service (Genesis 4). Let me add, I don't believe that the offering was the issue. It was the attitude of the heart that was the problem.

This brings us to an important matter concerning worship. God has always looked at the heart. He has been seeking people who will worship Him in spirit and in truth. God is looking for people of integrity and surrender who will come into His presence. Of course, He begins with people everywhere who haven't a foggy idea about entering into His presence. We all were there at some time in our lives, but He will not leave us there. He wants to set us free from the bondage that holds us to the world and liberate us into a life that honours Him and enjoys His presence.

As the Spirit of God brings us into maturity, one of the very important lessons we need to learn is that of acknowledging the Lord's power, love and majesty. This should be expressed by our words and actions in ways that humbly demonstrate our surrender to Him as His servants. That's where the attitude of our lives becomes very important. It is true—there is no One like the Lord. There is no greater power. Everything that exists is a result of His plan and workmanship. All the honour, praise and glory belong to Him. Besides that, His faithfulness endures forever and He works with us to develop higher plans than we could ever accomplish on our own. We need to learn to Worship Him with a clear understanding (in spirit and in truth) that our God is Awesome and completely worthy of our praise.

How, then, should we worship?

1. *It must all begin in the heart.* We need to recognize the important principle: "Without Him we can do nothing." That's a humbling process.

2. *We should live our lives in such a way that our considerations will always put Him first.* In each situation we encounter we should ask ourselves the question, "What would Jesus do?"

3. *We ought to learn about the power of our words.* Our expressions of worship and praise cause the gates of Hell to tremble. Speak out your worship!

Worship takes us directly into the presence of the Lord. We should learn to wait on the Lord. In case you didn't know, wait means *wait.*

▌ **THE LAW OF LOVE**

*"Love is patient, love is kind. It does not envy, it does not boast,*
*it is not proud. It is not rude, it is not self-seeking,*
*it is not easily angered, it keeps no record of wrongs."*

~1 Corinthians 13:4-5

Wouldn't you know that it would be 'foot in the mouth' Peter who would ask the question? "Lord, how many times shall I forgive my brother when he sins against me? Up to seven times?" (Matthew 18:21). The truth is that he already had vengeance in his heart but was waiting for the legal/right moment to arrive before he released his anger. He wanted to draw the line in the sand and remind his "brother" that there are limitations to how much anyone can get away with.

The question comes to my own mind. Did Peter think that forgiveness is an item that you measure out in grams and kilos or centimetres and meters? His question was, "How much is the allowable personal limit for each offence or offender?"

Jesus set a pretty high figure of permitted transgressions, but, in fact, the number is not important. It's the principle: forgiveness comes in super, extra-large, double-roll quantities that should be liberally administered under the gracious name of Jesus Christ because that's exactly what He would do. You see, the fruit of the Spirit, that should be a developing part of our Christian character, leads us to a greater tolerance of the offences, failures and inadequacies of others. Jesus spoke about suffering for His sake as being a part of our Christian witness. The whole principle is contrary to what the world believes. But then again, so is the Love of God. God sets the example by pouring out His patience, kindness, love and mercy through endless occasions and under some pretty grimy circumstances on our behalf. I think it's high time that we learned to practice that kind of lifestyle. It may not alleviate the hurt and pain that others cause us, but God has promised rewards for those that will live by His principles.

My mother used to say, "It takes two to make a fight." Her message was simple. If one does not respond in anger, the fight is over and the time for rebuilding has arrived. Perhaps we are too sensitive in our own expectations concerning the intrusions of others upon our kindness and not so sensitive to the needs of others who don't have the same experience we have with the Lord Jesus.

I think Peter eventually learned his lesson, because later he wrote, "Above all, love each other deeply because love covers over a multitude of sins" (1 Peter 4:8). That sounds like a public confession to me.

▌ **I WANT YOUR LOVE**

The Living Bible translates the spoken words of as…

*"I don't want your sacrifices…I want your love. I don't want your offerings, I want you to know me."*

~Hosea 6:6 TLB

It's obvious that God wants us to have a sincere heart affection and a personal relationship with Himself. I almost hear a tear in His voice as He cries these words to a people who had totally missed His plan.

What appears to have happened is that the believers, somehow, continued what they interpreted as an obligation in their giving and sacrifices, but had at the same time disconnected their hearts from what they were doing. To them, it was a simple case of "pay your dues and you'll be O.K."

We should know that we can't do that with God because He wants our whole heart and soul. Not just the effort, but the heart. Not just the silver and gold, but the will in surrender to Him. If what we do or give to God is not wrapped up in trusting and loving God, then all we do is in vain.

Jesus warned the Pharisees of their hypocrisy. —They were very precise in caring for their tithe but had forgotten to be concerned about "justice, mercy and faithfulness" (Matthew 23:23). We too, can get caught up in making sure we do everything according to 'hoyle' but at the same time neglecting being compassionate with others and personal with our God. The heart of the matter is the heart. Someone has said, "The important things in life are not things."

As we come to the house of the Lord, we pause in our rush to catch a fresh glimpse at the example of our Lord, who was willing to give His all, a true illustration of sacrifice with heart. He gave Himself completely as an offering to please the Father, but at the same time, in complete love for mankind. There was no separation between the sacrifice and the true worship of love. I repeat, it's an example, an illustration of what we should be doing as well. Could we call it, "anointed duty?" That's doing what we know we ought to do but always based on the principle of our personal relationship with our Lord. We do things because we love Him. This is not based upon our feelings and emotions but is a decision of the heart. Let's learn to put something of ourselves into what we do for God, to combine our love with our service. Even as we listen to the ministries of Music and the Preaching we want to do it in a loving and worshipful attitude. We come to Him to let Him know that we love Him and appreciate His kindness to us.

As we bow to worship, let us thank the Lord for His faithfulness in giving us another opportunity to begin again. I trust that our hearts will reach out to Him in sincere gratitude. What a wonderful Saviour we serve!

▌ **LOVING OUR CHILDREN**

*"He took the children in His arms, put His hands on them
and blessed them."*

~Mark 10:16

You can't help but admire the prayerful concern of the mother who came to Jesus on behalf of her boys to plant the suggestion that she would be so pleased if Jesus would allow one of her boys to sit on His right hand and the other on His left (Matthew 20:20). She had no intentions of laying claim to the centre throne. She understood and respected that position, but as far as she was concerned, she would be "eternally grateful" if Jesus would just "arrange" this little matter for her. Well, that's a great mother for you!

Who hasn't dreamed great dreams for their kids? We want only the best for each of them. That's part of the loving desires of every good parent. I'm sure that if there was any way that you could fix up the same arrangement with the Lord as the request of that dear mother, you would do your utmost to make it come to pass. The response of Jesus was courteous, but direct. Those places are reserved already and the Father knows all about it. That may appear to be bad news unless you interpret His answer in a positive way. God knows all the kids in the world and yours might even be the ones that occupy those positions in Heaven.

Let me give you some suggestions for preparing our kids for that possibility.

1. "Train a child in the way he should go and when he is old he will not turn from it" (Proverbs 22:6). That position is not given to just anyone—it belongs to the one who goes through the training processes first.

2. Teach your children to respect their parents, as well as their elders, under all circumstances. "'Honour your Father and Mother', which is the first commandment with a promise." (Ephesians 6:2)

3. Set a godly example for them to follow. May your steps often lead to the house of God, to the Word of God, to the place of Prayer, to the works of Service, to the place of Worship with your tithes and to a Compassionate attitude toward the lost of the world. Let your lifestyle be above reproach. Somebody is watching you.

4. Love your spouse with all faithfulness and devotion. A healthy love relationship teaches a child to be that kind of person too.

5. Let your faith be so practical that you use it at home, at work and where you do business as well as in Church. You can not separate what you are (a Christian) from who you are (a parent and a citizen.)

It is very possible that what we invest in kids today will bring them closer to the Lord than we could ever have imagined.

| **LOVE IS HARD WORK**

*"Love is patient; love is kind."*

~1 Corinthians 13:4a

Poets, through the centuries, have sought for words that could describe love. They talk about flowers and chocolates, of birds that twitter a joyful song, of starlit nights and bright moonbeams.... and their search goes on. Now, all of these things may have something to do with Romance, but that's not love.

Love is best spelled out in 1 Corinthians 13 in the words of the Holy Spirit. God sees love as commitment, sacrifice, faithfulness and loyalty. There may be no kick in the heart to talk about these kinds of things, but when it comes to working for enduring relationships, they are the necessary ingredients that make for a strong bond. In plain and simple words, true love requires a lot of work. Prime Minister Churchill during the Second World War "encouraged" the people of Britain that they would win the war by "blood, sweat and tears." You might say anything that is worth much is worth fighting for. It's simply plain hard work.

But I'm not sure that we view the Church and each other with that kind of love. As much as we profess that we love one another we can easily let things slip so that our commitment to each other and to the Church is not so strong. You see, I believe that we need to work at strengthening our relationships. We need to apply effort—the kind that goes the second mile, and forgives when we fail. The kind that reaches out to the weak and encourages them to carry on. It's the kind of effort that does not grow weary in well doing because we know that there is a great reward following. It's the kind of effort that takes us out of our comfort zone to where we can be a blessing to others. Sometimes that's simply hard work. But please don't shy away from it, because this is the thing that is closest to the heart of God.

Jesus demonstrated His love for us by coming into our situations and rescuing us from the drudgery of life. He came to give us "life to the full." But what a price He had to pay. He was willing to pay the price for our best interests, not His own. Let's reach out to each other and give some love away—not expecting anything in return but the satisfaction that if Jesus would do that for us, surely we could do the same for Him.

44

▌ **SHOWING LOVE**

> *"This is love: not that we loved God, but that He loved us*
> *and sent His son as an atoning sacrifice for our sins."*
>
> ~1 John 4:10

It was love at first sight. From the hillside he watched her as she brought the sheep to the well as she had done so many times before. In the words of the Bible, "She was lovely in form and beautiful."

Rachel was the younger of the two daughters of Laban, but the favourite choice of Jacob. "I'll work for you seven years in return for your younger daughter, Rachel," he offered. Laban agreed. A warm handshake, a big bear hug, a roast of lamb and the deal was set.

Let me see. With my calculator and a little bit of practical information I come up with the cost of the arrangement: 7 years of wages. Around a quarter of a million dollars by the average worker's salary today. It appears that, to Jacob, he was still getting the best part of the arrangement. As a matter of fact, as the story goes, he was willing to work an additional seven years in order to have her as his wife. Make the whole agreement a half a million dollars and he would still say, "She is worth her weight in Gold." Now that's a true picture of what falling in love may cost a fellow.

My father-in-law told his daughter that she would not be allowed to marry until she was twenty-one. However, when she was nineteen I asked him for her hand and he agreed that I could have his daughter as my wife. We were married when she turned twenty and all I had to do was say "thanks." Mind you, I've been paying the price ever since. (joke) At this writing we have passed the 42-year mark of married life together.

My question is, "How much are you willing to pay for true love?" You see, when God wanted to demonstrate His love, He was willing to pay a great price to show what value He placed on the arrangement. When I, sincerely, consider what He was getting in return, I think the price He was willing to pay for me and you was still too high. But it is not what I see my worth to be that determines His willingness to go to such an extreme price—it's what He sees me and you to be worth that ultimately tells me how much He values our eternal relationship. On the other hand, in return for such a fabulous expression of love, what should I do in return? What price should I be willing to pay to show how much I love my Lord? Silver and gold don't bring Him any pleasure. Neither do the sacrifices of lambs and goats. There is, however, one thing that He desires more than anything else that would serve to satisfy the longing of His heart. It may sound simple but it must become a lifestyle. BE HIS! Committed, devoted, adoring, trusting, serving, seeking, pure and separate from the world. That should be no big deal when you consider the eternal arrangement He has reserved for us in "His house." We're going to move there, soon.

■ **LOVE IS BLIND**

*"Above all, love each other deeply, because love
covers over a multitude of sins."*

~1 Peter 4:8

Someone has said that "Love is blind, but marriage is the eye opener." Now, I would never say that, nor do I necessarily agree with that statement, but the fact of the matter is that Love should be blind to the weaknesses and failures of others and we should not be quick to condemn anyone, especially in a marriage relationship.

However, we should be aware that we live in a very imperfect world with a lot of imperfect people (except me and you, of course!). We need to recognize that the relationship we have with each other was designed in heaven by a Loving Heavenly Father who has purposed that we all be a part of His Church. It is a very humbling thought that when God speaks of His Church as a Bride—radiant, without stain or wrinkle or any other blemish, but holy and blameless (Ephesians 5:27)—He was speaking about the potential in every one of us. Is it possible that God sees more in the people of our generation than we do? We ought to be satisfied to let the weaknesses and frailties settle into the blind spots of our vision. Those are the things that we can recognize as not being the priorities of our lives. We are regrettably inclined to major on the negative rather than being consistent to emphasize the positive.

Peter summed up the matter concisely when he wrote, "Above all, love each other deeply, because love covers over a multitude of sins." You see, the depth of our love is not in that we explore to discover the faults of others but in that we work at concealing others' weaknesses. Isn't that what Jesus did when He wrote in the dust as the self-appointed judges awaited the passing of the sentence of condemnation upon the woman caught in adultery? "If any of you is without sin, let him be the first to throw a stone at her" (John 8:7). Talk about "silence in the Church" that day! It was deafening. There must have been a lot of self-inspection that suddenly shamed the congregation into honest inactivity. The love of the 'Dust-writer' reached out to one who was given another opportunity to change the direction of her life. We've all been there. At least I have, and I'm grateful that His love reached out to cover me.

So, really, "love is blind." May God grant us hearts that have learned to be longsuffering and patient, kind, faithful and always willing to follow His example. May His love flow through us to reach out and accept the wayward into the kind of relationship that we have already found in Christ Jesus. May our love become an action word that compels us to care for others.

46

▌ **REAFFIRM OUR LOVE**

*"Be devoted to one another in brotherly love.*
*Honor one another above yourselves."*

~Romans 12:10

We take a lot of things for granted in our lives. Blessings and favours we receive are accepted with no second thought. We know this is especially true about the wonderful things God shares with us on a regular basis because God is good. But it's also very true on the human level that "most people" are very kind and considerate. It's when we run into someone who is obnoxious or inconsiderate that we realize that not everyone is polite and gracious. However, don't let that be an excuse to become negligent in expressing your appreciation to those you should love. Paul wrote to the Corinthian church and said, "I urge you, therefore, to reaffirm your love..." (2 Corinthians 2:8).

Paul's letter was written to a church with a lot of problems, but it seems that one of the main issues that he wanted to address was the lack of the love that should be displayed in Christian circles, too. We often think of our relationship with God as being the total focus of our spirituality, but the Bible teaches that next to loving God we ought to love our neighbour as ourselves. When the Apostle Paul mentioned this matter as one of the things they lacked, he urged them to take positive steps toward declaring and displaying their love. The situation merited a reaffirmation.

Reaffirming our love means that we should double up on our efforts to show our love for the Church family. It is strange how easily we can take family for granted when they fulfill such an important role in our lives. A reaffirmation of our love could take many forms: a gracious "thank you;" a warm handshake or quick hug; a letter or card especially written to express appreciation in a thoughtful manner; a phone call to just keep in touch during the week; a flower and lots of other ways.

People need to know they are appreciated. No one should be taken for granted. The saying goes that "the squeaky wheel gets the grease," but that intimates that the silent ones are neglected. There are a lot of folk, especially in our families and in the Church, who go about their duties without a complaint. If they would fail to do what they have been doing, we would notice with great regret. They need to be recognized from time to time with expressions of gratitude. That's the kind of care and concern that shows an affirming love. It becomes an energy builder, a spirit encourager, a purpose director, and a reward for faithfulness. We all know that true love is a rare ingredient in our world today, and it's the real stuff that we all need. Love is a lot like a smile—you can never give it away—for like a boomerang, it keeps coming back. You see, as a smile begets another smile, so love given receives love in return. Let's reaffirm our love!

▌ **LUST AT FIRST SIGHT**

*"Greater love has no one than this, that he lay down his life for his friends."*

~John 15:13

Would someone please stand up and tell this generation the difference between the "love" of romance and the "love" of service? The world has these matters confused. The Bible gives us clear teachings and examples for us to be equipped for both.

Usually, when people tell me that it was "love at first sight," I believe that what they really intended to say was that it was "lust at first sight." That is not all bad, because it could still be the beginning of a permanent lasting relationship as long as a lid is kept on the lust until a more mature love in romance is developed. Without the "rush" that comes into the lives of people who "fall in love," the follow-through that develops a loving relationship will be built on duties and responsibilities without the necessity of the thrill or spark of excitement. I speak with the authority of personal experience plus the observation of thousands of couples through the years of my ministry. What I've discovered is that true love is willing to wait, serve and sacrifice with no view of recompense. That kind of love is willing to give and forgive without remembering the weaknesses and frailties of those we love.

It may be hard for some, in their youth, to comprehend that for a loving relationship to endure it must be based on the principle of giving and surrendering rather than the "what can I get out of this?" principle. As a matter of fact, a lot of marriages today could use an adjustment in refining these facts. Too many homes have delegated responsibilities according to gender. "Dish washing is a woman's job." "Mowing the lawn is a man's job." "Vacuuming the house is a woman's job." "Washing the car is a man's job." I don't believe that legislation of these matters is right. For a husband and wife, Love must view all these concerns as "ours" as and dictate that we equally work together, because it is for our mutual benefit that all these things be taken care of as efficiently as possible.

True love makes us all servants/slaves. True love looks for ways to ease the load of others. We count it a privilege to give of ourselves for the better of others. You've probably discovered that some people are hard to love. That is quite human and natural, but nevertheless, we still need to work at the difficult as well as continue doing what comes easy to us.

I would remind us that the love of romance should lead to the love of service in our homes. And, let me add, real brotherly love should show the same willingness to usefully serve those we are in contact with on a regular basis. Take the time to show some "real" love in your home, in your workplace and in your Church. We'll all be the better for it. "Love is patient. Love is kind." (1 Corinthians 13:4a)

**WHAT DOES GOD WANT?**

*"Teach me to do your will, for you are my God;*
*may your good Spirit lead me on level ground."*

~Psalm 143:10

The important matter is, "What does God want?" The funny thing is that in our hurry to do our own stuff we sometimes forget that, in everything, He is interested in all the details that make up our lives. He does have a perfect plan for us that includes His protection and provision in order to fulfill His purposes if our lives are put into His care. The bottom line is that when we do it God's way, we will be blessed and He will be glorified. The big issue occurs with the battle on the inside. We want God but we want Him our way. We want His blessings but we want Him to bless our choices. It doesn't always work that way. You've probably discovered that on your own.

What does God want of you and me? Let me start by saying I don't think that He wants us to be puppets that are without intelligence and limp in His hand. As yielding and surrendered as that may sound, that is not what God had in mind when He formed us. He has created us with emotions, a free will and a measure of intelligence in order to be His representatives on earth. What God is looking for is for us to exercise our free will to surrender our choices to Him. That doesn't happen "once for all." The tests are laid before us daily, and the devil will do his best to persuade us to disregard the prior claims that God has on our lives so that we make the choices we want for our own pleasure. That game backfired on Adam and Eve and the rules of encounter have not changed since then. Here is a basic suggested list of regulations that we all need to learn and practice every day:

1. Let God know that you want to serve Him in every area of your life.

2. What does God's revealed will through His Word say to us on this matter? Once we know that, the choices should be easy. (Example: "Do not be yoked together with unbelievers" 2 Corinthians 6:14). If you need an explanation on that one, you're not listening very closely.

3. When the Word doesn't clearly spell out God's counsel, it is wise to seek the wisdom of mature believers. (Example: Should I buy a new car with my present budget?) Be honest and let wise people give you advice.

4. When that isn't easily available, we should proceed in the direction of our heart with a willingness to back up if His prompting speaks of His disapproval. There is nothing wrong with making mistakes if we learn a lesson from them and then get back on track. The Spirit of God is good at rescuing us and extending the mercy of God to us in what seems to be a failure. This can be a very intimate experience with God as He speaks to our hearts.

49

**| ON BEING LOST**

*"Rejoice with me; I have found my lost sheep."*

~Luke 15:6b

We had just returned from four-and-a-half years in Argentina a couple of weeks before Christmas. Our son was only three years old, and apart from "cookie please" his complete vocabulary was Spanish. We took him to shop with us in one of the biggest stores in the city, amongst the crowds of the seasonal rush and push, everyone hurrying to get their Christmas gifts together as quickly as possible. As we sought out the presents that would bring delight to our family on Christmas morning we suddenly realized that Kevin was no longer with us. Panic filled our hearts. Somewhere in the crowd of shoppers, our little boy was lost. He was, of course, too short to see us. There was too much noise around, so he could not hear us. English was a foreign language to him so that whatever he did say to anyone around him, no one would understand, nor would he understand anyone who tried to communicate with him. We moved quickly through the crowd, calling his name, searching under clothing racks that had become hiding places for him and around the tables and bins loaded with merchandise. At some point, he would realize that he was without a Father and Mother; that all the people around him were strangers. His protection, care and nurture were gone. He may have thought farther than that—his home was gone; his family and those who loved him were gone. In the business and rush of the people that were all around him, he was all alone and it looked like no one seemed to care.

At one moment, the crowds parted and I saw our little boy, with tears streaming down his cheeks, one finger clicking on his front teeth, but not a sound coming from his lips. Our embrace was nervously joyful.

I think I learned a personal lesson on "lostness" that day. Would someone who suddenly came to the realization that they were helplessly, hopelessly, without a home for eternity feel the kind of emotions that a little three-year-old must have felt? Then again, there are many who only become aware of the despair of their "lostness" after they've been found. What of the multitudes of our world today who have never heard the story of God's searching love and provision of a home for them in heaven? What of the generations in our own land who have given up listening to pompous sermons and watching the empty phoney faith of believers who have not learned to exercise their trust in God? The truth is, they may not be asking the questions that we think should concern them, but they are looking for answers that would bring solutions to the confusion around us. Jesus Christ is the only answer to man's "lostness."

We need to carry this message, wrapped in sincere love, and whether in foreign lands or right here at home, make it clear that there is a God in heaven who cares about us.

50

█ **ETERNALLY SECURE**

*"LORD, you have assigned me my portion and my cup;*
*you have made my lot secure."*

~Psalm 16:5

Security has become a big issue to this computer generation. Information that flies around the world in a matter of seconds can be tapped into by invisible intruders who know how to convert personal information into a new identity. Then, through electronic processes they can divert finances and shares in stocks and bonds into their own accounts and simply disappear. It has become a high-tech game. Computer companies are continually upgrading anti-virus programs to monitor and control the unseen invaders from entering and changing their programs. Someone has said that the best place to be secure is to put your savings in a sock and stick it under your mattress. Now, that is not my personal recommendation, but obviously, there aren't many perfectly secure places in the world anymore.

That reminds me that Jesus said, "Do not store up for yourselves treasures on earth, where moth and rust destroy, and where thieves break in and steal. But store up for yourselves treasures in heaven..." (Matthew 6:19-20). Treasures in heaven?! That is an interesting concept. Is there a more secure place in all of creation? Consider, after all the effort we put into many things in this world, it is terrible to think that someone can come along and take them from us and we have no way of getting them back. What a waste of time and energy! No wonder they call it criminal.

But Jesus is looking at the matter in a different light. There are some things that you can store to enjoy at a future date. His concern was that we get too involved in building, possessing and saving things that will eventually disappear. He reminds us that there is another option. We can begin to put away things that are of eternal value that will bring us benefits in heaven. For example, the Bible teaches that intercessory tears are saved in heaven; that prayers ascend before God like precious incense. I believe that the gifts of tithes and offerings are noted in God's book of records of things done in the body that will be evidence of our trust and confidence in God. Jesus said, "A cup of cold water to one of these little ones...will certainly not lose his reward" (Matthew 10:42). I know that Jesus does not intend to tell us that working for earthly things is not important. I understand that He did express concern that we are so taken up with gaining earthly treasures that we forget they will fade away and that what is done for the Lord will remain to bring us eternal benefits. It has been said that you cannot out-give God. Any investment in His kingdom in even small ways will bring great rewards. It takes faith to see that as a possibility. The carnal mind will struggle with it, but the mind of faith will say, "If God said it, I believe it."

Now let's get out there and try it. The process involves investing our earthly goods to prosper heavenly principles.

❙ **YOU CAN RUN BUT YOU CAN'T HIDE**

*"But if you fail to do this, you will be sinning against the LORD;*
*and you may be sure that your sin will find you out."*

~Numbers 32:23

He sat on the edge of his seat as the prophet related the message. His emotions rose to anger as the sermon progressed. He could never remember seeing the prophet so involved in an illustration. His own emotions, from his Shepherd and Warrior years, rose into a fury of anger as the sermon progressed. It was all so vivid to him. How could anyone commit such an injustice?! The rich farmer was abusing the tender love of the poor farmer for his solitary lamb while he himself possessed an abundance of sheep. "Stop! That man does not deserve to live!"

If it weren't so serious, we would say it's almost funny. David had never felt a message so personally as he did this one and had never reacted so judiciously. He noted the nervousness of the restless prophet as he took another deep breath, paused for but a brief moment; then with a dramatic piercing look Nathan replied, "You are the man!"

David was caught in the message, hook, line and sinker. He was the man who had abused his rights and privileges. He was the man who had taken another man's wife and had her husband killed. His was the plan to hide his sin. It was his lust, fear and deceit that so far, had gone uncovered. BUT GOD had seen it all. He could argue that he was not to blame; that it was the woman who caused him to fall. He could have silenced the voice of the prophet with a simple command to "take off his head." He could have persuaded his leaders and his kingdom that, as king, he had every right to all that was under his royal domain. He could have insisted that other kings had done worse things than this and that it was quite acceptable by all worldly standards. Instead, he bowed his head and cried, "I have sinned against the Lord." His own confession became a song in the hymnbook of Israel. He tells his own story of repentance in Psalm 51, as he humbly wept his way into the presence of God and cast himself upon His mercy and forgiveness. As you read this Psalm, you feel his pain as, broken, he seeks for God's favour to return upon his life once again.

My mother used to repeat an old proverb to us: "Oh, what a tangled web we weave when first we practice to deceive." The Bible says, "You may be sure your sin will find you out" (Numbers 32:23). That can be a very humiliating experience. I think we all need to remember that the Devil is an evil taskmaster, deceiving us into thinking that pleasure is the real reward of what we do. Sin has other consequences that we may not see at first.

Be assured, child of God, God loves you too much to let you get away with sin. He most certainly wants you to get it out and repented of before it's too late. It is not in His pleasure to condemn anyone, but it is His joy to stop the ravages of sinning that robs us of the joy and fellowship of His presence. God is LOVE and He still forgives those who come to Him.

❚ **REAL LOVE**

*"...God is love."*

~1 John 4:8b

This is the most simple and profound explanation of who God is. It explains who He is and why He does what He does. Now, it is true that we don't always see the emotion in God that we expect from a loving relationship, but the long-term evidences are to be seen throughout history. Many are the stories throughout the scriptures of the Lord exercising patience and kindness to a people who were rebellious and unthankful. He has been faithful to His promises and sensitive to the cries of His people in need. Generations attest to the fact that God is a tender, loving, compassionate Friend who cares for His people. The psalmist David drew on his years of experience through the good and the bad times to say, "Give thanks to the LORD, for he is good; his love endures forever" (1 Chronicles 16:34). That is God!

When God created humanity in the beginning He had expectations that man, made in His image, would somehow reflect the same characteristics of His Divine nature. However, after less than one generation of human existence Cain, fresh from a "worship" service, in a fit of anger killed his brother. Generations since have carelessly neglected the developing of the kind of love that God IS. No wonder Jesus would say, "A new command I give you: Love one another" (John 13:34a). Notice that it is not worded as a suggestion. Although it is not listed with the other ten commandments of the Old Testament, it is clear that all of the details of the Decalogue are superseded by this commandment. "The entire law is summed up in a single command: 'Love your neighbour as yourself'" (Galatians 5:14).

Love was not intended to be a romantic experience only. It is a lifestyle. We have confused it with the theatrical terminology of Hollywood influence. Around Valentine's Day the world of commerce takes advantage of the oozy, lovey-dovey sentiments that we think are the true expressions of love. However, the kind of love that God expects from us is not measured by the value of a gift but by the attitude of our day-by-day lifestyles. Please don't be snowed by the rant of commerce that invites you to spend $50+ dollars for a dozen roses that are supposed to say "I love you." There is no escape from the fact that true love takes on the attitude of a servant; it forgives, is patient, restores, holds no grudges, blesses, surrenders, speaks no evil, thinks only the best and gives of oneself. If all of this is supplemented by the roses, then it's O.K. But there isn't a gift you can put in a box that will replace the lifestyle expressions. Love is intended to reach to everyone who can be influenced by our gracious conversation and benevolent acts. The bottom line is that God wants us to love like Jesus does and there is no substitute.

"...let us love one another, for love comes from God" (1 John 4:7).

**❙ DESCRIBING LOVE**

*"But when the kindness and love of God
our Savior appeared, he saved us…"*

~Titus 3:4-5a

Poets through the centuries have tried to describe love in terms of endearment and romance as from the heart of a lover. Most will admit that there is no way that one could properly portray the bubbling emotions of the heart and the dreams that fill the minds of two who have "fallen in love." When it comes to explaining the love of God, the task becomes infinitely more difficult. We know that we are dealing with someone whose basic nature is love. And, because He is God, we are dealing in infinite values. We have difficulty finding words that will adequately portray the magnitude of the love of God. There is no thermometer, barometer or other kind of gauge that can measure the fullness of His love. We can use some of the things that He has said to help us understand more about Himself and His love for us. For example:

"'For I know the plans I have for you,' says the LORD, 'plans to prosper you and not to harm you, plans to give you hope and a future'" (Jeremiah 29:11).

"Many, O LORD my God, are the wonders you have done. The things you planned for us no one can recount to you; were I to speak and tell of them, they would be too many to declare" (Psalm 40:5).

"The LORD himself goes before you and will be with you; he will never leave you nor forsake you. Do not be afraid; do not be discouraged" (Deuteronomy 31:8).

"…I have loved you with an everlasting love; I have drawn you with loving kindness" (Jeremiah 31:3).

Jesus came into the world to be a living example of the Love of the Father. All the things He said and did represented the feelings and emotions of God towards humanity. He came as the Healer, Supplier, Teacher, Counsellor, Miracle-worker, Companion, and Friend. His actions confirmed the compassion and mercy of God as he reached out to all kinds of people, from the "uppermost" to the "guttermost," across the span of generations and nationalities. He came because He loved people and knew that there was no other way they could be brought into His Father's presence without His intervention. That's the reason why He came to my "house" one day, and why He came to yours.

During one of His teaching sessions He shared a principle that He intended to live by. "Greater love has no one than this, that he lay down his life for his friends" (John 15:13). He showed the whole world the full extent of His love by becoming the servant of God and the substitute of man by taking the consequences of all our sin upon Himself on the cross at Calvary. Because of His love, He was willing to be the replacement for all mankind and pay the absolute price that would make a way for us to be brought back to God. That's what we remember each Holy Communion service. The cost was high! He paid it with His own life out of His love for each of us.

54

**OLDER TREASURES**

*"Rise in the presence of the aged, show respect for the elderly
and revere your God. I am the LORD."*

~Leviticus 19:32

Growing old is both a pain and a pleasure. The joyful side comes from the recognition of the lessons learned through the many experiences of life. Both the good and the foggy memories of the bad become the fuel of the quiet times. The examination of how things used to be compared to how they are today remind the older folk that growing old is a real accomplishment worthy of special recognition. There ought to be a hero's badge given to those who have traversed the years to becoming a Senior; to those who have kept the faith and retained their joy. After all, just surviving life is a kind of war in itself.

Probably no generation in all of history has witnessed such dramatic changes as from the "simple" but often strenuous way of life of past years to the dynamics and often confusing ways of modern technology. And there is still more to come. The painful part comes with the realization that these bodies weren't designed to live forever. Every Senior knows that. Although on the inside, they feel there is no change from the earlier days of life, when it comes to moving the outside part to fulfill the youthful activities of the mind they discover that physically it's just not there anymore. It's at that stage of life when the scriptures remind us, "...though outwardly we are wasting away, yet inwardly we are being renewed day by day" (2 Corinthians 4:16).

It's the inward part that is spoken of in this passage that needs to be acknowledged as truly being a hidden treasure that should be discovered and enjoyed. Some older folk have given up and have stepped out of the arena of "life." Let me remind you, you are not a "has-been." You are capable of being a spiritual activist by the exercise of your faith in the God who is the Ancient of Days. We are told that most things get better with age. Never is that more true than when we are talking about people. Lessons from life's experiences are invaluable, and our Seniors hold a treasure house of wisdom gleaned from years of struggle and stress. Add to that the factor that our Seniors have centuries of cooperative involvement in trusting and proving the faithfulness of the Lord through some very troublesome times. Theirs is the kind of contribution that needs to be recognized in a generation of changing values. God has not failed to be there through the struggles and stresses of past experiences, and He will still be available for those of this and future generations, because God never changes. Our Seniors will tell us that God still answers prayer. They will remind us that the pleasures of the world cannot compare to the joy of keeping the pledges of commitment to honouring God.

When it comes right down to the sunset side of life, believers will tell us that there are no regrets for those who have served the Lord. God is good. I believe that the Bridegroom has saved the best wine to the last. (John 2:9,10) A final word to all Seniors and wannabe Seniors – enjoy yourself! I say, "Rejoice in the Lord always" (Philippians 4:4a). God is faithful.

| **WHAT A DAY THAT WILL BE!**

*"Look, he is coming with the clouds, and every eye will see him,*
*even those who pierced him...So shall it be, Amen."*

~Revelation 1:7

Jesus is coming back again, just like He said He would. The event will take a lot of people by surprise in spite of the fact that Pastors and Prophets have been sounding out the message for centuries. For the Church, we look forward with eager expectation to His returning and to the clear triumph of the procession of the saints who will be caught up to meet Him in the air.

What a day that will be! There will be family reunions with loved ones who have walked through the valley of the shadow of death. Together our physical frames will be changed into "spiritual" bodies that will be able to enjoy God's presence for timeless eternity. Those who struggled with physical disabilities will be set free with new, transformed abilities to see, hear, smell, touch, taste, leap and hold as never before. Pain and sickness will be left behind. Sorrow and discouragement will be history. The struggle against the Tempter and the Destroyer of our souls will be finished. His sting and his power will have no effect on us any longer. We'll be caught into the presence of the One who loves us with an everlasting love. He will take us to His Father's house where we will humbly bow in grateful praise and worship for Who He is and for all He's done for us. We will be embraced by Boundless Love.

The beauty of that place is beyond our present ability to understand. The Apostle John, in his description of heaven in the book of Revelation, struggled for adequate adjectives to paint the heavenly portrait. Suffice it to say, "No eye has seen, no ear has heard, no mind has conceived what God has prepared for those who love him" (1 Corinthians 2:9).

Without a doubt, the most wonderful part of the whole transition will be the moment we see our Saviour face to face. Yet, I imagine that the longing I have to see my Master is greatly overshadowed by His desire to present us to the Father in heaven. He's the One who loves us, came into the world to set us free from sin, who died and rose again, who ascended into His Father's presence to prepare a place for us. He's the One who intercedes for us at the Father's right hand, and He's the One who will welcome us Home. After all His suffering on our behalf, what a joy it will be to be able to express our appreciation without the limitations of our present weaknesses.

Jesus is coming back again. Let's be watchful and doing what He has left us to do. He may return today.

56

▌ ## THE REAL GENTLE GIANT

*"Taste and see that the LORD is good;*
*blessed is the man who takes refuge in him."*

~Psalm 34:8

We are first introduced to the Spirit of God as He is reportedly seen in the darkness, over a formless and empty world (Genesis 1:1). Like a gigantic Eagle fluttering over a bunch of sticks that would soon become her nest, the Holy Spirit hovered over the earth. He was about to begin a project that was going to be the object of God's special attention for centuries to come.

We meet the Holy Spirit many more times throughout scripture as He works in human lives, calling sinners and empowering saints each for special purposes in the Divine plan of God. He often exercises His supernatural abilities to give wisdom and to anoint those who were chosen for extraordinary responsibilities. It is obvious that He has a continuing occupation of developing exceptional evidences of God's interest in humanity. One of His primary focuses at this time is directed toward the Church.

1. *He works on the hearts of sinners to make them realize their need of a Saviour*—impressing, convicting and calling to repentance. He then makes them a part of the Church universal.

2. *He works in the Church to make us more like Jesus in the daily routine of our lives* (i.e. nurturing love, joy, peace, long-suffering, gentleness, goodness, faithfulness, meekness and self-control). If you don't think this is an extraordinary purpose, you haven't met some of the people that I know who are still growing in their spiritual walk with God.

3. *He works with individuals to empower them with special giftings that make evident an exceptional ability for a particular task* (ex. healings, messages, faith, wisdom and special insights into situations.)

4. *He comes into the lives of believers in an experience known as the Baptism of the Spirit,* (being filled with the Spirit), where the believer surrenders to the Lord in praise and worship with the evidence of speaking in other tongues by the Spirit.

He always works as an "absolute Gentleman" in the things that He does. He forces no one; He speaks in gentle tones, heard more by the heart that the ear; He nudges as He leads us by inner promptings rather than by pushing and shoving; He is a Comfort to us when we are in distress. He is a Faithful Friend and Counsellor.

▌ **Be Real**

> *"...stand up and praise the Lord your God, who is from everlasting to everlasting...Blessed be your glorious name, and may it be exalted above all blessing and praise."*
>
> ~Nehemiah 9:5b

When Jesus was upset with people He did not hide His feelings. Most often His indignation was against the self-righteous religious leaders of His day who would give the outward appearance of deep devotion but who inwardly were spiritually dead.

I believe it is imperative for the Christian to be "real," through and through. We are to be the kind of people whose integrity is beyond question; whose lives are not just words or an act, but whose faith is built on a real experience with a wonderful, living Saviour. After all, we are who we are by the Grace of God. This is not a day to step back from letting the world know what has happened in our hearts. It is very possible that some are hesitant to make a public statement of their faith because they suspect that there may be an adverse reaction to their testimony.

The counsel of a wise King may help some to be encouraged to be true to their Lord. "The fear of man will prove to be a snare, but whoever trusts in the LORD is kept safe" (Proverbs 29:25). The situation in Jesus' day was that people professed to be what they were not, and Jesus knew it. I wonder if that is any worse than not professing what we really are because we're afraid of what people will think. The point I want to make is that we have received so much from the Lord that we, in humble gratitude, ought to demonstrate what we really are and what we really believe. Be real! That should not change with the weather or the company we keep.

Perhaps you've heard of the Bible College student who found summer employment in a logging camp. When he returned to College in the fall, some asked him how he survived the summer in such ungodly circumstances. His response? "Oh, that was easy. No one even suspected that I was a Christian."

I'm afraid that kind of hypocrisy must be very upsetting to the Lord. Plain and simple, we are called to be the light of the world. Our lives need to fearlessly reflect the light of the SON. Something about Him should be seen through us on a regular basis, or else we are bad examples of a good God. Paul wrote to Titus saying, "I want you to stress these things, so that those who have trusted in God may be careful to *devote themselves to doing what is good*" (Titus 3:8, emphasis added).

You see, a true Christian experience is demonstrated through our deeds as well as our words. Verbal profession without the lifestyle is like clouds without rain. (Jude 1:12)

May the Lord help us to be all we were called to be and nothing less.

▌ **JUST IN TIME**

*"There is a time for everything and a season for*
*every activity under heaven."*

~Ecclesiastes 3:1

I've always wondered who we are trying to fool by changing the clocks ahead one hour during the spring and back in the fall. It seems to me that the day is still twenty-four hours long. They tell me that you're supposed to get an hour more of daylight to enjoy in your waking hours, but I've discovered that I still wake up in the dark and go to bed in the dark, so what's new? The truth is we have so much control over time, and still, so little control over time. It's obvious that we have the responsibility to regulate what we do with every moment of our life, and yet, time moves on and waits for no one.

When the Bible refers to "Redeeming the time..." (King James Version) the modern translations read "..making the most of every opportunity" (Ephesians 5:16), and the thought is to remind us that time will come to an end at some point. Whether it's through the process of dying or at the beckoning of the trumpet call of God, time will cease to exist. At the same time, any opportunity to do something in this world for God will be history. We need to plan our lives in such a way that the opportunities to serve God do not slip by without an effort on our part to do what He has created us to do.

I always find it interesting that God, who is timeless, designed us with time limitations but also established His program so that His only begotten Son would be confined to the same conditions. Can you imagine what it would be like for God, who never slumbers nor sleeps, to be suddenly bound to a daily schedule like every one of us. He knew the time of day and the eating habits of society, so He provided lunch for the people around him at least two times and breakfast at least once. He knew when it was safe to go to certain places and when to delay His arrival, all for very special reasons according to His reading the clock.

But most importantly, the Bible makes it clear that He came into the world, "when the time had fully come" (Galatians 4:4), to be the Saviour of the world. He came just in time. He came to die at Calvary, just in time. (It was the feast of the Passover). Instead of a little lamb dying for the annual covering of sins, Jesus became the Lamb of God to take away all the sin of the world at one time.

It's about time that we recognized what Jesus Christ came into the world to do. His death was to give us access to the Father who longs to pour out living blessings upon those who trust Him. We must not delay the wonderful opportunities that He offers us to be a very blessed people. Soon the timelessness of eternity will claim us as we join the saints of history in a great reunion in the Presence of our Eternal Lord.

▌ **CALL TO PRAYER**

*"When [not if] you pray... "*

~Luke 11:2a

Occasionally, in Church, an invitation is extended for a special week of prayer emphasis. We want God to do what He wants us to do in the Church and prayer is always the starting point. We need to learn to place ourselves before Him in order to hear His voice and to learn the lessons that He wants us to learn. We are a needy people living in a needy world. God alone has the answers to the many problems that perplex our society as well as each congregation. We need to hear from Him. Each believer should set aside a special time to make the extra effort required to be a part of an united emphasis to seek the Lord from time to time. Prayer is time invested into the spiritual development of His Church and each believer in the world. It is also the beginning process of reaching the "lost" of our generation.

We have many promises in His word that remind us that when we seek the Lord, He will hear and answer prayer. "If my people, who are called by my name, shall humble themselves and pray and seek my face and turn from their wicked ways, then I will hear from heaven and will forgive their sin and will heal their land" (2 Chronicles 7:14).

"You will seek me and find me when you seek me with all your heart" (Jeremiah 29:13).

1. I believe in the importance of private times of prayer when we are alone with God. Jesus often spent quiet times alone with His heavenly Father.

2. I see, as well, the value of a united prayer effort when we do our best to meet together to encourage each other in prayer. The early Church believers had a regular plan for united prayer where they ministered to each other and waited on the Lord. It's times like that when we have a sense of belonging to a wonderful, caring body of friends.

I think that it is important to be built up in the Lord through our personal prayer lives on our own, but it is so much more of a blessing to the whole church when we are prepared to build up others by making the extra effort to being "together" in a group sharing one another's burdens and cares. After all, that's one of the reasons that the Lord leaves us here on earth after we come to know Him. We need to learn how to encourage each other in prayer.

God answers prayer.

**| BE A HERO**

*"This cup is the new covenant in my blood, which is poured out for you."*

~Luke 22:20b

It is a fact that the sight of blood makes some people sick and others faint. However, Doctors and nurses get used to seeing wounds and abrasions and have learned how to stem the flow of this very valuable resource of our lives.

The Canadian Blood Services holds clinics for people who are willing to give blood to be used in giving life to others who have been involved in serious accidents or are in need of surgery. Their motto is: "Be a hero. Give life." Many rise to the challenge and take the time to give a part of themselves for others they do not know.

If that is the description of a hero, then I know the greatest hero of them all. Jesus gave His life-blood to grant life to every man, woman and child through His death on the cross over 2000 years ago. The truth is that only His precious blood can deal with the issue of sin that is a plague upon all of mankind. There is no other medicine that offers a cure for the problem of sin that lies within every one of us. The Bible says, "... the blood of Jesus, his Son, purifies us from all sin" (1 John 1:7b).

This is intended to be a "Good News" announcement. There is a solution to deal with the greatest issue of life. Jesus said that He came into the world "to seek and to save what was lost" (Luke 19:10). The lost are those who need His forgiveness in order to live life "... to the full" (John 10:10b).

The blood of Jesus Christ is a remedy that will wash away all our sins and grant us peace with God with eternal life as a result. The key is that we need to apply to Jesus, personally, for the cure that will give us these benefits. At some time, we all need to face the fact that without Jesus there is <u>NO</u> hope for us until we ask Him to wash away all our sin. The Bible makes it clear that we "all have sinned and fall short of the glory of God" (Romans 3:23). But there is a life changing experience that we receive when we invite Jesus Christ into our lives. That's where the blood of Jesus comes into effect in our lives. God declares us clean of all sin when we ask for His forgiveness.

He's the real hero.

▌ **SHARING OUR FAITH**

*"Come, follow me," Jesus said, "and I will make you fishers of men."*

~Mark 1:17

Reaching the lost has always been the great interest of the Heart of God. I think it's important to continue to keep "reaching out to sinners" in proper focus because this is the reason that Jesus came into the world. There are people "out there" who need to know the Lord in a personal way. We have the experience and we need to make it known. Here are some things we can continue to do:

1. *Pray* for those outside of the Church. Jesus said, "Ask the Lord of the harvest, therefore, to send out workers into his harvest field" (Matthew 9:38). Almost everything that God does is begun with our coming to Him first, telling Him our concerns or asking Him to intervene. We need to intercede for the lost with compassion as Jesus did for us in John 17. Winning souls has always been His heart's desire.

2. *Be prepared* to speak of the things that God has been doing in your life. "Always be prepared to give an answer to everyone who asks you to give the reason for the hope that you have. But do this with gentleness and respect" (1 Peter 3:15b). Think about it beforehand. You don't need to speak a lot of theology. It is most practical to relate your personal experiences with the Lord.

3. *Watch for opportunities* to express your faith. Your life and your speech are the best sermons that most people will ever hear. How you live and your reactions to all kinds of situations will tell a very important story of what God means to you. Be attentive to the prompting of the Spirit of God to speak a kind word in brotherly love. Let them see the joy that Jesus gives.

4. *Don't cut yourself off from unchurched people.* Most Christians lose contact with the Mission field of the unsaved by cutting off any friendship with those who still need the message of God's love. We must learn how to be friendly in worldly situations without compromising our example and our message. We don't have to agree with the position of the world to reach into it to rescue those who will respond to His call to repentance. There are many who are looking for answers to the ache of their hearts, and we hold the key to finding those answers. God loves them more than we could imagine and it's time that the people in the world recognized that. We need to express our love and friendliness in a stronger way. We may be the only Gospel that they will ever meet in their world of confusion. Jesus left heaven to come to our world to rescue us. Now it's our turn to do the same for those who are lost.

| **TRUSTING IN PAIN**

*"When I am afraid I will trust in you. In God, whose word I praise, in God
I trust; I will not be afraid. What can mortal man do to me?"*

~Psalm 56:3-4

Everyone heard the call for help. The crowds that gathered around the
Master all heard her cry, but "Jesus did not answer a word" (Matthew 15:23a). I
suppose you've wondered, occasionally, as have I, whether God is deaf. I know
that there have been many calls to Him for assistance in some pretty important
matters to us, and God does not seem to respond. The truth is that the testing of
our faith sometimes carries a lot of inner pain. We struggle with our own self-
worth, our standing in Christ and our ignorance about, "What is God doing,
anyhow?"

Let's learn to rest in a number of very basic principles:

1. "God is love" - He cares and is concerned about every detail that comes
into our lives. He feels the pain we feel and He knows the battles of the mind that
tend to bring us down, but we need to learn that some of the discomforts that
come to our lives are for our good. It may be like a visit to the Dentist who needs
to jab us with his needle in order to do what must be done to relieve the pain we're
going through. He might as well say, "You've got to get worse before you can get
better." We understand that kind of reasoning until the Doctor is God. Let's be
patient in affliction because He has a way of making, "all things work together for
the good" (Romans 8:28a).

2. "God is love" - and His desire is that we meet with Him often because He
has so designed us for fellowship with Himself. Even if the pain does not go
away, many will report that His presence and blessing in time of need have
developed a new trust and confidence in God that makes it all worthwhile. His
delays in responding may be His method of prolonging the process of communion
in prayer. A relationship with Him is better than getting the answer to our prayers.

3. "God is love" - and it is important to Him that you appear sincere and
"real" with those around you. There are too many good-time believers who are
happy to serve God when everything is going right. However, it takes a real
man/woman of God to stand strong in faith when it seems that God is not
answering prayer, today. The lesson learned may not be for you but for someone
who is watching you. So, let the whole world know that you serve a wonderful
God, who is awesome in the things that He does, even when He doesn't do
anything. That's a real test of faith.

**█ LET'S GET EXCITED**

*"Then Miriam the prophetess, Aaron's sister, took a tambourine in her hand, and all the women followed her, with tambourines and dancing."*

~Exodus 15:20

The Gaither's made famous a song that goes like this: "Get all excited, Go tell everybody, that Jesus Christ is King." There is nothing that attracts a crowd like genuine excitement, and I believe that we have a lot to be excited about. God has been good to us in so many ways—in our own lives as well as in the life of the Church. I've discovered that excitement is not only because of what has happened in the past but also for what we anticipate is going to happen in the future. We have both kinds. We get excited about what He has done, who He is and what He will yet do. I don't think anyone in the world can express that kind of joy and excitement like those who believe in Jesus Christ as Lord and Saviour. Sometimes it takes great faith in order to believe what you do not see. That is what is meant by "glorifying the Lord."

Let me remind you of some of the wonderful benefits of knowing the Lord:

1. Your sins are forgiven.
2. You've been adopted into a wonderful family.
3. You personally have access to the awesome presence and power of God.
4. Your future is a part of God's eternal plan and heaven is your eternal destiny.

Hey! If you can't get excited about that, you should remember that Jesus Himself said, "Rejoice that your names are written in heaven" (Luke 10:20b). This is a wonderful fact, a present joy and our future hope, and it is worth getting emotional about the things that God has done.

Besides that, it's time to get excited about what God is going to do in our world and in His Church. His Spirit is moving in very precious ways. You have a Church family who are absolutely wonderful and who desire to see the Lord do what only He can do. Let's be excited with them. Let's be expecting. Let's be faithful to do what God wants us to do and sensitive to what He is saying to each of us.

We can be anticipating a real visitation upon us as we catch the vision of what God wants to do in our community and through each of us. Please, be prayerful, because we want to reach out with the joyful message that God loves our world and every hurting and heart-broken person that we meet. Let's get excited!

█ **COME ON BACK**

*"Not everyone who says to me, 'Lord, Lord,' will enter the Kingdom of heaven, but only he who does the will of my Father who is in heaven."*

~Matthew 7:21

There was a generation in Biblical history that had forgotten their responsibility to the Lord. After many years of blessing and God's intervention in the matters of their nation they left God and His directions and began to trust in themselves. "...everyone did as he saw fit" (Judges 17:6).

It seems that commitment to the plans and purposes of God had become irrelevant. The people decided they didn't need anyone, God or king, to tell them what to do. They were prepared to make up their own mind about important matters and, unknowingly, live with the consequences.

Now that sounds a lot like our generation. Respect for God and His requirements and respect for people in authority are definitely not at the top of the list of people's priorities. Could that be true in the Church as well? Whatever happened to the call to, "Seek first the kingdom of God...?" Why are we so caught up in doing things that please us and giving little thought to what God thinks about our lifestyle and our worship? I am grateful for those who are faithful to seek the Lord and who live their lives honouring Jesus as Lord. There are still many of them. But Jesus said, "When the Son of man comes, will he find faith on the earth?" (Luke 18:8b). Why would Jesus pose such a question unless it was meant to stir some individual soul-searching on our part? You be your own judge.

The people that know God ought to be responsible citizens of His kingdom and recognize that there needs to be a brand new resolve to putting Him first above all else. We live in a very immoral and materialistic generation whose philosophy is "If it makes me feel good can it be bad?" You would think that we would learn some of the lessons of history. When Israel decided to make their choices with selfish motives they paid an awesome price. They became dominated by other nations. Their children were taken as slaves. Their wives and daughters were abused and sold in the market. They lost ownership of the things they called house and home. Their personal pride was driven from them and they became a distraught and discouraged people.

Maybe the parallel to our time does not fit all those terrible details, but I send out a call. Come back! "Trust in the LORD with all your heart and lean not on your own understanding; in all your ways acknowledge him and he will make your paths straight" (Proverbs 3:5-6). That's a call to submission and obedience—it may not always be the expectation of the world. It may not even be comfortable to you, but God will honour and bless that kind of confidence in Him.

Sometimes it will be a step of faith because we need to learn to obey before we see the results. But God will not fail. He is faithful and more willing to give than we are to receive.

**▌ WALK IN THE LIGHT**

*"Blessed are those who have learned to acclaim you,*
*who walk in the light of your presence, O LORD."*

~Psalm 89:15

No one "turns on" the darkness. It just happens when the light goes out. Night comes when the sun goes down. Darkness is the result of the absence of light.

We used to get after our children for leaving lights on when they left a room. For a time, we had to bribe them with rewards for turning out the lights and being more considerate of the bills that we had to pay. However, I do not remember once telling them, "When you leave the room, turn on the darkness so we don't waste the light." We know what happens when the lights go out on a stormy night; we search for matches and candles so we can see something. Free activity is very limited. Vision and direction are stunted, and stumbling results. It may seem funny, but in absolute, total darkness it's easy to become disoriented and lose your balance. It's easy for your imagination to play tricks on you when the lights are out. We are creatures who are made for the light. For millennia, we have looked for options that will help us deal with the darkness. Fire, wax candles, oil lamps, gas lanterns, glow material, batteries and bulbs and electricity all became tools that we use to fight back the gloom and shadows.

It is true, though, that darkness does serve a very positive purpose. We sleep better when the lights are out. Rest comes easy when our eyes are no longer effective. However, darkness can be used for very evil purposes as well. The Bible says, "But men loved darkness instead of light because their deeds were evil" (John 3:19b). That describes the base nature of humanity. People would prefer that no one see what they are doing when they are practicing what comes natural to them. When the light comes on and reveals the things that people do in their darkest hours it can be very embarrassing and uncomfortable.

That is what the gospel message is all about. The light of the truth of the Word of God helps us to see where we are going. It even helps us to see where we have been. The Light of the World can shine in our hearts to challenge the darkness of sorrow, discouragement and despair and drive it away. It is the presence of God and His love that invites us to step out of the Kingdom of Darkness into His marvellous light, where purity and wholeness, through His forgiveness, become realities. It is also in His presence that we understand the true purpose of why we are alive and where we are going in the future. We don't need to feel our way around, guessing at probabilities. We have the assurance that a life surrendered to God is a life that can experience the light and freedom of His love. Invite the Light of the World into your life and let Him teach you His ways.

▌ **ONE DOOR**

*"I am the gate; whoever enters through me will be saved."*

~John 10:9a

It does concern some that we might be very narrow-minded when we say that, "there is no other name under heaven given to men by which we must be saved" (Acts 4:12). We have learned that Salvation is through the name of Jesus and no other. Some would like to widen the road to heaven to include the name of Jesus along with other gods and prophets. They argue that there are a lot of good people in other religions that believe they are going to a heaven of some kind. They would insist that we should be open to encouraging them to continue on their path of choice to their "hoped-for destination." After all, as someone has said, "Every coin has two sides." That is true, but when you're talking about the eternal soul of man and living in heaven or hell I believe that it's very important to know that there's only one way to get to heaven and a thousand ways to go to hell.

Someone else has said, "All roads lead to heaven." The truth is, any other road is the wrong road and it may lead you to many places, but definitely not to heaven.

When Jesus came into the world with the full intent of dying on the cross, it was because there was absolutely no other way to bring salvation and eternal life to mankind. He came because He is the only way! We don't need to be embarrassed to declare that truth anymore than a fireman needs not to be embarrassed who points the way to the only available exit from a burning building. He is doing us a great service in giving us good directions that will lead to a longer, safer life.

The truth of the matter is that there isn't a lot of time to debate the fact of how to be saved or whether there are other possible options. We must believe the Word of God and respect the directions that He has given us. The philosophers, wise men and those with good intentions who think about eternity have got to stop trusting in their own ideas and come to accept the plan that God has given for us to follow.

That's the message that needs to be told. We should speak it with confidence because we are living in a world that is seeking for solutions to what happens to us when we leave this world behind. At some time in each person's life each one needs to have an adequate presentation of the Gospel message shared with them. This is the message of the Church to the world today. It is not shared to exclude others but rather to welcome all to be a part of God's solution to the real necessities of mankind. Jesus is the answer to our world in need; there is no other and we are the ones to tell that story. A world of lost souls should have the opportunity to hear the message and then to make their choice.

Jesus said, "I am the way, the truth and the life."

**TOO LATE**

*"Then I beg you, father, send Lazarus to my father's house,*
*for I have five brothers. Let him warn them..."*

~Luke 16:27-28

Did you hear the story of the young couple in India, believers in one of the religions of the Orient, who in their quest for peace sought the counsel of their priest? They had tried everything they could think of that would satisfy the desires of their heart. To them, no sacrifice would be too great. As they shared with their spiritual leader they were shocked and dismayed to hear him say, "If you really want true peace, you must take your little child and throw him into the Ganges river as an offering to our god." Brokenhearted, but willing to risk all to gain the satisfaction they were longing for, they made their way to the riverside. On the banks, with a final wail and a sob, they cast their little newborn treasure into the murky waters of the Ganges. They clung to each other in sobs hoping that the depths of their sorrow would birth the peace that they long had sought after.

A stranger, seeing their tearful embrace but ignorant of what had just transpired, approached them. "May I pray with you? I serve a God who loves you and understands your sorrow and who longs to give peace to every man." He shared his own testimony of how Jesus Christ had come into his heart and washed away all his sins and that Jesus continued to add blessings to his life. His life was now in the Lord's hands and he had a peace that passed all understanding. He asked the young couple if they would like to ask Jesus to come into their hearts. He bowed his head and prayed the sinner's prayer with them. With the amen, the young lady, wiping the tears from her face and with a pleading look at the stranger, asked the simple question, "Why didn't you come sooner?"

That's a big question. The truth is, there are multitudes who stand on the banks of life searching for peace. Some are prepared to do anything to find the peace that we know. It takes a heart that weeps for them in their loneliness, in their sorrow, in their addictions and in their broken relationships to reach out to each; not with a sermon, but with a story—the story of God's love. Someone has said that the biggest obstacle to Missions is the lack of concern of the people in the Church. That couldn't be true of a people who have experienced the Grace and Mercy of a loving God, could it? Is it possible that we have been satisfied so long that we do not see the pain of others? Jesus saw the multitudes as sheep without a shepherd and He wept over them. They still need to be told the Good News. Will you look, see, go, and then tell your story before it's too late? Look today.

| **TELLING THE GOOD NEWS**

*"Indeed, the very hairs of your head are all numbered. Don't be afraid;*
*you are worth more than many sparrows."*

~Luke 12:7

Jesus asked the question, "What good is it for a man to gain the whole world, yet forfeit his soul?" (Mark 8:36). That could be the answer to the question, "How much is a soul worth?" Have you ever given that much thought? I'm sure that you know and understand the price that was paid to freely provide your Salvation. We are reminded often, in times of worship and under the sound of God's Word, that Jesus gave His life on the cross so that we could be part of the Divine family of God. I'm sure that you understand that the story and the application of those facts are God's gift to us, not based on anything more than the truth that God loved us while we were still sinners and enemies of God. We can't boast of any accomplishments that would make us worthy of receiving that marvellous gift.

The principle is simple. When we realize that God gave so much and that all He asks of us is to accept that wonderful offer, we are welcomed into a brand new relationship with an awesome God.

But let me press this a little bit further. We could never repay what Jesus did for us on the cross. The cost was too high. We owe a debt to Him that should be repaid by our loyalty and commitment to do the things that He wants us to do. That's a call to faithful obedience.

The thing that is closest to His heart is to broadcast the message of His wonderful love and what He has done, so that more would come to love and trust Him. In other words, we need to tell the story; to reach the lost; to share His life with this generation; to be bold in our living because we have been made a part of His heavenly family. We dare not hold back the truth. There's a world "out there" that has read all the bad things about "Christians." It's time they learned the truth. We're a body of believers who have had our sins forgiven and have a regular relationship with our living Lord. The experiences we live are joyful and exciting. We're not long-faced morons. We care for the wounded and hurting of our generation. We're sorry for the bad impressions that some have made who claim to be what we really are and we want to make it clear, 'Serving God is wonderful.' That's what the good news is all about.

▌ **COMING CLEAN**

*"But if we walk in the light as he is in the light, we have fellowship with
one another, and the blood of Jesus, His Son, purifies us from all sin."*

~1 John 1:7

No matter what we were doing during the day, one of the rules that we
learned as children was: "You don't come to the dinner table until you've washed
your hands." For a long time I was sure that was a verse in the Bible. It was
preached often to us as kids but I never learned where, exactly, it was found. I
think it's in the book of Hezekiah. (Don't look for it!)

Cleanliness and strict rules of separation were principles that the Nation of
Israel had to learn as they walked through the desert wilderness. These are
primarily the lessons that the book of Leviticus deals with. To us, it seems like a
lot of rules and regulations that touch almost every area of life. The clear message
through all of the details was that God is "holy" and requires that His people be
"holy" (without sin, righteous, clean).

I'm not going to get profoundly theological on you at this time, but being
holy is what being clean is all about. God has a treasure house of blessings that He
wants to share with His people every day. But the problem is that we need to be
clean when we come into His presence or we will remain unable to receive and
understand what His blessings are all about.

You see, my mother wasn't way out when she insisted that I have clean
hands before I ate my dinner. Her principle is easy to understand. You should
never eat good, wholesome food with dirty hands. God's principles should be
received in the same manner. If we sincerely want God's blessings we need to
come in a way that is pleasing to Him, because, in the end, it's good for us. The
psalmist asked the question, "Who may ascend to the hill of the Lord? Who may
stand in his holy place? He who has clean hands and a pure heart." (Psalm 24:3-
4b)

God wants to meet with every sinner in the whole, wide world to let us all
know that we can be made clean and pleasing to Him. All the things that offend
our wonderful, loving Lord can be washed away under the precious blood of
Jesus. That cleansing agent is what takes care of all the spots, stains and
uncleanness of a life that is not pleasing to God and brings us to holiness, for
"...without holiness no one will see the Lord" (Hebrews 12:14b).

The process is free for the asking. No matter where you've been or who you
are, God loves you and invites you to come to Him and be made clean.

God longs to share His divine presence with us, but the requirements must be
met. Simply, we must believe that when Jesus died on the cross, He provided a
way that we can all be made clean of the things that displease the Father.

"...the blood of Jesus, his Son, cleanses us from all unrighteousness." 1 John
1:7b

▌ **SERVING OTHERS**

*"We who are strong ought to bear with the failings of the weak
and not to please ourselves."*

~Romans 15:1

You've got to keep your eyes wide open all the time. I mean, it's a dangerous world out there. Now I'm not trying to scare anyone, but I do want to encourage us all to be on the lookout for our brothers and sisters. You see, we are our brothers' keeper, and the Lord has advised us, "Be devoted to one another in brotherly love. Honour one another above yourselves" (Romans 12:10).

You've heard it said that the proper order of service is "Jesus first, Others second and You at last." That is how you spell JOY, and it is totally contrary to the way the world thinks. Sometimes we get caught up in making our own lives comfortable and schedule our agendas according to what is convenient. Think of others. It's a fact that we are not all at the same level of maturity in our walk of Faith. There are a lot of folk who are a couple of steps behind us. We could scold them to hurry up. We could berate them because they take so long to enter in to the worship the way we do, or we could condemn them for being distracted by their struggles against the enemy. The fact remains that we need to look out for them as loving brothers. We must care for their condition and help them in their growing experiences. It's care they need, not lectures. It's love, not rules. It's patience, not insistence. What do we gain by making them angry because they are not like we are? They need to know that we love them right where they are.

We do a great service to the Kingdom of God if we will take time to call a word of encouragement to the stragglers; or give a warm embrace to the discouraged; or just a plain, sincere, 'How are you?' Someone has said that the best medicine against personal depression is to be an encourager of others. We need to practice that kind of remedy for ourselves.

*It is shameful to think that many people only come to Church to get a blessing?* No, I didn't say that's wrong and I'm not swinging on any chandeliers. Somehow, we need to learn that people are blessed when we are a blessing. That is, we come together to give a blessing and to serve people and the Lord. It is a fact that more people become committed to a Church because someone cared to demonstrate love to them than by many of the great sermons of many preachers. We need a change in attitude from "serve us" to "service."

Reach out and touch someone today. It's a dangerous world out there and we need to be on guard...for our brothers and sisters.

71

▌ **BECOMING LITTLE CHILDREN**

*"He said to them, 'Let the little children come to me, and do not hinder them, for the kingdom of God belongs to such as these.'"*

~Mark 10:14b

Jesus used many things as object lessons for His sermons. He spoke of yeast and its infiltrating powers; of the tiny mustard seed that grows to be a large tree. A coin became a lesson on values between the kingdom of heaven and Caesar's on earth. He taught about laying good foundations on solid rock rather than shifting sand. He used salt, candles, foxes, birds, lilies, and sunsets each to convey a special message to the people He taught. But one day, He took a little child and with the attention of every Mother and Father, brother and sister focused on Him, He said: "I tell you the truth, unless you change and become like little children, you will never enter the kingdom of heaven" (Matthew 18:3).

Do I hear you say that as a child you've been there and done that, too? After all, we argue, we have become mature adults and we put away all childish things. Maybe that's the key to the major problems of our world. We have become independent and self-sufficient. We are educated and capable of working through our own problems. We are strong enough to defend our rights and we've arrived to where we are by the sweat of our brow and our ingenuity.

Hey, that's not what Jesus wanted us to see. How far we have fallen from a total dependence on Him. We've lost sight of the Father and our need of His supply for the burdens of life. Worse, we have arrived to "maturity" and don't need God anymore.

Society is the proof that most people believe they can make it to heaven on their own. We need an attitude change. Jesus said that we needed to become like little children. Look at the innocence and the trusting beauty of little children as they walk hand in hand with a parent or skip along the street to the beat a children's song. Visit a playground or a park and watch the lively antics of these little treasures who bounce with boundless energy, until bedtime.

There are lessons to learn:

1.  We need to humble ourselves and acknowledge that we need the help of our heavenly Father. He's waiting for us to call.

2.  We can't get to heaven unless we come to the Father as trusting little children and commit our ways to Him.

3.  There are times when we need to drop our guard and let those around us have access to what is happening in our lives.

4.  But most important of all, we need to exercise simple faith and trust in our Heavenly Father who loves each of us as His own children.

MARCH 13 ▎ **YOU, TOO, ARE FAMOUS**

*"What good is it for a man to gain the whole world, yet forfeit his soul?"*

~Mark 8:36

Word has it that a famous hockey player is worth 9 million a year. That's probably more than all of us combined will make in a lifetime. I wonder, do you think that God is impressed by his hockey prowess? Do you think the angels in heaven will stand in line for his autograph if he makes it through the pearly gates? In God's eyes, how many of you would it take to make the value of that famous hockey player?

Hey, let me remind you that when the last puck is shot and all the hockey sticks are returned to their place in the dressing room and the role is called up yonder, you will stand in the presence of God as His own child while any famous sportsman, unless he's born again, will stand on his own. You see, the transition from the dressing room to the Palace of the King has a way of changing a lot of things that seem to be valuable and important. The king of hockey or the fastest racer has no more honour in the courts of heaven than the lowly beggar on Granville street in Vancouver.

You see, when Peter says that we are bought, not with corruptible things such as silver and gold but with the precious blood of Christ, a lamb without blemish or defect, he was talking about real value. Dollars and cents could never buy my Salvation, nor does being worldly famous give me extra credits in heaven. God was willing to let His own Son die as the only price that could set me free from sin and give me access to His Divine presence. That means, in God's sight, my personal value has increased an awful lot by the value that was necessary to pardon my transgressions. You see, because of what Jesus did in my place, the Father in Heaven looks upon me as one of His family. That puts me in line for a tremendous title and inheritance plus a very special relationship with our Heavenly Father when I finally go to His house.

However, the day of accountability will call us to report on what we've done with what we've got and how we have related our lives to His plan. The famous and the not so famous will have to stand before Him to give account of Spiritual worth, not monetary worth. The bottom line is that He loves you and me, not for what we do or have done, but because we trust in Him. The Bible speaks of the day of rewards as including crowns and laurels and commendations for running the race faithfully. You are worth a lot more than any famous sports person on earth simply because Jesus is your friend.

| **HE GAVE THANKS AND BROKE IT**

*"Therefore, as God's chosen people, holy and dearly loved, clothe yourselves with compassion, kindness, humility, gentleness and patience."*

~Colossians 3:12

He "...gave thanks and broke it..." It was one of those very special occasions when Jesus was alone with His disciples, eating, teaching and just visiting with them; and then..."He gave thanks."

He gave thanks because He was grateful that His daily needs were met by a wonderful, Heavenly Father who cared. Anyone who has been without food for any length of time knows how blessed we are to be able to eat whenever we want. But His gratitude went a lot deeper as He gave thanks. Holding the bread in his hands, knowing that within hours those hands that had been laid upon many a sick and weary person, would be pierced by Roman spikes, He gave thanks.

He gave thanks that salvation could become a reality to a world of lost humanity. He knew the price that must be paid and the pain that would be involved, but He looked forward to that moment with joy because He would be able to present each of us to His heavenly Father, pardoned through his sacrifice on the cross. He "gave thanks and broke it..."

The bread had to be broken to be shared. He wasn't just thinking about Himself. He had the needs of all of those around Him on His heart. A selfish person would have thought only of Himself, but He broke the bread and passed it to His disciples. Each one must have a share of what He gave. It was a gift from Jesus to be received, held and then personally taken. He did not come as a relic to be revered, studied and relegated to some bookshelf. Could you imagine the disciples putting the bread in their pockets to be consumed at some future date? It was to be eaten...NOW.

There are some who know all there is to know about Jesus and the cross and have treated those facts with dignity and respect because they believe they're an expression of a true gift of God. But their lives have not been changed. Jesus wants the principles of His life-giving sacrifice to be acted upon and received personally. In those moments with His disciples it was as though He held his own body in His hands and broke it to give Himself to His followers.

There are some who know all there is to know about Jesus and what He accomplished on the cross and have treated these facts with respect because they believe they're true. There is another step to take. That is to live like He has become a part of our daily routine; at home and in the work place. He gave Himself. Have you received Him?

74

▌ **GOD'S PEACE GIFT**

> *"For the wages of sin is death, but the gift of God*
> *is eternal life in Christ Jesus our Lord."*
>
> ~Romans 6:23

Don Richardson, one of the first missionaries to reach into unexplored Papua, New Guinea, tells us of his experiences in reaching the Natives and adapting to their culture. He discovered that deception was considered a virtue among these very primitive people. Their greatest pleasure was in befriending members of other tribes and leading the new friends, under the guise of goodness and kindness, into a trap where the unsuspecting person would eventually be murdered. Needless to say, the details of the process that led to the homicide were recounted, again and again, around the campfires amidst the laughter of the men in admiration of the killer's astuteness in accomplishing the "wonderful" deception. The problem was that the other tribe was not content until vengeance was measured upon the perpetrators of the foul deed. Thus, the history of the tribes was often stained with the blood of innocent victims who died in the execution of the virtue of deception.

However, in their unwritten laws, there was a provision to stop the carnage. By mutual agreement of the leaders of the warring tribes, a newborn son was taken from each of the tribes and a ceremony exchanging the "Peace Child" was celebrated. Peace would rule with the understanding that one of "ours" now lived with the other tribe and therefore harmony should be respected.

The Holy Spirit quickened the heart of Don Richardson as he recognized that the ceremony of the Natives had a clear application in the gospel message that he had struggled to convey. God gave us His only Son for the very same reason that the tribes exchanged their children: to make peace with mankind. Suddenly, the truth of the reason Jesus came into the world was seen in a different light. He was God's "Peace Child" who came to be the expression of God's love to each of us. The war is over! The Son of God came to live among us so that we could be reconciled to the Father.

Once a month, we remember the Lord's death through the Holy Communion emblems. Without Jesus' sacrifice on our behalf, we remain at war with the will and purpose of God. There is nothing that we can humanly do to stop the war because we cannot offer God anything that would justify a peaceful relationship with Himself. However, God took the initiative and extended a Peace offering to us in Jesus Christ. The moment we take the step of faith and accept Jesus into our lives, the war comes to a conclusion. We are brought into His family by virtue of the gift of His Son and welcomed to live under His pardon and forgiveness.

Invite Jesus into your life today and allow the Holy Spirit to be your Friend, Guide and Helper each day.

**PART OF THE TEAM**

*"To each one of us grace has been given as Christ apportioned it."*

~Ephesians 4:7

Missions is very important because reaching the lost has always been the plan of the heart of God. The amazing thing is that He invites us to participate in His project to bring all men to Himself. Without exception, we are all drafted into His service. Our areas of personal responsibility may be very different, but like a well-prepared and trained army, if we all do what we are supposed to do when He asks us to, there is no enemy that can stand in the way of the Church of Jesus Christ. We need to learn the value of each one of us doing our part. We often feel like we are very insignificant cogs in the great workings of God. The fact is that without everyone carrying part of the load, the work will only be delayed. Without exception, everyone is important to the working of God's purposes in the world.

What you and I do may appear to be very small in the overall picture of God's plan; but all that the Lord asks of us is to be faithful with what He has committed to our responsibility and care. It may take the form of concentrated prayer, special giving of our finances, or going to someone, in love, to tell them that Jesus died for them, or just being a loving, available shoulder to cry on. We must work in cooperation, as one body, or the task would be too gigantic to tackle. There is great power in the unity of a body of people who are moved to become a part of the program of God. God does add His blessings as a reward for our faithfulness.

As one giver to another, we need to pool our Missions offerings with other congregations in other places to meet the needs of those who are ministering in foreign lands because, "… how can they preach unless they are sent?" (Romans 10:15a). Our giving helps to meet the needs of those who are on the front lines of the battle to take back the world from the enemy of the souls of mankind. Missionaries are not our substitutes, as we've heard some describe them. They are another part of the team that are depending on us to fulfill our part on the home front. We shall all get our rewards, in due time, because we share in the harvest of the lost. Let's also remember to pray for these who have become our extended family and are serving the Lord far from their homes and the comforts that we enjoy. They need to know that we have not forgotten them. Our prayers for courage, comfort and strength may be necessary to keep their hearts focused on their goals. They also need our prayers because they rely on the power of the Spirit of God to drive home the message of the Grace and Mercy of God.

God bless you as you remember the reason for the Cross of Calvary was to reach the Lost.

▎ **THE MASTER AND THE COOK**

*"Let us not give up meeting together, as some are in the habit of doing,*
*but let us encourage one another—and all the more*
*as you see the Day approaching."*

~Hebrews 10:25

A PARABLE OF A FAMILY

In ancient times there was a great and wealthy Master who was blessed with many wonderful children. He loved each one of them very much and desired nothing but the best for them. He provided his shelter and protection as they grew up and made himself available to them whenever they needed his counsel or assistance. Because he wanted only the best meals for his children, he appointed a cook who had received special training in order to provide the very best food, properly spiced and cooked so that his children would grow up to be healthy and strong. Each day he personally gave directions to the cook on the progress of the development of his children with personal recommendations to help the cook do his appointed task with all diligence. It so happened that the cook was very obedient in following the Master's instructions and very committed to doing the work that was his responsibility. He applied himself conscientiously because he, too, had come to love the Master's children. Each child became very special to him and his efforts for their provision and sustenance were labours of love. He applied himself to understanding the individual needs of each of the children and prepared meals that were designed to help them in their growth and development. He knew that sometimes he would have to prepare things that the children would not like but which were necessary for a balanced diet. He even tried new recipes, occasionally, so that they would have a variety of good things that were provided by the Father.

However, he noted that although he worked very hard at his duties, from time to time some of the children were not coming "home" for their regular meals. This caused great concern to the cook and also made the Father very upset. The Father felt very strongly that meal times were meant to be shared with the family and that it was the duty of each child to respect the wishes of the Father—to be at home when the meals were prepared. He knew that the cook had worked very hard to do what was expected of him and that both he and the cook had only the best interests of the children upon their hearts. He knew that no one else could possibly care for them as well as he, although the children might believe otherwise. He did expect his children to be at home in their proper place, on time, as a part of the family. The children realized that what their Father wanted them to do was for their own good, because he loved them so much. And because they loved him, too, they were willing to honour his request.

Pastors/ministers/priests often work many hours in the preparation of a Sunday sermon only to find that some of their congregation members are not there to receive what God has laid upon their hearts. Let's be diligent to be at the meeting place at the appointed time.

█ **A SHOT IN THE AIR**

*"All that the Father gives me will come to me,*
*and whoever comes to me I will never drive away."*

~John 6:37

He was still a young man. He had grown up in the home of a caring, loving father and mother. He and his younger sister lacked nothing in this world. They had the security of a home, food, clothes, education, and fellowship with a Bible-believing congregation. But privately, his father described him as "a shot in the air." As far as his father was concerned, his son was a waste of a life. He would never amount to anything. In spite of the monetary investment that was intended to bring a healthy young man into the world of maturity and responsibility he had turned out to be nothing but "a bum." After twenty-four years, his father gave up on him. He was a hopeless loser. It was a heartbreaker for the parents who felt so frustrated by the situations that had captured their son and denied them the fulfillment of their desires and dreams.

I've learned that God does not give up, under any circumstances. People may deny His existence and curse His name, mistreat His Son and malign His message of love, but God does not surrender when the situation seems impossible. To God, no person is "a shot in the air." There is value in each one. He patiently works upon the hearts of the rebellious and the prodigals of life. He still reaches into the hearts and homes of people who have been written off by society. He cares for the bitter, the hurting, the angry, the proud and the worldly mighty. Until life's final breath, He will consistently and persistently be on their case; neither in judgment nor condemnation, but in love.

God sees and longs to develop the powerful potential in the life of every individual. That is why the lost must be found and the wayward brought back into a loving relationship with the Master. God is industrious as our Creator and Developer. If He can take a lump of clay and make it one of the most beautiful things in all of creation, you better believe that He can work that same miracle in the rejects of our world. There is hope. Some of us have loved ones who have shown absolutely no appreciation for spiritual matters. That person could be your spouse, your child or a close friend. God knows and He cares. But let's remember that God calls us to work together with Him.

1. Our *praying* for others is one of the main processes to prepare the hearts of people to receive the work of God.

2. It's our *watching for opportunities* to speak God's <u>Word</u> into their lives that is the process of sowing good seed that will result in the transformation of others.

3. Our *example* of a living faith makes a clear pattern for others to follow to know the same Lord we know.

4. And finally, our *trust in God,* in spite of the passage of time, demonstrates our confidence that a life placed in the hands of a loving God through a spiritual commitment will always result in a benefit beyond our understanding. God is faithful!

78

▌ **FIGHT LIKE A REAL MAN**

*"Fight the good fight of the faith. Take hold of the eternal life
to which you were called when you made your confession
in the presence of many witnesses."*

~1 Timothy 6:12

During these days of wars and rumours of wars, economic unrest, terror in the streets throughout many communities around the world, and people living in fear of diseases that, as yet, have no cure, we are smelling the breath of the dragon. He's the one behind it all. We don't see him, but we see what he does and the effects of his actions on all of humanity, and he's not finished yet. More than anyone else he knows that his time is short. I don't know if he seriously thinks he has a chance to win this war, but I see the evidences of his malignant intent to destroy as much as he possibly can while he has time. His efforts are not just in the realm of the physical, but much of what he does is intended to hurt the spiritual part of every one of us. His intention is to distract us from trusting God; to overwhelm us with the sorrow and tragedy so that we begin to lose the reason of faith.

There are three options for us to follow under these circumstances.

1. We can just ignore the situation and hope that it will go away. (I think this is the option that most of the world is choosing.)

2. We can try to hide by withdrawing from any public activity and being very selective in our friendships.

3. We can call on God to intervene in all the matters that are such a grave concern to our society and then live in confidence that He is still in control and that He is going to show Himself through all the situations that cause us apprehension.

From our vantage point it appears that we are totally helpless in resolving the present world crisis. Not so! We may feel insignificant in light of the monstrosity of the worldwide effects of our enemy's actions, but prayer is a resource of power that equips the weakest saint and makes him a giant-killer. Someone has said, "Get down on your knees and fight like a real man." The Bible reminds us that, "The weapons that we fight with are not the weapons of the world. On the contrary, they have divine power to demolish strongholds" (2 Corinthians 10:4). Strongholds include the foxholes and caves of the physical enemy as well as the shadowy side of Satan's habitation. God knows them all.

There are groups of believers around the world who are becoming aware of the need for seeking the Lord in earnest intercession as a call for His intervention in earthly affairs. We have neglected prayer as a weapon of war. It is a powerful tool that plugs into an unlimited resource, across unlimited distances to accomplish unlimited tasks in the name of the Lord. Do you want to see what God can do? Do you want to see a resolution to the international problems that have gripped the world? If there ever was a contribution that believers could make in a spiritual conflict it's through prayer and it's now!

▋ **THE GUIDE OF THE FUTURE**

*"Consider the ravens: they do not sow or reap,*
*they have no storeroom or barn; yet God feeds them.*
*And how much more valuable you are than birds!"*

~Luke 12:24

Ira Stanphill wrote,

"Many things about tomorrow, I don't seem to understand;
But I know who holds tomorrow, and I know He holds my hand."

Those words were born out of a quiet confidence in the power, protection and provision of our Lord as Ira went through some difficult times. God has purposed, in His wisdom, that the future be a mystery to us. There are many details that are hidden from our understanding that are well known to Him. You see, He knows all the happenings of every tomorrow because, to Him, they are just as clear as this present moment (Jeremiah 29:11). That's why it is important to trust Him and not to fear what may come our way. Of course, there may be things that will be concerns to us that we are totally unaware of at this instant. There will also be wonderful times that will make such great memories for "future reference." Throughout all the experiences to be discovered in these coming days, let's be assured that God has never surrendered control of His creation and that "our times" are in His hands (Psalm 31:15).

He has promised that He will never abandon us and that He will always remain a Loving, Heavenly Father who faithfully cares for our every need (Hebrews 13:5). For people who don't know the Lord their search for answers to future situations has led them to consult teacups, palm readers, horoscopes and other kinds of fortune-tellers. But we know there's nothing that gives the kind of peace of heart and mind like a growing faith that "in all things God works for the good of those who love Him" (Romans 8:28b).

As believers we have an additional matter of blessing for the future as we live in expectation of the return of our Lord and Saviour, Jesus Christ. He has promised a latter rain experience for those who hunger and thirst for Him and for those who are willing to seek His face so that His promises may be fulfilled in our time. I believe that when the Church leaves this old world behind we are not going to leave with our tail between our legs but in Triumph because the purposes of God will be accomplished according to His plan. We're on the victory side and the enemy knows that. Let's believe and live like the conquerors we were designed to be. I count it a great joy to be in fellowship with others of His Church who get excited about the opportunities to serve the Lord in these days.

As we enter a new day/month/year, let's do it with confident faith that these are going to be wonderful days as we experience the power of God released into the world in preparation for His return.

80

| ## THE GOOD NEWS IS STILL GOOD NEWS

*"I rejoiced with those who said to me,*
*"Let us go to the house of the LORD."*

~Psalm 122:1

There's not a lot of good news in the papers these days. Besides the trashy stuff, the papers are full of accidents, murders, robberies, reports of wars, bad political decisions, and the list goes on and on. You might get the impression that nothing good is going on in our world today. The truth is that you don't sell newspapers with good news. People are more interested in the blood, gore, crime and deception. Society wants to find out who else has been victimized today. That's what makes the news.

If you want to hear some good news, you'll have to go to Church. There you'll hear that it's the good news of the gospel of Jesus Christ that will give you a life-changing experience. If we could take the time to interview the folk that gather there I'm sure you would hear stories of deliverance, healing of body, soul and spirit, and the faithfulness of God to supply our needs. There are folk there who have gone through deep trials but now have a new story to tell.

The message of the Gospel is a message of hope and new life. Jesus Christ came into the world to make a difference in our lives. His word promises that "old things will pass away and all things will become new." Jesus said that He came to "bring us life and that more abundantly." There are transformations that occur when Jesus Christ comes into our lives. Our Sunday gatherings are times of celebration where our joyful praise and worship expresses our gratitude to the Lord for the wonderful things that He does in each of us. Sometimes we praise Him by faith because we believe that He is going to answer our prayers in spite of how we "feel" today.

God is good—all the time! Even to the discouraged and depressed, the message of His wonderful love and power encourages us to leave the stresses and strains all around us and find a place of rest in Him. There is good news in the house of God. He knows us best, but He still shows us He loves us the most.

This same gospel message can change our society. Drugs, alcohol, thievery, murders and rapes will become a part of history as one by one the heart of each citizen responds to the transforming power of the Gospel of Jesus Christ. There is coming a day when Jesus Himself will reign over all the earth. There will be universal peace and harmony because all of creation will be under His direction. What a tremendous day that will be! But even today we can begin to know the power of His presence as we give ourselves to Him. There is Power to Change in the message of His love. If you haven't discovered that yet, give your Pastor a call and have a little chat with him.

Don't delay. Do it today. God wants to make this a day of Victory for you.

▌ **THE VALUE OF FAITH**

*"Be on your guard; stand firm in the faith; be men of courage; be strong."*

~1 Corinthians 16:13

How much would you be willing to pay for a kilo of Faith? Well, if an amount the size of a mustard seed can move great mountains, I imagine a kilo would be worth quite a bit. Faith is what brings the hand of God to intervene in the matters around us. Someone has said that faith is the coin of heaven, but it's made to be usable while we live here on earth.

When Jesus was teaching His disciples about end time events, He asked them a rhetorical question. "When I return shall I find faith on the earth?" (Luke 18:8). That's a good question that only the last generation can answer. I guess the best way to ensure that there will be lots of faith is to exercise the faith that we already have and pass the Word along so that others will do the same. That becomes a heritage to the next generation. As we read His Word, believe, trust and test the promises of God, our faith increases. Let me remind you that it doesn't just happen by itself. There is something that I must do. Like exercise that builds good muscles and strengthens the bones, so the exercise of our faith builds a strong spiritual body. I heard someone say, "I gave up exercise because it makes me tired." What he didn't say was that the lack of exercise is also fatal. We need it to grow and keep strong and healthy.

Where does faith come from?

1. "Faith comes from hearing the message, and the message is heard through the word of Christ" (Romans 10:17). It comes through the ear gate on the message of the Gospel. Presenting ourselves to being attentive to the Word as it is preached puts us in a place where our faith is built up.

2. God has given everyone a measure of faith. (Romans 12:3) This is a heavenly gift that will bring us heavenly blessings when we invest it back into His kingdom. You've got it already. What we do with that gift is up to us. Let me suggest a couple of things.

3. Get into the *Word*. There is no way that a two-hour dose of Church on Sunday is enough to keep us growing in God for the rest of the 166 hours of the week. We need to be into the Word every day.

4. We need to press in to prayer, earnestly believing that God has a perfect plan for our lives and that we need to get to know Him better to understand what that is. Prayer is one of the means of exercising faith. As our needs come to us, we lift them into the Father's presence and believe that He will answer as He said He would.

These are exciting days to be alive and to see the gracious hand of the Lord doing so many wonderful things for us. Let's learn to *be* people of faith—not living off the faith of others but *being* people of faith. There is a difference.

| **ABOVE ALL ELSE**

*"For you, O LORD, are the Most High over all the earth;*
*you are exalted far above all gods."*

~Psalm 97:9

We need a move of God's holy presence upon us. There is absolutely nothing that can take the place of His blessing upon our lives and in our Church. We need Him! It's strange how our focus can be so altered by the things and experiences of the world that misdirect us from seeking His face to seeking our comfort and our good. You see, most of us have issues that the devil drops into our laps that are seemingly important. It could be hurts or temptations. It could be financial or relational. We need to learn to lay them all before the Lord and remember that we are designed to seek Him. The confusion comes when we seek Him for what He can do for us and not for who He is. He is the King of Kings. He is the Lord of Lords. He is worthy of our praise, all the time.

The writer of the book of Hebrews puts it concisely when he says, "…let us throw off everything that hinders and the sin that so easily entangles, and let us run with perseverance the race marked out for us. Let us fix our eyes on Jesus, the author and perfecter of our faith…" (Hebrews 12:1-2). Did you hear that? Our eyes should be fixed on Jesus and not on any other thing that could distract us in our service for the Lord.

How do we do that in a practical way? Please allow me to give you a few suggestions:

1. The Lord loves us with an everlasting love. This is unchangeable. There is no one who cares for our eternal welfare like Jesus. We are "the apple of His eye." He is not interested in us because of our beauty, intellect or financial status—He loves us because He is love.

2. He has created us to develop a relationship with Himself. He wants us to understand that no matter what experience we face in life He is more interested in building a trusting confidence in His ability to work out all things for our good than in simply answering our prayers. Jesus asked the question one time, "Which is easier: to say, 'Your sins are forgiven' or to say, 'Get up and walk?'" (Luke 5:23). To Jesus, the healing problem was nothing compared to the relationship that the forgiveness of sins would bring.

3. If we have trouble reaching out to God it is possible that the enemy has dropped a few things on us that have become the cumbersome stuff that entangles us and hinders our vision for Him. The answer? A simple but sincere prayer: "Dear God, I love You and want You to help me through the obstacle course of life so that I never lose sight of You through all the twisting and turnings of my journey." Then trust God!

4. We need to put ourselves in a place where we can open our hearts to worship Him, in spite of feelings, and tell Him that we love Him and need Him more and more each day. Worship is the key. We are blessed when we practice the art of worship.

▌ **SMILE A WHILE**

*"Rejoice in the Lord always. I will say it again: Rejoice!"*

~Philippians 4:4

Our "faith" is worth getting excited about. We've got good reason to be enthusiastic about what the Lord has done for us, for what He does in each of us and for what He is about to do in this world. We are a very blessed and privileged people. I heard someone say once, "Even on the worst days of my life, I am very blessed." Isn't that the truth? We have so much to be thankful for and so many reasons to be joyful in spite of the disappointing things that happen in our world today. The most important things that the Lord has done for us are done inside of our lives where no one notices. I believe it is time that we showed some of the joy and the peace of His kindness on our countenances. We are the book that the world reads concerning the practical aspects of believing and trusting in God. As people watch us, they ought to see something that would attract them to Jesus by the things that we say and do. It's not right that we should hide His grace in our hearts and keep the world guessing about what it is that is so important to us. The Psalmist said, "This is the day the Lord has made; let us rejoice and be glad in it" (Psalm 118:24). The prophet Isaiah wrote, "Surely this is our God; we trusted in him, and he saved us. This is the LORD, we trusted in him; let us rejoice and be glad in his salvation" (Isaiah 25:9).

The image that many in the secular world have of "believers" is not very complimentary. But then, they can't be blamed, totally. Check out some of the folk around you and see if they are any different than those that don't know the Lord. Aside from the fact that we are human and have our problems like everyone else, we do have a resource that the world does not possess. Let me remind you that we used to sing a little chorus in Sunday school that goes something like this: "Smile a while, and give your face a rest..." There's not much theology in that phrase, but some good counsel just the same. There is a saying that a smile given away will receive a smile in return. Paul wrote to the Philippian Church and exhorted them to "Rejoice in the Lord." (Philippians 4:4a) I think it's interesting that Christians need to be told to be a joyful people. Come on! There is too much sadness in this world and we need to get our society back on track. There is a reason to have joy in the Lord. There is a wonderful benefit to possessing a trust and confidence in a Mighty God who loves and cares for those who believe in Him. The unwritten gospel message that is read on our faces ought to be a message that attracts enquiring interest in what makes us tick. A loving smile can make the difference. Someone has said, "You have a face that would stop a clock." That can change, with a little effort. The telephone company has given courses for receptionists and one of their bits of advice is that people can tell if you are smiling when you talk on the phone. That is a pleasant conversational tool, especially for Christians.

**HE SEES THE END FROM THE BEGINNING**

*"For you have delivered me from death and my feet from stumbling,*
*that I may walk before God in the light of life."*

~Psalm 56:13

He is an awesome God. History tells the story of His loving investments in the needs of humanity. It stretches our minds to think that the Creator of all things, the Maker of heaven and earth, would take such profound interest in any of us. After all, as human beings, our track record for good behaviour is atrocious. I'm sure that if we had the authority of God we would have taken the fast, easy way to bring a solution to the constant bickering and waywardness of mankind. But not so with God; even in our personal rebellious ways He is still a very faithful and loving friend. After all, He is love. That never changes despite the emotional swings of mortality. He is the unchanging Rock of commitment and affection who plans methods of restoration and not destruction. That's why the stories of history demonstrate His very special interest in each of us.

Even the times of judgment are written lessons of His loving correction that would serve a dual purpose:

1. to get us back on track in ways that please God, and
2. to develop the things that are best for us.

It may appear that God is selfishly imposing His will upon us and exercising His power and authority over us against our free choice. The truth is that all of God's choices are, first of all, for our good. He sees beyond the reasons of our choices to the final results, and knowing the end from before the beginning, He exercises His will for our good. Sometimes that may be sorrowful for us, but the end result will always be to benefit us for timeless eternity. To encourage your heart, listen to this: "If the Lord delights in a man's way, he makes his steps firm; though he stumble he will not fall, for the Lord upholds him with his hand" (Psalm 37:23-24). God knows all the "details" and "derails" that are involved in the decision processes that we go through, and He will affirm what is best for us. That ought to bring encouragement to us. It is sometimes hard to explain the fact that God's intervention in the matters of our lives is not with selfish motives but with an eye to increase our joy. His very character would not allow Him to be anything less than a very loving, patient and caring God. We need to trust Him! Although we do not take pleasure in all the things that come our way, there are, sometimes, unseen purposes that God wants to develop. The Bible says, "And we know that in all things God works for the good of those who love him..." (Romans 8:28). Many of the miracles that He has done prove that He is God, and at the same time they demonstrate His compassion for each of us.

There is nothing impossible for Him to accomplish, and He cares for you (1 Peter 5:7).

❚ **WHY?**

*"Those who know your name will trust in you, for you, LORD, have never forsaken those who seek you."*

~Psalm 9:10

He's the Lord of glory! He has all power and wisdom to do whatever He wills. That may be a mystery to us sometimes, because we don't understand why God does some things and doesn't do other things. That is the side of God that we may never fully understand until we reach heaven. It's in those kinds of situations that we need to trust Him and believe that He is righteous and does all things well. We may have a lot of questions when it comes to some very personal dealings with Him, because He doesn't always do what we want Him to do. To be honest, it may be confusing to us, but we need to recognize that it's His privilege because He is God. Trusting Him when we don't know what He's doing is the hard part of the walk of faith. However, knowing Him in a personal way does bring a settled assurance that He does what is best. That's the lesson we need to learn.

Now, I've heard it said by some "influential" speakers that whatever you declare and believe—that's what you'll receive. I'd like to think that is true, but I've discovered that it doesn't always work out that way for the simple reason that I don't know all the details involved that God does. So, His not answering some of my prayers is because He is a merciful God who will not give me what is not good for me even though I think otherwise. That brings me to the big issue of healing. If there is any area of mystery and controversy in modern theology it lies here. Why are some people healed and others not? Why do some good people die young and some bad people live long lives? Why is pain and suffering so common when we know that Almighty God has the ability to speak a word and remove all the discomfort that has invaded our society? Why are there so many plagues and other such problems in the world that cause universal concern? Who knows the answers to these questions? I would like to tell you that I do! Notice I said, <u>I would like to</u>...but I don't understand all these things either. I have learned, however, that God has never lost control of any situation. He is still all-wise and all-powerful, and even though He does allow some things to happen that look like disasters He is always a merciful and compassionate friend to those who trust Him.

In a more personal way, whatever situation may come, delight in the good experiences and learn to trust God in the uncomfortable ones. He loves you with an everlasting love. There are lessons to learn. The biggest one is to trust Him when the road gets rough and believe in Him when we can't see the end of the journey. I can assure you of one fact—God is a Wonderful God and the journey is almost over. He is bigger than all my problems; bigger than all my fears; bigger than all the tornadoes that sweep this globe; bigger than all the worries that I can't resolve. He is an awesome God!

▌ **RESURRECTION POWER**

*"Martha answered, 'I know he will rise again
in the resurrection at the last day."*

~John 11:24

I've never seen it happen. From our human perspective, Death is the end of the road and the possibility of someone coming out of the grave is unbelievable. I think I'm pretty safe in saying that you haven't seen anyone come out of their tomb either, no matter how good their life was and no matter how much money they had in their bank account. We all expect that one day we'll take the route that leads to the cemetery and be carried by six strong men who will deposit our remains into the empty spot especially prepared for that moment. Personally, I haven't made up the details of the schedule for those final moments of my earthly existence yet, but I do know this one thing (hang on to your hat): I will rise again! I'm not bragging when I let you in on that little secret, but I do know my rights. Paul said that Jesus was "...the firstfruits of those who have fallen asleep" (1 Corinthians 15:20). He was Number One in the process of the resurrection and after Him come the multitudes who believe that the plan of Salvation provided by Him on the cross of Calvary includes the hope that we shall rise again when the time is right. This earthly journey is very brief at best, but it is only a painful pilgrimage in time until we begin to live eternally.

You see, when Jesus came into the world His intention was to bring us through the valley of the shadow of death into a timeless eternity of life in the presence of God and under His full blessings. When Jesus died on the cross, He paid the full price for all of our sins. He took the consequences of our mistakes upon Himself, which made us free to enjoy our new liberty in Him. You may remember that way back in Genesis that Death became one of the natural results of sin. Adam and Eve could have avoided death if they had been obedient to God's Word. From their initial sin, death entered into the life-span of humanity because all have sinned. However, when Jesus paid the price in full through His death, it meant that Death has no permanent claim on my life any longer. I view "Death" as a doorman who must open the way to eternity as I pass through his territory. Death is not a final resting place. Jesus changed that. Death has become a gateway that leads to the Father's eternal presence.

But then, I've neglected to tell you that some will not walk "through" the valley of the shadow of death. When Jesus returns to this world, there will be the sound of a loud trumpet and the shout of an angel that will call all Believers, living and dead, to a meeting in the air and we shall all be caught away. (1 Thessalonians 4:13-18) I'm looking forward to that moment with great anticipation. That's one of the reasons that Easter is my favourite time of the year.

▌ **AMONG MANY, BUT ALONE**

*"So Jacob was left alone, and a man wrestled with him till daybreak."*

~Genesis 32:24

God deals with us in personal ways. We are not all bunched up like a can of sardines. We do appreciate the times we are together and are able to unite our voices in praise and worship and assent to the Ministry of the Holy Spirit in our lives through the preaching of the Word, but it is interesting that we can all be a part of the worshiping body and yet each one receives something personal through the ministries. That's because God knows our hearts and what we require, and He is able to give one message that meets a variety of needs. The Holy Spirit is the One who enlightens us and distributes the blessings according to the openness of our hearts. Each one is special to Him and how He ministers to you will be totally different from the brother or sister sitting beside you.

Do you remember when the Apostle Paul was sharing his testimony with an angry crowd? He told them how Jesus came to him as a bright light on the road to Damascus. Listen to his words: "…my companions saw the light, but they did not understand the voice of him who was speaking to me" (Acts 22:9). All who were in Paul's group had a fantastic experience that day, but it seems that Paul was the only one who got the message. God had a personal matter that He wanted to deal with in changing Paul from being an angry persecutor into one who served Jesus Christ in a very special way. The congregation may have been small at that moment, but God was there and He saw exactly what Saul of Tarsus needed in order to bring him into the ministry and to commission him into His service. The others could say that something strange had happened on their way to Damascus, but Paul alone could say, "Lord what do you want me to do?"

Let me assure you, God knows your need. He understands the stresses and pressures that you go through, and He cares for you. When we come into His house to worship and learn of Him, we should keep our hearts free and open to hear what He has to say to us. There may be many others around us who are 'there,' but none will receive exactly the same message that the Lord wants you and me to hear as the Spirit applies the Word. The key is to guard ourselves so that the channel of communication with God is kept clear and open. We can quickly plug up the lines that feed our hearts with spiritual food simply by thinking that everyone has to be on the same page as we are. Our God is a personal God. If you were the only person in the world that needed a Saviour He would still make Himself available for you. If you come to a Church service and you are the only one that has a longing to meet with Him, He will be there to meet with you. I can say that to everyone that comes under the sound of the Word of God because I believe that God has more to say to us than we are prepared to hear. Open your heart and let His Word speak to you.

**GOD KNEW IT ALL ALONG**

*"He makes wars to cease to the ends of the earth; he breaks the bow and shatters the spear, he burns the shields with fire."*

~Psalm 46:9

It happens over and over. We pray for peace but it looks like war again. There are always serious decisions that have to be made at those times. Some decisions may involve the lives of the youth of our nation and the horrors of open military conflict. With the terrible implements that may be used to destroy the lives of so many so quickly, we need to be people of compassion and intercession to invest some of our prayer time in asking God to intervene.

We understand that what we are seeing lived out in our world today was foretold centuries ago. "When you hear of wars and rumours of wars, do not be alarmed. Such things must happen, but the end is still to come" (Mark 13:7). It is a sign of the end time. Another military conflict is not a glitch in the plan of God. He knew it was coming and that it could be used as a warning sign for the believers.

The war to end all wars is yet to come. We read about Armageddon in the book of Revelation as one of the final conflicts between righteousness and evil. I believe we are seeing the alignment of loyalties that will come against the nation of Israel for that battle. Chapters 38 and 39 of Ezekiel describe the nations in Old Testament terms that will form their alliance to come against the nation of Israel. (*Check it out for yourself.*) This will be time for the nation of Israel to remember the words of their prophets spoken almost three thousand years ago: God will be their defence. The Bible says, "...my hot anger will be aroused, declares the Sovereign Lord" (Ezekiel 38:18).

It appears, today, that Israel is not involved in the debate concerning other countries in the Middle East. They are preparing for a defensive war but are not at all a part of the discussions related to the whirlwind of war around them. Let the people of God be aware that in such serious moments of history we ought to guard ourselves in preparation for the grand exodus that is sure to come. God has promised that His signs would be a signal for His second coming. We don't know the day nor the hour, but obviously we are in very dramatic times that have been accurately foretold and are coming to pass before our eyes. You need not be surprised.

What should the righteous do in times like these?

1. Let's be people of prayer. Let's pray for righteousness to prevail in every area of conflict. Remember the innocent ones, the children who have no choice in where they are, so that God's comfort and protection will surround them.

2. Let us watch for opportunities to tell the world that we are not surprised at what is going on although we grieve for peace as much as any other person.

3. Let's be people who live our lives knowing that God is on His throne and in absolute control of the events of our world today.

Let's remember that a generation that forsakes their God will be a generation of people who will pay the consequences of that choice.

▌ **DEEDS OF KINDNESS**

*"What good is it for a man to gain the whole world, yet forfeit his soul?"*

~Mark 8:36

In Luke 16, Jesus told the story of the man who wanted to send a "Special Delivery" message from Hell. The man's life on earth had been one of affluence and pleasure. During his earthly existence he appeared to be oblivious to the needs of the people who lived around him, especially the beggar who sat by his front door. He shouted back his warning from the searing flames of the torments of Hell. Although there is no crime mentioned in the brief account of this man's life, it becomes unmistakably obvious that there were at least two things that Jesus wanted to make clear to those who heard the story. These were matters that were recorded as warnings to anyone who thinks "they've got it made."

Lesson # 1: You cannot expect to ignore the needs of others and not pay a high price yourself. It is possible to shut ourselves in to our sweet and precious comfort zones and disregard the pain, hurt and suffering of so many of those who would be pleased if we would only cast a crumb of concern and recognition their way. The truth is, for many people it doesn't take much to encourage them. Jesus is addressing the problem of selfishness that excludes any concern for the needs of others. In another of His stories Jesus expressed this sentiment through the words of a King, "I tell you the truth, whatever you did not do for one of the least of these, you did not do for me" (Matthew 24:45).

Lesson # 2: The important things in life are not things. As important as things may appear, there never is a time to neglect the welfare of the soul. A personal experience with the Lord is a far greater treasure than all the accumulated wealth of this world, and that experience is free! As rich as this man may have been, he took none of his wealth with him. He had somehow neglected the true riches that the Lord offers to all. To some there is a personal sense of accomplishment in knowing what it is that we are leaving behind. As laudable as that may be, where we are going after we are through in this world is so much more significant. We need to confirm that location before we leave this one.

In summary, it is so important that you have an outward look toward the needs of others. It is also very important that you have an inward look, in preparing your own heart to meet with God. It's the in-between the outward and the inward look that causes us the most problems. Take care! We are people on a Mission.

**NOT OUR PLAN, BUT HIS**

*"Give and it shall be given unto you…"*

~Luke 6:38a

Paul heard the call, through a vision, from a man in Macedonia, "Come over and help us!" (Acts 16:9). It was an urgent call that redirected the missionary heart of Paul to a new field where people were hungry for the gospel message. Macedonia was a long way from where he was and where he intended to go. It would require weeks of traveling on foot, but there were people there who needed to know that Jesus came into the world to save all sinners. Paul pulled out all the stops and immediately headed in the direction that the Lord had laid on his heart.

Times have changed, but the real need of mankind remains the same. Without the message of Jesus Christ, the Saviour, what hope does anyone have? There are multitudes today that can be reached through the means of modern technology if the support of prayer and finances would be directed toward a concerted effort to reach the lost.

We have heard of recent climatic catastrophes in many parts of the world. Stories are told of the failure of crops and of increasing unemployment that causes many financial difficulties for the Pastors and Evangelists who live by faith. It has been reported that some are surviving by making a stew out of blades of grass in order to find some nourishment.

The average Canadian is living a very prosperous life compared to the standard of living in many parts of the world. With the economic situation as it is, the Canadian dollar is in a favourable position so that a Pastor in another country can live, fairly comfortably, on $25 (Canadian) per month. The call, as clear as the Macedonian of centuries past, has caught our attention. These may be unprecedented opportunities to reach out to people who are looking for answers to their personal and social problems. Equipping the national pastors with our support at this time may be the beginning of a great revival as they give themselves completely to preaching the gospel message.

Remember to occasionally share in a special gift offering (above your tithes) for the ministries of so many who reach the millions of people living on the edge of poverty today. You may not see the results of your investment until you stand at the judgment seat of Christ and hear of how much was accomplished by your generous gift.

Let us learn how to make "sacrificial" giving a part of our worship and believe that God can increase our gifts. It's wonderful what God can do when we place our offerings in His hands. He has a way of multiplying them to become useful to multitudes and to satisfy the hunger of many. Let's continue to pray that God would add His abundant blessing to what we do today!

91

**HARMONY**

*"... that they may be one as we are one."*

~John 17:22b

If I told you that $1 + 1 = 2$, you would tell me that I have learned the first basics of elementary Math. If I told you that $1 + 1 + 1 = 1$, you would know that I have learned the basic principle of God. A Mathematician may disagree with that formula, but when it comes to the revelation of God, is there really any scientific method that explains God better than that? When God describes Himself, He has revealed Himself as three persons in one. He is spoken of as "plurality in unity."

Jesus put it another way. He said, "I and the Father are one." (John 10:30)

There is something very mysterious about that kind of relationship that God wants to see evidenced in His Church. We are all created as unique individuals with different personalities, opinions and fingerprints. In spite of this, God has designed a plan that we should all be able to live in unity and harmony.

You see, many centuries ago, people decided to try to duplicate the works of God by their own wisdom and abilities. What they intended to do, at Babel, was to show God that He was not the only Creator. God viewed their actions as rebellion and disobedience to His authority. We can name their actions with one word, plain and simple: SIN. God sent confusion upon them and they were scattered from the plain of Shinar to the far corners of the earth. Sin always separates, harms and hinders relationships.

But when Jesus died on the cross, He made a way for all men of all nations to come together in unity and harmony. He prayed to His Father, just hours before the cross, "That all of them may be one, Father, just as you are in me and I am in you...that they may be one as we are one" (John 17:21-22). The plan of salvation was designed to bring us together as one body, to serve the Lord in UNITY. The scattering because of sin has been dealt with. It's time to hear the voice of the Spirit of God calling us into harmony as we do the will of God. And yet, it is a personal decision that each of us must make to guard that unity. "Make every effort to keep the unity of the Spirit through the bond of peace" (Ephesians 4:3). Make every effort! You have probably already discovered that sometimes that means a lot of work. That's what effort is.

So, whether you are from Canada, New Zealand, Malaysia, Singapore, Hong Kong, Guatemala, Nicaragua, Columbia, Ecuador, South Africa, Spain, Germany, Italy, England or the Czech Republic, you are a part of us.

Check my math, if you like. Although we are many in number, we have been called to be one in Christ.

█ **TRIUMPHAL ENTRY**

*"Hosanna! Blessed is he who comes in the name of the Lord."*

~Mark 11:9b

Jesus came into the world to make a difference. The enemy of our souls had robbed God's creation for too long of the joy and peace that we were designed to possess. Selfishness and sin had taken their toll upon mankind and burdened all of us with needless cares and countless struggles because we were not living in the victory planned for humanity. Jesus said, "I have come that they may have life, and have it to the full" (John 10:10b). Jesus was not at all interested in half-way joy. His offer is fullness of joy—living life to the full. Let's not be content with anything less than what God wants for us.

But let's be real! There is a joy and a pleasure that the world knows. It's the kind of stuff that the people demonstrated nearly 2000 years ago when they welcomed Jesus into Jerusalem with great cries of rejoicing and acts of celebration. It was done in His honour and Jesus was worthy of all of it. But less than a week down the road the same voices that were lifted in jubilation were changed to angry tones, and "crucify Him!" filled the dusty air of that early Friday morning. What on earth happened?

Emotion can be a wonderful thing, but when it is based on selfish desires or the "bless me now" attitude it stands on an unsure foundation. The lasting joy that Jesus offers us does not depend upon what we get out of Him but what we give to Him. This is a day-by-day experience as we surrender ourselves to Him. You see, Jesus is honoured more by our lifestyle than by our vocabulary. If we stop praising Him when we don't get what we expect, we become embittered, prune-faced, lemon-lipped, spoiled little brats. However, when we learn to praise Him through every circumstance, then the "joy of the Lord will be our strength." That's the kind of life He wants us to have all the time.

Our special joy at this time of the year is based on the fact that, just like Jesus, for the Christian every valley of the shadow of death has a resurrection experience that will liberate us from the encumbrances of these days. This will be true of every trial and test in our lives. We ought to rejoice in the truth that God lovingly cares for us, and His promises are sure. "Let us rejoice and be glad." Our God is good. He is a Faithful friend.

"Do not let your hearts be troubled. Trust in God....if I go and prepare a place for you, I will come back and take you to be with me" (John 14:1, 3).

**PALM SUNDAY**

*"I saw heaven standing open and there before me was a white horse,
whose rider is called Faithful and True."*

~Revelation 19:11a

He is coming back again, but next time He won't be riding on the back of a young donkey. He'll come back as the triumphant leader that He is. Those who have committed their lives to serving Him will be caught away to meet Him in the air. The Bible speaks of the departure of the Church from this world to meet our returning Lord and to move the celebration from earth into the courts of heaven. There will be a great time of rejoicing as we enter into the inheritance provided for us by the Lord. Pain, distress and disappointment will all be noticeably absent. The conflicts of the ages against sin and the enemy of our souls will be terminated. The angels of heaven will join us in a chorus of gratitude for the amazing grace of God that has determined a way to bring us into God's presence through the victory of the Cross. There will be endless days of enjoying the purposes of eternity free of sickness and weariness. What an awesome moment awaits us! That's why scripture encourages us to keep looking up in anticipation of that wonderful day.

On Palm Sunday, we remember one of the last days of Jesus' earthly ministry as He came, in the role of a triumphant General, into the city of Jerusalem. It appears that at long last the people recognized Him for who He really was, "The King of Israel," the son of David. Emotion ran high as the multitudes expressed their gratitude for their Deliverer who had come with miraculous signs and wonders, which He did among the people. What they did not understand, although Jesus had instructed them through the months of teaching, was the fact that He knew from His early childhood that the greatest miracle that He would ever do was going to happen at the point of His death on an old rugged cross, outside of the city of Peace. His death would make it possible that every one of us could be transformed from the sinners that we are into members of the family of God. It would be an awful price but He was willing to do it.

It would have been difficult to tell the people who wanted to "party" that in a matter of days they would be angrily calling for His funeral. But it was all a part of His plan. He would die that weekend to pay the price to set us free from the condemnation of sin, but He would come back again to continue the celebration at some future date. There will be no shadow of the cross looming on the horizons on that day. It will be a day of pure triumph. I believe He's coming soon. We must be ready.

▌ **THE PATH OF THE PALMS**

*"Hallelujah! Salvation and glory and power belong to our God,*
*for true and just are his judgments..."*

~Revelation 19:1b-2

Hey! The King is coming! It's time to rejoice and be glad. It's time to let go of the unnecessary and focus on the importance of being in that group to extend a sincere welcome to Him. He will appear in the magnificence and glory of the King of Kings and Lord of Lords. The radiance of His presence will affirm His most honourable title. All doubts and questions about His authority will be resolved as He commands His Church to come to His eternal residence. He alone is worthy of our praise and adoration. We need to be aware that the kingdom of darkness and the kingdoms of this world are only temporary arrangements, but His Kingdom will last for eternity. Another would have us believe that he also has a kingdom and is worthy of praise. But, when all is said and done, it will be clear that only Jesus is Lord of all. He will rule over the hearts of believers and His power will overcome every adversary that has ever come against Him and His glorious Church.

Television brought us the action as the statue of the "king" of Iraq fell in the central plaza of Baghdad. I was reminded that, one day, every king will bow in the presence of the One we worship. He has long been a neglected Ruler, disposed of His Kingdom by the choice of His own creation, but nothing is going to stop His return and the following days of accountability.

He has given us ample assurance that He is at the door of time, to make His physical presence known so that the whole world will take notice of Him. Those who are loving and serving Him will be rewarded for their faithfulness because He is mindful of the sincerity and commitment of those who put their trust in Him.

The real point of what I want to say is that He will be given the recognition, finally, that He has been deserving since He went away. He designed us in the beginning to be people who worship. He was, always, to be the object and focus of our adulation and adoration. He is the One who is worthy to be crowned King over all. He should be the theme of our rejoicing and the message of our victory because of His Triumph over Sin, Death and the enemy of our souls. Even now, the authority of His presence has become the banner over our lives. He has honoured us by delegating us to be His representatives in the world to demonstrate to a lost generation that He is the Ruler of this world. He may not be acknowledged as the King of the Universe but He is the King over this piece of "real estate" that I call my body. Let's rejoice in His victories and be expressive of our joy as we gather together each Lord's day to worship Him. This is a day to be glad. Pull out the stops and proclaim that Jesus is Lord and He is coming again.

**SPEAKING OUT HIS PRAISES**

*"Praise the LORD. Praise God in his sanctuary;*
*praise him in his mighty heavens."*

~Psalm 150:1

Who wants to be out-done by a stone? Should we let the stones cry out to set an example of praise (Luke 19:40)? I've heard of pet rocks, with painted faces, sitting on a shelf as adornments, but to think that someone would choose to have the heart and personality of a stone, blows my mind. For that reason, when it comes to praising the Lord, I want to be in the category of those who worship with heart-felt praise, with feeling and emotion, if for no other reason than the thought that a stone might do a better job than me.

I want to learn how to worship in spirit and in truth. This principle comes from the lips of our Saviour as He made His way to the temple for what we could describe as His farewell party. There was the excitement of celebration in the crowd that day. We believe there were a lot of people in the crowd who didn't have a foggy idea of what was happening. However, when you remember the size of His congregation when, twice, He fed them with a bread and fish lunch, there must have been many who were expecting more of the same. Add to that the many who "heard Him gladly," as well as the many who received a healing touch from Him and then those who were there to criticize Him, and you have a pretty big gathering.

You had better believe, according to the critics, that they were not in a whispering mode. They were shouting out grateful expressions from their hearts. You couldn't keep them quiet if you tried.

I always wonder if the Holy Spirit did not orchestrate this farewell party in heaven. Part of His ministry is to always uplift the precious name of Jesus. I wonder, too, if the people felt strangely moved upon in their exuberance of proclaiming His directive of ministry. " Blessed is the king who comes in the name of the Lord. Peace in heaven and glory in the highest!" (Luke 19:38). This was a praise and worship service out in the countryside that had not been seen since those glorious days when David brought the Ark of the Covenant into Jerusalem.

And the Pharisees knew it. They shouted, "Jesus, rebuke them to be quiet!"

"I tell you," Jesus replied, "if they keep quiet, the stones will cry out." To tell you the truth, I would have liked to see that, too!

The lesson is clear. Let the critics complain. Meanwhile, we have so much to be thankful for. There should be times in our life when we praise the Lord with "all that is within" us. So, when you worship, don't be stony stingy. Let's just praise the Lord. It's a day to speak our praise for the triumphs of our God. They say the best is yet to come. That's His promise, and for that we praise the Lord, too.

▌ **THE SPECIAL SACRIFICE**

*"He was pierced for our transgressions, he was crushed for our iniquities;*
*the punishment that brought us peace was upon him,*
*and by his wounds we are healed."*

~Isaiah 53:5

We all stand on common ground as individuals who have fallen far short of God's desires for His creation. The One who made us had high purposes in mind for us. To those who were willing to allow Him to have His way, He was willing to add His richest blessings to fulfill His perfect plan. In spite of His loving concern for all mankind and His personal interest in our day-to-day situations, we have all done things that have greatly displeased Him. Simply, we blew it! Every one of us has sinned and offended a Holy God. Even so, His love cannot deny that we were made for His glory.

Years ago He set in motion a plan that would provide a shelter from the condemnation that we deserve, through the substitute judgment upon an animal sacrifice. The principle was simple. The animal was the substitute for the sinner. Upon confession the offences of the sinner were figuratively laid upon the animal that was then condemned to death. The sinner was temporarily free of any condemnation because of his substitute. That ceremony needed to be repeated every year in a public ceremony because that same judgment was required every time the sinner did something that offended God. The fact is that the only covering for any offences and wrong choices was through the shed blood of the substitute, who died in the place of the sinner. This was a part of the Loving plan of our Creator. God was not willing to let us go on our way in sin without the provision of this temporary rescue operation. The perfect plan, to eternally cover our sins, was withheld for hundreds of years as God taught His people the importance of trusting in His plan for redemption and the principle of substitution. When those two matters were inscribed in the history record of God's word and obeyed, then Jesus came; the perfect, spotless, loving Lamb of God, to take away the sins of the world. He was willing to leave Heaven and His royal throne to become the one and only sacrifice that could deal with all the sins of mankind. We all need the Saviour and the covering that His death on the cross can provide. He willingly came to die as our substitute, in our place. There is no other way of dealing with our sin problems and being restored to His favour.

We must return to the same two basic principles:

1.  We need to trust God's plan, and

2.  We must recognize that Jesus is the only substitute who is able to pay the penalty price of our offences.

From before the very first offence that was committed, God had this plan ready to go into motion in order to bring us back to Himself.

▌ **MAYBE NOT SO BAD?**

*"Then I acknowledged my sin to you and did not cover up my iniquity.*
*I said, 'I will confess my transgressions to the LORD'*
*—and you forgave the guilt of my sin."*

~Psalm 32:5

"For the wages of sin is death." Perhaps not very inspirational, but a fact nevertheless. There is a consequence to doing things that offend God. It is true that He is very patient and that He is described as "God is Love."

Let's begin with this matter by looking inside of ourselves before we talk about what God is going to do about "them." You see, I believe that one of the major difficulties with dealing with Sin is that we have a different opinion of what Sin is than God does, and unfortunately we are prepared to make some compromises that Christians should not take liberties to make. When the Bible clearly states, "Avoid every kind of evil," (1 Thessalonians 5:22), that should serve as a clear enough guideline to help us keep out of some troubling situations. We can also judge each situation that the Holy Spirit brings to our attention. It is a process, reminding us that what we do may not be wrong by itself, but it could be perceived to be wrong by the assessment of others. Be careful there! It's so easy to try to justify our actions, but we need to be aware that some things we do could affect another's experience if they misunderstand what we do. For that reason, we should be caring enough of our brother or sister to be willing to forego what is all right for us but does not seem right to someone else. It is good advice to evaluate the things we do.

The other matter of concern is when we as believers do things that we know displease the Lord. Theologians through the years describe the problem under two special terms.

1. They speak of the sins of "OMISSION" because we don't do what we should be doing. "Anyone, then, who knows the good he ought to do and doesn't do it, sins" (James 4:17).

2. Then there are the sins of "COMMISSION" that are deliberate choices we make to do things that displease the Lord.

Sometimes we are tempted and we fail. Other times it is simply surrendering to what others are doing or not making a decision to please God. We are responsible for failing in either case, but the promise of God's Word is still, "If we confess our sins, he is faithful and just and will forgive us our sins and purify us from all unrighteousness" (1 John 1:9). There is no reason why we have to tolerate sin in our lives. We do ourselves a big favour when we come to the Lord and confess our failures to Him.

We've all been there, without exception, but some take a little longer in responding to the Spirit's call to clean up our acts. I wonder if Revival isn't hindered because we as Christians are not ready to be used by God because of our poor relationship with Him in this matter. "Let a man examine himself."

| **GOOD FRIDAY**

> *"Why question me? Ask those who heard me.*
> *Surely they know what I said."*
>
> ~John 18:21

Within three days the boisterous laughter had died down and a frightening rumble of anger began to stir in the streets of Jerusalem. During that time, the attitude of the people had changed. Jesus spent the daylight hours in the temple teaching the people. In parables, He taught His followers that He would be returning. His message emphasized two basic principles.

These were:

1. That the whole law of God was wrapped up in one important regulation that we should love the Lord with all our heart and our neighbour as ourselves.

2. That we have to recognize our personal responsibility to be involved in serving God where He has placed us, with the understanding that there is coming a day of accountability.

Those were gentle reminders to all of us. No one should have been upset by what He said because He simply established a short list of requirements that we should guard in preparation for His return.

However, in no uncertain terms, He did give a public scathing for the hypocritical attitudes of the religious leaders who had proudly held to their own set of rules and judged anyone else who did not do as they did. Jesus said, "They do not practice what they preach." (Matthew 23:3b)

If I could briefly assess what turned the tide from joy to anger in those few days I think I could sum it up this way:

- *Firstly*, sometimes people don't like being told that they are personally responsible for the consequences of their lifestyles.
- *Secondly*, when it comes to matters of religion, you probably have discovered that the most dangerous person in the Church is a hypocrite. You can't tell them anything without a terrible reaction.

So Friday came, and with it, the crucifixion. But as you know, there's a Sunday that comes after Friday. I'm glad that Jesus had the last word on the whole matter and that the anger was turned to joy once again. The resurrection spelled out TRIUMPH, not only for Jesus, but for all of us as well. The resurrection also spells out new life. There is an opportunity for a new beginning. It is Jesus' intention that we learn to live in the joy of the resurrection. We have been freed from all condemnation and the tyranny of ordinances to serve the Lord in loving liberty. Let us rejoice in His victory!

▌ **WHEN YOU JUST DON'T FIT**

*"Do not love the world or anything in the world. If anyone loves the world, the love of the Father is not in him."*

~1 John 2:15

We are called to serve God; to be in the world but not of the world; to be different in a peculiar way. Our lifestyle should demonstrate the high privilege of being the Sons of God.

I used to think that we were not meant to be weird in the world we live in, but I think I've changed my mind. I mean, being weird according to whose standard? If the world thinks we are strange by the things that we say and do that ought to be all right. I don't have any intentions of conforming to their standard anyway. Now, that may trouble some people but I think it takes a real "gutsy" person to be free from measuring up to what the world's expectations are, anyway. The truth is, who sets the right standard? If I read the Word of God correctly I believe that there ought to be a moral and ethical standard that measures my conversation, my manner of dress, the things that I do with my body and my devotion to honouring God above all else. That may not put me in a magazine of modern fashions or be an example of what the "new generation" expects, but I think it's time that we stood our ground and called foolishness for what it really is.

Paul wrote to the Church in Rome with these words: "Do not conform any longer to the pattern of this world, but be transformed by the renewing of your mind" (Romans 12:2a). That is a clear call to separation from the imposition of the worldly standards upon the believer. If there is anything that we are called to resist it is the "fitting in" to the pattern of the world. It is time that the Church set the standard of purity and righteousness to a wayward and lost generation. This holds true in every aspect of our lives. Let our homes and marriages be strengthened by the Biblical standards of sacrifice and commitment. Let our work ethics reflect our integrity and sense of honest industry. Let our thoughts and the matters that entertain us be purged by the standards of purity and righteousness. Let our conversation be clean and wholesome, saturated with the love of God. Would Jesus do what we tolerate or what we do?

It is not my intention to be judgmental of others in my assessment, but I wish to offer the opportunity for me to judge myself and for you to judge yourself by Biblical standards. What is the reason we don't make a difference in our modern world?

We don't often speak of holiness, but that ought to be our purpose for personal examination. The Bible says that we ought to: "Make every effort to be at peace with all men and be holy; without holiness no one will see the Lord" (Hebrews 12:14). If we want to please God above all else, I think we need to hear what He is saying to us about these matters even if the world does not approve. We want to honour the Lord above all else.

100

**EASTER WEEK**

*"Death has been swallowed up in victory."*

~1 Corinthians 15:54b

There were all kinds of evidences that proved, beyond any doubt, that He was dead.

1. The professional "killing machines" of the Roman army were satisfied that the nails and the cross, the whipping and the buffeting had taken their toll. The spear in His side was the final test. To them, one less troublemaker had been eliminated from disturbing the Pax Romana.

2. Those who took Him down from the cross, doing all that was necessary to free His cold body from the rough wood, were witnesses that He was truly dead. They quickly wrapped His remains in a burial shroud, winding the linen tightly around Him with spices between the folds. His head would be hurriedly bound up in a special piece of cloth according to the customs of the time. He was treated just like the dead in every other burial ceremony. To those who held Him, there was no question that He was dead.

3. Guards were placed at the tomb to make sure that no one would break the Roman seal placed on the great rock that blocked the entrance way. Their assignment was to guarantee that no one would get <u>into</u> the tomb to steal the body of Jesus, lest it be interpreted that He did rise from the grave.

*However*, when the ladies came early Sunday morning to more respectfully care for the body of Jesus they discovered: no guards, a broken Roman seal, a rolled-away stone and an empty tomb. I said, AN EMPTY TOMB. This was not what they expected. It wasn't supposed to be like that. If representatives of the most powerful country in the world could not keep track of a dead body in a cold, damp, stony tomb, what was the world coming to? Suddenly, two angelic beings stood beside them dressed in garments that shimmered like lightning. "Why do you look for the living among the dead? He is not here; He has risen," they said (Luke 24:5b-6a).

Now, listen! Others may delight in demonstrating their gods of stone and the tombs that have claimed some of them. We don't have either. Our Lord is alive and well and His tomb is empty. There will never be a tomb for Him. For, although He was dead, He is alive for evermore. The fact that He demonstrated His power over one of the darkest foes of humanity gives us hope that He will do it again. Those who die knowing Jesus Christ as their Saviour have this assurance—we will rise again just like He did. He is described as, "the firstfruits of those who have fallen asleep" (1 Corinthians 15:20b). When it says that He was first, it means there will be seconds and others as well. That is our hope. Jesus overcame the claims of the grave over our frail bodies. Today, we remember His VICTORY!

**EASTER SUNDAY**

*"He is not here; He has risen! Remember how He told you,*
*while He was still with you in Galilee."*

~Luke 24:6

The disciples of Jesus didn't believe it, but the hypocritical religious leaders and the Roman forces believed it. Jesus had said that He would rise again on the third day after His death. I wish that the disciples would have had their act together and gathered at the tomb, according to Jesus' schedule, and welcomed Him back in a joyous celebration. Frankly, they blew it. It was even difficult for those who saw Him, alive and well, to persuade the others that the resurrection was a fact. You see, this was no simple fairytale that was being told. People, whose very lives were threatened with a similar death, wanted proof. They wanted the evidence. They would not accept some made-up, fool's dream. This matter had to be determined as factual. The story demanded an examination.

Jesus knew all of this, and so, He came to speak to His followers on a number of occasions. He ate with them, conversed and traveled with them, instructed them on where to catch fish, prepared a breakfast for them and invited them to touch His body to know that it was really Himself. Paul, speaking about the resurrection in his letter to the Corinthians, states that, "..he appeared to more than five hundred of the brethren at the same time" (1 Corinthians 15:6).

I always think it's interesting that when the Roman guards told their superiors the personal eyewitness accounts of what really happened in the twilight morning hours of that day, they decided to make up a story and hide the facts. They should have run out to find the disciples, surrendered their lives to Jesus, and become the first evangelists. What a story they had to tell! None of the believers saw what they saw.

Let me just summarize two points that I think are very important today:

1. This is a day for a great celebration. The disciples missed it, but we're going to rejoice. No greater miracle has ever happened than the one we celebrate today. Our Lord is risen, just like He said. He is alive after overcoming Death and the Devil's anger. He is the Conqueror of the dark and dreaded domain.

2. This is a day to remember that Jesus died for our sins. It's a day to acknowledge that He is OUR Saviour. If you have never given your life to Jesus Christ, I don't know a better time than right now. In a simple prayer, invite Him to come into your life today.

| **DEATH BY SURRENDER**

*"The reason my Father loves me is that I lay down my life—only to take it up again. No one takes it from me, but I lay it down of my own accord."*

~John 10:17-18a

Funerals are rarely happy occasions. We always identify those moments with sorrow and pain. At times there is the mixture of sorrow with the confidence of our hope, however, saying farewell and experiencing the separation from our loved ones is never easy. When it's a matter of sickness there is often a little more understanding about that process. When the death is the result of an accident or tragedy there are always thoughts about how such a misfortune could have been avoided.

However, the laws of the land are very serious when the death is planned and a murder has been committed. The local police, and the Interpol of all the nations become involved in catching the person who has committed such a terrible thing.

Why then, was no one tried for the death of Jesus? Does the washing of hands remove the guilt of a heart and mind that had condemned to death a good man? You can't possibly describe the sorrow and pain of the beloved friends that had shared such a big part of His life. You hear the stories of the women who wept for him and the men who mourned his passing from the shelter of a firmly locked upper room. This was worse than an accidental tragedy. This was the murder of an innocent man.

But there was more to it—the death on the cross was designed by the one who hung there. He came to take away the sins of all men and it was "time" for the sacrifice that would pay for the guilt and crimes of all men of all generations of those who would believe in Him. It is right to say that the condemnation of death fell upon all men, beginning in the Garden of Eden, because of our disobedience and our sins. However, Jesus took that death upon Himself. Because He was a man He could die. And because He is God His death became more than equal to the death of all sinners of all time; that is, for those who would confess their sins to Him.

We look back to the cross through the emblems of the communion service. With sorrow we remember that it was for our sins that He died. At the same time we rejoice because, by His death, we have been freed from the consequences of sin. Eternal life in a loving relationship is our hope beyond the grave.

▌ **VICTORY IN THE BATTLE**

*"This is my body, which is for you; do this in remembrance of me."*

~1 Corinthians 11:24b

Remembrance day is a date that was designed to keep our memories alive to the tragedies of past wars, so that they may never happen again. We may take for granted the benefits that we've received as results of the conflicts of two World Wars and the Korean conflict. There was a time when everyone knew someone who was lost to the horrors of those awful years. With the passing of time we don't know a lot of people who were directly involved in the dreadful engagements that took the lives of so many young men and women of our nation and permanently scarred so many others.

Regardless, let's do our best to REMEMBER that there were people who were willing to face the brutalities of war in order to provide dignity and freedom to our generation. We express our gratitude to the veterans of those days and give thanks to God for the freedoms we do enjoy in Canada today.

But let me remind you, perhaps needlessly, that not all the wars are over. Until the Prince of Peace comes to rule over the hearts of all men and our world, some very sad battles will continue to be waged around the world. The most tragic of all of these conflicts are on the battlefields of our own hearts. Many walking wounded survive, in pain, unrecognized by the average person, but enduring some terrible conflicts. Let me advise you, if you are in that number, Jesus is the answer. Your battle scars may be from a failed marriage, rebellious children, unfaithful friends who've betrayed you or the loss of a loved one. Whatever the conflict might be, Jesus is the Healer, Restorer and Supplier of every good and perfect gift. There is no one who understands your situation quite as well as He does. He lived during a period of conflict between Rome and Israel when He walked among men. He always reached out to the hurting and the sorrowful of His day. We are told "Jesus wept" as evidence that He cared and that He was "moved with compassion" when He saw people struggling with the pressures of life in an oppressive generation. But the most valuable tool to hold on to is the fact that He came into the world as a "Warrior" to take on the one who would seek to destroy, harm and hinder each of us. He stood up as our Champion, and at the cost of His own life, conquered the enemy of our souls.

The results are in. Jesus won the war and offers to us the power to overcome sin, the privilege of being a part of His royal family and the future hope of being with Him on His own territory to spend the rest of timeless eternity where sickness, pain and sorrow do not exist.

He is coming back again, soon, as the Triumphant Captain of our Salvation. That is something we should never forget.

104

**THE EMPTY TOMB**

*"But thanks be to God! He gives us the victory
through our Lord Jesus Christ."*

~1 Corinthians 15:57

I was there. The tomb, where two very brave men laid the body of Jesus, is empty. The stone was rolled away that first Easter morning so that we could see inside. The soldiers guarding the Tomb were upset that neither did their dead captive abide by the laws of nature nor did He give consideration to the seal of the Roman government that was to serve as a security device. The seals of authority of the world ruling power, placed on the stone, were completely disregarded. That must have caused some concern in Rome, because if One person did that, who was to stop everyone else from doing the same? He wasn't supposed to leave the prison cell of the grave without permission.

Graves have been known to keep their captives in permanent detention. No one else has ever been able to disobey that law since the beginning of time. But even His followers could not grasp the fact that He had broken that rule and had risen from the grave. Some believed that the Romans or the Gardener had taken His body to some other location in order to discourage His followers from promoting His teachings. It took Jesus Himself, alive and well, sharing personally with those He loved, to demonstrate that, "All power" belongs to Jesus; that He is "The Resurrection and the Life." He was dead, but now He is alive forevermore. He is the firstfruits of those who have fallen asleep. He shared in our humanity,"... so that by his death he might destroy him who holds the power of death—that is, the devil" (Hebrews 2:14).

Death is supposed to be the ultimate enemy to hold captive the highest object of God's creation. But Jesus has power to do what no one else can do. On that resurrection morning, He demonstrated that there is no area where His dominion does not have authority. All other powers must bow before Him—even Death no longer possesses a sting and the grave has lost its victory. We can rest in this fact: He has Overcome all of the obstacles that would hinder us from reaching God, our loving heavenly Father. The empty tomb remains as a continuing promotion of the truth of the Resurrection. You, too, will rise again. Many years ago, an earthquake broke open one of the walls of the tomb where Jesus was buried. Someone took the time to rebuild the broken wall with bricks and then hung a wooden door to preserve the sacredness of the site from acts of vandalism. Then someone was careful to place a sign on the door to let the whole world know. "He is not here. He has risen." What a triumphant message that holds hope for all of us! Whether we are alive and await His coming or we pass through the open door to life eternal, we possess this assurance, the trumpet call will summon us into His living presence. What a day that will be!

**OPENED FOR ME TO SEE**

*"There was a violent earthquake, for an angel of the Lord came down from heaven and, going to the tomb, rolled back the stone and sat on it."*

~Matthew 28:2

He didn't need to open the tomb. He could have walked right through the stone; at least that's what He did when the disciples had the windows and the doors locked in fear of the persecution of the religious leaders. He just appeared in their midst and gave a clear witness of His resurrection. With that in mind, I don't think He was in the grave when the stone was rolled away. The tomb was empty. Jesus was no longer there and there was no need of the stone that blocked the entrance. It was the mercy of the Lord that sent the angels to move the stone from the entrance. There is no need to guess or wonder. You can check it out for yourself.

If the stone was still sealed, the soldiers would still be standing there and Jesus' followers would insist that a monument should be placed in remembrance of their fallen hero. But He is risen. The grave is empty. The Father wanted all to see that His Son was no longer in the grave. He sent His servants, the angels, to open it up for all to investigate. The earthquake that the soldiers felt was a demonstration of the power of the resurrection. Jesus was no longer bound by death's cords. By His holiness and power He was able to step out of the valley of the shadow as the Conqueror of Death, Hell and the Grave. Jesus had left the temporary resting place of the stone tomb chamber.

1. The soldiers knew it and it was serious business that they had let the "dead man" escape from their custody.

2. The women knew it because they heard the angel say, "Why do you look for the living among the dead?"

3. The disciples discovered the truth quickly when Jesus stood among them and invited them to check out the wounds and the scars. These guys who once ran from their persecutors suddenly became very brave in their proclamation that Jesus was alive and well and had ascended into heaven. The tomb is empty.

I was there a number of years ago and checked it out for myself. Someone has made a wooden door where the stone once stood. Carved into the door someone has written, "He is not here, He is risen." The resurrection is also a prophetic announcement to all Believers. "For as in Adam all die, so in Christ all will be made alive. But each in his own time: Christ, the firstfruits; [that's the prophetic part that tells us that there is more of the same to come] then, when he comes, those who belong to him" (1 Corinthians 15: 22-23).

There is no stone or tomb that can keep us from joining the Lord in the power of the Resurrection.

106

**THE RESURRECTION**

*"Look at my hands and feet. It is I myself! Touch me and see; a ghost does not have flesh and bones, as you see I have."*

~Luke 24:39

In case you thought you needed proof that it really was the Lord, remember that you are not the first to think that way. It was Thomas who provoked the examination, and his doubting was for our benefit as well. He just could not believe that His Master had risen from the dead, and so Jesus appeared into a closed room and was willing to offer a personal inspection to his disciples of the scars on his wounded body.

If you remember, it was this group who had hoped that Jesus would be the next king in Israel because He had the answers to all the needs of men. He could teach, heal, feed multitudes, change water into wine, raise the dead, find tax money in a fish's mouth and stand up to the "religious hierarchy." But He died. If anything could dampen the enthusiasm of a happy bunch of confident followers it was the fact of the suffering and death of the One they had trusted would be the liberating Messiah.

They would not be fooled a second time. They were not ready to be deceived by any invented stories of a resurrection. It had never happened before, so why would it happen now? The disappearance of the body of Jesus must have another explanation that they had not discovered as yet, and it had to be a reasonable solution. Into this situation Jesus showed Himself and offered to prove that He indeed had risen from the dead.

The proof stood before them. He was visible. He was touchable. All doubt must vanish at the evidence before them. They were so persuaded in their belief that this truly was the Lord that they were willing to lay down their lives in future ministry to tell the story of the resurrection. For forty succeeding days Jesus appeared, spoke and fellowshipped with the early believers.

Paul reminds us, "...he appeared to more than five hundred of the brothers at the same time, most of whom are still living, though some have fallen asleep" (1 Corinthians 15:6). That's a group of witnesses large enough to persuade the Supreme Court of the fact that Jesus is alive and well.

But remember this, one of the best evidences of Jesus' resurrection is a personal experience with Him. Next to the truth of the Word of God, the proof of Jesus' claims to be the risen Lord is in the relationship that we may have with Him today. The proof is in His presence. The Holy Spirit works in the lives of believers to help us to be sensitive to the Lord in our day-to-day experience. Jesus is alive!

107

**ONLY THE LAMB IS WORTHY**

*"In a loud voice they sang: 'Worthy is the Lamb, who was slain,*
*to receive power and wealth and wisdom*
*and strength and honour and glory and praise.'"*

~Revelation 5:12

Deeply moved, everyone at the conference stood to their feet as the soloist sang, "I pledge allegiance to the Lamb." It was another special moment as our hearts were challenged to express our loyalty to the One who laid down His life for us. This was one of those instances in life that required action, not just words. There seemed to be an unspoken call to be committed to serving the Master. The Congregation rose to their feet in humble respect and reverence of the King of Kings and we pledged allegiance to the Lamb. In those moments our hearts felt the drawing of the Spirit, as one body, to a fresh vision of the purpose of the Church in these days to be more than observers. We were being called as Soldiers of the Cross to stand behind our Captain and pledge our undivided loyalty to Him. It was a humbling moment as we recognized what our Leader had already done for us and that generations of faithful ones had followed Him in service to various parts of the world. In a world and time when people are not prepared to commit themselves to anything that does not bring them pleasure, this became the hour of decision to either rise in demonstration of an understanding of the call of God or to sit back and let others do it. The same call reaches out to you for your decision.

After all, let's consider that we are indebted to Him because:

1. We owe our very lives to Him because He is our Creator.

2. We owe our hearts of gratitude to Him because of the work of the cross where He willingly took our place and suffered and died. He paid the penalty and the consequences of our sinning.

3. We owe so much to Him because, daily, He watches over us to lead, guide, protect and help us to grow in spiritual understanding and maturity. He is the Chief Shepherd of our souls and He intercedes for us at the right hand of the Father.

4. We owe an unspeakable debt because He has promised us a wonderful home in heaven where He has reserved blessings beyond our ability to comprehend at this moment. He has gone to prepare a place for us, but He will be coming back again to take us to Himself.

More than words, it is time we begin to demonstrate by our lifestyle that we are committed to honouring Him with all that is within us. The martyrs of past generations were willing to lay down their lives in order to share the message of God's love. They did so under severe circumstances. We enjoy liberties because of their faithfulness. Can we do less than honour Him with all our hearts? He is worthy.

APRIL 18 ▌ **A MATTER OF PRAYER**

*"Here I am! I stand at the door and knock. If anyone hears my voice and
opens the door, I will come in and eat with him, and he with me."*

~Revelation 3:20

God answers prayer! There is nothing that can be done best until we have
prayed. Someone has said, "We are often found seeking the hand of God to do
things for us, but we need to learn to seek the face of God for who He is." It is that
kind of drawing near, to know the Lord, that brings the most lasting results in our
own lives and in the situations we face.

God is faithful to hear all of our requests because He is a God of love and He
cares for the things that cause us concern. But we also want to learn the other part
of praying so that we can know how to bless Him and bring joy to His heart. It
seems we're always on the receiving end of His favours because He does so much
for us. I want to learn how to give back to Him the things that He wants us to
bring. I believe one of the things that blesses Him is my willingness to slow down
long enough to talk to Him and let Him know that I love Him and that I give
myself to Him. I don't believe it is possible to do that to the full until we learn to
patiently wait in His presence, shutting out the clamour of the world and stilling
our souls in prayer.

Allow me to emphasize the word *patience*. We need to learn to take the time
that is needed to do a good job in telling the Lord that we love Him and want to
serve Him. It is very important to take (or make) time to spend with Him. Apart
from saying "grace" at the table and "Good Night, Jesus" it is very possible that
praying is not an easy piece of work for us to perform. Yet praying is not designed
to be difficult. It is supposed to be a personal conversation with God in terms of
an expression with which we are comfortable. I believe that there is nothing that
brings more joy to the heart of God than the fact that I purpose to spend protected
time with Him; that I won't let anything interrupt my designated prayer time.
After all, He has been on the giving end of blessings so many times through the
years; it's about time that we did something about returning the favour. Seriously,
it is time that we did something personally to bring joy to His heart.

I want to challenge each of us to examine our prayer life and to do
something that will revive a fervour in seeking the face of the Lord with the
attitude of worshipful gratitude. We owe that to Him for His faithfulness. Every
one of us can pray. God wants to hear our own hearts, and though the words we
speak are not like those of the Theologians, He accepts the simplicity of our day-
to-day speech. It may seem impossible to say adequate words to bring joy to His
heart, but believe me, things said in simple fashion please Him, too. Be yourself!
Tell the Lord today what you really feel about His loving you just as you are and
caring for your every decision. God loves you and wants to spend personal time
with you, alone. Talk to Him. He's waiting for you to call.

APRIL 19 | **GOD IS TALKING**

*"There will be great earthquakes, famines and pestilences in various places, and fearful events and great signs from heaven."*

~Luke 21:11

It was another earthquake. We knew it was going to happen sooner or later. It wasn't the expected big one but it was a "waker-upper." Everyone has been talking about the shaking that caused people to get out to the streets. Christians everywhere had opportunities to talk about the Lord during that time. The tsunami that hit Indonesia, Sri Lanka and India will long remain in the memory of those who experienced the terror or knew of someone who was there.

It's interesting that these things are difficult to predict and impossible to control, just like the weather. There's not a thing you can do about it. Those are matters that are in the hand of God alone.

We are awed by the power and impact of these uncontrollable activities that have been occurring around the world in these days. I don't view these as prophesies of doom because they are some of the signs of the end times that are given to remind us of our Lord's return. God has been giving us evidences of the fulfillment of His promises. Jesus is coming back again! It's as though the rocks are crying out for the coming of the Saviour to bring the final redemption to the world. "…the whole creation has been groaning as in the pains of childbirth…" (Romans 8:22). When we ignore the purposes of God and refuse to heed His calling, then extraordinary things will happen in nature as creation gives expression to the longing of having the Lord as ruler of this world. To every believer it's time to pull out the stops and believe God for great things to happen in His Church. I believe that God has divinely ordered the Second Coming of Jesus to the ingathering of the harvest. When the last soul is won, as He alone understands, then Jesus will descend on the clouds of the sky and catch us away.

These are designed to be days of the harvest. Time is short! Evangelism and Missions must become our lifestyle. We watch for opportunities to share our faith and we encourage those who are serving God in ministries around the world by our prayers and faithful giving. There is a world to be won. There is an enemy to confront and defeat. Jesus said that He would build His Church. We must present ourselves as tools in His hands and be available to touch lives with love because that's how it happens. The Church is people, right here near home and around the world. Every once in a while the Lord has to ring the bell to get our attention. It's a reminder that things are soon coming to a close. What needs to be done should be done quickly. We can work with joyful expectancy that He rewards with blessings beyond words and that His return will be a triumphant exodus from this world into the Kingdom of God's dear Son. Jesus is coming again.

**▌ JOY IN THE HARVEST**

*"How, then, can they call on the one they have not believed in?*
*And how can they believe in the one of whom they have not heard?*
*And how can they hear without someone preaching to them?"*

~Romans 10:14

Harvest time is always a joyful season. There's a lot of work, of course, but the fact that the earth brings forth a rich reward from the sowing season through the summer rains and sunshine to the shorter days of the fall is cause for great delight. It's the increase through the gathering that is the proof of a job well done. We get excited when missionaries come from their fields of service to let us know what is happening out there. We hear of the challenges and obstacles that need to be overcome as well as the triumphant victories as trophies of God's grace are brought to know a wonderful Saviour. It's all done through teamwork.

1. It's the missionaries on the front lines that are at the greatest risk. They are right where the battle is the fiercest. Daily, far from the contacts of home, they seek for opportunities to share the message of God's love. We admire the commitment and dedication of this force of faithful servants who are willing to go to where the need is the greatest. They are great men and women of God who have answered the call to GO. At the same time, they are very human and subject to the same kinds of life problems that we are. Without them, where would the project of reaching the lost in other lands be?

2. Then there are the supporters who bring their offerings into the house of the Lord to be administrated in His service. It still takes money to be able purchase equipment and to reach out to the world through various means of evangelism. Those who feel the project of reaching the lost is God's plan invest their finances to support the workers in various parts of the world. They know that the missionaries are God servants and can only accomplish the job if we give them the proper tools. Prayer is the lifeline that connects us together across the distance that separates us as we believe God for His care and provision for their daily needs. The lifeline needs to be held in the hands of people who know how to pray and intercede.

3. Then, of course, the Lord is involved. He is the Master of the harvest field. He invests His interests in reaching the lost by His rich anointing and blessing that prepares the hearts of the people to receive the ministries of His servants. It's His word that is carried to the lives of those in need. It is the Holy Spirit who quickens the words that are spoken and impresses the kind of conviction that brings repentance. It is the Holy Spirit who becomes the guide and teacher in the hearts of new believers.

We are a team. When we each do our part, great things will be accomplished and the waiting harvest will be gathered in while there still is time. I'm sure that the Lord of the harvest is tallying up the tasks performed for the Reward Ceremony, coming soon.

┃ # THE CONCLUSION IS CLOSE

*"But mark this: There will be terrible times in the last days."*

~2 Timothy 3:1

What a time to be alive and serving God! These are exciting days as we see so many things that God is doing in our world. There are untold opportunities for the sowing of the gospel message in our generation that we have never heard of before. It is true that the enemy is doing his best to distract the world from the blessings of the Lord, but at the same time there is a new hunger in the hearts of people who are open to discuss spiritual matters that they have neglected for so long. It is true that the power of the uncontrollable has caused a lot of concern in many parts of the world. Earthquakes, tornadoes, famines, AIDS, flesh-eating disease, the weather in general, mad cow disease, hoof and mouth disease, etc. have suddenly dramatically influenced our modern technological generation in apocalyptic proportions. If you can see these things going on and not question that God may be speaking to this world, then there really is something wrong. Jesus advised his disciples that there would be signs that would announce the nearness of His return. He could not have spelled it out more clearly than by way of the headlines of the newspapers and the "Top story" of the national news taken from the verses of Matthew 24. What is God saying?

Let me tell you a few things that I believe are foremost on His agenda:

1. It's all coming to a conclusion. This world was not designed to exist in this fashion forever. The devil would like you to believe that it's always been this way since the beginning of time. Not so! He promised that He would come back to earth again and that He would give clear signs before that happened. The signs are there!

2. God desires a personal relationship with each one of us, more than anything else in all of creation. If we need to be "shaken up" to make us think of God then so be it. The end result is what He is after.

3. This is not a time to be half-committed to serving Him. It's all or nothing. Fence-sitters will get a fence-sitter reward. The committed will hear, "Well done good and faithful servant." (Matthew 25:21a)

4. The Lord is holding back some of the most powerful demonstrations of His judgment until the harvest is gathered in. There are still lost souls who have not yet had a clear declaration of the gospel message presented to them. Some of them are in your workplace and others live next door to you. They are all loved by the Lord and He wants them to be a part of what He is doing.

Be prayerful and watch for opportunities to share your faith. There's not much time left.

█ **BEING YOUNG**

> *"...young men and maidens, old men and children.*
> *Let them praise the name of the LORD, for his name alone is exalted;*
> *his splendour is above the earth and the heavens."*

> ~Psalm 148:12-13

We all were young once. I know we think that some people were born old but that's not true. We have good memories of those early years when the worries of paying taxes and the supper menu were not a part of our program. We might even remember those serious times of concern when parents wanted to know everything about where we were going, what we were doing and who we were with.

I've discovered that those are chronic questions that probably every generation of moms and dads have asked since Cain and Abel went out to play. Parents struggle with how long to hold on and how soon to let go of the decision making process for their kids.

At some point, young people need to know that there are rewards and consequences to all choices and decisions. I think it's fair to say that parents want their kids to experience the rewards and avoid the consequences, and that is the reason for those many questions. But let me say, I've met some pretty mature kids in my time. They're the kind that you can trust to make the right decisions and who aren't afraid or embarrassed to ask for advice when there is some doubt. We can't put all the kids in the same box 'cause it simply does not fit everyone. I always hope that young people will realize that older people are not enemies and that we don't believe that the youth of our day are hopeless.

I sincerely believe that God wants to do some very special stuff in the lives of our youth today. They've got energy, educational resources and the desire to be people of influence. It encourages my heart to believe that God will call some of them to some very specific purposes in life. The next generation of leadership is already in formation and soon will take over the duties and responsibilities that the older folk will lay down. To every young person under the sound of my voice/writing I want to remind you that the Apostle Paul many years ago said, "Don't let anyone look down on you because you are young, but set an example of the believers in speech, in life, in love, in faith and in purity" (1 Timothy 4:12).

The intent of his counsel was to call young people to believe in themselves and take the initiative to be real, true-blue, committed believers who do not compromise for the world's standards. He is saying, "Be gutsy!" God is still calling young people and we want you to feel free to respond to what the Lord is saying. Don't be intimidated by the older folk who might not understand what you're doing. The truth is, they were young once, too, and had to learn by trial and error. We love you and know that God has a wonderful plan for your life!

| **HE KNEW HE WAS THE WINNER!**

*"Therefore he is able to save completely those who come to God
through him, because he always lives to intercede for them."*

~Hebrews 7:25

It's not wise to celebrate the victory before the battle. Who knows what surprises you might encounter in the midst of the conflict? The end results are never known until the last moments of the war. One great general in history surveyed the battlefield littered with damaged equipment and wounded and dead soldiers. He understood the tremendous price that had been paid through the conflict in the lives of his precious young men. Tearfully he said to his officers, "One more victory like that and we shall lose the war."

There are a lot of things in life that just don't matter. Then there are some things that are worth fighting for. We sometimes don't have our values straight and end up fighting for the wrong things because of our own personal interests. We may win, but with regrets because we discover it really wasn't what it seemed to be. You heard the story of the woodsman who said, "A dog can beat a skunk in a fight anytime, but some things are just not worth it!"

Jesus knew what was worth fighting for and He was willing to do whatever had to be done. On the human level He saw the need for a champion to challenge the powers of evil and so He offered Himself. He came into this world to make inroads into the kingdom of darkness and to conquer it. The process, He knew, would be lonely, painful, shameful, degrading, humiliating and would end in His death. But the battle would be won through the sacrifice of His life! The prize was worth it all. He would rise again from the dead and offer a plan that could lift every man, woman and child from the powers of darkness and place them in the perfect love of God with the promise of an eternal reward.

The motive behind His plan was based on love and whatever the cost, He would be willing to take on all the forces of darkness. He knew that without His intervention, all of creation would be under the wicked domination of "the god of this world" whose one goal is to destroy anything that God has created. That, of course, includes all of humanity. The Bible says concerning Jesus, "...for the joy that was set before Him He endured the cross, despising the shame..." (Hebrews 12:2). He knew from before the beginning of the project that the plan of Salvation would be successful. There was no way that the enemy could defeat Him on His mission. The purpose of God would be fulfilled and everyone would have an opportunity to choose to be a part of the Victory that Jesus provided on the cross. It's for that reason, days before the cross of Calvary, Jesus came into Jerusalem in a triumphant procession that we know today as Palm Sunday. This was a celebration in anticipation of the ultimate victory that He would accomplish at Calvary.

We continue to rejoice in the victory that has been passed on to us. Our freedom in God was won through Jesus Christ.

**OUR GREATEST EARTHLY RESOURCE**

*"But Jesus called the children to him and said,*
*'Let the little children come to me, and do not hinder them,*
*for the kingdom of God belongs to such as these.'"*

~Luke 18:16

There is no question that the most valuable resource of our country is not the wealth in the mountains, nor the oil on the plains, nor the trees of our forests, nor the fish of the sea. Our whole future as a nation depends upon the potential of the children of this generation. The greatest untapped wealth that will make our nation great and our homes secure lies in the hearts and minds of our children. We know that the little "rug rats" aren't going to be small all the time. Add food, education, moral principles and time and it won't be long before they will be governing our country and managing the affairs of our world. No wonder that Jesus would take the time to invite the children to come to Him and add His blessings upon their formative years.

Ministry to children needs to be recognized as one of the most important investments that can be made in our future. If we don't give our kids an opportunity to learn about the Lord and have a personal experience with Him, then the enemy of our souls will redirect their interests to things that could be very detrimental to their lives. You are wise in your planning for the future if you consider the real value of a Christian Education program that will influence your children in spiritual matters. Let me remind you, it won't just happen by itself.

I become very concerned when I hear that parents have their kids enrolled in all kinds of sports activities and hobby interests, but have not made Bible teaching a priority for their families. There will come a harvest day and some of the fruit that results from the seeds we have sown will come back to haunt us at some future date. Make no mistake, physical development is important and I believe that involvement in social interaction is a very important part of the growth of our children. However, if the price is that there is not enough time to have our children involved in spiritual interests, it is very possible that the "little rug rats" will grow up to be big monsters. Then it won't be their fault.

Parents, please allow me to give you some advice:

1. "Train a child in the way he should go, and when he is old he will not turn from it" (Proverbs 22:6).

2. Spend productive time with your children so they may learn that you are more than a legislator who lays down the laws. They need to know what makes you tick and that you value their little lives as worthy of love and patience.

3. Be on guard against the ungodly influences that invade our homes through television and computer systems.

4. Pray with your kids and read Bible stories to them. Let them know what a wonderful Saviour Jesus is to you.

115

| # A FAITHFUL FRIEND

*"A man of many companions may come to ruin,*
*but there is a friend who sticks closer than a brother."*

~Proverbs 18:24

You are never alone. No matter what paths, trails or roads you travel in life, you are not alone. The moment you accept Jesus Christ as your Lord and Saviour you are placed into a new relationship with the God of the Universe. As you seek and maintain your desire to serve and honour the Lord each day, you may know that He does have a very special plan and purpose for your life. The Old Testament prophet, under the inspiration of the Holy Spirit wrote, "I, the LORD, have called you in righteousness; I will take hold of your hand..." (Isaiah 42:6a). In the New Testament it is recorded that God said, "Never will I leave you; never will I forsake you." (Hebrews 13:5b) These are very rich promises that belong to those who put their trust in the Lord.

We may not "feel" that God is always that close to us, and I can assure you that the road may be rough ahead of you but God will be faithful to keep His word. We need to exercise our faith and trust Him when we do not understand what is going on around us or what His purposes are for us in strange situations. Rest assured that the only One who knows the future is also the Guardian of your soul. He has a way of bringing special resources into special occasions in ways that may surprise us, but sometimes we have to look for the answers ourselves. It is wrong to think that we can just lay back and wait for developments to unwind before us. Asking, seeking and knocking are terms that Jesus used to remind us that we must get involved in seeing God release the answers to our personal concerns. We need to invest time and energy in being obedient to Him as much as we possibly can. When we reach the limits of our attempts, God can take over and many times He rewards our searching with heavenly benefits.

Let me tell you some of the places to look for His companionship:

1. His Word is often His voice speaking to us. It is an unchanging source of wisdom and guidance that we should make an important part of our lives.

2. Prayer is taking the occasion to talk to the God of all of creation who has promised to hear us before we even call. It is also an opportunity to stop and listen to what God may be prompting us in our hearts. He speaks in Prayer.

3. Seeking the advice of mature believers opens the door to what God has been saying to others, sometimes through lengthy periods of time, and allows us to hear what God would say through their wisdom. God has been blessing His people through the ages, and shared experiences are God speaking to us again. Please don't let your session with "the wise" become a pity party. Tell it like you see/feel it and let God speak to your heart through the other.

You don't have to walk alone! There is Someone who cares.

**❙ SOMETHING BEAUTIFUL**

*"No one whose hope is in you will ever be put to shame…"*

~Psalm 25:3

It's a very romantic story that is filled with intrigue, mystery and miracles. It's the story of the choosing of a wife for Isaac, the son of Abraham. It's found in chapter 24 of Genesis and involves the commitment and dedication of a willing servant, the guidance and direction of God Himself and the total surrender of a very beautiful, modest lady who wanted only to please the Lord and submit to His plan. The interweaving of prayer, trust in God, desire to serve, diligence and faithfulness bring the story to a fairy tale conclusion. Just think! God knew a young lady across the mountains, rivers, forests and deserts that would be the right girl for a young man that was willing to leave the choice to God. That young man did nothing more than wait, pray and meditate until the whole process was completed. He finally received his bride; and she was a beauty, if you don't mind me saying so. The story includes another important detail: "…he loved her."

It's not my intention to give you any pre-marital counselling today, but I do want to remind you that there are some very wonderful things that God wants to share with those that put their trust in Him. You know that God can see over the horizons of our lives and into the best situations that we could ever dream of if we will but trust Him. Sometimes the process requires patience on our part as we wait to see what God will do. At other times He expects diligence and effort in the pursuit of His purposes and knowing His will. The key is to not get overly concerned about arriving at our goals as much as to be desirous that in the process of living we want to see what God can do when He is given control. Jesus said, "But *seek first* his kingdom and his righteousness, and all these things will be given to you as well" (Matthew 6:33, emphasis added). Making the pleasure of the Lord our primary goal adjusts the focus for the other important things of life. Many times we resort to a different process: if only I had this or that then I would serve God. That's not the way it works. That puts everything backwards. God first, what I want afterwards and, of course, patience to let God do "His thing."

I think it's fair to say that waiting for/upon God is a very difficult matter for most of human nature. If we would pause to consider the rewards that He had reserved in historical settings for those that took the time to trust Him, I think that we might learn some lessons about what really is most valuable in life and whether or not it is all worth waiting for. The truth is that God is not in a rush. We shouldn't be either. But while we wait, let's maintain our confidence, because He does all things well and He sees beyond the mountain ranges that obscure our vision. He has something beautiful reserved for you. You may be surprised at what God has prepared for you.

▌ **HE CARES FOR YOU**

> *"All that the Father gives me will come to me,*
> *and whoever comes to me I will never drive away."*
>
> ~John 6:37

Most people can identify quickly with the story that Jesus told of the one lost sheep. Who hasn't been completely "out of it" at some time in their life? We have felt the need for a caring person to come alongside of us to hold us close and give us the strength to see our way out of the trials and temptations that, too often, befuddle us. "You've been there, done that and bought the T-shirt," as the saying goes.

Real care is a missing element that we hear people asking for today. Whether it's a request concerning their Doctor or their Pastor, the Mechanic at the garage or the Social Worker, every one wants to feel important and understood by others.

But let me remind you that Jesus thinks that you are very important—so important that He left His heavenly home in glory to come to this world for one particular reason...He cares for you (1 Peter 5:7). He cares for me. He cares for those who don't care for Him and those who couldn't give a "hoot" about what He did on the cross for all the lost of this world. He still cares.

That may not bring a lot of consolation to you when you feel alone unless you grasp the reality of His promise and recognize that, "He will never leave you nor forsake you" (Deuteronomy 31:6b). He's always near to those who trust.

But then, there are the lost. These have not heard that there is a Loving Saviour, who gave Himself to help them out of their sin and to bring them into the family of God. There are many who need to hear that God does not intend to condemn those that come to Him. The Good News is that His love reaches out to all mankind because the Lord wants to pardon, restore and heal all that will come to Him. That's the reason for Missions. That's the reason why some leave their homelands and go to countries where they have to learn new languages and customs. That's the reason why we support them with our giving and our prayers. Somebody needs to share the story of the Caring Shepherd. We have a part in sending the wonderful story of God's love to our neighbours and to the uttermost parts of the earth.

That's what Missions and Evangelism is all about. We demonstrate our concern for those that the Lord loves that have not heard the message yet. There is so much sorrow in our world today and people are searching for solutions in the wrong places. We become partners with Missionaries as we pray, give and share the message of God's love.

That happens because...we care. Don't we?

**UNSEEN BENEFITS**

*"No eye has seen, no ear has heard, no mind has conceived what God has prepared for those who love Him."*

~1 Corinthians 2:9

You've heard the question asked, "If a tree falls in the forest and there is no one to hear it, does it make a noise?" What a crazy question!

The truth is that the most important things that happen in life may not be detected, and yet they have eternal benefits. When I asked the Lord to forgive me of my sin, in an instant, all of the things that I had done that offended God were completely washed away. My name was recorded in heaven in the Lamb's book of life and I was made a son of God. That allows me special privileges of inheritance for now and in the future. In an unseen moment, I was snatched from the kingdom of darkness by the grace of God and granted full landed immigrant status in the kingdom of God's dear Son. I was also adopted by the Heavenly Father, who welcomes me to often return to Him, by way of prayer, where I may leave all my cares and concerns with Him. I became an heir of God and a joint heir with Jesus Christ. In a flash, "the old has gone, the new has come!" (2 Corinthians 5:17).

Unseen, but very real, the Holy Spirit moved into my life to be a Guide through all the experiences that lie ahead. Invisible, He prompts me when I make mistakes, brings joy when I am faithful, fills me with wisdom for the special tasks that fall across my way and grants a very special channel to the Father through prayer. You didn't see any of that happen, but each of these miracles occurred when I believed that Jesus died for me.

When I remember His death on the cross of Calvary I remember that what He has done for me is the same provision He would grant to every one of us who will acknowledge our need of a Saviour. God has given us the opportunity to weigh His offer and either to accept it or to leave it alone. It happens by faith. I believe in His Word and accept His offer. However, leaving it alone doesn't mean that it is going to go away. He will return to offer anyone the same benefits that I claim as mine. But the choice belongs to each of us. Choosing to "not choose" is a choice as well, and the result is the same as a rejection. To go into eternity without the unseen affairs in order is to enter into the terrible alternative. Hell was not created for man but "for the devil and his angels" (Matthew 25:41).

The choice of whether someone goes to heaven or hell is a matter for each individual to decide. We are wrong to blame God for sending anyone to hell. We are ultimately responsible for making that decision ourselves, or rather, refusing to choose to give ourselves to Him. Although He will do everything possible to make the options plain and simple, He will not force His will on anyone. He never has and never will.

**AN ESTABLISHED STANDARD**

*"Heaven and earth will pass away, but my words will never pass away."*

~Matthew 24:35

We're living in a generation of ethical variables. What was once valuable to us is no longer important to our modern society. There are religious organizations that teach clear moral virtues for the building of better families, however, if they are dealing with someone outside of their group, it is okay. to lie, cheat and defraud. That's the kind of double standard that has come to be quite acceptable to some today. We've also heard of "situational ethics." That means your standards can change according to the company you keep. If the people you are with smoke marijuana, it's okay. If they are against it, you must be too. You could call this the "herd syndrome" where you fit in with whatever the crowd is doing. After all, isn't it easier to let go of your standards than to fight for them?

Please let me remind you that God's Word "stands firm in the heavens" (Psalm 119:89). That's the standard we should live by. Peter reminds us that, "the word of the Lord stands forever" (1 Peter 1:25).

Thank God, there is something in our world that does not change with the times but is consistent through the generations as a monument to the unchanging standards of God. Jesus made it clear to the people throughout His ministry that the religious leaders had set a level of righteousness that was a very high standard that even they were not able to attain. He offered a substitute that was not popular to His generation but that would demonstrate the expectations of God in everyday life. He spoke of divorce, anger, financial integrity, future planning, pride in public display, and of lust and social responsibility. He taught principles that had not changed since the Garden of Eden and are the only way to please God. I guess it all comes down to one simple question that we all should ask. What does God say about the issues that are so important to us, as well as the things that we don't think are important at all? We've got to learn that the only One that really matters in any crowd is God.

Let me come back to emphasize the importance of knowing God's Word and learning what His expectations are for our lives in this upside-down world. It's time that Christians realized that it is more important now than ever before to stand upon His Word as the rule that regulates our lives. If you are ever in doubt about those things, look to a mature brother/sister and get some wise counsel. May your solutions be born in the Word of God because, "Your Word is a lamp to my feet and a light for my path" (Psalm 119:105). It is imperatively important that we make the reading of God's Word a daily part of our lives. It serves as an unchanging magnetic pole that points us, always, in the direction that God wants us to go. Without it, we have no compass to give us a sure bearing through the experiences of life.

▌ **WHATEVER YOU WANT, I'LL GIVE**

*"Whom shall I send? And who will go for us?"*
*And I said, "Here am I, send me!"*

~Isaiah 6:8

It was when the dagger was in his upraised hand that Abraham clearly heard the voice of God. "Do not lay a hand on the boy" (Genesis 22:12). Abraham was prepared to give his son as an offering to God upon the altar he had made on Mount Moriah where the Mosque of Omar stands today in the city of Jerusalem. It was another step of obedience that Abraham was willing to do. God had asked him to give his promised son upon an altar. It must have seemed crazy to Abraham to hear God make such a request. But the test was designed to prove Abraham's complete trust in God.

He passed with flying colours. There was "NO" thing that would stand between him and the Lord. Nothing was more important than doing what the Lord had asked of him, no matter the cost. But you know the rest of the story. A substitute was provided for Isaac in the life of a mountain sheep that was caught in a thicket. Abraham was committed to honouring the Lord with all that he possessed and with all his heart, and so God provided a substitute sacrifice. That was the key to his relationship with God and his wonderful walk with the Lord. "Nothing between the Lord and the Saviour." Abraham's actions were a demonstration that whatever the Lord has need of he was willing to surrender it to Him—even his beloved son.

But then, so was the heart of the Heavenly Father as He saw the need of fallen man. His plan was to give His only begotten Son to be the substitute for all sinners, for all time.

Jesus came into the world as the Lamb of God that would take away the sins of the world. It was an arrangement whereby all my sin was laid on Jesus and His righteousness became mine. It is a fact, today, that all my sins are gone and that there was no other way to do it. It did not come to me because of anything special that I did, but by the free gift of God. While I was a prodigal and rebellious son, God was willing to allow His Son to be my substitute so that I could have the liberty to serve Him with the beginnings of eternal life. We are now free of all condemnation and invested with a new authority as the Sons and Daughters of God so that we can choose to honour Him with the rest of our lives. His gift was because of our need.

I always think it is so interesting that what God would not let Abraham do, (give up his son,) God Himself was willing to do.

| **MISSIONS**

*"And this gospel of the kingdom will be preached in whole world
as a testimony to all nations, and then the end will come."*

~Matthew 24:14

The Keystone of the founding of the Fellowship of the Pentecostal Assemblies of Canada was the uniting of a group of Pastors who had a common vision for a Worldwide Missions Outreach. Through the past number of decades their Missionary emphasis has been a priority in their Churches across the Dominion of Canada, and God has added His blessings to the fulfillment of that vision. Missions giving is necessary to fulfill the mandate to, "Go into all the world and preach the good news to all creation" (Mark 16:15).

Missionaries are sent to various parts of the world to preach and teach the gospel. They are people who respond to a very special calling, yet they are just like we are and have needs like the rest of us. Some have children who, obviously, require special attention for their education and support. Needless to say, they depend on us working with them by our prayer support and by providing for their daily requirements. Only eternity will reveal what your faithful giving and praying has accomplished. You may not have thought of it in a personal way, but what you give together with others is the size of the tool that is used to reach the lost. Without the tools, what could our Missionaries accomplish? We want them to be able to efficiently do the most possible in the shortest time available so that the job of reaching the world will be completed before Jesus comes back again. It will be a tragic moment to find out, when Christ returns, that we could have done the job a lot better and faster if only we would have given in a more committed fashion. Let's do what we can do with what we've got so that we may hear, "Well done, good and faithful servant."

Giving to Missions:

- is a gift of faith. We release our finances but don't see where they are going or what they are accomplishing; regardless, we give to the Lord.

- is a step of faith. We could use the money ourselves but we invest in the Kingdom of God by surrendering our finances to the Lord.

- is a vote of faith. We may never meet the recipients of our giving but we believe that God has called quality people to do His work in Missions and our giving is a vote of confidence in God's choice.

- is a declaration of faith. I want to be a part of what God is doing in other parts of the world, and although I may never see where it is being used, I declare that I trust that God is able to use this gift for His glory.

Remember the words of scripture: "How can they preach unless they are sent?" (Romans 10:15a). Let's do some sending by our faithfulness.

122

❚ **PRAYER**

> *"The sacrifices of God are a broken spirit; a broken and a*
> *contrite heart, O God, you will not despise."*
>
> ~Psalm 51:17

Prayer serves as a direct connecting line from your heart to the heart of God and depends more upon your right attitude than your right words.

Jesus gave a clear illustration in Luke 18 when He spoke of the pride and the ego of the Pharisee, contrasted by the humble approach of the Tax-collector. The Pharisee was a religious leader who had all the credentials for doing things right and for fame and fortune, but his heart was taken up with himself. It appears that he came to God to proclaim the credits of his accomplishments and his personal worthiness of God's special consideration. Meanwhile, the Tax-collector, standing at a distance, beat on his breast and cried, "God have mercy on me, a sinner" (Luke 18:13). Jesus said that it was this man who went home justified that day. God heard his prayer because of his attitude and his humble confession.

Let me remind you of the ACTS approach to prayer. These are four steps that should occupy our regular prayer times.

A - stands for Adoration. We acknowledge God for who He is and we worship Him. It involves making our hearts approach His throne as humble and contrite people who have audience with the Most High. He is worthy of our praise because He is God.

C - stands for Confession. We open our hearts to tell God the truth about what goes on inside. He already knows, of course, but the fact that we are willing to acknowledge our weaknesses and failures brings us into a right attitude with God. We seek His forgiveness for things that we have done that we know displease Him and we receive His pardon.

T - stands for Thanksgiving. Not the "let's eat turkey" kind, though. Thankfulness is an acknowledgement of His faithfulness and the kindness of His daily provisions for us. He has done many wonderful things for us and we should be faithful to express our gratitude. We come into His presence with gratitude for the many blessings that we already have received and then move on to thank Him for those that will come through His promises.

S - stands for Supplication. Everyone has needs. This is a time to lay our burdens down. It is time to intercede on the behalf of others and their needs. It is time to call out to God because we depend upon Him for so much in our lives.

It is important to remember that it's not the wording of our prayers that makes them powerful. It's the attitude. "If my people, who are called by my name, will humble themselves and pray..." (2 Chronicles 7:14a). The step that must be taken before we pray is to humble ourselves. That's the time to check our attitudes. Let's learn to pray and do it God's way.

**BORROWED NUGGETS**

The rich man wasn't in Hell long before he became an ardent believer in Missions:

*"...I beg you...send Lazarus to my father's house, for I have five brothers. Let him warn them, so that they will not also come to this place of torment."*

~Luke 16:27-28

"There are ninety and nine that safely lie,
In the shelter of the fold,
But millions are left outside to die
For the ninety and nine are cold.
Away in sins delusive snare,
Hastening to death and dark despair
Hastening to death and none to care,
For the ninety and nine are cold!"

Livingstone said, "God had only one Son and He was a Missionary."

Every heart without Christ is a Mission field.
Every heart with Christ is a Missionary.

A Missionary does not necessarily go outside of his or her country, province or community. A true Missionary needs only to go outside of himself or herself.

Down beneath the mighty ocean,
Divers (missionaries) plunge for treasures rare,
But men (us) hold the ropes above them
So they breathe the upper air.
Seeking pearls (the lost) of richest value,
Braver hearts have dared to go,
But our hands must every moment
Hold the ropes that go below!

"Many will never reach the Mission Field on their feet, but all of God's children can reach it on their knees."

Today we focus a little more closely on Missions and the challenges of sharing the gospel to our generation. I'm not sure that we grasp the importance of everyone having a heart to see the lost brought to Christ. That is the passion that brought Jesus to this world and made the Apostle Paul declare: "For Christ's love compels us..." (2 Corinthians 5:14a).

Let's continue to commit ourselves to being Missionaries!

# THE PRIVILEGES OF PRAYER

*"He said to them, 'When you pray, say:*
*"Father, hallowed be your name…"'"*

~Luke 11:2

A single word or thought lifted to the Father through the name of Jesus is given access to the throne room of heaven. The freedom of entrance is granted to the pauper and the rich man, to the simple and to the wise. It does not depend upon our material resources nor our good looks. God extends to us the privilege and pleasure of prayer, where we can lay our burdens down and trust Him for the answers. Jesus taught us that God is our Heavenly Father and that He cares for us as His own dear children. He already knows our needs but invites us, just the same, to come before Him and share our heart's desire, as a little child. The number of words that are used in the request does not matter. He is most interested in the attitude of the heart and reads the motives and intents there. His greatest desire is that we learn to come to Him with all our needs and dreams and tell Him about them. There obviously should be many times that we come to Him with Praise and Thanksgiving for the many things that He has done for us, mindful that He has designed us to be people of Worship and Praise.

It is interesting that those who have learned the discipline of prayer find that praying brings great blessing. Those who have not learned to exercise themselves in this way, however, may find prayer dry and difficult. God does add blessings to those who seek His face. He is a Rewarder of those who earnestly seek Him (Hebrews 11:6).

A wise man so wonderfully stated the truth: "More things are wrought by prayer than this world dreams of." God answers prayer. He longs to do more for us than we can imagine, and He has given us the key, through faith, to open the door to His presence and His treasure house. The responsibility of laying our burdens and cares before Him rests on our shoulders alone, yet Jesus, Himself, is the one who intercedes for us (Hebrews 7:25).

When we are not sure how to pray, the Holy Spirit comes alongside of us and helps us in our weaknesses to say the right things at the right moment (Romans 8:26). The sounds of that kind of praying may be unfamiliar to our normal conversation, but they are true expressions of the Holy Spirit, who knows the need and carries it before the Father in a form that we do not understand.

Then there is the privilege of praying in the Holy Spirit (Jude 20), where the Holy Spirit uses another language to lift our verbal expressions to God. Besides that, He shares the joy of His presence with the one who prays. What a privilege it is to come to the Lord in Prayer.

Let's learn that any effort invested in prayer is well invested and brings a great increase. We have prayed.

Now let's be aware of what God is going to do in our midst.

▌ **MOTHERS' TRAINING**

*"Her children arise and call her blessed;*
*her husband also, and he praises her."*

~Proverbs 31:28

The old adage is still often repeated, "The hand that rocks the cradle, rules the world." It has become increasingly more obvious that the Mother's role is becoming a very strenuous task. In our day, as moral values are shifting, it is progressively more difficult to raise our children with Christian standards. There are all kinds of messages that are being fed to our families through television, the education system and through the pressure of their peers. Having said all that, let me remind you of the positive side. The Apostle Paul commended Timothy for the faith that he possessed that was first evidenced in the life of his grandmother Lois and in his mother Eunice (2 Timothy 1:5). He was a third generation Believer. The faith of his grandmother and his mother eventually became his faith. I never thought of faith as something you could give away, however the example of faithfulness does teach many lessons, and that is something we all need to learn to share, freely. It may sound like a "call" into the ministry when I say this, but I believe that Mothers need to exercise their faith in the home scene in a greater way than ever before because of the counteracting influences of the world.

We have often said that the Father is the Priest of the home, and although I would never stop insisting that this is God's plan, I think it is important to recognize that it is a shared responsibility as important as changing diapers, doing dishes and vacuuming the house. We need to make room for family prayer, good old gospel singing and reading the Word to demonstrate to our kids that there is a healthy alternative to the trends of society. Speak well of your spiritual leadership and make it clear by your faithful attendance that Church is more than a community club. Speak often of answers to prayer and the importance of trusting God when things don't seem to be going the way we want them to. Pray with your children about their school problems and their relationships with their friends. It's all a part of sowing faith in the tender hearts of our children. I believe that God will honour us as we are faithful to give him room in our homes as well as our hearts.

Mothers, don't let go of the cradle. We need Mothers who will be godly to influence this generation and the next. The things you say and do are an investment that will be passed on to future generations. If things continue as they should, according to this pattern of scripture, you may see the dividends lived out in your own grandchildren as they become people who trust and serve the Lord.

█ **WOMEN IN MINISTRY**

*"They all joined together constantly in prayer, along with the women and Mary the mother of Jesus, and with his brothers."*

~Acts 1:14

If you thought for a moment, you could probably name most of the disciples who followed Jesus during His earthly travels. But could you name the ladies that supported His ministry? You probably would remember that there were three Marys and a Martha who were very good friends of His and who seemed to always be nearby. Did you know that one of the first times the Word "deacon" is used to describe a ministry it was related to the contributions that a number of ladies did to assist Jesus in His activities and travels?

Luke 8:3 names Mary, Joanna, Susanna and "many others." What they did is simply described as, "These women were helping to *support* [Greek - '*Diakoneo,*' from which we get our word 'Deacon'] them out of their own means." They were servants to Jesus. Handmaidens who helped supply the needs of the ministry of Jesus as He traveled the dusty roads of Israel. This passage focuses on the liberal commitment of a number of ladies who obviously worked to support the Master and His disciples. The historical record honours the involvement of these wonderful ladies in their efforts to provide for the day-by-day needs of our Lord. There is no record, though, of any bills being submitted to the finance committee for review. They served in love. It is interesting that many sermons have been preached on each of the disciples and, in detail, their personalities and endeavours are examined. But I have never heard a sermon about Joanna or Susanna. Then again, the ladies often do things in the background and don't get much credit for their efforts and their labours of love. We may have missed that point, but the Holy Spirit made sure that a record was made of their actions and it is recorded in this gospel message.

Women have played a very prominent role in the development and progress of the Church. The book of Acts often relates accounts of the women, whose faith was strong, who were committed to the progress of the gospel and the spiritual life of the primitive Church. There were Dorcas, Priscilla, and Lydia as well as Philip's four daughters who prophesied. Others are named in the greetings at the conclusion of each of the Apostle's letters to the Churches as Paul expressed his gratitude for the faithfulness of those who became a part of his ministry to reach the lost.

We appreciate the fine work our ladies of this generation are doing as they are involved in praying and caring for many of the tasks of the local Church. Stop for a moment, today, and think of those who are involved in your Church, and be faithful to express your appreciation for each as they share the burdens of ministry. Many of them are the reason our Churches are successful and growing with influence in our community.

▌ **TRUE SERVANTS**

> *"...Deborah arose, arose a mother in Israel."*
>
> ~Judges 5:7b

She was obviously a housewife and not out to build a kingdom for herself. She just used the giftings and talents the Lord gave her to do a job that needed to be done in Israel at that time. Her office was under a palm tree where she met with people who had problems and needed advice and counsel. Deborah learned how to listen to the Lord and was bold to speak whatever the Lord had laid upon her heart. It was through this lady, the wife of Lappidoth (Judges 4:4), that God gave direction on how to bring the nation out from under the dominion of their enemies. She had neither throne nor crown to demonstrate any worldly authority. It doesn't appear likely that she lived in any palatial estate to confirm her position to the nation; but people knew that when Deborah spoke, they must stop and listen. She was everybody's mother (Judges 5:7)—people from all over the nation gave her that kind of respect. She was a woman who heard from God and who obediently shared His message wherever it was needed. She was "A Mother in Israel" by Divine appointment. Her children were all those who had need of a comforting word at the right time.

There's probably a lot of women in the world today, like Deborah, who don't grasp after the power of authority but who wisely, in lady-like fashion, are faithful to be the godly people that God has designed all of us to be. The ministry that God has committed to all of us is, simply, to be available to touch the hearts of those who see our witness and are looking for answers to life's pressing questions. We don't need a sceptre and robe to let people know our position. Sometimes those objects can become objectionable. But the simple, committed lifestyle of a Mr. or Mrs./Miss Average Person can be seen as more accessible than we could imagine. Whoever we are and wherever we serve the Lord, there is a task that needs to be done and it is ours by God's appointment. It may not be the deliverance of a nation, but definitely, there is a war out there that is directed at destroying the lives of people in our neighbourhood.

This is not going to be deep theology, but let me make a few suggestions about being like Deborah:

1. Let's take time to become people who hear from the Lord.
2. Let's take time to become listeners who hear the hearts of people.
3. Let's take time to be practical in our witness for the Lord.
4. Let's take time to explore/determine what our special talents and giftings are.

▌ **THE FAITH OF OUR MOTHERS**

*"I have been reminded of your sincere faith, which first lived*
*in your grandmother Lois and in your mother Eunice*
*and, I am persuaded, now lives in you."*

~2 Timothy 1:5

A little girl on the playground, huddled among her friends, turned to a little boy and, loud enough for everyone to hear, she shouted, "I love you." In embarrassment, he ran for the cover of his friends. It was those three words that gripped my thoughts for a few moments. I wondered if she understood *anything* about what love really is.

There is a saying that, "puppy love is real to the puppies." How many other boys would be the objects of her "love" before she met the one that would be the love of her life? I wouldn't want to demean the innocent intentions of those words used in the context of her understanding. I'm sure that to her, the matters of commitment and endurance had not quite developed in her mind. Saying "I love you" can be something nice to say to your family and friends. But as you grow up, those words have a very special meaning.

Real love requires patience, persistence and plain hard work. To talk of love is to speak of sweat, sacrifice and surrender—not very much exciting romance in those thoughts. Who would have ever expected that something so beautiful as love would have such down to earth, practical applications?

Nowhere is the significance of those words more real than in the routine of a Mother who spends endless waking hours of her day in the concerns of her husband and children. Her day sometimes stretches into the midnight/midmorning feedings, diaper changes, meal planning, housecleaning and laundry chores. All that began when she "fell" in love. You see, love is a choice to be willing to serve others at our own personal cost. I, like you, enjoy the emotions that are sometimes connected with a love relationship. However, if we live only on the emotional level, we have missed the true meaning of love.

Let a Mother teach you. Let her example be a lesson to us all. Let her lifestyle direct us to what love is all about. This is not kid stuff!

Mothers, we honour you on a special day, once a year, for the faithful demonstration of your love. We recognize that we cannot repay a good Mother for all the time and energy invested in our lives. The very fact that you are in Church on any Sunday is a witness to your commitment to honouring the Lord and directing the spiritual life of your children. You are a special treasure to us. Even Jesus recognized the importance of Motherhood, and while He hung on the cross, one of His last concerns was for His Mother. John, known as the Apostle of love, was delegated the responsibility for her care. Mothers, we wish to honour you today!

**WE HONOUR MOTHERS**

*"Many women were there, watching from a distance.
They had followed Jesus from Galilee to care for his needs."*

~Matthew 27:55

They may not have been the only ones who sustained Jesus' ministry, but it is clear that the ladies made a tremendous contribution "out of their own means" to cover the expenses involved in carrying on the spread of the good news that a Saviour had come into the world (Luke 8:3). Their involvement was noted on many occasions throughout the gospels as they humbly ministered to Jesus and His followers.

1. It appears that the home of Mary and Martha had an open door of hospitality for Jesus and the disciples whenever they were in the area. Their home was available as a place where Jesus and His followers could find food and rest (John 12).

2. It is interesting to note that when Jesus was making His final journey to Calvary His only recorded conversation from Pilate's judgment hall to the cross, was when He paused to speak to a group of ladies who followed Him, mourning and wailing for Him (Luke 23:27). Obviously, they were expressing deep concern for the way that matters had turned against Jesus. The guys, who were supposed to be the brave defenders of the faith, were nowhere to be seen. It was the ladies who shamelessly demonstrated their disapproval of the treatment of the Saviour. They did what they could do and Jesus recognized that.

3. It was the women who followed Joseph to see where His body was laid. They were the first visitors to arrive at the tomb on the resurrection day. They were the first to let the world know that He had risen from the grave and that an angel had spoken to them. The distraught disciples who were still in mourning thought their story was "nonsense," but the record says that the women "remembered his words" (Luke 24).

4. It was a lady opening her home in Philippi to the Apostle Paul that brought the introduction of the gospel to the western world (Acts 16:11-15). It all began through the door of a woman named Lydia, and has been advancing in that direction from the Middle East to the Far East and back again since then.

Mother's Day is our opportunity to express our appreciation for that kind of leadership in our homes by godly ladies who have been faithful to honour the Lord in various forms of service. They have often given leadership in spiritual matters and we are blessed by them for the wonderful contribution they have made in our lives.

▌ **MOTHER'S DAY AND OUR MOTHERS**

*"Her children arise and call her blessed; her husband also and he praises her: 'Many women do noble things, but you surpass them all.'"*

~Proverbs 31:28-29

From his raised position he could easily see almost everyone in the audience. They came from many nations to be a part of the celebrations planned for that weekend. There were rich and poor, young and old, all with their eyes focused on him, awaiting the words he might say or to see the things he might do at this very important time in his life. As he scanned the crowd, more aware now of their needs than ever before, he paused and looked into the eyes of his own, dear mother.

He knew the story of how, as a very young lady, she had been found "with child." She had survived the terrible stigma laid upon her because she wasn't married and there was no way to successfully explain that. Of course, all the neighbours had done their share of criticizing and condemning, but she had decided that she would bear this infant even under those awful circumstances because she believed that God had given her this child.

The story never went away, and from time to time people would throw that back at Jesus. He was an illegitimate child (John 8:41), born without a father through some apparently shameful circumstance. But his mother was like most other mothers. She was there for him. She did the buying of the groceries and the meal preparation; the cleaning of house and belongings. She personally made many of his clothes with her own hands. She was his counsellor, nurse, chauffeur, protector and very best friend. She taught him to pray before he went to bed and before each of the meals that she so lovingly prepared. Her own spiritual life began to set patterns for his own until he came to understand more clearly the direction that his Father in Heaven had planned for his life. His name was often on her prayerful lips when he did things that she could not understand. She longed for fame and success to follow his endeavours, like every other mother does. As a matter of fact, she was there, many times, as a vote of support and encouragement when he faced the crowds of people who wanted what he possessed...until the very end.

And now, from his vantage point, on the cross, he remembered the kind, sacrificial, thoughtfulness of his mother. "John," he said, "Behold, your mother." He wasn't going to be there for her in her old age, so Jesus would do the best he could for her. He chose the youngest of the disciples, the disciple of love, to take care of his mother; as though sharing the prized family possessions as an inheritance, he gave his most valuable asset to his best friend.

We cannot count the true value of godly mothers, but we thank you today.

**▌ IN HONOUR OF MOTHERS**

*"Many women do noble things, but you surpass them all."*

~Proverbs 31:29

There is no question that by all appearances Timothy's greatest asset was the input of Faith passed on from his mother and grandmother.

"I have been reminded of your sincere faith, which first lived in your grandmother Lois and in your mother Eunice...." (2 Timothy 1:5a)

Timothy may not have always been aware of the real value of their faithfulness to leave a spiritual heritage for him and train him to love the Lord. Others could see the tremendous contribution that had been invested by them in giving direction to Timothy's life. Paul was the one who brings this to our attention, with a gentle reminder to be thankful for godly parents.

I always think it's interesting that there was no reference to Timothy's father or grandfather, and I wonder where they were and what effect they had upon this young man. We are not told, but it makes me think. To be on the positive side, let's not forget the power of influence that is committed to every mother on earth. Although times have changed and many mothers need to work outside of the home in order to meet the family budget, it is still recognized that a mother's influence is imperative for developing a family that understands true spiritual principles. We love you for that, Moms!

Let me just share a few things that are really important for all parents to pass along to their kids:

1. Teach them how to pray, when to pray and TO pray (that is, the method, the reason and the will to pray). Prayer is one of the most important ingredients in the development of a life toward spiritual maturity.

2. Teach them by having them read Bible portions to show them that the Bible is the Word of God and it is important to read and to memorize it. They should see and hear you reading as an example to them. Let them know that you appreciate when they make the effort to read their Bible as well. You'll be eternally grateful ("I have hidden your word in my heart that I might not sin against you" Psalm 119:11.)

3. Teach them to be courteous under all circumstances. That is, to respect their elders and those in authority. Though older folk may have a different viewpoint than they do, the wisdom of experience is still one of the best teachers they will ever find.

Your own list probably goes on... We love you and wish to honour you today. God bless you! Your task is great and God is able to give you His guidance every day for each of your own personal needs and desires.

**┃ BEING A LOVING MOTHER**

*"Many women do noble things, but you surpass them all."*

~Proverbs 31:29

Allow me to state the obvious: parents can adopt children but children have no choice in who will be their real parents. There are some situations where the arrival of a child in the home is viewed as a tragedy. They are sometimes called "unwanted" children. That truth should not be related to the babies who had no choice in being born. That kind of situation should instead be called "unwanted motherhood." These children are still very precious in God's sight, as is every child. Jesus demonstrated this in a number of sermons when He would take up or point to a little child and express the teaching of the heart of the Father toward them.

Being a mother is a choice. Being a loving mother is also a choice, whether it be by birth or by adoption. We cannot express the seriousness and commitment that such a calling requires. Loving motherhood doesn't run on an eight-hour shift. It's a 24-hour-a-day job that sometimes requires wearisome night shifts and tiresome days. A mother's involvement and interests vary from the dreary drag of dirty diapers to balancing the finances of home budgets. When you speak of mothers you had better recall the exploits of "super woman" who, with boundless energy and wisdom, was capable of resolving all issues. To say they can leap over tall buildings with a single bound would be an understandable exaggeration, but to enumerate their tasks and routine accomplishments, although true, would also appear to be a great exaggeration. It has been said that the energy that a mother expends each day in the faithful, loving care of a family far exceeds the effort that a father puts into an eight-hour shift of manual labour.

Godly motherhood is a special gift to future generations. Each child is an important investment in the direction of our future. They will, too soon, become the leaders of businesses, our communities and perhaps the government of our nation. They will be the ones who have input into the moral fabric of our society.

It was through his mother's teachings that Timothy became an important man of God to his generation. It was that kind of influence that began with Grandma that was passed on through the ages to make such an impact down to our time. Perhaps it all began over a kitchen table, at some child's bedside or in a children's Bible class at Church.

Of all the things that a mother does there is probably nothing that will share such long-term impact as committing a true faith and trust in God. Talking Bible thoughts and praying with your children are the keys to a lasting loving motherhood influence that will give children a right perspective on God's purpose for their lives. Training children in godly ways and planting the Word in their hearts are two of the promises of God that will bring eternal dividends.

Your children will rise up and call you "Blessed."

133

█ **THE GIFT OF THE FATHER**

*"On one occasion, while he was eating with them, he gave them this command: 'Do not leave Jerusalem, but wait for the gift my Father promised, which you have heard me speak about.'"*

~Acts 1:4

Jesus had spoken about the gift of the Father that the disciples would receive, but they had to wait for the promise in the city of Jerusalem. I'm sure that they had no idea of what to expect as this was brand new territory for all of them. I have a feeling that there was an air of anticipation as they tarried together in times of prayer and praise. They had no time schedule that they could establish as the possible moment of the arrival of "the Gift." They had no idea of what appearance the promise would have. I'm sure that every knock at the door was a lift in expectation as they opened to receive the unknown mystery "present." Did they believe that another physical Jesus would come to be their new leader? If so, would He be dressed in regal robes and crown accompanied by a military contingent?

As much as Jesus had often spoken of the coming of the Holy Spirit, it must have been difficult to conceive of this Wonderful Person coming in the sound of a rushing mighty wind and with tongues of fire on top of the heads of the Believers. Then they all burst into praise in languages not known to them. The Gift of the Father moved into the hearts of those who were gathered together in the upper room in the dynamic, unseen form of the Holy Spirit.

Something about His arrival, invisible but accompanied by phenomenal signs, filled the hearts of the 120 with great joy to such an extent that the whole community of Jerusalem heard about it and knew that something strange and wonderful was going on. The streets were filled with sincere but confused spectators as they heard and saw the reaction of the Believers. "We hear them declaring the wonders of God in our own tongues!" (Acts 2:11). They did not understand everything that was going on because they, at first, thought that the Believers were all inebriated; but they did recognize that God was being glorified. There obviously was something of a Divine encounter that was happening with these people. That's the way the Holy Spirit came as God's gift from heaven and that is how He works in the hearts of believers today. Peter said, "The promise [*of the Father*] is for you and your children and for all who are far off—for all whom the Lord our God will call" (Acts 2:39). That's an invitation to receive the same experience that the early Believers received and to become witnesses to our community. Whatever happens in our lives, let God be glorified!

According to the Bible record, it wasn't long before the "spectators" became participants, and following repentance, "about 3000" made their decision to accept the Lord and become a part of the new body of believers that became the Church of Jesus Christ. We need that kind of experience again!

134

*"However, as it is written: 'No eye has seen, no ear has heard, no mind has conceived what God has prepared for those who love him.'"*

~1 Corinthians 2:9

It started out like one of the many side trips that Jesus took with Peter, James and John. Away from the crowds and the regular banter of the rest of the disciples, they climbed up a high mountain. They weren't used to this kind of strenuous excursion, but as they huffed and puffed, they obediently followed Jesus to "who knows where." He was always pointing out bits of interesting information and relating things to His Father's creative and loving hand, so it was not unusual that Jesus would take them aside to give them a private lesson or to show them some new thing.

When they finally reached the summit, unexpectedly, everything about their friend Jesus was changed. They had walked with Him for about three years and had seen Him do some fantastic things, but never the likes of what they saw this day. His flesh was transformed into a radiance brighter than the sun. His clothes became effervescent white. The whole scene was the kind of thing that one would imagine in heaven, and it reached far beyond their expectations. Moses and Elijah joined Him, dressed in heavenly robes of the same brilliance. Peter, James and John had suddenly become a part of a Divine council meeting called to order by the Creator of all things. They listened intently to the conversation concerning Jesus and the "Exodus" that He was going to accomplish at Jerusalem. They didn't understand that part of the conversation, but were overwhelmed with the glory and ecstasy of the moment of heavenly visitation. This was a mountaintop view of God that no one had ever seen since the day Moses saw His glory on Mount Sinai.

It may be difficult for us to comprehend the kind of experience that occurred that day on the summit. Our imagination can't translate the kind of beauty and glory that heaven holds in reserve for those who will arrive there. Paul wrote to the Corinthian Church: "Listen, I tell you a mystery. We will not all sleep but we will all be changed. In a flash, in the twinkling of an eye; at the last trumpet…we will all be changed" (1 Corinthians 15:51-52).

We shall be changed into the same likeness as Jesus had on the mountaintop. It doesn't seem possible! But that's one of the promises that the Lord is holding in reserve for the day we leave this old world behind. That is a part of the plan of God that begins at Calvary and ends with us standing in the Father's presence for the rest of eternity. We'll be changed—transformed! As much as I love the house I've been living in for these many years I know that there still awaits me the promise of my personal change. I trust that you long for the trumpet signal that will lift us out of our world of sorrow and sickness to live in a permanent place of peace and joy in the presence of the King of Kings transformed into the beauty of God's sinless creation. He's coming soon, for you, to make that change!

135

MAY 15 **THE UNCHANGEABLE**

*"I am not ashamed of the gospel, because it is the power of God*
*for the salvation of everyone who believes..."*

~Romans 1:16a

Anyone who has spent the major part of their life in the last century knows by experience what changes have done to our society. We have moved from the horse and buggy lifestyles to Rapid Transit and the rocket generation. Those who have been a part of space exploration are literally flying faster than a speeding bullet. Candlelight has been taken over by the incandescent, fluorescent and halogen bulbs. It is interesting that when we want to get romantic, the candle is still an important item on the dinner table.

The change in moral values is one of the items that has brought a different shade of life to healthy family relationships. Today, things are said publicly that were a shame to speak even in the privacy of the clubhouse. Paul spoke of this matter with concern and hesitancy: "For it is shameful even to mention what the disobedient do in secret" (Ephesians 5:12). Our generation has lost all sense of shame. Please, please, give me back the old-fashioned prudence and grace of embarrassment. Times have changed! I wish we could say that things are getting better, but I don't feel comfortable with some of the things that Society accepts as being "normal."

I want to reaffirm my joy in the fact that there is one unchangeable that has made the difference in my life. Jesus said, "Heaven and earth will pass away, but my words will never pass away" (Matthew 24:35). Feelings, the weather and moral standards may change at any moment, but the security of the unchanging Word of God has blessed me through the years. I have read sermons by Jonathon Edwards (1704–1758), John Wesley (1703–1791), Charles Spurgeon (1834–1892), Billy Graham (1918-) and the Apostle Paul (0010–0064) and I've discovered that the message has been the same through the years.

There is a standard of right and wrong that's not based upon the trends and fashions of society. If anyone cared to look, God has not changed, and what He expects from us is still the standard that will bring us peace and lasting enjoyment because of His approval. Let the world blow in the winds of popularity, pleasure and apathy, but God will not bend to seek their approval. He will continue to remind us that, "There is a way that seems right to a man, but in the end it leads to death" (Proverbs 14:12). The bottom line is still this: We serve a God of love and He seriously cares for each one of us. That is why He has given us a true moral guide in the words of inspired scriptures. Let the debates of human reasoning continue, but the fact is that God will have the final word. He has not changed, and we should understand that although He allows all of us to make our own choices, there is coming a day when we will all appear before his throne to give account of ourselves according to His standard. Maybe, before we get there, we should prepare for that day!

MAY 16 ▌ **YOU CHOOSE**

*"'Come now, let us reason together,' says the LORD.*
*'Though your sins are like scarlet, they shall be as white as snow;*
*though they are red as crimson, they shall be as wool.'"*

~Isaiah 1:18

There is no question in my mind that God is worthy of all honour and reverence. I'm acquainted with His deeds and I've seen the majesty of His works and there is no doubt whatsoever that we ought to approach Him with absolute respect, trust and confidence. But I am always amazed at the respect that He has for each of us. I'm sure it is an outflow of His loving nature that holds Him back from any forceful intrusion into my life. I appreciate the fact that He does care in many unseen ways and that He has a plan that He seeks to develop in my life. I appreciate that He makes situations and conditions to work out for my good even though I am oblivious of how that all happens. But when it comes down to the final decision concerning His continued influence in my life, I understand that He wants me to make the choice.

He does not force us to follow Him, although to do otherwise does have consequences. He often lets us see the options and then allows us to go the direction that we want to.

Needless to say, many of our lives bear the scars of our own stubbornness, and some of the memories of wayward experiences may haunt our nightmares. God has created us as free-will human beings. We can choose what we want to do, where we want to go, what we say and how we say it. We can choose what we think about, what we put on and in our bodies, where we will live and many other important decisions of our lives.

And then there is the most important decision of all: Will we serve God as He asks us and receive the reward of an eternal destiny in His presence or not? You see, going to Hell is a choice we make. That will be the inevitable result of other bad choices we make throughout our lifetime. If that is what you want, God will do everything He possibly can to help change your mind, but the final choice is ours. We shouldn't be surprised, then, when we get to the judgment seat when earthly life is through and find out the result of our life choices.

Please allow me remind you that there are promises that express God's desire to guide us in the direction that will best profit us eternally. His Word says, "You will seek me and find me when you seek me with all your heart" (Jeremiah 29:13), and again, "Come near to God and He will come near to you" (James 4:8a). It appears to me that God and His plan are just one step away. Although God has done so much for us we need to make that first step ourselves. That is our decision. No one else can make it for us and He respects us too much to force us to make that choice. To make that choice is to open up an entirely new set of options that will benefit us with His provision, protection and promises...but the Choice is yours.

137

**THE CHOICE: TO GO OR STAY**

> *"Even so, when you see these things happening,*
> *you know that it is near, right at the door."*

~Mark 13:29

It is our hope, although we don't often think about it; Jesus is coming back again! There remain a couple of unfinished tasks that need His attention and only He can accomplish them.

1. Without question His primary reason for returning would be because of His great love for those who believe and trust in Him. There is nothing in all of creation that is more important to Him than those who have committed their lives to Him.

2. Obviously, He cares for the lost as well and is prepared to demonstrate, audibly and visually that He indeed is the Lord of all creation.

The Bible describes that at His return a trumpet call and the voice of the archangel will precede the Lord's descent in the clouds where we will be caught up to meet Him in the air to be taken into heaven (1 Thessalonians 4:17). It will definitely not be a secret. You see, the world may doubt the reason for our hope and so they postpone their decision to accept Jesus into their lives. But God is prepared to give them a dynamic and dramatic demonstration that will cause multitudes around the world to believe in Jesus Christ and to be willing to die for their faith. Chapter 7 of the book of Revelation describes a great multitude that comes out of the Great Tribulation.

Now, if you had a choice, and you do, wouldn't you prefer to go with Him when He returns rather than lose your life during the terrible times of the great persecutions through the Tribulation period? One of the main reasons that He hasn't come back yet is the fact that there are still people that need to make that important commitment of giving themselves to the Lord. He is patiently delaying His return to extend opportunities to them; but there is coming a day when the waiting time will be over. It may be soon.

He is coming again:

1. to show His love to the believers by taking them back to heaven where He will present us to His Father with great joy.

2. to demonstrate to the unbelievers that our hope for His return was not in vain.

3. to remove the Church from the world and allow a clear demonstration of the wickedness of the devil and the sinfulness of man. (Then God's justice will be known to be true and righteous.)

There is a place of beauty and harmony that awaits those who have put their trust in Jesus Christ. We call it Heaven. Jesus called it, "My Father's house." The God who created the magnificence of this great Universe has reserved the best for the last and we shall be there to enjoy it with Him.

**He Knows Those Who Are His**

*" 'Can anyone hide in secret places so that I cannot see him?' declares the LORD. 'Do not I fill heaven and earth?' declares the LORD.*

~Jeremiah 23:24

Most everybody likes to be recognized by those around them, except, for sure, those who are doing something they shouldn't be doing. It's always good to be in the company of friends who share the same interests and to feel the warmth of belonging. There is nothing in the world as special as those times.

The strange thing, though, is the fact that even the best of friends can put on a "mask" to hide their true feelings. Some even attend the same Church we do and sing the same songs we do and pray with the same kind of fervour that we do but it's not from the heart. It's put on. I've been fooled many times through the years. But then again, I'm not supposed to be the judge of those matters. That's God's business. We need to continue to show them the same kind of love whether they're "real" or not. The truth is that God knows all the details because He reads the hearts of men and understands all the motives that are a secret to us. Paul wrote to Timothy and said, "...the Lord knows those who belong to Him..." (2 Timothy 2:19).

Do you remember the story of the man who came to the wedding celebration and the King recognized that He was not properly prepared to be a part of the festivities? He was summarily thrown out (Matthew 22:12-13). My question would be, "Why didn't anyone else notice that 'the stranger' was different from all the other guests?" I don't need an answer to the question but it does teach me that I need to know for sure that I'm ready, because when I stand before the King on that last day, He will see through my mask to the depth of my heart. There can be no hidden thing that will rob me of the joy of being a part of whatever He has reserved for those who trust in Him. I become ultimately responsible for what I've guarded in my heart.

Now, it was not my intention to cast doubt upon whether or not we are going to be a part of the future rewards that the Lord has prepared but I certainly do want everyone to know that the Holy Spirit will help us, right now, to be ready to be welcomed as part of the family of God. You see, it's His job to speak into our hearts and let us know if there are things that grieve and disappoint the Lord. He is the One who brings it to our attention when things need to be fixed up. He doesn't do that because He takes pleasure in laying a guilt trip on us, but rather, He lets us know that our Lord, who is a loving God, is willing to pardon and heal/restore us so there won't be any wondering as to whether we've passed the test or not.

Take a moment, every once in a while, and present yourself to the Lord for His review. If there is something that the Lord brings to your attention that needs to be dealt with, don't put it off. Fix it up. Most often a simple prayer for forgiveness will resolve the matter completely.

**TRUSTING IN THE SHADOWS**

*"He will keep you strong to the end, so that you will be blameless
on the day of our Lord Jesus Christ. God, who has called you into
fellowship with his Son Jesus Christ our Lord, is faithful."*

~1 Corinthians 1:8-9

You don't have to be a rocket scientist to know that the sun is always shining even though we don't see it because of the clouds and the darkness of the night. We know that the sun is continually doing what it's supposed to do. Sometimes it is clearly seen on the other side of the world while we are covered with darkness. We understand that is the way things are. It is not a question of privilege or right, but rather a constant process for everyone that best helps us to develop and grow in a healthy fashion.

It's funny, though, that in life we think we should always live in the sunshine of joy and happiness and have things the way we want all the time. It isn't always that way. The truth is that God has created us to enjoy Himself all the time, even in the dark times, because He never changes and He's always there. However, when the sun isn't shining on us, the dark and trying hours that we sometimes encounter do serve us for very important and practical purposes. But that doesn't change the fact that God is always there.

"For the Lord is good and his love endures forever; his faithfulness continues through all generations" (Psalm 100:5).

"Indeed, He who watches over Israel will neither slumber nor sleep." (Psalm 121:4)

Heroes of the faith, through the centuries, have believed that the victory is not in our feelings or emotions but in our trust in God. He is the Rewarder of those who confidently rely on Him at all times.

"…weeping may remain for a night but rejoicing comes in the morning."
Psalm 30:5b

We will face the dark hours of struggle and disappointment but God will not leave us alone. He has promised to be with us always. The Psalmist says: "He brought them out of darkness and the deepest gloom and broke away their chains" (Psalm 107:14). We have to lean upon the promise of His Word and believe that our loving heavenly Father is aware of every detail of our lives. He turned His back on Jesus when He bore our sins on the cross, but He will never turn His back on us, ever, because of the forgiveness we receive in Jesus Christ. There is coming a day when the storm clouds will no longer hide the face of the One we have learned to love and trust. It will be a great day of rejoicing as we are caught up to be with Him into His very presence where we will enjoy the light of an eternal day. We are never alone. He is a faithful friend.

140

▊ **GOD ANSWERS PRAYER**

*"I cried out to God for help; I cried out to God to hear me.*
*When I was in distress, I sought the Lord."*

~Psalm 77:1-2

"The prayer offered in faith will make the sick person well; the Lord will raise him up" (James 5:15a). We should expect that God will answer prayer. He has invited us to seek Him through prayer and to cast our cares upon Him. It should only be natural, in a supernatural way, that God would respond to those who obey Him and trust Him for solutions to their discomforts and difficulties. Add to that the fact that He is the Creator of our bodies and knows how every molecule and atom fit together to function with every other part of the body, and it should be obvious that He is able to return order to a system that is not doing what it was created to do.

There is no question that the enemy of both God and our souls would try to disparage the name of the Lord and His healing power. We have all, at some time, entertained some doubts concerning God's lack of involvement in the healing processes that would ease our distress.

Let me confess—I would be the first to admit that I do not understand everything about healing and why God allows affliction to come upon His sons and daughters. The fact remains that He has promised to never leave us nor forsake us and that there are Divine purposes in what God does and what He allows to happen in each of our lives.

Don't despair! God loves us with an everlasting love and will be our guardian in every experience of life; even THROUGH the valley of the shadow of death (Psalm 23:4). Let's examine our hearts and allow the Holy Spirit to do something brand new in us when we don't understand what He is doing. If we discover that there's nothing wrong let's allow our faith to be stretched as we seek God's face and learn to trust Him and His wonderful purposes. We believe He heals because the Bible teaches that "He is the Lord" who heals us (Exodus 15:26). Most of us have seen or known someone who has been touched by the Lord and the miraculous has occurred. He is a God of the impossible and there is no thing that is impossible to Him. Believe Him for your own personal miracle.

The Lord wants everyone to know that He is God of the universe and that all of creation is still under His dominion. His Word bears witness that He wants to reveal Himself to us in the natural world and in the miraculous. Let's believe that when we pray God hears in heaven and is moved by the things that move our hearts. Whatever happens, bless God! He is Faithful to His promise.

"O Sovereign LORD, you are God! Your words are trustworthy, and you have promised these good things to your servant" (2 Samuel 7:28).

▌ **TRUST GOD**

> *"Trust in the Lord with all your heart*
> *and lean not on your own understanding."*
>
> ~Proverbs 3:5

I guess you've discovered that sometimes it seems a lot easier to lean on our own understanding than it is to trust in the Lord. At least that's what most of us do. Is it that we are not prepared to wait for Him to work out His purposes or is it simply that we would rather exercise our independence and stick to our own ideas? I've asked myself this question many times in my ministry, "Why on earth do we find it so hard to trust God?" It's probably true that we don't have so much trouble trusting God for the BIG STUFF, but we wrestle with God over the little stuff. We believe that He pardons our sins when we confess them to Him and that our names are written in the Book of Life. We can trust Him for healing in impossible situations, but we find it difficult to trust Him in areas where we can influence the outcome by our own choices.

Let me give you a couple of examples:

1. How many young lives have been led through some very painful situations because they were in a hurry to marry somebody who wasn't the right person for their lives? Though parents and Pastors advise "Do not be yoked together with unbelievers," there's always somebody with a 'better idea.' Listen! We need to trust God for His choice because it's His best. We've all seen that mistake made and though we try to counsel to wait, the "love bug" bites and none can stop the infection. Only as we truly trust God and His word are we able to make the right kind of decisions. It's those kinds of situations where we need to learn that you can never win if you go against God. Trust Him!

2. When the Word clearly describes the desire of God to, "Bring the whole tithe into the storehouse... test me in this..." (Malachi 3:10), we should understand that God is inviting us into an opportunity to TRUST HIM and not lean on our own understanding. How many other ideas are out there? I can't afford to tithe; I will pay my tithes as soon as I pay the mortgage; I need a new TV and God understands. There are so many excuses that I couldn't count them all. But it boils down to a simple principle; if we don't obey His Word and tithe, it's because we don't trust God, plain and simple. He sets the challenge for us to prove His faithfulness, and yet so many are not prepared to obey Him. God offers the test so that we may experience His abundant blessings because we choose to obey and trust Him rather than make up other excuses. Trusting Him will always bring more blessing.

You may have other kinds of tests that are pressing on you. The choice will still be yours. You can commit your way and trust in God or otherwise.

We serve an Awesome God and One who is worthy of our utmost confidence. Trust Him! He will not fail you.

▌ **TO PLEASE GOD**

> *"Great is the LORD and most worthy of praise;*
> *his greatness no one can fathom."*
>
> ~Psalm 145:3

We love to worship the Lord and we enjoy coming into His presence to express our gratitude for the many good things that He shares with us so liberally. There is no question that we are blessed as we worship the Lord. We honour Him with our praises and express our adoration because He is worthy of our thanksgiving and our worship. We have often felt that there is nothing that is so sacred to God as the worship that we bring to Him. We are challenged to shut out all the voices of the activities of the week in order to get close to God, unburdened and free, to enter His presence.

I would like to challenge you today with another aspect of our coming to God. I am with you on the fact that God is worthy of our praise and that He still "inhabits the praises of Israel" (Psalm 22:3 KJV). However, there is one thing that blesses God more than the words, dances and enthusiastic expressions of our times of worship. I'm sure you're going to say, "Tell me what that is and I'll do it!" I've discovered that when God gets blessed, we do, too. Do you know what I mean? I think we ought to re-evaluate what motivates us to come into His presence and for what purpose.

Most of us are happy to get from God whatever we can. We are absolutely confident that God approves of our method of approach to Him as long as we offer "the sacrifice of praise," but I'm not so sure that is always true. Listen to what He told a great king through the voice of a prophet: "...to <u>obey</u> is better than sacrifice" (1 Samuel 15:22). Now, that may not be comforting one little bit, but I wonder how many times we are blessed because we do praise Him—and God is faithful to reward us for that—but it becomes a substitute for what we ought to do. What God wants, more than anything else, is obedience to His Word and obedience to His Will. That's what brings great joy to His heart. We could never calculate the variety of rewards that God will give to that kind of committed effort that is seen as more than lip service. He said to His disciples, just before He was crucified, "If you love me you will *obey* what I command" (John 14:15, emphasis added). Our true love for God is measured in our obedience to Him. True worship can be a result of the benefits we receive when we do what He wants us to do. The two can move, hand in glove, as we serve Him each day in worship and obedience. We'll have many opportunities, in these days, to prove that His promises are true.

We are blessed! Let's be obedient to serve Him so that the end result will be a focus on His joy. That's when we become very blessed.

▌ **HE BRINGS JOY**

> *"For you make me glad by your deeds, O LORD;*
> *I sing for joy at the work of your hands."*
>
> ~Psalm 92:4

Jesus performed His very first miracle at a wedding celebration in Cana of Galilee. He was an invited guest amongst many others. It could have been a family connection, because Mary was there as well. What part Jesus played in the ceremony is unknown, but His concern for the joy of the married couple becomes obvious. He was prepared to get involved in order to avoid a cloud of embarrassment that could have spoiled the festivities. I think it very interesting that He would create "stuff" that would contribute to making people happy. I know that His primary purpose for coming was to make us holy through His precious blood that would, later, be shed at Calvary, but I shouldn't be surprised that He would want to bring us happiness as well.

Peter was one of those close observers of Jesus' day-by-day activities. He reported to those gathered in Cornelius' house how "God anointed Jesus of Nazareth with the Holy Spirit and power, and he went around *doing good* and healing all who were under the power of the devil because God was with Him" (Acts 10:38, emphasis added). The end result of all that Jesus did was to relieve pain, guilt, and discouragement and bring us into a loving relationship with His Father. When Jesus prayed to His Father just before the experience of the cross, He made it clear that one of His concerns was that those who trusted in Him would know His joy. "I am coming to you now, but I say these things while I am still in the world, so that they may have *the full measure of my joy within them*" (John 17:13, emphasis added). On another occasion He said, "Until now you have not asked for anything in my name. Ask and you will receive, and *your joy will be complete*" (John 16:24, emphasis added).

I think there's something there that we should remember. Jesus is not a joy spoiler—He's the joy giver. Why is it, then, that there are so many unhappy Christians today? Well, as you know, I don't have all the answers, but let me suggest something that I believe is important. The closer we get to Jesus and knowing Him, the more peace and joy we have. There is no better place to find the joy that is permanent than being where He is. We can do that by being in the house of worship at each opportunity; or by being with those who love the Lord. His promise is still true, "Where two or three come together in my name there am I with them" (Matthew 18:20). The Psalmist said, "...you will fill me with joy in your presence, with eternal pleasures at your right hand" (Psalm 16:11b). Joy is one of the fruit of the Spirit, and like all the other fruit it continues in us if we keep up our personal maintenance program. That is, we need to come to Him for a regular refreshing and recharging in order to be what He wants us to be.

**HE STILL LOVES SINNERS**

*"Then the master told his servant, 'Go out to the roads and country lanes and make them come in, so that my house will be full.'"*

~Luke 14:23

When Jonah had finally cleaned himself off and gotten his bearings straight, he headed towards the second-to-last place on earth he wanted to visit. He had just returned from the worst place and had learned a very hard lesson that has since been passed on through generations. God wants "to seek and to save" those who are lost. Although He doesn't like the things that sinners do, He still loves the sinners. Like a lot of folks today, the people of Nineveh may not have been aware that God was concerned about them in spite of the wickedness within the city walls. He knew exactly how many little children lived in their city and cared for them. He was not prepared to give up on them without an effort to show them His love. Someone needed to let them know that their sins were destroying them. In order to know God's love they needed to repent and ask for forgiveness.

Into that picture moved Jonah. From thousands of kilometres away God directed Jonah to go to the most wicked city in the world, to a people who spoke a "foreign" language and to a people of strange, rude customs. His message was simple—repent or judgment would fall upon Nineveh. Jonah didn't want to go. As a matter of fact it would have made him happy to read in the morning newspaper that Nineveh had been destroyed. But God cared! When no one else would give two hoots, God cared. They were a people hopelessly lost but God wanted to change that. He had higher plans for them as He does for all of lost humanity. As far as God is concerned "He is not willing that any should perish" (2 Peter 3:9b KJV).

It doesn't matter where they live, God cares! That's what Missions is all about. We are modern day Jonahs who are able to know that modern day call to reach the lost. It's important that we hear what God wants us to do and that we obey. There are a lot of modern Jonahs surviving in our world today. They won't release their finances to do God's work in distant parts of the globe. There are others who have never spent much time in prayerful concern for the lost where the message of God's love has not been told. And then, there are others who have felt the Spirit's tug on their hearts to get involved in reaching out to the lost, some right here at home and others in distant lands. Perhaps some of us need a "Whale of an experience" to get us going in the right direction. God wants us to be involved in doing His will. There is nothing that is more important to Him than reaching those who may be living in the darkness of indifference to His love. Whether He asks for our life's service or prayers or finances, He wants to reach the lost. He cares!

Do you think that the Lord can bear the thought that His redeemed will refuse to tell the story of His love? Watch out! There are "great fish" all around.

**▌ STILL THERE THROUGH THE SHADOWS**

*"So keep up your courage, men, for I have faith in God
that it will happen just as He told me."*

~Acts 27:25

Most of us struggle from time to time with the matter of walking by faith. We may know the theology of how to describe what faith is and know many stories of people of faith who have come through deep trials with great success, but there are times when that is of little consolation to those who are going through deep trials.

The problem is that we live in a sensory world and natural things sometimes become obstacles to believing God in the invisible world. I acknowledge that there are times when I need to wrap my head around Bible principles and get a hold on God's Word in order to find comfort or assurance for some of the tough situations that we all face. Trusting God isn't always a happy time, although I believe that we can experience a deep settled peace and a calm assurance that things will work out just fine in the end.

I'm pretty sure that the walk up Moriah's slopes was more than just a difficult climb for Abraham. He knew that he was about to surrender his greatest asset, his greatest desire, upon an altar of sacrifice. The recorded conversation with his son Isaac is very brief   Nothing is conveyed in words concerning the emotions that must have been racing through his head and heart. Nevertheless he held this confidence: "God Himself will provide the lamb" (Genesis 22:8). Next to walking into a fiery furnace this has got to rate as one of the greatest tests of faith recorded in scripture.

But look at the results!

1. Abraham learned that obedience to God would bring blessing in spite of heartache and duress.

2. He learned that God would be the supplier of his need, just in time.

3. He learned that a God-given substitute will satisfy God's requirements.

4. He learned that the tests of faith deal more with the willingness to obey from the heart than the actual accomplishment of any deed.

5. He learned that God would still give him the desire of his heart.

6. He learned what it meant to have God as his friend (better than any other).

Somehow we need to learn to trust God *absolutely*. Every situation that comes our way still requires some decisions and choices on our part. However, we need to look for God's purposes and seek to do His will. He will never ask us to do anything that would be immoral or contrary to His Word. He will ask us to possess our souls in peace and to believe that when the final chapter of the story is written, whatever the experience might be, that there is great blessing in serving such an Awesome God. Doubt, fear and impatience become our enemies when we come to prove the promises of God. Stand fast, therefore and believe God. He cannot fail!

**BE THE CHURCH**

*"Then the Church throughout Judea, Galilee and Samaria enjoyed a time*
*of peace. It was strengthened; and encouraged by the Holy Spirit,*
*it grew in numbers, living in the fear of the Lord."*

~Acts 9:31

Bill Gaither penned the words to the song that states, "Let the Church, be the Church. Let the People rejoice." It speaks of the achievement of the fact that we have been placed on the Victory side of the great triumphs of God's grace. We're talking about the Church of Jesus Christ today. It's not the building; it's the people that love the Lord. That's the group, trans-denominational, that extends beyond the borders of countries and across the seas. They are the ones who know their Redeemer and Lord; those who trust in the name of Jesus and serve Him faithfully. Every congregation that honours Jesus Christ as Lord is a part of the Universal Church. Each group of believers may have a different way of expressing their devotion in both their Worship and Proclamation of the story of God's love. That's great! I believe that it is very pleasing to God when we can recognize our differences and that they really don't make a difference in our fellowship as a part of the Body of Christ.

To each of us the Lord has committed a trust in the form of talents and abilities. They come in such a variety of expressions that one fellowship/denomination would not be able to contain them all. These giftings were not given to us to make us feel proud or better than others, but rather, are for the purpose of honouring Him in our own unique way. Through the centuries God has raised up groups of people with a renewed emphasis on some particular truth to call us all back to the basics of the faith that we may have overlooked. Yet it is true that the success or failure of the Church on the local level depends upon the faithfulness of each one in that congregation doing his or her part.

Here's a call to everyone: do what God wants you to do because you are a very important part of His Church. He has promised that His Church will be beautiful and triumphant when He returns. He has promised to add His blessings as we serve Him faithfully. The devil trembles when the Church stands upon the promises of God. Therefore, "Let the Church, be the Church." As we go through the routine of our weekly schedules, let us be sensitive to what God says to us and obedient to follow His promptings. Let us choose to take a part and get involved where we can. Be bold, be strong! These are great days to be involved in what God is doing in the world through His Church. I'm confident that the Lord will pour out His Holy Spirit upon the people that honour Him by responding to His will. We are His Church.

▌ **CLEANING HOUSE**

*"Create in me a pure heart, O God, and renew a steadfast spirit within me."*

~Psalm 51:10

It's the clutter of stuff that makes a home look unkempt. When things are not put in their proper place it doesn't take long before the mess is noticeable. It's important to remember that it's not the amount of possessions that one has but whether or not there is a place where they belong and whether or not they are useful. Garbage, of course, belongs in the garbage can, and good stuff should have a space where it can be stored for future use.

Minds are like that. Peter wrote, "The end of all things is near. Therefore be clear minded and self-controlled so that you can pray" (1 Peter 4:7). With all the things that are going on in our world these days it's easy to get a cluttered mind with endless amounts of needless stuff. There's garbage on TV. There's garbage on videos and CD's. There's garbage in magazines and the gossip papers by the check-out counter. There's garbage pressing to reform our laws to be more tolerant of things that God calls sin. The piles of stuff that are not of God that clamour for our attention, are becoming a stench in the land.

Integrity and morality in public service are at an all-time low. Our youth are caught in a web of pressures to conform to things that we have been opposed to, and they are spiritually suffocating, ignorant that there is a place of purity and wholeness in Jesus Christ.

The evidence that we are living close to the end of all things is becoming more obvious as the signs of the times are being fulfilled around us every day. Jesus is coming again. It's time that we got our minds in focus and cleared out the junk to be able to be released to hear what God is saying to His Church body. We need to free ourselves of the things that would distract us from hearing the voice of the Spirit of God. The importance of that becomes more obvious as we recognize the seriousness of these days.

If you'll check back to the passage we just read, it will remind you that we need a *clear mind* in order to be people of prayer. It is easy for us to go with the flow of society and allow the clutter of the world to press us into their mold. If we want to be people who are led by the Spirit of God, we should appreciate the importance of possessing a clean heart and mind. Perhaps it is because we are so preoccupied during our waking hours with the junk around us that God's message in the last days to humanity will come through dreams and visions. We are called to serve God with self-control and orderliness of mind and heart in such a fashion that the worldly "stuff" won't possess us. We need to be leaders in spiritual discernment, and a cluttered carnal life will not be the kind of vessel God can use. We need to make some clear choices to honour the Lord in all our ways rather than desiring the ways of the world.

Jesus is coming back again. Have you heard from Him lately?

**OUR MISSION FIELD**

*"Ask of me, and I will make the nations your inheritance,
the ends of the earth your possession."*

~Psalm 2:8

The work of Missions and Evangelism needs to be revived in our hearts. Reaching the lost was the passion of the heart of Jesus and the early Church, and it has always been the passion of God from even the beginning of time. He was the One who came to seek out Adam when he had sinned. God took the initiative and came to speak to Cain to warn him of the path of sin he was taking. The Bible teaches that God even loved those who were not thinking about Him. He sent Jonah to Nineveh and used Lot in Sodom and Gomorrah because he cared for those who were lost and wanted them to turn from their evil ways.

Let me tell you a very important and up-to-date fact: He cares for your neighbours and the people you work with. He cares for the "down and out" as much as the "up and out." His desire is to see all mankind come to the experience of His salvation. The method He uses? You and me! We are the bait on the hook that will capture people for Jesus. We are called to be witnesses to the lost. Like it or not, God is counting on us to live our lives speaking when opportunity presents itself and being examples of godliness in our world. Where do we start? Let me give you a few suggestions:

*We need to begin at home.* How we live behind the closed front door and curtained windows is what we really are. What we really are is what the world will perceive when we get out where the action is, so let's start there.

1. Let's be people of prayer—the private kind. We need to learn the value of a personal encounter each day with Jesus in a quiet time. He is our very best Friend. Telling Him that we love Him and want to serve Him brings our lives into proper focus. Things may not go the way we expect them to all the time, but He is there as a Comfort and Strength for all our experiences.

2. Let's teach our families that uniting together in prayer is the glue that will hold us through the crises of life. Tell each other how God has answered prayer and encourage one another to believe for God's blessings when we pray together.

3. Organize a family time to read and discuss passages of the Bible or one of the many Bible stories that have been a blessing through the ages.

4. Watch your conversation so that it is positive, uplifting, encouraging, free of criticism, loving and patient. We are responsible for the attitude of our hearts. No one else can govern what we are on the inside, not even our enemies.

With the help of the Lord we are in control of the way we behave. Our family and friends will recognize that.

MAY 29 ▌ **THE PROMISE**

*"All of them were filled with the Holy Spirit and began to speak
in other tongues as the Spirit enabled them."*

~Acts 2:4

The first time that Moses went up the mountain to meet with God, the Lord spoke to him softly as a friend to a friend. He promised Moses that if the people of Israel would be obedient that they would be God's "...treasured possession...a kingdom of priests and a holy nation" (Exodus 19:5-6). Moses came down and told the elders about his conversation with God and then people responded, "We will do everything that God has said." When Moses returned to the mountaintop God told him that He would again meet with him, but this time it would be in a way that *people would never forget*. They would hear God speaking with Moses and put their trust in him.

On the morning of the third day there was thunder and lightning and it looked like the mountain had turned into a volcano. Smoke billowed out as from a blast furnace, the mountain trembled violently, and the sound of a trumpet grew louder and louder (Exodus 19). That was the day that the Ten Commandments were given to the people. It happened fifty days after the Passover experience in Egypt, when the children of Israel left captivity. This was the first Day of Pentecost, sometimes called the Feast of Weeks. God spoke in an audible voice accompanied by some tremendous demonstrations never seen before.

On another day of Pentecost, two thousand years later, the silence of the place where the disciples were gathered was shattered by the sound of a blowing violent wind; tongues of fire sat upon the heads of each of the 120, and they began to speak in other tongues as the Spirit enabled them. God was speaking again through a group of believers. One of the interesting aspects was that the experience of speaking in tongues was repeated as a continuing blessing upon the Early Church. It is God's gift, described as the Promise of the Father, given as fulfillment of the prophecy of Joel. The Apostle Paul encouraged the believers to "be filled with the Spirit" (Ephesians 5:18). He taught the early believers that a part of his prayer life was speaking in tongues. He said, "I thank God that I speak in tongues more than all of you" (1 Corinthians 14:18). It appears that the people who committed themselves to Jesus were encouraged to seek this added dimension in their lives in receiving the Gift of the Holy Spirit.

God is once again meeting with His people. He does it in a way that makes us recognize that it is a Divine visitation as He did in the days of Moses.

I believe that He wants every one who acknowledges Jesus Christ as Lord and Saviour to share the same experience. As you pray, invite the Holy Spirit to fill you with His presence in this spiritual refreshing.

*"But you will receive power when the Holy Spirit comes on you;
and you will be my witnesses in Jerusalem, and in all Judea and Samaria,
and to the ends of the earth."*

~Acts 1:8

The whole place was filled with the roar of a rushing wind. Flames of fire, like candlelight, settled over the heads of each of the believers and they all spoke an unlearned language of praise to God. This was Pentecost. Nothing like this had ever happened in any religious revival in the history of Israel. The Holy Spirit came upon the followers of Jesus who had waited with prayer and expectation for the arrival of this heavenly gift. The Holy Spirit was not just an influence at work in the universe. He was now present in each life and had begun to demonstrate that He was there, not just as a Visitor, but as an indwelling Partner to work the works of God through the faithful. No one could have adequately described these happenings to Jesus' followers before they actually came to pass. The joy and ecstasy of the experience was a visible witness to the unbelievers that God was confirming His presence in the lives of "the Church." There were many others in the city of Jerusalem that day who were spectators of this move of God. They heard and saw visible manifestations of a Dynamic influence that they could not understand working through this small group of people. When Peter stood up to explain what was going on, this great congregation of onlookers were touched by the power of the Holy Spirit.

Two things were involved. It was the combination of:

1. the move of the Spirit **in** the believers and

2. the witness of the preaching of God's word **on** the hearts of the spectators. Three thousand were added to the Church that day. The key was that the Holy Spirit had come upon Jesus' followers and they now lived their lives in that Pentecostal experience.

Revivals of this kind have come like waves across Christendom throughout the history of the Church. There have been many dark years in that history as well, but when God's people became concerned about the spiritual coldness of their generation and began to seek the Lord, God answered their hungering prayers and satisfied their hearts.

This last century has witnessed many special visitations of the presence of God. Various congregations and groups of believers have been wonderfully blessed by what God has been doing in their lives. At a time when there are such large numbers of Christians in a world of six billion people, we should be expecting that God would, once again, do dramatic and dynamic things today.

Pentecost Sunday is a date that follows 50 days after Easter. Both dates remind us that we have been saved because of the work of the cross and that we may be empowered by the Spirit for service until Jesus comes back again.

| **AT THE END**

*"In the last days, God says, I will pour out my Spirit on all people.
Your sons and daughters will prophesy, your young men well see visions,
your old men will dream dreams."*

~Acts 2:17

There are two events that are clearly on God's agenda for these times. Both are related to the promises that He has made for those who will trust Him and both express the love that He has for His Church.

1. *He has promised an outpouring of the Holy Spirit upon the whole world.* The promise goes way back to the Old Testament with references to the latter rain, which was recognized in Israel as being essential to prepare the fields just before the harvest. That term is interpreted as referring to the rain of the Holy Spirit upon all flesh just prior to the end. We have experienced this already in refreshing showers, but we long for the deluge that will bless the discouraged and challenge the hearts of he Church to repentance and commitment to His service. The harvest of souls awaits the outpouring that will prepare the lost to receive the gospel message. At the same time, the outpouring will bring an endowment that will equip the Church to do the job that must me done. There is no question in anyone's mind today that our world needs a Mighty visitation of the power of God. We can't be sitting on our hands to await this experience. There is a price to pay. That price is to get serious about wanting the Lord to do something special in our world. We need to seek Him with all our hearts and be prepared to surrender our wills and plans to His purpose.

2. *He has promised that He is coming back again.* He has not forgotten the Apple of His eye. The plan of Eternity has always been that we be in His presence, without the limitations of the body. We will be changed. In a moment, in the twinkling of an eye, we will be caught up to meet the Lord in the air and we shall be like Him for we shall see Him as He is. We are the Bride of Christ, but if we think that our love for Him is stronger than His love for us, then we don't fully understand the heart of God. The point is, that He has the power to change all things and to call us into His presence whenever He wills.

The responsibility on my part is to be serious about my relationship with Him; to demonstrate, by my devotion and lifestyle, that I am looking forward to His return. That involves my obedience to one of His last commands: "Go and make disciples of all nations" (Matthew 28:19a).

The last days of the Church on earth should be days of triumph and victory as we do our part to bring the lost to know the Lord as Saviour. Amid tragedies and catastrophes, the signs of the times sound an alarm to the world that we all need to look for supernatural intervention in the matters of our world. At the same time, the book of Revelation describes the triumph that awaits us as we are caught up to be with the Lord forever. What a wonderful day that will be! It may be today.

# BEING AN EXAMPLE

*"To this you were called, because Christ suffered for you,*
*leaving you an example, that you should follow in his steps."*

~1 Peter 2:21

You will never read that Jesus used a proper classroom setting as His teaching style, but it is obvious that most of his disciples, except one, learned their lessons well. They didn't have chalk-boards or overheads but they were still grounded in the life-changing principles that are the foundation of the Church. The learning process was through the example of Christ's lifestyle and the chats and conversations that were a constant part of the group's banter as they moved from community to community. They became the ones who related the stories recorded in the Gospels and the teachings of some of the Epistles.

When the scriptures speak about the simplicity of the gospel we are reminded that "a little child will lead them" (Isaiah 11:6b). We have strange ways of complicating the whole gospel story that was intended to communicate the tender love of a very kind and generous Heavenly Father who gave His Son to be our Saviour. We break it down into the basic doctrines and then we pick at every word to explore the grammatical roots of the words that are spoken. We take apart the parables in our attempts to discover what all the symbolic phrases could mean and on and on it goes. I want to assure you that I think it's important to understand clearly what Jesus intended to say in each of His messages so that we can convey truth to those who will listen to us. However, I think the pendulum of life should swing to the side of demonstrating the message through practical life experiences.

Jesus taught His most powerful lessons by how He lived, and His disciples were witnesses of that. His gospel was one of demonstration of the heart of the Father applied to a world of tremendous hurts and needs. Words became simple pictures to bring a piece of heaven to the hearts and souls of mankind. St. Francis of Asissi put it right when he told his students, "Go into all the world and preach the gospel to every creature. If you have to, use words." That's quite different from our expectations today. It seems that we are more satisfied with hearing a sermon than seeing one lived out before us. I think that people in the world are tired of rhetoric and are looking for the reality of what Jesus would do if He lived in our time. Believers ought to be "acting out" the message of God's love every day. It really takes a different lifestyle to give impact to what the Spirit of God has done in our lives. That's what the world is looking for more than our lectures on morality and our pious sermons that criticize the deficiencies of our world. Jesus came to demonstrate the love of the Father. His actions spoke clearly of compassion, forgiveness and mercy.

"Let your light shine..." (Matthew 5:16).

153

▮ **A PASSION FOR SOULS**

*"Pray continually."*

~1 Thessalonians 5:17

I've borrowed a quotation from Charles Spurgeon:

> "We cannot go on as some churches do without converts. We cannot, we will not, we must not, we dare not. Souls must be converted here, and if there be not many born to Christ, may the Lord grant to me that I may sleep in the tomb and be heard no more. Better indeed for us to die than to live, if souls be not saved. If sinners will be damned, at least let them leap to hell over our bodies. And if they will perish, let them perish with our arms about their knees, imploring them to stay. If hell must be filled, at least let it be filled in the teeth of our exertions, and let not one go there...unwarned and unprayed for."

This reminds me of the prayer of the Apostle Paul, who cried, "For I could wish that I myself were cursed and cut off from Christ for the sake of my brothers, those of my own race..." (Romans 9:3).

Moses expressed that same concern: "But now, please forgive their sin—but if not, then blot me out of the book you have written" (Exodus 32:32).

There's passion in those words. Their hearts reach out to a generation of the lost who have not been warned that judgment awaits the transgressor, and that the Grace of God pardons the one who sins but seeks His forgiveness. There is hope. There is a way that people can be freed from guilt and condemnation. Christ is the answer. He is willing to forgive anyone who will call on His name, but it takes people to tell the story and stand in the gap on the behalf of those who have not yet heard the message.

May our hearts hurt for the true needs of those who live around us and across the seas. May there be a swelling of soul to encompass the broken and the bruised of our society with the compassion of the Grace of God. May our spiritual eyes be opened to the opportunities of these days to reach out to those that Jesus loved enough to lay down His life.

We've a story to tell and we need to step out and do exactly that. Time is short and the task is great. Only as each of us does our part will the souls of men be won. The greatest battle we may be facing in the matter of soulwinning is our apathy to the needs of men and to the call of God.

▌ **A LIFE IN THE MASTER'S HAND**

*"Jesus, knowing their thoughts, took a little child and had him stand beside Him. Then he said to them, 'Whoever welcomes this little child in my name welcomes me; and whoever welcomes me welcomes the one who sent me.'"*

~Luke 9:47-48a

If you would have seen the block of granite, you could never have dreamed that Michelangelo would have been able to visualize the figure of King David inside that chunk of stone. But he did; and after months of chipping and slicing, the statue remains to our generation as an artistic feat of ingenuity.

If you would see the diamond as it's washed from the clay banks of an African hillside, you would never believe that such an ugly rock could be used to adorn the finger of a beautiful bride and reflect a million light beams for generations afterwards.

If you would have seen the lump of clay as it was slammed onto the artisan's table as a dirty, slimy, mass of useless dirt, you could not have imagined what the Master Craftsman would do to shape and colour his work into a beautiful Ming vase that would be treated as a valuable treasure for centuries after.

When you see a little baby, born amidst the wailing of mother and child (and sometimes Daddy, too), you cannot envision all the potential and possibilities that lie within that little life. We only know that in the beginning stages there's a lot of crying, complaining and thoughtless actions at all times of the day and night. It may be hard to believe that each child has the potential to become a great scientist, Prime Minister, Military leader, Missionary/Pastor or teacher or whatever.

Jesus knew this and He loved the little children. Time and again, He reached out to a little child and drew that little life into His sermons and teachings. He understood the value of each one of them, the contribution that each would make to our world and the eternal worth of their souls. Pottery, gems, jewels and statutes fade into insignificance beside the lives of little people who will make a difference in our world. No wonder that we emphasize the importance of children's ministries in our Churches. We are not just caring for the present but we are laying up treasure in the hearts of the children who will become the leaders of the future.

Will you be a part of an outreach to your community in volunteer service for the children in the various departments of your Church? Everything we have learned about God was given to us to pass along to someone else. You've probably discovered that there aren't a lot of big people that care to talk about God, but the little ones are open to learning about Him.

You may have heard that 85% of all people who claim to be Christians, accepted the Lord before they were eighteen. That sets a priority emphasis upon the direction for the outreach of a Church. Plan to be a part.

**❚ GOD CALLS, WE SEND**

*"So we all agreed to choose some men and send them to you
with our dear friends Barnabas and Paul."*

~Acts 15:25

Giving to Missions is a work of faith. It is an investment in the Kingdom of God in areas beyond our control. We are always happy when the call of God rests upon someone to go into the ministry and do the things that we know are important to the heart of God. We don't always understand the principle of cooperation that is involved in the call of God. Paul wrote to the Romans, "How can they hear without someone preaching to them? And how can they preach unless they are sent?" (Romans 10:14-15). For us today, the key word is "SENT."

There needs to be the sending by the Holy Spirit, who works in the hearts of His servants impressing the 'called' with a sense of urgency to do God's will and then prepares them for ministry. Like a written letter placed in an envelope, God's message is wrapped up in the life of a messenger we call "a Missionary." At this point, two people are involved in God's plan—the Holy Spirit and the potential Missionary.

It is then that the Holy Spirit begins to lay a concern for the fulfillment of His plan upon the hearts of others who will care for the sending, to make sure that the letter is sent and received at the proper destination. Generally, that call is placed upon people who are willing to share themselves by way of their praying and their giving. These are senders who are working in cooperation with the Holy Spirit. We are given an opportunity to be partners with God in seeing His project come to completion. He counts on you and me to do our parts in making sure the message gets to the area of need. Of course, there is a cost involved, because "How can they preach unless they are sent?"

Imagine a letter with wonderful news inside, of a wealthy inheritance being held at the Post Office for lack of postage. Could you imagine God's message being held up because of a lack of finances to send the messenger, when all along God has given you and me the ability to expedite the process through our giving to Missions? The truth is, we are a part of a great band of senders who have felt it is important to do God's work while there is still day. The success of God's plan is hanging on to the principle that everyone must do his or her part.

"Give and it will be given to you. A good measure, pressed down, shaken together and running over..." (Luke 6:38).

█ **COME AND FOLLOW**

*"If my people would but listen to me, if Israel would follow my ways, how quickly would I subdue their enemies and turn my hand against their foes!"*

~Psalm 81:13-14

Anyone who has ever made a decision to come to Jesus has discovered that there is forgiveness for sin and that the Lord, in His own loving way, does not condemn us for our past offences. The Bible clearly teaches us that confessed sins (to God) are forgiven because Jesus died to pay the penalty of our sins so that we might be free to serve Him. That all begins when we respond to His invitation to "come" to Him. What a wonderful privilege and honour for us to receive such a tremendous experience!

However, I want to draw your attention to the fact that when Jesus said "come" He also said "follow me." Most of us are happy to stop after the first word because there is very little effort involved in that step. It's the "following" part that is difficult.

I think it's time that all Christians shake their heads and recognize that one of the main reasons that Jesus invites us to come to Him is to follow Him in daily service. Being the kind of people He wants us to be requires dedication, commitment, loyalty, faith, and may I say, "effort." Sometimes it takes us out of our comfort zone to leave a clear witness of the change that has occurred in our lives.

The process that follows is living our lives as Jesus would have us do. That may mean a change of schedules, for example, to honour the Day of the Lord. It may mean changing our lifestyle in terms of conversation. It could be that we need to review the things that are influencing our lives and make choices to select spiritual input in place of movies, videos, music, and other forms of entertainment.

The Bible tells us that the believers were first called 'Christians' in the city of Antioch (Acts 11:26). When critics saw the people who believed in Jesus they were amazed at the likeness between Jesus and His followers.

Our world needs that kind of demonstration again. Not just the "comers," but the "followers" who purpose to let Christ-like attitudes and actions be seen through their lives. He's still calling (Mark 1:17). The obedient who continue to follow Him soon learn that, although the road may be rough on occasion, there is nothing like the joy of being His servant and knowing that what we do has been patterned for us.

The Apostle Paul said, "Follow my example, as I follow the example of Christ" (1 Corinthians 11:1). This is another principle that we need to be aware of—others, perhaps our children or good friends, may end up doing what we do and generally imitate us. In other words, I need to follow the One who is worthy to follow and trust that those who follow me will all be going in the same direction.

❚ **THE HEALER**

*"Great crowds came to him, bringing the lame, the blind, the crippled, the mute and many others, and laid them at his feet; and he healed them."*

~Matthew 15:30

He walked down the aisle with his arms extended in front of him as he hurriedly made his way to the front of the Church. He felt his way along the altar to the stairs and made his way onto the platform. The Evangelist called him to come closer, and following the sound of the voice, the blind man made cautious steps toward the place of prayer. A brief interview followed as the young man explained that he had been this way from birth but that he believed that the God who still does miracles would heal him today.

The Evangelist laid his hands on the head of the blind man and prayed a simple prayer. In a moment a miracle happened. There was a notable change in the appearance of the blind man. His smile shone brightly and the sparkle in his eyes betrayed the fact. His eyes were as big as saucers as he moved his head from side to side in utter amazement at the wonderful world around him.

The Evangelist said, "I want you to count the lights on the ceiling." With his hand extended, he pointed; "One, two..." That's the way I saw it, as a young child at my first miracle service. Since then, I've seen and been the recipient of the miraculous healing power of God. One of the Old Testament names of the Lord was, *Jehovah Rapha*, 'I AM THE LORD YOUR HEALER.' It's consistent, then, to understand that God is the One who heals. If we believe in the many miracles that brought the world, the stars and life into existence, it should be no great thing to believe that God can heal today. He is the Designer and Maintainer of all things, from the small one-celled little creature to the planets that hang, rotate and shine in space. I confess that there are many mysteries about Divine healing that I may not be able to resolve. The fact remains that the same God who created all things out of absolutely nothing is able to speak His word and bring His healing power into every one of us. He demonstrated the extent of His healing power when He ministered to the many who were brought to Him, who sought Him out and who called for His help. He turned none away. It's the same Jesus that we come to when we pray and it's the same Lord who has healed before and will do it again. When all is said and done, I trust that you'll reach out to Him for your own physical needs and live believing that the day of miracles has not passed us by. Let's be a people brave to trust the promises of God. When we don't understand why we are not healed instantly, let's be confident that God does all things well, even though we won't be completely satisfied until we have persistently tried everything in our spiritual arsenal to see the Power of God released upon the needs of men. Live expecting a miracle. Seek to be a miracle, today.

| **HE CAME FOR THE LOST. ALL OF US.**

*"He told them, 'The harvest is plentiful, but the workers are few. Ask the Lord of the harvest, therefore, to send out workers into his harvest field.'"*

~Luke 10:2

The reason Jesus came into the world is summed up in His own words. "The son of man came to seek and to save that which was lost" (Luke 19:10). That was His Mission. It is the expression of the heartbeat of God. He was willing to go to any lengths to bring lost humanity back into a right relationship with Himself. One of Jesus' last commands was the Great Commission: "... go and make disciples of all nations" (Matthew 28:19). The first and the last of His earthly ministry shared the same challenge. Then He made it clear that one of the main reasons He would send the Holy Spirit was to give us all power to witness—to witness to the whole world, beginning in our hometowns and then to all the nations.

The early Church understood the challenge and began to reach out beyond their borders to the provinces and nations of the world in spite of the persecution of the day. It could be said that "you couldn't keep them quiet." They were commissioned to tell the most wonderful story ever told. Everywhere they went they gossiped the gospel. "Those who had been scattered preached the word wherever they went" (Acts 8:4). What they had to share concerning their experience with the Living Lord was worth more to them than their very lives.

Are lost souls really worth the effort and the cost? In a modern world that focuses on the comforts of life and doing things to please ourselves, the primary aim of God's purposes has been deflected. We shelter ourselves in the sense of security that we, the Church, are more valuable to God than the lost multitudes of this world. I wouldn't advise anyone to push that idea with God. Do you remember the story that Jesus told of the 100 sheep? It seems that He was saying, "One lost sheep is worth ninety-nine in the fold." Am I stretching the point? We covet being comforted and nurtured in Churches that serve to be nothing less than incubators for immature believers while God calls us to be obedient to His commands. Jesus said, "If you love me, you will obey what I command" (John 14:15).

We have been privileged to have Missionaries share their calling and vision with us from time to time. They are the ones who are listening most closely to the heartbeat of God. They are people who are working on the front line both for God and for us, because we should be a part of the team. The work will only be done if each of us in our own way will do the things that God asks us to do. The lost of our communities are our Mission field. God's call to reach our neighbours is just as real as the call of a Missionary to some foreign country. Look around you today and see the ones that need the Lord. Don't neglect to pray and seek for opportunities to reach out to them. God's counting on you!

█ **THERE IS A WORLD LEADER COMING**

*"Who is the liar? It is the man who denies that Jesus is the Christ. Such a man is the antichrist—he denies the Father and the Son."*

~1 John 2:22

The Prophets have been telling us so for a long time. It's all coming to an end. That is, this whole world system as we know it today is in for a big surprise. They will wake up one day and discover that all those "Christians" will have vanished in some unexplainable disappearing act.

That, of course, is no secret to us. We've been talking about the coming of the Lord for a long time, and we'll continue to do the same because it is one of those Bible truths of the future that the Lord has openly declared. There may be some mysteries about how it all comes together and there are differences of opinion about the timing of His return, but every Bible-believing person ought to be fully aware that He is coming back again. It is true, we don't know the day or the hour, but there are enough signs described in scripture to give us adequate warning that His time is "about now." It is very possible that the next world leader has already been born and is presently being educated or is already working in some office in preparation for his great day of revelation. Don't be surprised when you hear of some great wise man who begins to dominate the attention of the world with his solutions to the problems that have plagued us for centuries. He may pass himself off as a gift of God to this generation for such a time as this. There's no question about the fact that he will not only have some great solutions for the situations that have not been resolved through the centuries, but that he will also be able to exercise supernatural powers that will cause even some believers to be deceived and to accept him as being God's answer to the needs of mankind. We need to be ready! We need to be prepared to be able to discern who this guy really is and not fall for all his impressive methods.

Remember, the bottom line is always that Jesus Christ is the One and only Saviour of the World and that we have a heavenly hope because He died on the cross to set us free from sin. There is no other. Don't fall for the lie that God would not punish us because He is love. Nor the lie that we're all going to the same place, so any religion is good religion. Nor should anyone be deceived by someone who comes along and gives flowery discourses or performs some miraculous deeds. It's all a part of the deception of the enemy of our souls to make us believe that Jesus is not the only one who can do these things.

Let me remind you, if you miss the coming of Jesus to this earth you've got a real tough row to hoe.

Be on guard! Jesus is coming soon. Be, now, what Jesus would want you to be when He comes back to earth again. Be committed to the responsibility of declaring that the one and only way out of this world is to believe that Jesus Christ is Lord. He's coming back again to prove it! Maybe today.

**WHO DID DIE?**

*"For Christ died for sins once for all, the righteous for the unrighteous,
to bring you to God."*

~1 Peter 3:18a

As Barabbas sat on the cold dungeon floor he could hear the crowds gathered outside the prison walls. Their furious shouts drove shivers up and down his back. "Crucify him! Crucify him!"

He imagined the hate the Romans must have felt towards him because of the things he had done. Stories of his exploits, robberies and murders were the scary midnight tales that were told around the campfires. His lifestyle had brought him to this place, and his execution was about to be completed along with his two friends.

By the sounds of the mob, it would happen any moment. There it was again, "Crucify him! Crucify him!" He knew that the people were calling for the Roman method of torture and judgment. He had seen the crosses many times on the roadsides of Israel during his nefarious career. Everyone in Israel hated seeing those crosses. That was the way the Roman law could publicly demonstrate, throughout the land, the price that is brought on by disobedience and rebellion to their purposes. It was inhumane. Death was slow. Suffering was maximized as the prisoners were beaten, goaded, reviled and ridiculed. Barabbas knew that as violent as his life had been against the Roman Imperialism, this would be his sentence.

But could it be that the Jewish people would be so thankless of his efforts to free them of the Roman invaders that they would demand his death on the cross? Oh, the dread of the pain.

Barabbas heard the boots of the soldiers as they approached his cell. This was it. The moment had arrived. Death awaited just outside the door and a little way down the road. They threw open his cell door, unlocked his chains, pushed him roughly through the hallways and into the bright, blinding, morning light outside the prison walls. The door slammed shut behind him. He was alone and free! No walls surrounded him. No bars, no chains, no soldiers.

Who was this One, then, who would die on the cross? What crime did He commit that would cause the people to condemn Him to a death on the cross?

Whoever He was, He was going to die in Barabbas' place and mine and yours...

█ **BE A MAN**

> *"... fathers tell their children about your faithfulness."*
>
> ~Isaiah 38:19b

You'll find all kinds of fathers in the Bible. Each of them teaches us a lesson about lifestyles that will affect future generations. The truth is, history has a way of making examples of all of us. You would probably like to know what effect your life will have on your kids and the society of the next generation. Most of us would like to be remembered for the kindness, goodness and wisdom that we shared while we exercised our influence.

It must be very humbling for baseball players. When they make errors during a game, the loudspeakers at the stadiums blare out, "Player #42 made an error." It is registered on the scoreboard and goes down in the record books for posterity to review.

Now, we have all made mistakes and we all acknowledge that. Sometimes it's noted in the minds of our kids, who may never forget, or in the memories of our closest friends, or on the ledger of the police blotter, but always on the register in heaven. You may not realize it, but being a father is pretty serious stuff. I always think it's strange that there isn't one specific chapter in the Bible that tells us how to be good fathers. I believe that God wanted us to know how to be good in ourselves, to please Him, and that would flow out into being what God wants us to be as fathers. Building a strong personal relationship with HIM makes for great potential for becoming a good father. However, it might surprise us that some who know the Lord really well do not practice the "art" of being a good father. It's sometimes easier to leave being a father up to mother. She then needs to fulfill a dual role in the home. Gentlemen, let me advise you that there is no reward for relinquishing the responsibility of being a good father. We sometimes tremble to perform our duties because, if there is a failure in the home, "the buck stops here." Better to let someone else handle that one—but hold on!

Let me give us some advice:

1. God still answers prayer and it is by no means defeat to leave all our burdens with Him and let Him work out some of the situations in our homes. You really don't have all the answers. God still works miracles for those that seek Him.

2. When you lack wisdom, ask God for guidance. He has promised to supply (James 1:5).

3. Being head of the home does not mean that you are always right, or that you have to prove anything to anybody.

4. Submission is not a swear word, nor is it only the responsibility of women and children. The Word is, "Submit to one another out of reverence for Christ" (Ephesians 5:21).

5. If you are a man...be a MAN. Be real!

6. Lastly, from time to time do what Jesus did— He took the children in His arms and laid hands upon them and blessed them. Be as a Prophet to your family.

▌ **THE FATHER DOESN'T GIVE UP**

*"Be at rest once more, O my soul, for the LORD has been good to you."*

~Psalm 116:7

It was the young man who gave up on the Father in the story of the prodigal son. The parable describes the Father as a patient and prayerfully anxious man who was a great provider for his family and for the servants that worked for him. The wayward son remembered that while struggling with the pigs for food. The Father didn't give up on the son. It was the decision of the son to leave the Father.

What drove that boy to make the kind of decision that would throw away the security of a wealthy home and the careful provision of a loving Father? We can only imagine. Many young people have gone that same route. The tragedy is that some have not made it back from the pig pen. At least, not yet. I've seen some of them in downtown Vancouver begging for money to be able to buy themselves a bowl of soup. I've heard that they sell their bodies to be able to continue to live away from the comfort and shelter of loving parents and home. Many of them go through tremendously tragic circumstances of sickness and disease, and they take on a "might makes right" mentality. It may be their method of rebelling against the rules and guidelines set down to shelter them from the very situation they are in. They want to try it for themselves with no rules and their own kind of freedom. We hope they will learn before it is too late. Some do and some... The sad part is that 'experience' is a bad teacher because it gives you the test first and then the lesson afterwards.

Then, there are some who live at home and enjoy the comfort and security of having all their physical needs supplied but they are as far away from the Father as anyone could be. That is just about as dangerous as the one who has chosen to live on the street. It is only a loving relationship under proper discipline (self or imposed) that will build healthy character and supply adequate resources for proper social skills to succeed in the world. That's equally as true with our earthly relationships as it is with our Heavenly Father. There is no question that Jesus' story was intended to reveal the attitude of His Father toward those who are not in fellowship with Him. Let me make it clear—the Father never gave up on anyone. Those who are not loving and serving Him have made their own choices to go in the direction of life that they want. The Father allows that to happen but He is watchful for the first inclination to return. Sometimes it is pride that keeps people from admitting that they really need the Father to help them make something important of their lives. We've all been there. We know that the Father loves, more than words can describe, and He is ready to reach out to whoever reaches up to Him. There's always room for those who choose to return.

*"The Father of a righteous man has great joy..."*

~Proverbs 23:24

The book of Proverbs is a book of advice for all kinds of life experiences. Most of these words of counsel come from the wisdom of Solomon, and were intended to give special insights into a variety of situations so that his own sons would have a book of direction to help them as rulers of the nation. It is obvious that Solomon had explored and discovered the righteous and the carnal sides of life, and had developed special instructions for avoiding doing things that would displease God and destroy a man's integrity.

Solomon does give many words of advice that serve our generation, as well. Listen to this: "Many a man claims to have unfailing love, but a faithful man who can find?" (Proverbs 20:6). You've probably read that passage many times and passed over it quickly. I thought we should examine the intent of these words more closely in the light of Father's Day. I have not yet met a man who deliberately determined to be a bad Father. I have been the witness at many a marriage altar where men have pledged their undying love and faithful commitment to the most beautiful women on earth. No, I confess, I don't know what was going through the minds of these guys at the time, but I don't think they ever got a clear picture of what they were committing themselves to. You see, it's easy to say the words because we know how to say what is expected of us, but the test comes when the tuxedo is returned, the flowers have faded and the practical routine of life takes its toll of blood, sweat and tears.

The pledge of unfailing love is the kind that Jesus showed when He came into this world to live among the mass of humanity that had long disposed of the importance of God in the daily schedules of life. He came anyway, to teach us that God has never stopped loving us in spite of our neglect of Him. Husbands and fathers need to get that kind of motivation back into every part of our lives. There are some very special people who look to us for that type of unfailing devotion.

I guess my question is, in this generation, where are the guys who pledged their faithfulness "'til death do us part?" I wonder why so many homes are breaking up and why we, as men, have not taken the leadership in reaching out to God for some of the solutions that He has for our situations. Why are we so slow in picking up our responsibilities as Spiritual Leaders in the home? And why do the wives have to put up with so much, for so long that their patience has come to an end? The big question is the one that Solomon puts to us: "...a faithful man who can find?"

Before anyone thinks that I intend to condemn all of manhood, let me assure us all that God wants to make our relationships loving and our homes a refuge of peace. To make that happen we need to remember that we are workers together with God. He is the One who helps us to be men of faith and faithfulness. Let's be sensitive to hear what He has to say and obedient to what He wants us to do.

▌ **BLIND**

*"So we fix our eyes not on what is seen, but on what is unseen. For what is
seen is temporary, but what is unseen is eternal."*

~2 Corinthians 4:18

I've always wondered if blind people dream dreams and have nightmares.
Can they see monsters lurking in the darkness of their unseeing world? I've never
had the opportunity to ask anyone about it but I've wondered how they could
imagine what people look like or what encountering a dog would be like to
someone who has never seen one. I've wondered how they could imagine the
difference between the colours of red and yellow when they've never seen
anything like that. No matter how much you describe the details of brilliance,
shades and shadows, how could they ever know unless they had something to
compare with in their imagination? Is it possible that they can dream formless
thoughts and conversations? Does a blind person really understand what they are
missing that is so common to most of us?

How much did the blind man (Luke 18:35) understand about the Saviour
who could heal him and give him something that he had never had before? What
stirred his imagination when he heard the crowd and knew that Jesus was coming
that way? How did he know that Jesus was able to heal him and how did he know
that he was missing something that everyone else possessed? How could he
imagine that he was missing one of the five senses and that he was so deprived?

Can you understand that it is possible that people with sight are also missing
out on something that they can not see? They are losing out on the blessings of
the walk of faith that every believer experiences every day. It may be impossible
for unsaved people to comprehend what we see and experience because of our
relationship with Jesus. Our faith helps us to live in a world where moral values
and priorities are totally different. The world cannot know the kind of blessings
that we are privileged to have because there is no way that they can compare the
peace of heart and mind that we possess with anything in the world; unless
someone tells them! Even then, the Spirit of God needs to work in their hearts to
help them to understand the things of the Spirit. Someone needs to tell them!

There are better things in life than just living in the course of our world. Our
world is full of people who see but are blind to spiritual matters. They possess all
their 5 senses but are ignorant of the real purpose of life and the call of God that
reaches out to all mankind. Someone needs to tell them and then bring them along
to meet the Saviour! That's what Missions and Evangelism is all about. I've never
met a person who has truly committed their life to the Lord and returns with
regrets. God has a way of opening our understanding to new things and a new
hope.

| **WHAT A LOVING FATHER!**

*"How priceless is your unfailing love! Both high and low among men find refuge in the shadow of your wings."*

~Psalm 36:7

There is no father like our heavenly Father. His kindness and blessings, His mercy and patience, His giving and forgiving, His love for our future and all the details of our lives are far beyond anything that we can measure. I often wish there were a way that we could see His personal but invisible involvement in each of our lives every day. I'm sure that we often miss the degree of how much He is working out His plan through the details of our daily situations and circumstances.

Let me list just a few of the things that we know He is doing for us out of His Loving Kindness:

1. He is a faithful Counsellor and Friend.

2. His invisible hand is constantly working in us to make even the darkest of hours to be a blessing and benefit to us.

3. Great is the mystery of His exceeding mercy that sees the frailties of our humanity and the weaknesses of our lives and yet He loves us with an everlasting love.

4. How awesome to our understanding is the fact that of all the majesty and beauty of His creation, its order and created glory, His affection is focused on each of us as the prize and pride of His handiwork!

5. How magnificent the measure of His confidence and trust that He would commission us to represent Him here on the earth as Ambassadors of His kingdom and representatives of His love and concern for all of His creation!

6. How amazing that He would delegate to each of us to be the story-tellers of His plan and purpose in bringing Salvation to the world through His Son. He entrusts us with the testimonies of the pardon, peace, and promises of His workings in our hearts!

7. What a glorious hope of the joy that awaits us because the Father has provided a way that all who believe in His Son will inherit eternal life, without the restrictions and limitations of our human frame! (No more pain, sickness nor sorrow.)

What a wonderful thought that among the treasures that await us in heaven is the fact that we shall see Jesus! That is a part of His loving promise to us. We shall live in His presence and share in the light of His glory as one of those very special gifts of our Father who wants to share His very best with those who trust Him! Even now, He has promised to watch over us and knows the things that we have need of. He is a wonderful Father!

**GOD'S VALUED TREASURE**

*"Now if you obey me fully and keep my covenant, then out of all nations you will be my treasured possession. Although the whole earth is mine..."*

~Exodus 19:5

How much is a man worth? Joseph was sold for 20 shekels of silver. Jesus was sold for 30 pieces of silver. (I guess the cost of living had brought the increase.) I know a man who bought a slave on the market in the Sudan only a few years ago, in order to set him free. I've been told that you can rent a body in different areas of Vancouver for an hour or an evening. Minimum wage in the province in which I live at the time of this writing is $8.00 per hour, and your income can go up from there according to your education, job position and whatever the market demand is for your talents. But what is the real worth of a human being? Jesus said, "What good is it for a man to gain the whole world, yet forfeit his soul? Or what can a man exchange for his soul?" (Mark 8:36-37). It's one of those rhetorical questions that Jesus occasionally asked. The unspoken answer is, "There is nothing in this world that is worth the value of a soul." It is impossible to accumulate enough wealth, in this world to pay cash for your soul. That should increase the view of our own self-esteem/self-worth if we understand that God looks upon each one of us with that value scale in mind. There's nothing in this world that is worth more to God than you. Have you seen the picture of a little boy who says, "I'm important 'cause God don't make no junk?"

It's funny though, we can take ourselves off of God's stock and investment market—out from under His protection—and immediately another is ready to take possession of us. In the devil's mind, we're just trash. He's gloating for the day when those who are so valued in God's sight will all be thrown into the lake of fire. He's busy, right now, trying his best to keep us out of the Grace and Mercy of God that changes the trash into the treasures of heaven. But let me remind you, God has given us the power of choice. We can make the decision to be restored into God's purpose and His wonderful plan for eternity. God has given us the Holy Spirit, Who works with us to resist the attacks and accusations of the enemy of our souls and who makes us sensitive to the things that are important to God. It is only through Jesus Christ that we gain any real value in this world. You can't pay for it in cash; nor can you claim it by education. You can't claim it by inheritance nor by your heritage. It's who we belong to that gives added or less value to our lives. Becoming important to God comes through receiving Jesus Christ as Lord and Saviour and that has to be a personal decision each of us makes. Living without that kind of security is dangerous because we never know when "cash-in" day will come. For some, it could be today. For others, a week or two, or a little longer; but who really knows. I'm with those who have made the choice and are glad that He will be returning to catch us to be with Him for endless eternity. He has prepared a special place of peace and happiness for those who have come to trust Him.

▌ # IN GOD WE TRUST

*"My tears have been my food day and night,*
*while men say to me all day long, 'Where is your God?'"*

~Psalm 42:3

We are blessed! We serve a loving heavenly Father whose faithfulness knows no limit. His watchful eye is upon us for good as He surveys all of His creation "For the eyes of the Lord are on the righteous and his ears are attentive to their prayer..." (1 Peter 3:12a). In a world of constant turmoil and apparent injustices it ought to give us a great sense of peace to know that the Lord of hosts is taking care of His children. It is true that we don't always understand how He is able to make all things to work out for good, but our trust in Him is not based upon what we see with the physical eye but rather upon His promises. He knows best. We always think that we know best because we measure the blessings of God according to our comfort level. Listen carefully! I suspect that this is the process that most of us follow: If we feel good, God is good. If we don't feel so good, 'WHERE IS GOD?' The truth is that His loving kindness will not allow Him to permit anything to come our way except what is 'for our good.' It has been said that those who walk through the dark valleys understand this only after they've come through the valley.

It's like me, in the dentist's chair, and she's holding a very long needle in her hand behind her back while she's looking into my mouth. I know that what she is about to do is good for me, but I have a hard time telling myself that I'll be glad for what she is about to do. Of course, I'll be glad when it's all over but it's the "during the process" that I have to sell myself on the fact that this is good for me.

Let me remind "us" again. God is good and His care for us, through all trials and tests, is based on His eternal love. He knows every detail of our daily routines and is able to work miracles of grace in our lives. He invites us to "cast all our care upon Him, because He cares for us." He calls us, "Come to me, all you who are weary and burdened, and I will give you rest. Take my yoke upon you and learn from me, for I am gentle and humble in heart, and you will find rest for your souls. For my yoke is easy and my burden is light" (Matthew 11:28–30). It's obviously not His intention to leave us alone under any circumstance.

I think there is another side to the whole situation. If we don't learn to trust God in the difficulties, then the discomfort level rises; like two yoked animals where one does not want to go along with the other. The truth is, they both suffer. Better to learn that when we walk with the Lord in our daily experience things will go much easier on us if we can trust that He knows the route of our journey. So, let's trust Him.

The Psalmist says, "Praise be to the Lord, to God our Saviour, who daily bears our burdens." We are blessed because we serve an awesome God! "Trust in the Lord with all your heart and lean not on your own understanding" (Proverbs 3:5).

█ **THE ONLY WAY**

*"I am the gate; whoever enters through me will be saved."*

~John 10:9

It's only the precious blood of Jesus that washes away the stain of our sin. There is no other method nor any cleansing agent that can make our offences disappear. Whether we like it or not there are no other options. The bible makes it clear, "...without the shedding of blood there is no forgiveness." (Hebrews 9:22) And then again, "...the blood of Jesus, His Son, purifies us from all sin." (1 John 1:7b) We admit that many other religions have virtues that we commend because they demonstrate, in most cases, the desire of men to do what is good and right. But there is no other way to receive forgiveness of sins except through what Jesus did on the cross of Calvary. There is no other way to have peace with God with the promise of an eternity in heaven. Jesus is the only way! We are aware that the enemy of our souls will do anything for us to miss that point. It has always been his desire to destroy the things that God has done and to keep people from God. He extends other apparent spiritual options hoping that we will not make the 'right' choice until it's too late. That's why there are so many different religions in the world and also so many divisions in "Christianity." The enemy also tries to keep us 'too busy' to make the right choice right now because He knows that delay is as good as denial on the day of judgment.

We know that the Bible teaches that God has designed one plan to bring all men, women and children of all nations to Himself. We have that treasure of truth in the scriptures, not because we are good, but because God is Good and the record of His Word is the revelation of His truth. The fact is that none of us deserves the kindness of His favour that grants us forgiveness and pardon. His love has provided that for us and given us a way in spite of our ways. If Jesus had not died on the cross, we would all be responsible to make annual sacrifices that would cover our past sins until our next sin. The cost through our lifetime would be tremendous. The intent of the Old Testament process was to teach that sin has a high cost—there is no easy way out and there is no person that could ever pay such a price for all of humanity—that is, until Jesus came. Because He is the faultless Son of God His death was sufficient to pay for all of the penalties of the sins of mankind. His life was poured out as a free gift to all who will believe and to all who will receive His provision. There are no hoops to jump through; no cash down-payments; no mountains to climb; no oceans to swim; no penances to perform. The invitation to come to Him has been extended to all mankind through the generations and there is no other way. He simply asks us to BELIEVE that what He has done is a free gift to be received by faith and anyone can receive Him.

▌ **ADVICE FROM A WINNER**

*"For everything that was written in the past was written to teach us,*
*so that through endurance and the encouragement*
*of the Scriptures we might have hope."*

~Romans 15:4

We learn a lot of lessons from the experiences and discoveries of others. This is one of the most valuable purposes of communication. If others take the tests and teach us the lessons, then we are wise if we learn from them. This is a principle of the walk of faith that serves us in the learning processes of life. David was a great leader. He had a way of inspiring his followers because he had a reputation of being a winner. He had a few failures, like the rest of us, but it was his rising above his weaknesses that demonstrated the true success of this great man of influence. Today, I would like to look at a couple of words of testimony that he shared in Psalm 16:2, "I said to the LORD, 'You are my Lord; apart from you I have no good thing.'" I want us to look specifically at two things that he shares in this brief passage.

1. We know that David loved the relationship that he had with the Lord. He makes this public confession, "You are my Lord." He made a decision. God was going to be his Master by his choice. The fact that he was the leader, anointed for some very special tasks, did not fill him with pride. This confession is one of humble submission. He recognized a higher authority Who had a priority on his life. He, willingly, was prepared to surrender his position and accomplishments to the oversight of the Lord. His Commander in Chief was the Lord Himself. That is something that he practiced every day, which brought him the recognition of being a man after God's heart. That's quite a compliment. It all began in his yielding to the direction that the Lord had for his life. That's good advice for all of us. May there be more men and women, like David, who have a heart after God.

2. He, also, made a simple declaration of priorities that we should accept as wise counsel. Here it comes: "Apart from you I have no good thing." There are a lot of things in the world that entertain us or give us pleasure, but outside of the Lord nothing is really that important. We can easily be distracted by peer pressure or by our own desires and fantasies, but that does not always serve us well in our continuing life experiences. His advice for all of us is to make our choices the kind that will give us lasting benefits with no regrets. If the Lord is the centre of our activities and choices then all things will work together for the good... I hope that is not viewed as being super-spiritual. I think that even the routine and mundane things of life can be blessed by the Lord.

Leaving God out or our lives is asking for trouble. He wants to share "good" with us because He loves us so.

▊ **FATHER/TEACHER**

*"Let the little children come to me, and do not hinder them,
for the kingdom of God belongs to such as these."*

~Mark 10:14b

It really doesn't matter what your occupation is, if you are a Dad, you are called to be a teacher/trainer. Our primary responsibility, once we've brought a little child into the world, is to make sure that he or she learns how to go to heaven. We often forget that what we're doing to earn a living and provide for the needs of our families is only a temporary activity and that everything around us is only here for a moment. We have higher goals. We have begun a walk of faith that will never come to an end, but there remain many times of decision that young lives need to make. Some of those decisions will determine the direction of their lives both here and now as well as then and there.

As important as the things that are around us are today, they will lose their value eventually. Wise is the man who trains his children to understand this and who replaces the temporary with the unchangeable. It was a man of courage and faith who, speaking to other Father's of his generation, could say with confidence, "As for me and my household we will serve the Lord" (Joshua 24:15). Knowing that your children are going to serve the Lord by their own choice is the result of the spiritual investment that you make in the spiritual growth of your children. It won't happen by itself—there is a teaching and training process that is involved.

Gentlemen, we need to take this to heart and not step back from our responsibility. God has placed us as the heads of our households. You may find that it's simpler or more comfortable to let our wives do that task, and that may be the easy way out, but there has to be some of our influence shared with the children or they will interpret our silence as disbelief.

Let me suggest a couple of things that we, as fathers, should be doing on a regular basis:

1. *Pray for* your children by name.
2. *Pray with* your children
3. *Lead* them to the House of God
4. Let the *name of the Lord* be a part of your conversation to demonstrate your commitment to serving Him.
5. Be an *example* of a man of Faith.

The advice of scripture is clear: "Train a child in the way he should go, and when he is old he will not turn from it" (Proverbs 22:6).

**FATHER'S DAY**

> *"The quiet words of the wise are more to be heeded*
> *than the shouts of a ruler of fools."*

~Ecclesiastes 9:17

"Little Eyes Upon You"

There are little eyes upon you,
and they're watching night and day.
There are little ears that quickly
take in everything you say.
There are little hands all eager
to do everything you do.
And a little boy who's dreaming
of the day he'll be like you.

You're the little fellow's idol,
you're the wisest of the wise;
In his little mind about you
no suspicions ever rise;
He believes in you devotedly,
holds that all you say and do
He will say and do in your way
when he's grown up just like you.

There's a wide-eyed little fellow
who believes you're always right
And his ears are always open,
and he watches day and night.
You are setting an example
every day in all you do
For the little boy who's waiting
to grow up to be like you.

(author unknown)

"Sons are a heritage from the Lord, children a reward from him" (Psalm127:3).

It is a wise Father who recognizes the importance of his example. It is said that more is learned by observation than by hearing. Our children learn more from what we do than from what we say. It is said that experience is a bad teacher because we take the test before we learn the lesson. Better to hear the wise counsel of a godly Father than testing experience for ourselves.

▌ **MINISTRIES TO MEN**

*"That all of them may be one, Father, just as you are in me*
*and I am in you. May they also be in us so that the world*
*may believe that you have sent me."*

~John 17:21

It was an invisible congregation that the Prophet never saw. The fact that He felt He was all alone and voiced his complaint to heaven lets us see the human side of a great man of God. But God saw something that Elijah did not see. "Yet I reserve 7000 men in Israel whose knees have not bowed to Baal...." (1 Kings 19:18) That's a good-sized group of men. I believe that it was an encouragement to Elijah in his trying times to know that he really wasn't in the service of God all by himself. I think it would have been more encouraging to have those guys serving and worshipping God together with him. What a great congregation that would have made and what an impression it would have left on the ungodly had they all been there to stand together! !

Through the years, I believe there have been many servants of the Lord who have become discouraged because of the lack of input from men who, although they refuse to bend to the direction of the worldly winds, they don't stand up to be counted to back the Pastor. They are like the invisible 7000. The trouble with an invisible congregation is that you don't know who to count on for help when help is needed. I think that is one of the main reasons why God saves men in the first place. We are to work together to do the things that God wants us to do.

That is one of the main missions of Men's Ministries and HonorBound. There is nothing that is so encouraging to us as to know that there are other fellows who have the same kind of commitment as we have, who take/make the time to join heart and voice, body and spirit to get together to worship and serve the Lord. We need each other, and every one is an important part of the Body of Christ. Every man has a special but different calling in life and it's the coming together times that allow opportunity for us to develop together into the fullness of God's design. It appears that the women of our Churches have learned that lesson a lot more quickly than have the men. Yet, it appears that God has delegated certain responsibilities to guys as far as being spiritual leaders in our homes and in our communities. Only God knows what can be accomplished by a body of men who have learned to work together to serve the Lord. Our problem, too often, is that the invisible group of God-worshippers remain invisible when they should be seen and actively engaged in public activities together.

What an impact and what a force it would be to have the men of our Churches united to honour God.

173

| **PEACE, BE STILL**

*"I will lie down and sleep in peace, for you alone,*
*O LORD, make me dwell in safety."*

~Psalm 4:8

It is so good to come into the presence of the Lord with peace in your heart. It is refreshing to be able to open yourself up to the Lord when you know that you are right with God. There can't be anything in the world that is as comforting as knowing that there is nothing that stands between God and each of our lives. That is exactly what the enemy of our souls wants to disrupt. Many years ago, he snuck into the Garden of Eden to break into the relationship of Adam and God; to cause fear and shame to fill the hearts of our first generation of fathers and mothers. That's what sin does. It displaces peace and joy with fear and shame. Sin robs us of the sense of harmony that God wanted to instil in the heart of every human being from long before He created man.

God is a God of love. He has designed a plan that will restore "peace with God." He comes to us in mercy. You shouldn't fear that. He comes in forgiveness. You shouldn't be ashamed of that. His love embraces all that will come to Him. He is the only One who can restore peace to fallen humanity. As a matter of fact, He took the initiative to make sure that we could find a way back to His presence and the joy of communion with Him. The prophet Isaiah explains it simply; "This is what the Sovereign LORD, the Holy One of Israel, says: 'In repentance and rest is your salvation, in quietness and trust is your strength...'" (Isaiah 30:15).

The message is clear. Repentance brings restoration to our relationship, and rest is the natural result. It is then that we need to exercise quietness, to still our souls and to trust in the Lord. That's the package that adds strength to the heart of the believer.

Let's be confident that we are very precious in His sight and that He will do whatever is necessary to restore peace in our hearts.

Let's be confident that there is no power in all of creation that is sufficient to keep us from His love. "Who shall separate us from the love of Christ? Shall trouble or hardship or persecution or famine or nakedness or danger or sword?...For I am convinced that neither death nor life, neither angels nor demons, neither the present nor the future, nor any powers, neither height nor depth, nor anything else in all creation, will be able to separate us from the love of God that is in Christ Jesus our Lord." (Romans 8:35, 39)

That's the Rock of God's word. It's a firm foundation that we can hold on to when the enemy, with all his bluster and blow, comes to remove us from God's presence. We can possess a calmness in the midst of the storm because Jesus shouts, "Quiet! Be still!" (Mark 4:39).

"But the meek will inherit the land and enjoy great peace." (Psalm 37:11)

JUNE 23 ■ **IT'S ALL SO BEAUTIFUL**

*"...On each side of the river stood the tree of life, bearing twelve crops of
fruit, yielding its fruit every month. And the leaves of the tree are
for the healing of the nations."*

~Revelation 22:2

When Spring is in the air, the flowers are in bloom, birds are making their
nests, the trees are showing the handiwork of God in the greens, pinks and whites
of this miracle process of life that we are privileged to see at that time of the year.
What an awesome God we serve! It's all His idea. We enjoy the wonder of the
new birth as we visualize the transition from the dormant—waiting during the
winter chills—to the vibrancy of the life and colours of this season. As much as all
of this leaves us with impressions of wonder and amazement at the beauty around
us, God sees something of greater value in what He has made. All that we see,
appreciate and admire was designed as a temporary habitation for us until He is
ready to take us to His home in heaven. There the beauties that we enjoy so much
will fade into the glories of His eternal provision.

Paul wrote to the Corinthian Church and tried to give us a clearer focus on
what God has reserved for us. He wrote: "No eye has seen, no ear has heard, no
mind has conceived what God has prepared for those who love him" (1
Corinthians 2:9). Heaven will be a beautiful place. No pain, no sickness, no
sadness, no darkness and no fear. Loved ones will be there and reunions with
those who have gone before us will bring shouts of laughter amid tender tears and
loving embraces. Words cannot express the wonder of that place and the joy of the
company that will inhabit the Kingdom of God. That's the place we were designed
to possess. We're pilgrims here on passage to another destination. This earth, as
beautiful as it is right now, was never intended to be our final home. In God's
opinion, it's just not good enough for those who love Him.

But there is another side to the story. Not everyone you meet is going to go
there. You see, heaven is a 'destination of choice.' It doesn't come to us just
because we are living in God's creation today. The truth is, heaven is a free gift,
but it's a free gift to those who invite Jesus Christ into their lives before we reach
the end of our earthly journey. We all have to make that decision. Too many have
swallowed the line that once we die we all go to heaven—death is our passport.
Not so! People need to be told that God has prepared a better place and that His
love has made it simple to assure our arrival there.

That's what missions is all about. Someone needs to tell the story of God's
love because each of us needs to make an individual decision. Whether it's here
where we live or somewhere else around the world, the story is the same. Jesus
died on a cross to provide us forgiveness and the privilege of being a part of His
Father's Kingdom. Only accepting Him will guarantee an entrance into heaven.
Refusing to choose is like not accepting a life preserver when we are drowning.
There is no one else to blame but ourselves. Make your choice and make it Jesus!

175

▌ **THE GRACE OF GIVING**

*"For God so loved the world that He gave..."*

~John 3:16

When we talk about giving most of us think immediately of money and how it is our right to make our own decisions concerning our finances. I want you to notice the focus of the passage we just read. Giving was a result of God's love. The whole root of God's plan to give us His Son was His love for mankind. It was His love that promoted the whole process of giving the world a Saviour. He demonstrated the principle that true love has an evidence. You can't say that you love without giving. Ask any married couple who have walked life's road together for any length of time if that isn't true. The whole matter of living, loving relationships is the surrender of time, energy and resources, sometimes invested out of great sacrifice. The key to healthy giving is doing so with the right attitude. No matter what the gift may be, if the heart and motive are in the right place the gift becomes an expression of grace.

Some people find it hard to give. Usually those are the ones who should give the most. It is said that during the depression years on the prairies when times were tough people shared whatever they had with those who had need, regardless of whether they were friends or strangers. Potatoes became one of the most common food items and bartering tools for services and products. Humble folk shared their meagre resources with whoever had need. Their giving was based on their concern for the hardships of others. That's still called love in my language.

The early Church believers held a very challenging attitude toward things. "No one claimed that any of his possessions were his own, but they shared everything they had." (Acts 4:32) I have often wondered if there was a deep struggle in their hearts and minds to come to the decision that everything that they possessed really belongs to God and we are all called to be Stewards rather than owners. I have tried to envision the sight of a body of people who held on to the things of this world that lightly. They must have been a people who knew that whatever their need would or could be, God would supply either through the gift of a brother or through a miracle. Maybe this will stretch your own comfort zone, but I believe that God has to make us able for any situation that comes our way. The potential for the supply of all our need is either in our control right now or ready for distribution from the foot of the Throne of God. Each believer holds the key to their area of Stewardship and is ultimately responsible to God. We cannot give according to what others give. If we follow God's principle, then our giving of talents, abilities, resources etc. will come from our love for God and His Church. The Corinthian church had many miraculous evidences of the grace of God in the Gifts of the Spirit, but Paul had to write them to say: "But just as you excel in everything—in faith, in speech, in knowledge, in complete earnestness and in your love for us—see that you also excel in this *grace of giving*," (2 Corinthians 8:7, emphasis added) He wanted them to learn to Give.

█ **THE PASSING OF TIME**

*"Why, you do not even know what will happen tomorrow. What is your life? You are a mist that appears for a little while and then vanishes."*

~James 4:14

Each New Year, we cross another marker in the lifespan of our earthly existence. Time is a strange invisible commodity that affects every one of us. We only notice it by the ticking of the clock, the growth of our children and the marks it leaves on our bodies. It doesn't blow like the wind nor shine like the sun, yet everyone's life is measured by it in terms of birthdays and anniversaries. There is neither faucet nor dam that can stop the constant flow of the seconds, minutes and hours as they continue their relentless journey toward fulfilling their designed purpose. We face the unknown moments of time with a renewed anticipation of seeing the hand of the Lord in action in a world that needs to know their Maker. Before us the future lies as an unsolved mystery. There are unseen secrets that will be revealed to us as we journey the seconds and minutes of life. But God sees it all, until the end of time, as clearly as this moment. He already knows every detail that will affect each of us and He is actively working to fulfill His plan for our lives.

The psalmist wrote: "Teach us to number our days aright, that we might gain a heart of wisdom" (Psalm 90:12). He is speaking of opportunities that will present themselves to us to serve the Lord in a way that makes each moment a profitable investment for the Kingdom of God. How can I be a better servant? How can I be better prepared as an example of God's grace living in a world of spiritual indifference? How can I adjust my personal schedule so that God's priorities take first place and His purposes be fulfilled in my life?

Let me suggest a few things:

1. I must work on my prayer life. It will take time out of my routine, but it is God's method of strengthening my relationship with Him. I need to know the tug of the Spirit on my heart and mind. Prayer is still the fundamental process of communicating with the One who holds this day and the future in His care.

2. I must be diligent to read His Word and to capture its principles so that my life will have His direction through every experience of life. The Word is more than a composition of the letters of the alphabet. It is the revelation of His heart in dealing with mankind and the various conditions of the world.

3. I must learn to be sensitive to the voice of the Spirit of God as He seeks to influence my choices. I must be careful that I don't clog up the times that He wants to speak to me. And, I must be careful that I don't pass off His voice as an intrusion into my thoughts.

4. I must personally commit my ways to Him, whether I'm comfortable with what He allows to come my way or not. He is Lord! He is Loving and Wise! He cannot fail.

**JESUS IN THE OLD TESTAMENT**

*"And beginning with Moses and all the Prophets, he explained to them what was said in all the Scriptures concerning himself."*

~Luke 24:27

It's all about Jesus. The stories of the Old Testament often give us prophetic glimpses of Jesus and what He was going to do to bring us Salvation. The revelation of what Jesus accomplished on the cross is understood from the pieces of many of the historical records of things that others did. When the pieces are put together they give us a clearer picture of God's plan for His Son. For example, the book of Genesis gives us examples of what Jesus would fulfill when He came into the world. Other passages of scripture continue the same theme.

At Abel's death, his blood cried out. (Genesis 4:10) (The blood calls for justice and reaches the throne of God.)

Noah was told to build an ark. (Genesis 6:14) (The one and only way to be saved from the judgment that is going to fall upon a sinful world is found in Jesus.)

Abraham was called out of Ur to follow God. (We are called to serve Jesus, in the world but not 'to be' of the world.)

Abraham received the son of promise (Genesis 21:2) (Jesus came as the Son of the promise to be our Saviour.)

Abraham was prepared to offer his only son. (Genesis 22:2) (Our heavenly Father had prepared to offer His only Son from before the beginning of the earth.)

Abraham substituted a lamb for his son. (Genesis 22:13) (Jesus became our substitute Lamb and died for each one of us.)

Abraham commissioned his servant to find a wife for his son. (Genesis 24:3-4) (The heavenly Father sent the Holy Spirit to prepare a bride for Jesus who will come to live in the Father's Promised Land.)

Isaac was noted for opening wells. (Genesis 26:18-25) (Jesus is the provider of living water. John 4)

Jacob wrestled to bring blessing to his family. (Genesis 32:24) (Jesus faced the struggles of Gethsemane and Calvary in order to provide a future for us all.)

Joseph was a God-fearing man of integrity but was persecuted and condemned for things he did not do. (Genesis 37, 39) (Jesus was condemned unjustly of crimes that he did not commit but through his death was able to make an eternal provision for all those who would trust in Him.)

Joseph would not seek revenge against his brothers for their betrayal and for his being sold as a slave. (Genesis 45:4, 5) (Joseph said, "..because it was to save lives that God sent me ahead of you." Jesus said, "Forgive them Father for they know not what they do.")

Joseph wanted to live as the 'Protector' of his family. (Genesis 50:21) (Jesus said, "Do not be afraid... I will be with you.")

▌ **BE CAREFUL**

*"The righteous hate what is false,*
*but the wicked bring shame and disgrace."*

~Proverbs 13:5

Jesus said, "Be careful, be on your guard for the yeast..." (Matthew 16:6). Immediately the disciples thought about their lack of bread and their failure of foresight in planning the lunch menu. That was one message that went right over the heads of Jesus' little congregation. You see, some Pastors are in good company when the congregation doesn't grasp the direction of their sermons. Jesus rebuked His disciples for their lack of understanding concerning the point He wanted to make. Then, after careful consideration, they caught on to the fact that Jesus was sending them a caution about spiritual leaders. It was the teaching of the Pharisees and Sadducees that was the danger.

Let me show you a few things about their teachings:

1. Their main concern was not that people find God. The important matter was, "Will you be a Pharisee or a Sadducee?" Let's get your denomination clear here. (Is it really that important? ?)

2. They emphasized the importance of keeping the Old Testament Law, the traditions of the fathers, plus their additional rules and regulations that placed importance on minor details. To them, you needed to work to deserve God. You had to work at pleasing God, or else He would be angry; needless to say, we all struggle with that. (They never found the Grace and Mercy of God)

3. They stressed the need of "separation." That is, you don't mix with common folk or you might contaminate yourself with worldly things. They taught that they were superior to all others. (What did Jesus do?)

4. It is said that a Pharisee gave thanks, every day, that he was not born:

    a) a Roman,

    b) a slave

    c) a woman   (That must have made the ladies in Israel really happy.)

And the list goes on. Needless to say, their pride of position and their segregational arrogance drove people away from God. Jesus came to address them with clear terms. They were "whitened sepulchres," "hypocrites," "blind leaders of the blind," "snakes" and "vipers."

Jesus offered the truth:

-    that the Father loves us all, just as we are.

-    that He grants us forgiveness because we believe in Him, not because of our works.

-    that He is prepared to welcome us into an intimate relationship with Himself every day, not just on the Sabbath or holy days.

Jesus came into the world like a breath of fresh air to a generation sick of formalized religion and dictatorial domination. The Truth sets us free.

179

▌ **DIVINE BONDING**

*"That all of them may be one, Father, just as you are in me
and I am in you. May they also be in us so that the world
may believe that you have sent me."*

~John 17:21

Have you ever stuck your fingers together with 'crazy glue?' There is a bond there that is very difficult to break. It's as though every mark of division is erased and flesh is united with flesh. Sometimes surgery is the only answer. It's an ordeal to try to separate your fingers.

That bond is great for broken things and often restores the appearance of the damaged object into beautiful wholeness, once again, but it's hard on fingers that are supposed to operate independently.

Similarly, the blood of Jesus mends each of us who have been abused, beaten and broken by the deceitfulness of the enemy. There is no natural solution for the repairing of the soul of man, marred and scarred as we are through our sinful ways. We cannot become "whole" on our own. We have tried the crack-fillers of alcohol, drugs, immoral and/or good living, to no avail. There is nothing that brings us back into useful harmony with God like the blood of Jesus Christ. Every stain and blemish that is presented to Him by our humble confession is quickly eradicated as though it never existed. That's the super-glue of heaven. Then and only then can we have compatibility with the Father and His purposes for us become reality.

Judah describes that kind of relationship in the example of his father Jacob who deeply loved Benjamin. Judah basically said, "My father's life is bound up with the boy's life" (Genesis 44:30). His description of the bond between Father and son is one of unity to such a measure that to remove the boy from the father was to destroy the father. Now that's love! The blood of Jesus does that for us. "For I am convinced that neither death nor life, neither angels nor demons, neither the present nor the future, nor any powers, neither height nor depth, nor anything else in all creation, will be able to separate us from the love of God that is in Christ Jesus our Lord" (Romans 8:38-39). Do you get the 'super-glue' picture? There is a blending of lives to such a measure that two separate individuals become inseparable.

When we partake of the Lord's supper, it is through the emblems of His broken body and shed blood we are reminded that Jesus came into the world to bring us back to the Father as new creations in Christ Jesus—as though we had never sinned—repaired, patched up and brand new, just like His Son! All traces of the damaged product of our lives is completely eradicated by His sacrifice on the cross. He makes us one with Himself.

█ **VACATION TIME (1)**

*"Who satisfies your desires with good things
so that your youth is renewed like the eagle's."*

~Psalm 103:5

You've got to plan some time to "get away from it all." That's what holidays are all about, and summers are a good time to take advantage of the warmer weather and the beauty around us. Most of us don't realize what pressures we are under until we get to a quiet place for a day or two. Some folks show it by the stress lines on their faces or by sharp answers to simple questions. We were not designed to be perpetual motion machines. We're only human.

It appears that Jesus was concerned about the physical welfare of His disciples. He said, "Come with me to a quiet place and get some rest." (Mark 6:31) The people and the responsibilities were getting to the boys and they needed some time off. I'm sure that you understand what that is all about.

However, let me make one particular point that needs to be brought to our attention at this vacation season. When the disciples took their "day away" it was with Jesus. Some folks pack up the trailer or board the plane and any semblance of spirituality is left at home.

In order to have a true and healthy vacation I want to challenge you to take the Lord along with you. Let your travels be filled with the blessing of the Lord or you might be returning home for a rest instead of going away for a rest. We can get ourselves in such a rush to travel or to do something different that we miss out on the relaxation that we need so much. Have you ever had that kind of a holiday? Changing your location does not necessarily mean that you're having a rest.

Sometimes we need to still our hearts and minds and just plain "relax." Purpose that each day you will just stop the 'big rush.' Set up a lawn chair under the shade of a tree and read your Bible and then catch a few extra winks. It can be in those quiet moments that we are truly refreshed.

The Psalmist said, "Be still and know that I am God..." (Psalm 46:10). I found it interesting that the Hebrew word for 'be still' is *Rapha*. That's the same word that is used in *Jehovah Rapha*, one of the names that the Lord uses to describe Himself. It literally means 'I am the God who heals you.' (Exodus 15:26) Quieting ourselves and taking advantage of a time of rest is a healing and restorative process. We all need that.

If you are traveling somewhere this summer or just getting away from it all, don't neglect the Lord during your time away from your Church.

█ **VACATION TIME (2)**

*"He who dwells in the shelter of the Most High*
*will rest in the shadow of the Almighty."*

~Psalm 91:1

It's the holiday season. People are coming and going and enjoying times of relaxation and pleasures in the sun and rain. Holidays are God's idea. That was one of the reasons that He created seven days instead of six. Think what a change that would make in our lives. Jesus called His disciples to, "Come with me by yourselves to a quiet place and get some rest" (Mark 6:31). There's something about getting away from it all, once in a while, which is designed to be good for the soul as well as the body. However, some people when they go away for a holiday return home to get a rest. Does that sound familiar?

Let my grey haired experience give you some advice:

1. A holiday from work was not meant to be a holiday from God. Honour Him when you are away from your home Church. It may cost you a day, but you will be blessed and refreshed as you take time to wait on the Lord. Being in another Church can serve a double purpose:

   a) it makes you aware of how wonderful it is to be in the family of God with 'relatives' all over the world.

   b) you experience worship in a new way which could be a learning time to bring back to your own Church family.

2. Take time to relax. Don't think that merely getting a change of geographic location equals a holiday. Resting is important to rejuvenate and refresh the body and the mind. Good sleep is an excellent healer for the battles and stresses of the pressures of our daily routines and occupations.

3. Take advantage of the time to share your life with your family so that a closer bond can either be strengthened or developed. Converse with your loved ones. Play games with them. Take walks with them. Hear their dreams and learn about their desires. Find out where they are in life and what their plans are for the future. Share insights with them out of your own experience and allow God to use you to bless them.

4. Set aside some time to review and refocus on your personal relationship with the Lord and what it might be that God is saying to you in the coming days. You need some quiet time for yourself as well.

Be Blessed!

▌ **COME ON IN!**

> *"At that moment the curtain in the temple*
> *was torn in two from top to bottom."*

~Matthew 27:51a

It's an open door, the one that leads to Jesus Christ and God's forgiveness. The invitation has been extended to every generation since Calvary for all the wayward, hurting, burdened souls who know they need a Saviour. Jesus said, "I am the door." He also said, "Come to me, all you who are weary and burdened, and I will give you rest." (Matthew 11:28) The Love of God reaches out to the needy of our neighbourhood and of the world. It has always been a part of His plan to save the lost, to restore new life and to give new hope to anyone who will come to Him through the Open Door. The message is out—anyone who calls on the name of the Lord will be saved and his or her sins will be forgiven. We need to pass that message along. Too many people think of God as being far away from us and very angry. I think there's something seriously wrong when we call earthquakes, tornadoes and volcanoes 'an act of God.' I know that we have no control over those things, but we get the wrong picture of God if we believe that God only acts out of anger.

I've been the recipient of His love. I've known the touch of His forgiving hand and the blessing of trusting in Him. I've found Him to be a faithful friend in times of sorrow and despair. He's been there with me in the valleys of deep sadness and mourning. I've seen lives changed from hopelessness and despondency to confident, joyful trust in His power. He's been with me on the mountain peaks of great blessings many times in my life. He is a God who lovingly answers prayer and gives more than expected. To me, that's only some of the reasons why coming to Jesus has been such a wonderful blessing.

The Open Door is set for everyone as an opportunity to make a choice for a change of lifestyle and a better future. The choice should be simple; shall I choose to walk through it and accept Jesus as my Lord and Saviour? Or should I walk by and hope another opportunity will be presented to me? The truth is, there are no other options. To not choose Jesus is to be the loser of the greatest benefit of eternity. To postpone the invitation to come to Him is to neglect the summons of the Love of God extended to us. You see, "God is patient...not wanting anyone to perish, but everyone to come to repentance" (2 Peter 3:9b). That is to say, it is not God's will that anyone miss the Door. However, He will not force anyone to make that choice and require them to do what He wants them to do. Our free will was given to us to exercise that choice to serve God and to do His will as our own decision because that's what we want to do. Make your choice and make it now! "Anyone who trusts in Him will never be put to shame." (Romans 10:11)

> "...I have placed before you an open door that no one can shut."

~Revelation 3:8

▐ **WATCH OUT!**

*"Watch your life and doctrine closely. Persevere in them,*
*because if you do, you will save both yourself and your hearers."*

~1 Timothy 4:16

He had known what he was supposed to, but he didn't check his brakes before he took his loaded truck down the hill. It resulted in damage to many vehicles and the death of a young man as the momentum of his vehicle carried him into disaster. Some say it was a serious mistake of judgment that caused a series of tragic events. Some say that the mistake was simple neglect that could have been avoided had he taken a few moments to examine his brakes. He had driven his truck for many years over many kilometres and had never had a problem before. The lesson is: be on guard. You never know when the unplanned will break into your life. Success may be our regular routine but it's the surprises that can throw a wrench into our experiences.

This is true in the spiritual sense, as well. The writer of Proverbs reminds us: "Above all else, guard your heart, for it is the wellspring of life" (Proverbs 4:23). There may be some things that we can let slide and catch up to later on, but the condition of the heart needs constant maintenance. That's why we are admonished by the words "Above all else." We need to establish some priorities, and caring for the heart has got to be near the top of the list. Some terrible tragedies can occur if we neglect our responsibility in the welfare of our hearts.

Where we are in our relationship with God will be reflected in how we face the situations of life. Reading His Word, waiting in His presence in prayer, fellowshipping with other believers and being obedient to do His will are exercises that benefit a healthy heart. We need to guard those moments and plan definite periods for them within each day, or else they will be robbed from us by the "time stealers." The reason the care of the heart is so important is that it is the channel for all the rest of "who we really are." Our attitudes, our reactions, our quiet times, our focus and our dreams all have the heart as their source.

As Believers, we must be especially careful because the enemy of our souls will take advantage of our 'neglect' and sow seeds of disruption so that painful disasters occur that could affect us seriously or do damage to relationships with others around us. The key to being ready at all times is to form good habits to establish a spiritual routine that will prepare us for the 'surprises' of life.

The early "Methodists" were called that because they established personal goals that reflected a real method in their service to God. Their routines may have bordered on strict obedience to rules and regulations, but they saw this as their personal goal to keep themselves growing in spiritual matters. That's being "on guard," and it's a worthy example to follow.

184

| **Summertime**

> *"I said, 'Oh, that I had the wings of a dove!*
> *I would fly away and be at rest... "*

~Psalm 55:6

They call the hot days "the lazy, hazy, crazy days of summer." For many, it's holiday time and a great time to unwind and get away from it all. We've all heard of the person who is called a workaholic. They have trouble leaving their work at the office and sometimes they will be found sacrificing family time to stay at the office. Perhaps their feeling is: "This place would fall apart without me." The truth is, that is very unlikely.

On one occasion Jesus said to His disciples, "'Come with me by yourselves to a quiet place and get some rest.' So they went away by themselves in a boat to a solitary place." (Mark 6:31a-32) Jesus knew that they needed to get away from it all. The solitary place is not a lonely location. It's a place where the stresses of life and normal duties and responsibilities are left behind. Jesus knew that His disciples needed that kind of arrangement for a while. If there is anyone who knows the importance of holidays, it ought to be the One who designed us in the beginning. Rest was His idea, and there are a number of benefits that result from 'taking time off.'

Let me suggest a few:

1.   *The rest will do you good.* Everyone needs to be relieved of the common pressures we all face and that takes time. Don't think that a weekend away is going to be enough time to unwind. If you are anything like me it takes two or three days before you can relax. A holiday is designed to refresh you and to renew your energies and strength. Setting aside your routine cares for a change of pace will serve you well. It's like 'charging up your batteries' for future needs.

2.   *The rest will do everyone else good.* You will find that when you have time to relax and take it easy that you are a better person to be with. Relationships are strengthened and attitude changes toward difficult situations will give you an opportunity to view things from a different perspective. People will notice that difference and be affected by YOUR rest.

3.   *The rest will do your family good.* Some of the best memories of childhood will be of the times together as a family. Those are the times when you do things together. You laugh together. You become a full-time, twenty-four-hour-a-day parent for a number of days, away from the pressures of schedules and work-related responsibilities. Just spending the time together sharing a relaxed stretch of your busy life will add blessing to the whole family.

Let me add one more thing. *Don't forget to take God on your vacation!* Share a devotional time together. Find a Church to take in a morning service. Sing-a-long as you travel the highways. God will add His blessings to your life as you do. Happy holidays to all that are going to be away during the summer *dazes.*

▌ **RIGHTS AND RESPONSIBILITIES**

*"For we are God's workmanship, created in Christ Jesus to do good*
*works, which God prepared in advance for us to do."*

~Ephesians 2:10

We take many things for granted. At the same time, we know our freedoms and rights but are not as clear on our duties and responsibilities. Truthfully, one of our self-appointed freedoms is, "we don't have to do anything if we don't want to and there's nothing you can do about it."

This is not intended to be an exposition of my knowledge of civil law, but I think I can speak from experience to tell you that people who live claiming their rights but are not willing to do what their duty requires will soon lose their freedoms.

History dictates the stories of individuals and nations that have tried to live above the law of the conscience and have paid severe consequences. Once in awhile we need to take account of our own actions and measure them in the light of the Word of God. This is the standard that was established to keep us in a proper balance of which freedoms we have inherited and what we must do to maintain them in order to pass them on to the next generation. When the Bible reminds us that it is not sufficient to be hearers only of the Word but doers as well, we need to accept that as more than simply good advice. It is a rule. We often stop at the blessing of hearing messages, sermons and words of counsel and neglect to follow through with the practical aspects of what we have heard.

It happened in Jesus' day, and the hearts and attitudes of people haven't changed very much since then. He had multitudes that followed Him to hear Him speak, but when He came to the message of being a "cross–bearer" in order to follow Him, it wasn't long before His congregation disappeared. Doing the uncomfortable, or, for that matter, anything that requires a little bit of effort, somehow loses the "call of the Spirit" on our human nature.

Let me tell you that there is a definite reward to those who obey His direction. Not everything that the Christian is called to do is done on our knees or "in the Spirit." Some things need to be accomplished by a combination of faith and determination. It becomes a process of learning the principles of His Word and becoming obedient servants to do what He wants us to do. Let me tell you again, we know that heaven awaits those who have accepted Jesus Christ as Lord and Saviour—we know that we are "now" the sons of God and that eternity awaits us—but what should be the duties that we fulfill in order to pass those blessings on to others? I've heard it said that once you accept the Lord it doesn't matter what you do because you have a sure reward and home in heaven. That sounds like, "Come to the Lord, live like the devil and you'll go to heaven." I don't think so! His rewards are for faithfulness, not sloth or neglect, and that means that I exercise my faith to honour Him by doing things that demonstrate my gratitude for the liberties that He has given to me.

186

❚ **GOD IS IN CONTROL**

> *"'Do not be afraid of them, for I am with you and will rescue you,'*
> *declares the LORD."*

~Jeremiah 1:8

For all those who know that Jesus is in absolute control, there is peace in the midst of the storm. Perhaps we are alike, though. I look at everything that is around me and I struggle with the doubt, occasionally, that things have really gotten out of control. I wonder, sometimes, is it possible that the silence of the Captain is indicating that He may not be aware that things are as rough as they are? Well, if He wasn't in the boat with me, as He promised, that could be true; but His Word has assured me that He is with me at all times.

I think every one of us has a little bit of the 'back seat driver' syndrome. We want to tell the Lord how fast to take the curves and to watch out for the crazy drivers. We want to tell Him to slow down and watch out for the bumps in the road. We want to tell Him to move faster 'cause we're in a hurry. And the list goes on. He probably likes our input in these matters of life as much as you like someone else in your vehicle telling you how to drive your car. Do you know what I mean?

I know He has a lot more patience with us than we have with others who always seem to have a better idea or a better way. Hey, God is in control! I said, *"God is in control!"* He's an expert at all the traffic problems of our life's journey. He knows exactly how much a "vehicle" can take and what it was designed for. He knows where and how soon we will arrive at the destination if we continue at His speed. He may take an occasional detour along the route, but rest assured, He knows what He is doing. We need to trust Him.

By the way, we're not just going along for the ride. He does appreciate our company and fellowship as long as we don't get to criticizing and bickering like little children in the back seat. Conversation with Him along the way brings great joy to His heart. I am persuaded that He appreciates our expressions of gratitude for His faithfulness and commitment to see us through the darkest of valleys. Although we need to trust Him, I'm sure that He doesn't want us to fall asleep on the way because we might miss something that will be needed when we arrive at His house.

I've also noticed that He does have ways of making our journey exciting. It's in those exciting, scary times that I am especially grateful that He is in control. I know that when we arrive at the end of the road we'll look back and acknowledge that the trip was anything but boring. I have sometimes wished for a direct route to the Divine destination and I often wonder why the scenic route has to take so much of my time. Because He is the "Captain of my Salvation," every moment of the journey is important to Him and not designed just to fill in time. God's love for each of us is absolutely amazing. Even though there are billions of inhabitants on this earth, He has a special, particular road plan and purpose for you. Will you pledge with me to let Him have more control than ever before? I think I see the end of the road just up ahead!

▌ **GODLINESS WITH CONTENTMENT**

*"But godliness with contentment is great gain."*

~1 Timothy 6:6

True godliness can simply be described as 'God-like-ness.' It is a virtue that most of us do not have, naturally. However, it remains a goal that we strive for. The truth is that we begin the journey toward having His likeness observable in our daily living by coming to the cross and making the decision to allow changes to be made in our lives. There is no other place to begin. Every one of us needs to start at that point and make the determination to allow the Lord to deal with the things of our past.

From there we need to move on to a willingness to allow the Holy Spirit to teach us how to become more like Jesus. His inner promptings will speak a new direction into many of the areas of our daily routine that will demonstrate that God is at work in our hearts. For some people it is a simple task of willing surrender to please God. To others of us it is daily struggle with matters that want to keep us back in the old life and the old ways that were not at all pleasing to God. There still remains the partnership of "working together with God" so that the transformation be worked in our lives. We all begin the road to God-likeness at the same point and we all need to check ourselves, from time to time, to assess our progress. At all times we must remember that God loves us more than anything else in the world and is available to guide us into making the right choices for our lives.

You've noticed that the verse quoted above connects godliness to our attitude. This brings us to contentment. Godliness is a great treasure. Add to that the grace of contentment and you are a wealthy person. Contentment is another expression of peaceful gratitude. It is gratefully appreciating what God has already done, where He has placed us and what He has provided for us. Absent are the characteristics of impatience, envy, jealousy and bitterness. Prominent is the joy of knowing that our lives are in His hands and that He remains a faithful supplier for all of our needs. Someone has said, "Even on the worst day of my life, I am blessed!" That's the key to contentment.

God is in control! If He wanted other things for my life than I am experiencing, then working through me, He would have made it so. It may not be that I receive the fulfillment of the deepest desires of my dreams, but I am His and He cares for me, therefore, I am blessed. This is a day to be thankful. Our gratitude clings to the fact that God, out of His deep love for us, has called us to Himself to be part of His heavenly family, and that He is pleased to work His purposes in our lives. One day, greater than our fondest dreams, God will bring us to a place where all discomfort and personal need will be resolved as we stand in His presence. Until then, "Give thanks in all circumstances, for this is God's will for you in Christ Jesus" (1 Thessalonians 5:18).

█ **FELLOWSHIP WITH MAN**

*"Dear friends, let us love one another, for love comes from God."*

~1 John 4:7a

The Greek word *Koinonia* is used sixteen times in the New Testament. It speaks of 'fellowship' as in a close relationship with those you greatly appreciate. It was part of the lifestyle that existed in the early Church and was one of the marks that identified the Christians as being distinct from the world. "By this all men will know that you are my disciples if you love one another" (John 13:35).

Someone has said, "How can I love my 'brother' if I don't even know him?" Well, this is where it begins. At some point we need to meet the folk who are a part of the family of God. What better time and place than when the family gets together to worship the Father in the place of prayer?

The family of God is comprised of some very wonderful people. They come from all over the world, with various backgrounds, and each has had their own personal experience with the Lord. It's as we get to know them a little better that we begin to understand the magnitude and power of the love of God that reaches into our world to rescue us from our sins and makes us one in Christ. That is one of the reasons why we often take time during our gatherings to give people an opportunity to greet their neighbours. Some of them are shy and need us to approach them in order to break the ice. It may take a little effort to do that, but I believe that visitors will detect that we do love each other.

However, *that is only step number one.* A brief greeting is never sufficient to feel we know each other because it takes time to hear about and share our lives with each other.

*Step number two* - is what we do with our friendships after the Church service has been dismissed. There can be coffee times, lunches and dinners together, walks in the park and the camping times. All are important in developing a real sense of *Koinonia.* We've discovered that one of the important functions of the Home Bible study program in cell groups is to bring our friendships to another level of maturity. It's at Home meetings that we learn to seek the Lord together and pray for each other. It's at this level that personal concerns can be shared and carried by a smaller group of people. Once again, the early Church has set a pattern in this matter. It appears that Home prayer times were an integral part of their spiritual life.

We may meet each other as strangers, but we won't be strangers for long. As we get to know each other on a more personal level we soon discover that we are family and each member is very important to us. It's then that we understand that we are to bear one another's burdens because we want to care for each other. Our interest in others increases because we are cared for as well.

▌ **FELLOWSHIP WITH GOD**

*"And our fellowship is with the Father and with his Son, Jesus Christ."*

~1 John 1:3b

In God's eternal plan for His relationship with us, He has provided an opportunity to fellowship with Himself as a friend with a friend. We read about it in the book of Genesis when God came down in the cool of the day and met with Adam for their daily walk in the garden together. Those must have been very precious times of communion as God made Himself known to His creation. I'm sure, like any one of us, that there were a lot of questions on Adam's bright, pure mind. We don't know how long this personal friendship continued because there were no calendars in those days. Time was almost irrelevant until the day Adam stood beside his wife under the shade of the tree of the knowledge of good and evil and reached out his hand to take the forbidden fruit. He had been warned that his disobedience would be an act of suicide. He did not die physically, but the desire to meet with God suddenly vanished. Fear filled his heart. He did what many of us do when we are caught in our wrong choices; he blamed someone else for his actions. What he did not understand was that he had died spiritually. He stepped out of the protection of God by his disobedience, and stepped under the dominion of the evil ruler of darkness. His free will was not altered, but Satan had deceived him and robbed him of the position of authority that Adam once possessed as God's representative on the earth. That was then.

On the Cross, Jesus took the judgment of the sins of mankind upon himself. In His death as our substitute He paid the penalty that should have been ours so that we could come to God as did the very first Adam in Eden. The opportunity to have a restored relationship with God has been extended to all men. The offer is made to all freely as God's gift through His Son, but it does not happen automatically. Each of us must make our own choice to either return to God's plan as in the beginning and enjoy fellowship with Him, or to remain under the canopy of the god of this world. It seems foolish to even suggest that there is an alternative to serving God and fellowshipping with Him. Anyone can see, in the world around us, that any other choice is suicidal. We and our families need God's forgiveness and His protection against the evils that inhabit our world today.

God extends His love toward us with a Divine welcome to leave behind our guilt and condemnation in order to enjoy the peace of sins forgiven and the rich promise of heaven as our home. Even now God bestows upon us His wonderful blessings through the precious work of the Holy Spirit. Let's learn to acknowledge that God has done so much for us through His wonderful Son, Jesus.

**LET THE NATIONS KNOW**

*"Make known among the nations what he has done..."*

~Isaiah 12:4b

From the beginning of His revelation of Himself in the book of Genesis, God is known as the powerful Creator who calls into existence, from nothing, all that we see today. The world was designed as a beautiful island in the vastness of the universe where the stage was set for man to grow into a personal relationship with God.

The theory that man has developed by a series of fortunate accidents—from a fleck of dust that self-adjusted into becoming a human being—is absolutely preposterous. God has made us in a fearful and wonderful way. There is no question in my mind but that, in God's sight, the greatest thing He ever created was Man.

There is a difference. Everything else in all of creation turns and functions according to laws that govern orbits and conditions; but man was brought into existence with a free will to make decisions and choices. God has entrusted to us the sacred privilege of choosing the direction of our personal orbits of life. That is to say, we can accept His rules and laws and function in the way He wants us to, or we can break His rules and laws and move in different circles than He has designed for us. Nothing else in all of creation can do that.

Unfortunately, we see the effects some of our wrong choices have had upon our personal lives. The heartaches, diseases, catastrophes, plagues and pressures of life are all the result of moving in the wrong circles where sometimes even the innocents suffer the consequences.

Somehow, it must be made known to the nations that what is acceptable in our world today is not always pleasing to God. Jesus came into the world to reveal the insights of the Father in heaven so that we would not be conformed to this world. His death on the cross was to give us a new opportunity to begin again; to do the Father's will by our own choice.

Throughout the generations, He has been calling mankind to return to Himself and to submit to His Rulership. He has been both patient and faithful because He does not want to lose even one person. Each is of inestimable value to Him. He loves ALL of us in a way that is beyond satisfactory explanation. Once we've committed ourselves to serving Him the way we were designed to do from the beginning, we soon understand that one of the duties or privileges that we have is to become a roadblock to others who are on the road to destruction through their disobedience. There are many out there who are ignorant of the perils of their choices, and they need to be told. That's what Missions and Evangelism is all about. Tell the nations. Call them back to God. He has done marvellous things in answer to prayer.

▌ **FAITH ALIVE**

*"Show me your faith without deeds and I will show you my faith by what I do."*

~James 2:18b

Centuries of reformation battles have argued the intent of these words. Some have said that James was adding the need of works to the gift of God's grace in order to be saved. I don't think the matter of Salvation is even a part of this discussion. What I hear James saying to the Church is, "If you are saved by faith then that same faith should be seen in the things that you do."

Jesus put it another way. He said, "By their fruit you will recognize them" (Matthew 7:16a). My personal interpretation would be something like, 'what you've got inside should be demonstrated on the outside.' James adds strength to the statement: "... faith by itself... is dead" (James 2:17).

You see, our faith in God should be reflected by the things we say and don't say; by the things we do and don't do; by how we treat people or don't treat them. If no one can tell that there is something different about us, then there is something wrong. Faith in God becomes a lifestyle. Besides, the joy we have being in relationship with an Awesome God is balanced by the sense of duty to serve Him faithfully under all circumstances.

Here's a Biblical example. Peter and John were taken to court because of the overflow of their faith to the people in Jerusalem. After a lengthy examination it was determined that these were ordinary (like us), uneducated (like us) people, but, "they took note that these men had been with Jesus"(Acts 4:13b). Besides all the stuff that made them so much like any of us, what was the observable difference that amazed their critics? I can only surmise that when they were being judged, there was Peace on their countenance and an obvious expression of Wisdom in their words. I'm sure that they responded firmly, but in love; that there was a confidence in their faith as they declared what God had done and what they had personally witnessed. God is to be honoured because it is God who answers prayer and who heals the sick today. Their reactions made them appear to be just like Jesus.

I wonder if the Sanhedrin judges were shocked to see others that were exact replicas of the man they had condemned to death on an old rugged cross just months before. Would they be able to understand that the resurrected Jesus was alive and living in the hearts of His followers?

Now that's the demonstration of real faith that James is talking about. What would Jesus do if He worked where you work, lived where you live, met the people you meet and worshipped where you worship?

Let's exercise our faith and strive to be more like Jesus.

JULY 11 | **WORN AND WEARY**

*"I am worn out calling for help; my throat is parched.
My eyes fail, looking for my God."*

~Psalm 69:3

Take heart! Although He is Divine, Jesus knows what humanity is all about. During His earthly sojourn two millennia ago, He went through some of the same kinds of situations that you and I experience. The writer of the book of Hebrews states that He, "has been tempted in every way, just as we are—yet was without sin" (Hebrews 4:15b). He felt the limitations that hold us prisoners to our human frame. He knew what weariness was all about.

When Jesus and His disciples arrived at the well at Sychar He stayed to rest and relax while His friends went to get something to eat. The record says, "Jesus, tired as He was from the journey, sat down by the well" (John 4:6). Besides the matter of sticking together for security while they traveled in Samaria, they realized that there were special stresses upon Jesus that were greater than the average. It showed upon His body. One of His critics commented one day, "You are not yet fifty years old" (John 8:57). Well, you know the truth. He was just a little more than thirty years old, but looking at Him one would have guessed that the stresses that He felt added twenty years to His physical frame. Possibly the wear and tear of His ministry had left their mark on His outward appearance with lines of concern and compassion upon His face and a weariness in His walk.

Some of the pressures that He went through were mental and spiritual demands that took their toll on His energy. For example, He understood, by experience, what it feels like to be despised and persecuted when His intentions were to do good. He knew that some people hung around just to catch Him in disagreement over something that He said. He knew what it was like to be watched with a critical eye and for some to condemn Him as being the prince of devils when He was sharing the blessing of the Life and Power of God. To some in the crowds He was treated as the King in waiting, while others looked at Him with suspicion and fear. He knew how to handle the successful moments of life as well as the disappointments, but it all took a toll upon His humanity. He tasted what it is like to live as a human being.

What inspired Him to keep on in spite of the negative drag on His life? I believe there is one clear message to all of us. By experience, He understands how you feel. When you know you are doing what God wants you to do—when you are being what God created you to be—then you need to trust and find your approval in Him. Jesus relied on doing the will of the Father is spite of His physical limitations and the outward conflicts that waged against His soul. That truth was like food to His soul. I believe there are many living today who go through some of the same kinds of situations in life who will one day hear our Father in heaven say, "This is my beloved son in whom I am well pleased." I believe the end of the journey is not too far away.

Let's be renewed in His presence and get back to doing what pleases Him.

193

▎ **MISSIONS**

*"Therefore go and make disciples of all nations..."*

~Matthew 28:19

Missionaries are very human, like the rest of us, but they have a very special call upon their lives. Each time I hear one speaking and challenging our hearts I believe we are hearing the matter that makes the heart of God tick. After all, that is the main reason Jesus came into the world in the first place. He was interested in the lost souls of men all over the world who were dying without hope. Many are entangled in the bondages of the enemy who holds their lives in addictions, in diseases, in fear and torments. Let your heart be wide open to the messages of the missionaries of our time. Hear what burdens them in their ministry. Feel the unfinished challenges that carry them back to other parts of the world in obedience to the call of the Lord of the Vineyard. Capture the confidence of these loyal 'soldiers of the cross' as they lift up the gospel message in areas that have not heard the good news before. Some of you may hear the summons of the Lord calling you into fulltime service to a foreign land. Others may be challenged to serve the Lord in a new way through prayer, upholding the hands of those who are on the front lines of ministry. Others will feel the tug to give financially to our Missions programs in a more faithful manner.

Let each of our hearts be challenged with the urgency of the hour, because Jesus is coming soon and the harvest is not completed. We can share in the gathering of lost souls as we are faithful to be involved in some area of Missions. We may not stand on the front lines of ministry but we are equally a part of the outreach as we go, give and pray. When the Lord returns may He find us faithful to the commission to "Go into all the World."

Missions and outreach programs are what gives the Church strength and vitality. A lively congregation grows on the vision of reaching the lost while the opportunity still exists. We need to tell the story of God's love and expect that hearts and lives will respond to the message. We need to believe that God will quicken the Word that is shared and begin a transformation in the lives of the hearers that will lead them to know the Lord as their personal Saviour.

The early Church was scattered abroad by persecutions, but they moved from place to place with an enthusiasm of God's love to reach others. Each generation since then that has made "outreach" their purpose has prospered in blessing. Let's not let the past generation down, but maintain an increasingly greater enthusiasm for our common outreach ministry. The best way to receive blessing is to do what God wants us to do. Jesus said, "I tell you, open your eyes and look at the fields! They are ripe for harvest" (John 4:35).

▌ **SHARE A LITTLE LOVE**

*"But the greatest of these is love."*

~1 Corinthians 13:13b

How wonderful it is that we were created with the capacity to love. It is a part of the nature of God that He has committed, in trust, to His creation. We have inherited so many bad characteristics from our human nature that have brought nothing but pain and distress to our world. The fact that we can exercise love is evidence that God wants something of Himself to be seen in all of us.

Loving is a choice that we must make on a regular basis. It needs to be exercised particularly in difficult situations when the pressure is on and tempers are flaring. It seems strange to introduce such a special quality of Divine nature into the "ugly" of life, but that's exactly what Jesus came to do. He not only taught about love but He lived it. To the sick and diseased, to the poor and downtrodden, to the one caught in the very act of sin, Jesus practiced what He preached and demonstrated sincere concern, patience and forgiveness. He brought a piece of Heaven to the rougher areas of the world because that was what God was like.

There is a very special privilege that we all, particularly those who know the Lord, must exercise. We need to redirect our thoughts and actions to demonstrate that we are created to be channels of the Love of God. It is easy in the romantic setting of a Valentine's dinner, but we squelch when a real demonstration of love means to take out the garbage, help someone with their coat or open the car door for them.

Someone has said, "True charity begins at home." The fact is that one of the greatest opportunities to show love to the world is to live and encourage the practical expressions of love in the home. We used to feel that a man's pride was in his ability to be in control and be stoically emotionless in relationships. But true strength is in the ability to exercise love in a healthy fashion. One of the deepest revelations of the concern of God in His love for mankind is recorded in the shortest verse of the Bible. "Jesus wept." He wasn't afraid to show his emotions in public. Those who were standing there said, "See how He loved him" (John 11:35-36b).

Building on our love relationships is our committed duty in honouring God in our homes. Jesus charged a Church with the accusation that, "You have forsaken your first love" (Revelation 2:4). It is clear that He meant that in order to maintain a loving relationship it must be worked on. That is, when the glow of love diminishes, you can't ignore it. You need to do something about it. Walking away is never the answer because the very act of caring is the gift of God's love and that's what serving Him is all about. You can't wrap love in 'Chocolate boxes.' Love needs a human container to confirm the real meaning of love through day-to-day actions.

▌ **MADE IN GOD'S IMAGE**

*"If we have been united with him like this in his death, we will certainly also be united with him in his resurrection."*

~Romans 6:5

Consider the fact that everything that exists was made out of nothing. There are no factories on earth that can duplicate that process one more time. God simply spoke His will and His Word brought everything into existence. What a wonderful thing He did! We admire His handiwork in the sunrises and sunsets, the majesty of the mountains and the endless prairies. We stand amazed to view the starry heavens and understand that the closest star to us is 93,000,000 miles away, while the rest of the heavenly hosts are beyond that. The magnitude of it all is overwhelming. It is all beautiful to the eye and astounding to the mind. God is the initiator of it all.

But when God wanted to make something on earth that would resemble Himself, He made a man. Out of the dust and soil of the earth He fashioned the human frame and then breathed life into his nostrils. Something of the Divine was deposited into mankind that was not placed in any of the other creatures that God had made. It was this man who was designed to represent God throughout all of His creation. It was this man who was given authority to have dominion over all the things that God had made—except for the one solitary tree in the middle of the garden that was to remain under the jurisdiction of God and God alone. Everything else in the whole wide world was designated to Adam to freely use and administrate. Everything but that one single tree. In spite of all the other options, Adam and Eve stole from God's tree. They trespassed where they were not supposed to go. They blew it! The very ones who were to represent the Great Creator of all things became thieves, trespassers satisfiers of selfish desires and disobedient servants and breakers of the laws of God.

If you had someone working for you that deliberately disobeyed your instructions and stole from you, you would probably fire them immediately. You might even lay a charge against him and take him to court and have him thrown into jail. But God didn't. Sure, there were consequences to the disobedience, but God designed a way that His likeness could be restored in the lives of every man, woman and child. Jesus came into the world to replant His nature in every one of our hearts by His Spirit. Members of the early Church were called Christians because when the people watched the believers in action, they were reminded of Jesus. That's what the world needs to see again. The Church should be a body of believers who live in such a way that the world will take note that we have been with Jesus. Just as Adam's failure was his personal choice, so our returning to God must be by personal choice. It is time that we talked with the Creator and let Him know that our intention is to honour Him the rest of our lives.

▌ **THE HEART OF GOD**

> *"The LORD is good, a refuge in times of trouble.*
> *He cares for those who trust in him..."*

> ~Nahum 1:7

One of the things that is so obvious throughout the gospel accounts of Jesus' ministry is the fact that He loves people. He was moved with compassion for them. He wept for them. He ate with them in their homes and attended their funerals. He took their children upon His knees and blessed them. He healed their sick and consoled the discouraged. He knew the stresses and difficulties that were common to the average person of the day. He understood the temptations and weaknesses of humanity, but He didn't condemn any that came to Him. He accepted even the people who were societal misfits and outcasts. By contrast, the religious leaders treated the Publicans and 'sinners' as though they were a different kind of animal, while Jesus treated them as real people whom God loves.

This has always been the heart of God. He loves us. He loves you and me more than words could ever tell. He loves us in spite of our failures. He cares for us in spite of the fact that we have neglected Him and have not given Him the respect that He is worthy of. He has always wanted to give us His blessings and to demonstrate His concern for every detail of our lives.

It's interesting that we don't read anywhere in His life story that He ever had a real good laugh with His disciples concerning the events of His day. His humour was not recorded, but His concerns for the needs and the pressures of the people are often mentioned. This has not changed. To this day, the things that happen that are real concerns to us are very important to Him and no laughing matter.

But the issue that is of the greatest concern to God is to deal with the matter of Sin. I've told you already that He did not come into the world to condemn anyone. He came to provide forgiveness and pardon to anyone who calls on His name. His coming to earth was to fulfill a rescue mission that would reach the whole wide world and bring peace to the heart and soul of every man, woman and child.

This was so important to Him that He was willing to die on the cross, on our behalf, so that we could be forgiven. He stated His reasoning: "Greater love has no one than this that he lay down his life for his friends" (John 15:13). He proved this through His life and then the cruel death on the cross of Calvary. Some of His last words were spoken on our behalf. "Father, forgive them, for they know not what they are doing" (Luke 23:34).

Now He's seated on the right hand of the Father in heaven in a position of power and authority and yet He still cares for you and me.

▌ **TALKING TO STONES**

*"Do not be anxious about anything, but in everything, by prayer and petition, with thanksgiving, present your requests to God."*

~Philippians 4:6

Talking to wood and stones is a common practice in many parts of the world. I've done that occasionally, too, for example, when the nail won't stay still just as I swing the hammer. "Stupid nail!" (I'm sure that you've never done that, but I know some people who do.) However, when there are serious, troubling issues and people bow before a carved image to bare their hearts with pleas for assistance, there's something wrong with that picture.

We talk to a living God! He's the Owner and Ruler of all of creation. He can change the order of events far beyond anything that we could do for ourselves. He is the Master of resolving problems that trouble the hearts of His people. He is not like wood or stone, which have neither ears to hear nor hearts to be moved with compassion. Generations since the Garden of Eden have testified that God has heard their petitions and intervened in the matters of concern to those who reach out in prayer to trust Him. Seas have parted, storms have been calmed, the sun and moon have stood still, enemies have been defeated, fire has fallen from heaven, the sick have been healed and peace returned to troubled souls. The psalmist reminds us that, "As a father has compassion on his children so the Lord has compassion on those who fear him," and "From everlasting to everlasting the Lord's love is with those that fear him..." (Psalm 103:13, 17b). Love is the great difference that the Lord extends to those who come to Him. Needless to say a block of wood or stone will never ever give you those kinds of benefits. That's why we ought to be people of prayer. God is a living, loving God. It brings great joy to His heart that we would choose to seek Him whether it's for fellowship or because of our need. The fact that we come to Him is an acknowledgement of His Greatness.

We fail miserably when we think that we don't need to talk to Him. It appears that there are more stones in the world that get worshipful attention than the living God. "As for me and my house, we will serve the Lord." We need to plan purposeful times when we will respond to the Lord's invitation, "Come to me, all you who are weary and burdened and I will give you rest" (Matthew 11:28). Many of us have trouble focusing on the Invisible and speaking to Him as we would to a friend. However, faith overcomes our trust in our senses and brings us into the Court of the King of kings. Prayer is the key to a deeper walk with God. There is no substitute! I wonder how many things we endure because we fail to pray? I wonder what God would do if we were more diligent and "religious" about our praying?!

Lest I forget, let me remind you that one of the main purposes of prayer is to worship our Lord. Without complaint or petition we need to spend time thanking Him for His faithfulness, for His love, for His provision, for His creation, for His Son, for His promises, for His Word...and the list goes on. Prayer is a wonderful privilege that God has given to us.

▌ **GOD LOVES THE SINNER**

> *"Above all, love each other deeply,*
> *because love covers over a multitude of sins."*

~1 Peter 4:8

You've heard it said that, "God hates sin, but HE LOVES THE SINNER." That has always been a description of the heart of God. Time and time again He has been faithful to send prophets and messengers to declare this fact to each generation. From the experiences in the Garden of Eden and the days that followed the ejection from the Garden, God Himself spoke to Adam and then to his son Cain concerning the matter of sin. To the generation prior to the flood, God sent Noah, a "preacher of righteousness" (2 Peter 2:5) to warn his generation. Sodom and Gomorrah had Lot as their prophet, "living among them day after day" (2 Peter 2:8). They didn't listen, but God was faithful just the same because God is love.

The question is who is speaking for God now? Does anyone care what God is saying about sin today?

I suppose it brings us all back to self-examination and to an understanding that the Holy Spirit is at work in the hearts of men today to indicate the basic needs of the heart. Some have misunderstood what the ache inside the heart is all about and have turned to solutions in the needle or in the bottle. Others begin to occupy themselves in the pleasures of this world as though the joy and laughter of their activities will resolve the hidden turmoil inside. God is speaking to all of us, and it's time that we recognized that our world is in real need of an attitude of repentance, where we sincerely humble ourselves and seek His face.

Our world needs God! That's what Evangelism and Missions is all about. However, unless we seriously get the goods ourselves, what hope have those who do not know how to speak to God? It's a principle of scripture that our lives may be the only voices that the world will hear concerning how to reach God. It's time that every born-again child of God lived their life in such a fashion that the world would be influenced for change. It was a man of history who stated the fact that evil succeeds when good men do nothing.

We have a part in sending out the message to various areas of the world by way of the voice of people in our congregation. Whether the message is shared in far-off countries or to our next-door neighbours, it is our responsibility to let the whole world know that God loves them right where they are. It is His desire to help them face their struggles and to make them "overcomers" instead of "victims." Someone may be waiting to hear what you have to say as God speaks to your heart and you are faithful to speak to them.

▌ **DEPENDING ON OTHERS**

*"And how can they preach, unless they are sent? As it is written, 'How beautiful are the feet of those who bring good news!'"*

~Romans 10:15

It was a life or death situation. The plans were made; the men were ready; all that was necessary was to get Paul at the gate as he left the city of Damascus, where they would kill him and leave his body in the trash (Acts 9:23). That would terminate the ministry of the believers of the Way. If they could only get the Preacher, their problem would be solved.

But others had plans, too. In the darkness of the night, with ropes and a heavy woven basket, Paul was lowered down the wall to escape to freedom to continue his ministry for another day.

Obviously, he couldn't have made this escape by himself. He depended upon others to hold the ropes and gently lower him to the ground. The others are not named, but they have served as examples of the working supporters of the ministries of the Gospel through the generations. Many a godly service is dependant upon someone holding the ropes in compassionate concern that the Pastor, the Missionary or the Evangelist be granted the liberty of continuing his work.

We, too, stand on the wall as others go to foreign fields to carry the message of Salvation to the lost and dying. We stand on the wall with a firm hand on the value of intercessory prayer on the behalf of others who are carrying a message beyond our borders. We, too, stand on the wall as we give of our finances to support someone else in their service for the Lord. We are a part of the team. Failure on any one of our parts makes it difficult for the rest to fulfill their responsibilities. Willing and sometimes sacrificial effort is absolutely necessary if the task is to be completed.

It was four men who chose to make it their duty to bring their helpless friend to Jesus through the roof of the house where He was preaching.

It took thirty men to lift Jeremiah out of his private prison in a muddy cistern (Jeremiah 38:10-13).

It took an Andrew to bring a Peter to Jesus (John 1:41). It was a Barnabas who brought Paul into fellowship and into a wonderful life of ministry. Philip brought Nathaniel to meet the Lord. It was a couple of servants who brought Peter to Cornelius' house, and on and on the stories go throughout history.

The question is "How many undiscovered precious people continue on their hopeless journey through life for lack of someone to show an interest in them?"

We are a part of an important team and there are many who are counting on our support and involvement. Reach out and touch someone for Jesus!

█ **JESUS IS COMING**

*"Look, He's coming with the clouds, and every eye will see him."*

~Revelation 1:7a

Jesus said that He would be coming back again! There were reasons why it was necessary for Him to go away. He's gone to prepare a special place for each of us. He is seated at the right hand of the Father making intercession for each of us. But at the same time He promised that He would never leave us nor forsake us. That means, we will never ever be out of His thoughts.

His plan was to leave a clear representative of His kingdom on earth until He completed what He had to do. He commissioned the Church to spread the news of His love and to work for Him until He comes back again. It's true, He did not tell the day nor the hour of His reappearing, and setting dates is an absolutely foolish exercise. He expects believers to be obedient to His commission and faithful to spread the message of His offer of forgiveness and the promise of His return.

However, He did declare a number of signs that would precede His coming. Let me list a few from Matthew 24:

1.  Many will claim to be Christ (Father Divine, Jim Jones, David Koresh)
2.  There will be wars and rumours of wars.
3.  There will be famines, earthquakes...
4.  Believers will be persecuted. (try to take a stand against abortion, homosexuality or exercise freedom to read the Bible in school)
5.  Many false prophets will appear and deceive many (have you ever seen so many promotions for psychics, horoscopes and palm readers, etc.? If they can really tell the future, how come they don't win the Million dollar lotteries every week?)
6.  The love of most will grow cold (the word 'love' speaks of commitment, perseverance and loyalty.)
7.  There would be a proclamation of "Peace and Safety"...and the list goes on.

Jesus is coming back again!

a) Jesus said it and He is true to His Word.

b) The angels believed it and told the disciples that He would return just like He went away.

c) The Apostles believed it with all their heart and some of them died for proclaiming that message to a lost world.

d) Each of the New Testament books contains some reference to the blessed hope of Jesus reappearing with a tone of confidence that would cast out all doubt. He's coming back again for a people who are watching and waiting. That date could be today.

▎ **NOT UNCLEAN ANYMORE**

*"Therefore, my brothers, I want you to know that through Jesus
the forgiveness of sins is proclaimed to you."*

~Acts 13:38

It was His love for the lost that inspired His decision to leave His heavenly home to come to this world. All the beauty and splendour of His Palace and the host of attendants in their orderly function of ministry to Him could not change His mind. It was purposed that He would come to this earth—the earth that was made by His spoken word thousands of years before.

The object of His infinite interest? Me! You! Us! The reason? We needed help. That is, every one of us needed His help. You see, the sin of the garden of Eden has infected all of humanity and creation with a deadly virus. There is no earthly, scientific antidote to the plague that has befallen us. In spite of all human efforts, we have only succeeded in making a mess of our world and of our lives, and have been unable to find a human solution to the dilemma that came into existence through the bad choice of our forefathers. Add to the situation that we have compounded the problem by our neglect of God and our own subsequent bad choices. This is a general statement that fits every one of us.

Sin has done some terrible things with the minds and hearts of mankind. We have fallen short of the real purpose of our being on this beautiful planet, which was originally created for the glory of God. We need to acknowledge this as a personal fact in each of our lives. But Jesus came. He alone possesses the power and resources to deal with the Sin problems that plague our world.

His death on the cross assures us that our sins can be forgiven because: "... without the shedding of blood there is no forgiveness" (Hebrews 9:22). At each communion service we celebrate, we remember the Lord's death through the emblems of His broken body and shed blood. The cost of our salvation was paid by Christ on the cross of Calvary.

But let us remember one very important fact about the provision of His forgiveness; each of us needs to confess our sin to Him through prayer. He has been waiting for us to turn back to Him. He is prepared to give us His forgiveness and to cleanse us from the sin that has been plaguing humanity. His plan is to bring us into His Father's presence pardoned and free of condemnation. The key to the cleansing power is within us. We need to personally ask Him for forgiveness. He will wash away all the stains that have kept us from enjoying the goodness of God and fellowship with Him. Let me advise you—don't put it off. His love reaches out to you today.

■ **IT PAYS TO LISTEN**

*"He who has an ear, let him hear what the Spirit says to the Churches."*

~Revelation 2:7a

A Financial Investment Institution spent a large amount of money advertising on Television and in printed periodicals with the following main line: "When *.......* speaks, everyone listens." As you can see, this was no small boast. Their desire was to have everyone listen to their advice about making investments for the future.

I'm sure this company has a lot to contribute to novices who are searching for ways to prepare for retirement and future days of comfort and ease. There must be a lot of people using their informed counsel as they make a profitable business out of their experienced resources. "Everyone listens" is quite a statement.

But let me ask, what happens when God speaks? I wish that it were true that, "When God speaks, everyone listens!" This is a resource that we have just begun to appreciate when we come to the Lord in prayer and in the serious research of His Word.

The writer of the book of Hebrews says, "In the past God spoke to our forefathers through the prophets at many times and in various ways, but in these last days He has spoken to us by His Son, whom He appointed heir of all things, and through whom He made the universe" (Hebrews 1:1-2).

God has spoken; God is still speaking. Is anyone listening? Some have said that they have heard God speak in an audible voice. Others have said that God has spoken to them through a dream. Some have said that God used an individual to share with them and it was as though God was speaking through them.

But let me tell you the sure word of how God continues to speak to our generation. The Bible is His Word. It is the ultimate reference for what God wants to say to us today. Reading His Word gives the Holy Spirit an opportunity to make the words come to life as a personal message for each of us. The Holy Spirit works in cooperation with the written word to make the will of God known to us. The power and authority of that word will give direction, protection, encouragement and hope for our future.

God wants to make His message available to each of us for the variety of experiences that we go through each day. When we remember that God is Love, we must realize that He wants to speak to us to make His loving presence known. How much we want to hear what He has to say is determined by the amount of time that we are prepared to invest in the reading of His Word. It requires us to make time/to make the effort/to apply ourselves to listening to His voice through the written Word. God is still speaking to us, if only we will listen.

**TASTE IT AGAIN FOR THE FIRST TIME**

*"Give thanks to the LORD, call on His name;*
*make known among the nations what He has done."*

~1 Chronicles 16:8

It's a great day to be alive. We have so much to be thankful for when we review the details of our lives. Of course, there are still times when we aren't sure which direction is up, the finances cramp our dreams and the other "nitty gritty" things just don't come together the way we want, but it's still a great time to be alive. We are living on the edge of God's rich blessings and the promise is that He has more in reserve for us than we could ever imagine. Let's learn to let go of some of that stuff that makes us feel depressed and disappointed and look to the goodness of the many blessings that we share in every day. We can become indifferent to the good things that we have because they are just a part of our "normal" living. We have homes, warm beds, and special kitchen comforts that more than satisfy our daily needs. We have friends, family and good wholesome fellowship, to mention just a few of the blessings that we take for granted. Just imagine what it could be like if we had been born in some desert village where famine, AIDS and where terrorists roam freely. See, we do have a lot to be thankful for.

If we could only step out of our comfort zones, from time to time to get another "first look" at what we have become compared to where we began, I think we would have a greater appreciation of how blessed we really are.

If you know your Bible history you'll remember there was a time when the nation of Israel was taken away from their homeland to live as slaves in Babylon. After more than seventy years in captivity they were allowed to return "home." Can you imagine the joy of the return? Most of the people had been born in captivity and only heard the stories from their parents of the land that God had given to them. The old stories would tell them of the land that was flowing with milk and honey; where each family had their own home and a piece of property. What a dream! ! After days of crossing desert and wilderness they finally arrived at the row of mountains on the other side of the Jordan. Can you envision their delight when they came over the mountaintop and saw "their land" for the very first time? Listen to the words of one of those pilgrims: "When the LORD brought back the captives to Zion, we were like men who dreamed. Our mouths were filled with laughter, our tongues with songs of joy. Then it was said among the nations, 'The LORD has done great things for them.' The LORD has done great things for us and we are filled with joy" (Psalm 126:1–3).

Let me tell you once again; we need to see what God has given to us through the time of our spiritual growing as though it was for the first time. It's something worth getting excited about. We are a very privileged and blessed people!

204

**WE ARE BLESSED**

We are blessed! There is no question about it. God has been good to us. The Psalmist listed some of the reasons to praise the Lord in Psalm 103. Listen to some of them:

1. He forgives all your sins.
2. He heals all your diseases.
3. He redeems your life from the pit.
4. He crowns you with love and compassion.
5. He satisfies your desires with good things...and the list goes on!

Those who know the Lord have found that He continues to be a Friend. He's not made of stone or concrete. He is moved with compassion, He cares for our problems, our needs. There's no doubt that He's interested in every detail of our lives. "He who did not spare his own Son, but gave him up for us all—how will he not also, along with him, graciously give us all things?" (Romans 8:32). He is a loving and giving Friend, and blessing us brings Him great pleasure. We are the objects of His Divine love. When things don't go our way, rest assured He never leaves us nor forsakes us. We may not understand why some things come our way, but we can know that the heart of the Father is pained by things that hurt us and He will provide what is necessary. He is an awesome God and worthy of our praise.

## COME IN TO WORSHIP

We ought to remember that coming into God's presence is an awesome privilege. The fact that the Creator of all things would tolerate our presence is an absolute miracle. The truth is, He longs for us to meet with Him. Our times of Worship ought to leave us with a sense of His blessing, and yet, it's an honour to know that we bless God when we come together to worship Him. Can you imagine doing things for the simple fact of bringing joy to the heart of God?

Jesus said, "I always do what pleases Him." (John. 8:29) ALWAYS! We don't often think about the privilege it is to come into His Holy Presence. We gather together with other believers each Sunday to Worship Him.

1. Let us praise Him for Who He is! King of Kings and Lord of Lords; Author and Finisher of all things; the Lord God Almighty.

2. Let us praise Him for what He does! Saviour, Healer, Provider, Protector, Friend.

3. Let us praise Him because of His promises! He will never leave us nor forsake us. He will pour His Spirit upon ALL. He will be found of those who seek Him.

4. Let us praise Him that we can be a part of His Church to represent Him here on the earth; that He puts His Holy Spirit into our lives, to strengthen, to lead and to guide, and to grant special power and abilities for special situations.

**LIVING FAITH**

*"The unfolding of your words gives light:*
*it gives understanding to the simple."*

~Psalm 119:130

What is the bottom line of our FAITH? Is it based on what we "see," what we "feel" or what we "know?" Jesus expressed concern about last day Christians when He asked the question, "When the Son of Man comes, will he find faith on the earth?" Faith is a wonderful blessing that comes to us in either of 2 ways:

1. It comes as a direct gift of God, which allows us to believe for our Salvation as well as for other special miracles, or

2. It comes as a day-by-day experience of hearing the Word of Christ. (Romans 10:17)

The first process occurs when we are in a state of total dependence upon the intervention of God to help us in our inadequacy. The other puts some responsibility upon us to grow in our experience with God. We must do something. Effort and discipline are necessary to being strong in Faith.

I am dismayed at how little the average Christian is willing to invest into becoming a better disciple. The fact of the matter is that most of us feel that if God wants us in heaven He will get us there. Allow me to ask the question, "How badly do you want to assure that heaven is where you are going and that you have pleased God in the process of getting there?"

I am concerned that some very naive and innocent people are going to be deceived by someone who has a lot of good answers and does a lot of special miracles but whose goal is to lead people astray to serve false gods and arrive at false goals. Most of us would say, "Not me! He won't fool me!" but Jesus said, "For false Christs and false prophets will appear and perform signs and miracles to deceive the elect—if that were possible" (Mark 13:22).

Please let me give you some advice... Know what you believe and do not trust your feelings nor the things that you see that cause amazement. We need to get back into the Word of God. Read your Bible. Meditate upon it. Let the Word be your final standard of life for all you say and do. God is doing some very wonderful things in our world today and many are beginning to run to this place and that because of the message that God is here or there. That is exactly the kind of setting that the Enemy of our souls is waiting for. He is about to imitate a move of God with His deceiving tactics but "... we are not ignorant of his devices." Let your Faith be grounded in the Word of God and not in experiences, however great and wonderful they may be. Be strong in the Lord and don't lean on your own understanding. Let's get back to the Word of God.

206

| **STICKY FRIENDS**

> *"...there is a friend who sticks closer than a brother."*
>
> ~Proverbs 18:24b

These are the best kind of friends to have. Acquaintances are great and partners are tremendous assets but there is nothing that beats a really good friend. Perhaps our view of friendship is different in this generation than in the time that scripture was written, because almost all relationships today seem to be built on superficialities. The standard that the Bible establishes for a "friend" is clearly more exacting.

1. A friend is someone who will stand with you, through thick and thin: "a friend loves at all times" (Proverbs 17:17).

2. A friend is <u>lovingly</u> able to bring correction and reproof that is not viewed as criticism nor condemnation but as a solution to better a situation. "Wounds from a friend can be trusted but an enemy multiplies kisses" (Proverbs 27:6).

3. A friend is one who sincerely cares and always looks out for the betterment of those he loves. "...the pleasantness of one's friend springs from his earnest counsel" (Proverbs 27:9).

4. A good friend would be willing to lay down his life for his friend. (John 15:13)

It's hard to find that kind of friend today. We are all caught up in our own routines and have not worked at building the kind of relationships that the Bible speaks about. I believe that the computer generation has found faster ways of doing things and bringing solutions to life's business world, but at the cost of personal, lasting friendships. It's a fact that we need to work at this kind of inter-personal commitment. That's what kept the early Church together.

- They met together often.
- They shared meals with each other and went from house to house.
- They had confidence in those of their fellowship. They could share their deepest problems with others and have the assurance that their group of 'friends' would be available to help them through every difficult situation.
- Their intercession for each other was one of action and not just words. As the saying goes, "Words are cheap," Or, in a more colloquial way, "A friend puts his money where his mouth is."

It is interesting how often the Bible speaks about our human relationships as being a measuring rod for the depth of our relationship with God. For example: "The entire law is summed up in a single command: 'Love your neighbour as yourself'" (Galatians 5:14), and again, "For anyone who does not love his brother, whom he has seen, cannot love God, whom he has not seen" (1 John 4:20b). Let us love one another.

**CALVARY COVERS IT ALL**

*"But while he was still a long way off, his father saw him and was*
*filled with compassion for him; he ran to his son,*
*threw his arms around him and kissed him."*

~Luke 15:20

"Calvary Covers It All" was a hymn that was sung in the Church more than two generations ago. I appreciate the truth in these words as I grow in my understanding of the Grace of God that reaches out to us in our weaknesses and failures. The fact that God would extend His forgiveness to us so freely is a wonderful gift of His patience and kindness that goes beyond measure. It's as awesome as it sounds—He will never turn anyone away who sincerely seeks to be restored by His pardon. We would be fools to not take advantage of that every day, because He could return to earth at any moment to receive His own to Himself.

But let me make it clear, it is possible for a believer to sin in offending God and not seek the Lord's forgiveness, which obviously would be a very tragic mistake. Of all the people on the face of this earth we, Christians, ought to understand that God does not want His people to harbour sin or rebellion against Him and His purposes described in His Word. Can God fill a person with His presence if there is disobedience in their heart? Does His Grace reach into the lives of people who deliberately choose to do things contrary to His will and who are not willing to repent of their ways? Isn't that abusing the Grace of God, and shouldn't we expect that there will be a consequence to that kind of action?

Jesus dealt with this issue many times during His ministry. There were times when people came to Him for healing and He extended forgiveness first and then the healing afterwards. We want to switch the process around. We want to be whole to serve Him but we're not prepared to go through the process of getting right with God first. We shouldn't try to change the order. When our hearts are in a right relationship with Him, many of the difficulties that we face will lose their power and the joy of the Lord will be our strength. Allowing matters to build up walls against the Grace of God is to allow a toe-hold for the devil to climb up and rob us of the fullness of the Lord's blessings. I believe that's why there are bitter, angry, frustrated Christians today who are struggling to know the presence of God.

But God doesn't stop loving us, ever. He patiently waits until we open our hearts and dump out the garbage and allow Him to fill us and refresh us with His blessings. We've got to learn to let go of hurts and offences. We've got to turn away from things that we know are displeasing to Him. In plain and simple terms, we need to repent and seek His face. It's not too late! God wants to do more in and for us than we have begun to dream. We need to make ourselves available for His blessings.

*"Be on your guard! Be alert! You do not know when that time will come."*

~Mark 13:33

Reminiscent of the Titanic, at least 65 people lost their lives some time ago in a tragedy off the coast of Greece. Survivors said that they couldn't find the life jackets, and in the inky darkness of the stormy night, they didn't know where to go and no one was there to tell the passengers what to do. Ignorance is not bliss, as the saying goes; sometimes it's deadly. Our hearts go out to families who have lost their loved ones under such terrifying circumstances. It seems that the whole situation developed because of a total disregard for the rules and laws of the sea and a failure to heed the warnings that were planted centuries ago. There was a lighthouse on the rocks to caution of the obvious danger, but the crewmembers were busy—very busy—they were watching a football game on TV. Charges of murder were laid against the Captain and many of the crew of that vessel. Such negligence in the face of danger is criminal. They should have known better. The Captain should have left strict orders to be on guard throughout the darkness of the stormy waters. His commands should have defined the possibility of tragedy should the rules of navigation be ignored. There are no acceptable excuses because lives were lost.

Our righteous indignation boils inside at such incompetence. But hold on! I don't mean to upset the padded seats of our comfort zones as we see this kind of atrocity occurring but do you realize that this same process is happening around us every day because we are not sounding out a warning with clarity to our own generation? Souls are dying without hope, and few are weeping over the tremendous tragedy of the loss of so many lives. The ignorance of many and the wilful disobedience of others is going to have terrible consequences. Now, I know that there is no way that any one of us could get the job done by ourselves, but somehow we need to realize the importance of doing what we can to get the message out. "This ship is sinking and it's soon going to be all over."

There is some good news in spite of all the bad news. God is love. He has designed a plan that will rescue every passenger riding the face of this planet. He has sent a life preserver Who is capable of saving those who reach out to Him. Jesus came to seek and to save that which was lost. He did not come into the world to condemn the world but to save the world through Him. (John 3:17) That message has got to get out. We need to live our lives in such a fashion that men and women who are in the area of our influence will see the difference that the Lord has made in us, and then we need to let them know how it happened. God, indeed, has a wonderful plan for each of our lives and that includes having the security of His kind provisions for His blessing upon us, forever.

**BELIEVING WITH CONFIDENCE**

*"Because you have seen me, you have believed;*
*blessed are those who have not seen and yet have believed."*

~John 20:29

There was a time when almost everyone believed that the oceans beyond the western horizons dropped off to nothing. However, Christopher Columbus was sure that the world was round and he set out to prove his point. His crew was not always convinced of his sanity and almost persuaded him to return to Spain. But then, you know the rest of the story.

We look back and remember that we too, have crossed a new frontier, past the date of Y2K of the doomsday prophets and into a brand new millennium. Like Columbus, we passed into the unknown to chart our course where no one had ever gone before. I'm sure that each day of our future will carry similarities to each day of the past and that life will go on as "normal" as could ever be expected. The transition from the 1900's to the 2000's does remind us that time is marching on and that we have been privileged to live at a time of history that has brought the world through some tremendous technological advances. Scientists have learned how to map the genetic code of living things and are working toward reproducing mankind from a single cell. They are now exploring how to create life.

Let me remind you that there is one very special dramatic change that is soon about to take place that is often mentioned in scripture. *Jesus is coming back again.* Some may make light of it because He has delayed His return these last 2000 years, but I would like to restate what the Bible clearly expresses concerning this matter.

1. Jesus said that He would come back again. He said that it was necessary that He go away but that He would return and "catch" us to Himself. (John 14:1–4)

2. The Angels said that He would come back again. They said, "This same Jesus which is taken from you up into heaven shall come again in like manner as you have seen Him go up into heaven" (Acts 1:11).

3. The apostles preached that He was coming back again and were willing to lay down their lives because they sincerely believed it. Throughout their letters they remind the believers that Jesus is coming back again.

4. The signs that point to His return are being fulfilled in our time. The Bible teaches that the Lord would give warning signs to let us know when He is about to return. Many of these signs have been fulfilled already and others are seen as coming to pass.

This may sound like a crazy idea to some, but those who have trusted in the Saviour, until now, will not be taken by surprise. He is coming back again. What a change that will make for all of us. Be Ready!

▮ **MAKING WISE INVESTMENTS**

*"Dear friend, I pray that you may enjoy good health and that all may go well with you, even as your soul is getting along well."*

~3 John 1:2

I didn't mean to spoil his day, but I knew a little about his finances and the limitations that his income could provide for the needs of his family. He drove up to the Church in a huge, old Cadillac (about the size of a Boxcar). "God gave me this Cadillac," he bragged, meaning 'he got a good deal'.

Pardon me, but I admit my response was not very gracious. "I'm glad that God did not give me that Cadillac." The truth was, I knew that I could not afford the gas bill that the machine needed to keep it running. A couple of weeks later he decided the same. Was that really God's gift to him? And aren't you glad that God doesn't answer all our prayers the way we want?

Listen to me carefully. I believe that God wants us to be wise stewards of our finances. He has given us the ability to choose between our foolish wants and our real needs. Most of us have a wife/husband/father/mother or good friend who can help us assess the things that we think are really important and would be happy to advise us on the wisdom of our choices.

But it is God who is most interested in seeing us prosper because we learn to make wise choices. As a matter of fact, He has designed some guidelines to help us make proper investments. For example, He said, "'Bring the whole tithe into the storehouse, that there may be food in my house. Test me in this,' says the LORD Almighty, 'and see if I will not throw open the floodgates of heaven and pour out so much blessing that you will not have room enough for it'" (Malachi 3:10).

I don't think that anyone is more committed to bringing blessing to us than our Heavenly Father. I know that if He said He would bless those who follow His advice then He WILL.

We sometimes struggle to believe and practice the principle of tithing. God knows that. He is aware that we feel more comfortable with a dollar in our hand than holding on to 'a promise of blessing' that we cannot see. For that reason He said, *"Test me in this."* The real test of tithing is whether we can trust God or not. Let me tell you from experience that when we obey God, He does some very wonderful things for us that we could never have even dreamed about. He is Faithful.

He said, "Bring the whole tithe into the storehouse." The Jewish people of that day had no difficulty with that. The 'storehouse' is where you worship. There were rooms in the temple that were reserved to receive the tithes and offerings to be used in the services of the Temple and the maintenance of the Priesthood. But it was given as an offering to God. He is the One who returns the Blessings for those who are faithful to obey His command.

█ **BE WISE**

*"For in Him we live and move and have our being..."*

~Acts 17:28a

It is very foolish to not fear God. The Bible teaches us that "the fear of the Lord is the beginning of wisdom, and the knowledge of the Holy One is understanding" (Proverbs 9:10). It is wise to remember God and to reverence Him. After all, everywhere you walk, all the air you breathe, all the water you drink and all the food you eat belongs to Him. He could arrange to keep you from enjoying the things that He has made by His simple, spoken Word. We ought to live in appreciation of His kindness and in total respect for Who He is, for He is the Most High God.

I'm grateful for His willingness to allow a lot of these things to be so freely shared with each of us here in Canada. However, I can't take liberties to focus selfishly upon the abundance about me to the disregard of the title of ownership that belongs to Him, alone. All of creation speaks of His power, glory and wisdom in ways that even the wayward, worldly person can understand.

I need to remember, as well, that I will be held accountable on the Day of Judgment for how I have treated the life He has given me. He is the Owner of that, as well. In all that I think and do I use the faculties that He has given to me. I may not possess the talents and abilities that I see in others but that does not change the fact that I eventually have to tell Him what deeds I've done in the body that He has loaned to me.

I need to reverently, before God, acknowledge daily that my life is in His hands. The principle of fear is not the terror of thinking of Him as being a monster God, but rather the clear understanding that our God is an awesome God, Majestic and Powerful, but also Loving, Gentle and Kind. The very fact that He has patience with me, knowing who I am, ought to stir my respect for Him. This is the beginning of wisdom.

Did you notice that it is the "beginning" of wisdom? The end, obviously, will be the result of the choices I make at the beginning. Once I'm on track with a clear understanding of Who God is and I begin to serve Him faithfully, there will automatically be some changes along the way. For one thing, the destination of my eternity will change (from Hell to Heaven). For another, my value system will change (spiritual matters become more important than the material). And again, who I am will change (I become the habitation of the Holy Spirit, with authority to be called a Son of God).

Make the choice to respect and honour the Lord in all your ways throughout your daily routine. This is something that you have the ability to do that will bring great joy to His heart. Besides, He grants great blessings to those who put their trust in Him.

▐ **IN REMEMBRANCE**

*"But thanks be to God, who always leads us in triumphal procession
in Christ and through us spreads everywhere the
fragrance of the knowledge of him."*

~2 Corinthians 2:14

There are famous battlefields on every continent. Hardly has a generation been without the threat of war in some parts of the world. Today, we are saddened by the visual scenes of conflict in distant foreign countries on our television screen. We sorrow at the thought of the brutality and greed of the human heart and the lack of compassion for the innocent ones caught in a war that they did not invite. Remembrance Day (or Veterans Day) has been set aside to remember those of our own country who stood for the causes of justice and freedom and were willing to lay down their lives for these basic principles. As young men and women they stood on the front lines and saw what a real war is all about. We owe them a debt of gratitude.

At the same time, we need to be aware that a war of a different kind has been raging across the world in waves of iniquity for centuries. Sin abounds on every hand as mankind is swept onward in a tide of despair. But Jesus came! He came to take away the power of the enemy through His precious blood on the cross of Calvary. The tool that the enemy uses is sin. If he can influence anyone to succumb to temptation and to disobey the will and purposes of the Lord, he gains an advantage in the battle. His strength is in the fact that our guilt would drive us away from the God of love and leave us lost in enemy territory.

However, when Jesus took our place, He successfully provided the only cleansing agent that effectively cancels all sin. That leaves the enemy with no options to defeat us. We are cleansed by the Blood of the Lamb. We remain a part of the family of God, adopted by the Father, with title power that is superior to any guise or snare that the enemy may use against us. For us, the Battle is over. It was won on the old 'rugged cross,' a strange battlefield, where all the frailties and failures of men were heaped on the Son of God. He took care of them all.

If there is something brewing in your own heart that you know is not right, let me advise you to come by prayer and confess it to the Lord. There is absolutely no reason under heaven why you can't live in the victory of the cross. You were not designed to live with guilt and condemnation, but rather, to be full of the joy of the Holy Spirit (Romans 14:17). Please, please do not be satisfied with anything less than being right with God. After all, the battle is over and we are made "Overcomers" by the blood of the Lamb and the word of our testimony. Claim your freedom in Jesus' name.

**GOD LOVES**

*"If anyone says, 'I love God,' yet hates his brother, he is a liar.*
*For anyone who does not love his brother, whom he has seen,*
*cannot love God, whom he has not seen."*

~1 John 4:20

At a demonstration in Ottawa, the sign was clear and was obviously intended to be read by national and international television viewers: "God hates fags." I took exception because it is not true; God does not hate fags. Never, ever does the Bible speak that way about homosexuals. I confess that I personally have trouble with that kind of lifestyle, and I am aware that it appears that one of the principle reasons for the destruction of Sodom and Gomorra was the persistence of the people of those cities to permit homosexuality within their borders. Even so, I am still persuaded that God doesn't hate fags. Yes, what they do is an offence against God like every other sin that we could list. God does hate sin, but He loves people in spite of their sin. For that reason the Gospel message of His love and forgiveness reaches out to all who have done things that displease Him. He gives us all an invitation and opportunity to turn from our wicked ways and to do the things that please Him. He does not come to us in hate; never, ever. It is obvious that He cares very much about all of us. Again and again, He extends an invitation—draw near to Him and He will draw near to us; seek His face and He will be found; call upon Him and He will hear.

It is very unfortunate that we can not grasp the depth of God's marvellous love. We are very quick to expect God's judgment to fall on everyone who does things that offend God. I, for one, am very grateful that God is patient and merciful to all who have failed Him or else there would be no one in heaven.

Let me show you something:

Manasseh of 2 Chronicles 33 is noted as being the most vile, wicked, perverse, brutal king of Judah. The things that he did in his lifetime are listed as a living indictment against him. His crimes knew no boundary. But he repented (2 Chronicles 33:12-13), and God forgave him and restored him to his throne as King in Judah because he humbled himself.

To get back to the topic we introduced at the beginning, I believe there is hope for every sinner. Our Lord is a God of love and is able to save "completely those who come to God through him, [Jesus] because he always lives to intercede for them" (Hebrews 7:25). Jesus is on our side to help us to come to the Father.

Although God loves us just as we are, He is not prepared to leave us just as we are. His plan is to change us and to deal with the issues that displease Him whatever the matter might be. But remember, He always does it in LOVE.

▌ **WHEN HURTS REALLY HURT**

*"For in the day of trouble he will keep me safe in his dwelling; he will hide me in the shelter of his tabernacle and set me high upon a rock."*

~Psalm 27:5

When the news of the death of John the Baptist was brought to Jesus, the story tells us that He "withdrew by boat privately to a solitary place" (Matthew 14:13a). We all occasionally need quiet times in quiet places in our lives. I'm sure that the sorrow over the loss of a very powerful voice for the kingdom of God on earth was heavy upon His heart. The fact that another terrible injustice had touched the life of a wonderful servant of God, whose sole desire was to be no more than a steady, consistent voice in our world, made that loss so much greater. Hey, listen, bad things sometimes happen to good people. I guess you've discovered that already. How we handle our hurts and disappointments demonstrates the measure of trust and confidence we have in God. In some cases, it would be so much easier to take things into our own hands and try to do something about it as we judge best, but that is only one way to work towards a solution. Another way is the process that Jesus used: He just stepped back for a season of solitude and then came right back to do what He was sent to do. Things may never change around us, to our satisfaction, but we need to get it clear in our hearts and minds that God wants to use our lives in spite of everything else, and then we need to get back to doing what we know He wants us to do.

The passage we quoted above goes on to say that Jesus saw a great multitude, "and was moved with compassion." To Him, it was time to get back to work. There were people out there who were looking for someone to care for them. It wasn't time to bemoan that He, also, was hurting—that He, too, could not reconcile the injustices around Him with the final purpose and will of God. His focus turned out from Himself toward the needs of others.

In this way, Jesus established a pattern for the Church. The fact that there will always be problems in the Church is based on the fact that the Church is made up of very human and ordinary people. It is when we look at the needs of those around us and get involved in reaching out to those that need the Lord that the problems inside the Church fade into insignificance. If we resist the Holy Spirit's prompting to be a caring people, we'll become introverted and possessed by our own problems.

That's what kept Jesus' ministry so alive and vibrant; He didn't let persecution and problems hinder the direction of His life. He was prepared to do the Father's will and do what He had to do, regardless of whether He was acclaimed as a wonderful teacher or otherwise. The souls of the multitude are too precious to be sidetracked by feelings and emotions. The lost must be found. The bruised must be bound up. Those in bondage must be set free. This is our world too.

**HE IS COMING AGAIN**

*"And if I go and prepare a place for you, I will come back and take you to be with me that you also may be where I am."*

~John 14:3

Jesus is coming back again, just like He said He would. The event will take a lot of people by surprise in spite of the fact that Pastors and Prophets have been sounding out the message for centuries. As the Church, we look forward with eager expectation to His returning and to the clear triumph of the procession of the saints who will be caught up to meet Him in the air. What a day that will be! There will be family reunions with loved ones who have walked through the valley of the shadow of death. Together, our physical frames will be changed into "spiritual" bodies that will be able to enjoy God's presence for timeless eternity. Those who struggled with physical difficulties will be set free with new, transformed abilities to see, hear, smell, touch, taste, leap and hold as never before. Pain and sickness will be left behind. Sorrow and discouragement will be history. The struggle against the tempter and the destroyer of our souls will be finished. His sting and his power will have no effect on us any longer. We will be caught into the presence of the One who loves us with an everlasting love. He will take us to His Father's house where we will humbly bow in grateful praise and worship for who He is and for all He's done for us. We will be embraced by Boundless Love.

The beauty of that place is beyond our present ability to understand. The Apostle John, in his description of heaven in the book of Revelation, struggled for adequate adjectives to paint the heavenly portrait. Suffice to say, "No eye has seen, no ear has heard, no mind has conceived what God has prepared for those who love him" (1 Corinthians 2:9). No matter how delightful a situation your imagination can envision, it is still going to be far more beautiful.

Without a doubt, the most wonderful part of the whole transition will be the moment we see our Saviour face to face. He's the One who loves us, who came into the world to set us free from sin, who died and rose again and who ascended into His Father's presence to prepare a place for us. He is the One who intercedes for us at the Father's right hand and He's the One who will welcome us Home. What a joy it will be to be able to express our appreciation without the limitations of our present weaknesses. Jesus is coming back again. Let's be watchful and doing what He has left us to do. It may be today.

▌ **GOD'S GREATEST WORK**

*"How great is the love the Father has lavished on us, that we should be called children of God! And that is what we are!"*

~1 John 3:1a

All that you see and all that exists in the whole universe is the result of the spoken word of God. From absolutely nothing, He designed all things. This is hard for the natural mind to comprehend because we reason that, in order to build anything, you need to start with something.

Not so with God. He does the totally impossible. From my vantage point I would say that He has done a masterful job, as the beauty of creation so wonderfully displays. Artists often attempt to duplicate the beauty of His handiwork and, as marvellous as their results may be, they miss so much.

To me, it is what you cannot see with the naked eye that is so overwhelming. The miniature and the microscopic, when viewed under magnification, have such intricate detail and beauty of their own.

Let me take you a step further. If we could only see what God does in the hearts of men, changing us from natural dependencies to being in relationship with Himself, we would have a new appreciation of the detail of what God does in the lives of people who come to Him. There is a transformation that occurs in the inner man that is deeply profound. It could never be viewed by magnifying glass or microscope, but it is sometimes seen in the outward actions of the people. Painful faces are changed to faces of joy. Addicts receive the freedom to be themselves and once again be a productive part of society. Bitter hearts shine with forgiveness as old roots are severed and a new love for others begins. It is amazing what God can do.

The biggest part of what He accomplishes in the world today is revealed in the transformation of lives. So many people struggle through the effects and results of bad choices or bad circumstances but God offers the opportunity for all to know His recreating power and the joy of a new beginning. Jesus came into the world to make a difference in our lives. He demonstrated that the Father in Heaven is gentle, loving and forgiving and He is longing for us to know a real experience with Himself.

The choice is ours. God will not force Himself upon us but allows us to make decisions on our own. If we present ourselves to Him, He is prepared to do great things in our lives. The inside pain caused by guilt and condemnation can be erased. He can speak healing to the troubled soul and bring the peace that passes all understanding. Invite Him into your life to do a personal miracle for you. He is an Awesome God.

**I WILL NOT DOUBT**

*"'Have faith in God,' Jesus answered."*

~Mark 11:22

He is the Master of the Impossible. The Creator who made all things from nothing.

"I Will Not Doubt"

I will not doubt, though all my ships at sea
Come drifting home with broken masts and sails;
I will believe the Hand which never fails
From seeming evil worketh good for me.
And though I weep because those sails are tattered,
Still will I cry, while my best hopes lie shattered;
I trust in You.

*I will not doubt*, though all my prayers return
Unanswered from the still, white realm above;
I will believe it is an all-wise love
Which has refused these things for which I yearn.
And though at times I cannot keep from grieving,
Yet the pure ardour of my fixed believing
Undimmed shall burn.

*I will not doubt*, though sorrows fall like rain,
And troubles swarm like bees about a hive;
I will believe the heights for which I strive
Are only reached by anguish and by pain.
And though I groan and writhe beneath my crosses,
I yet shall see through my severest losses
The greater gain.

*I will not doubt*. Well anchored is this faith,
Like some staunch ship, my soul braves every gale;
So strong its courage that it will not quail
To breast the mighty unknown sea of death.
Oh, may I cry, though body parts with spirit,
*I do not doubt*, so listening worlds may hear it,
With my last breath.

Author Unknown

He will always remain a faithful Friend through all circumstances of life. Trust Him and talk to Him! He loves you more than words could ever say.

218

▌ **THE FOUNTAIN THAT SATISFIES**

*"The LORD, the LORD is my strength and my song; he has become my salvation. With joy you will draw water from the wells of salvation."*

~Isaiah 12:2a-3

He wasn't literally about to die of thirst, but he was in a desert place yet again. Memories of his childhood days in Bethlehem so contrasted with the frustrations of his nerve-wracking wilderness experiences that David cried out, "Oh, that someone would get me a drink of water from the well near the gate of Bethlehem!" (2 Samuel 23:15). There was something comforting and refreshing about that old well. His childhood days in his hometown were days free of responsibility and filled with childish pleasures. Most activities took place somewhere near the well, the focal point of everyday life, because everyone came there for water at least once a day.

Our experiences of the "good old days" often hold that kind of grip upon our minds. They make up many of the cherished treasures of memories from our growing up years. We like to come back to them from time to time and experience, in our imagination, what we no longer have in practice today. And we all like to dream a little bit.

Let me remind you today that there is an experience that happened almost 2000 years ago that changed the course of our lives. It was at the foot of the old, rugged cross that we laid our sins and burdens down, to find the supply of God's grace sufficient for all our needs. He granted us His pardon and welcomed us into His heavenly family. The joy of sins forgiven and the gift of a loving relationship with an Awesome God are the cherished treasures that hold us committed to Him. Like the old well, there remains a place where many wonderful experiences were lived and times of refreshing received.

The truth is, though, that we get so caught up in all of the hustle and bustle of daily living that we become exhausted with all the pressures and trials of life. As someone said, "We're caught in the rat race of life and the rats are winning."

Moments like those remind us of how important it is to get back to the well that brings us refreshing. That was one of the reasons that Jesus instituted the Lord's supper. It is urgent that we remind ourselves that the mercy of God is a wonderful, refreshing experience. By faith, not imagination, we return to the fountain of the kindness and love of God. The fact that we can pause to bathe ourselves in His presence and set aside the frustrations of our world to be cleansed anew by His precious blood and Gentle Spirit is a blessing beyond anything in this world. We need to "come back" from time to time and drink again of the wonderful provisions of our Heavenly Father.

▌ **MAKING OUR MOVE TO GOD**

*"I will call on you, O God, for you will answer me;*
*give ear to me and hear my prayer."*

~Psalm 17:6

"Who ever heard of winning a war by weeping and crying and brokenness?" These are the words of a song that is sung to challenge the Church to serious prayerful intercession. The scriptures remind us, "The weapons we fight with are not the weapons of the world. On the contrary, they have divine power to demolish strongholds" (2 Corinthians 10:4). There are issues today in the world, in our homes and in our lives that need to be addressed. If we know that Jesus is coming soon, it behoves us to get serious about these concerns and do something about them. Perhaps we're waiting for some special revelation from God on how to handle these matters that will bring us instant relief. Let me tell you that He has already spoken clearly about what has to be done and our lack of involvement is only delaying the solution.

There is no question that the kingdom of darkness is seriously pressing the battle to depress and defeat the work of the Lord. Let an army arise from the valley of lethargy to new life in God. It begins in our own hearts, where we become aware that the Lord fights the battles for those who seek His face and are prepared to be earnest in prayer and service. It is time that the world saw a living, vibrant, faithful band of Christians who believe in the love and power of God and who are willing to risk making an open declaration of faith. God is still on His throne. He will always be Lord of all and beside Him there is no other.

There is absolutely no reason why we should believe that waiting for God to make the first move is an intelligent decision. He has so often held back the solution to serious problems until we would get a sense of urgency in our soul to invite Him to become involved in the matters of our world and of our personal lives. His promise is, "If my people, who are called by my name, will humble themselves and pray and seek my face and turn from their wicked ways, then will I hear from heaven and will forgive their sin and will heal their land" (2 Chronicles 7:14).

Not getting involved is not the answer. Those who understand the power of prayer need to begin to exercise their faith in this way. Somehow we need to shake ourselves up to believe that nothing is going to happen unless we do something as workers together with God. How long can we wait while the enemy beats up our kids, causes dissension in our homes and destroys the morals of our nation? "Who ever heard of winning a war by weeping and crying and brokenness?" Do you really want to see what God can do? Let's set aside time to seek the Lord to appeal for His intervention and let God be God.

▌ **OLD TREASURES**

*"Because God wanted to make the unchanging nature of his purpose very clear to the heirs of what was promised, he confirmed it with an oath."*

~Hebrews 6:17

Contrary to what some may believe, "not everything that is old is worn out." We hope that in the maturing process Grandpas and Grandmas (Opahs and Ohmas) will have learned some very valuable lessons and discovered the patience and the wisdom to apply them in the right places. Getting old is not always "pain free" as many of you, of all ages, have discovered. But growing old will be as exciting as your attitude toward accepting the changes that are going on around us—on the outside as well as on the inside. Trying to fight those changes is like trying to hold back the tide. It's going to happen as sure as a new generation is born. Technology has done a lot to effect great changes in our generation already, and there are more changes to come.

Think back with me for a few moments. We no longer have to chop wood in order to prepare the dinner. If you remember what a wringer-washer is, you date yourself. Do you remember when the crank on the phone was on one side and the receiver was on the other? The refrigerator was literally "the ice box." Television was only in "Buck Rogers" comic books and two-way radios were in the dreams that made "Dick Tracy" so famous. Times have changed and will continue to change.

The Grandmas and Grandpas of today will remember a lot of that older stuff. The truth is, they had a lot of advantages in their day that kids now do not know. They had Sunday School, morning Bible reading and prayer in school, a different respect for the Lord's day and a clear understanding that the family that prays and plays together stays together. Work was to be desired, not shirked, and respect for your elders and those in authority was expected. Churches were left open for anyone to come in for prayer at any time, night or day, and the House of God was respected.

It's when I think of these latter things that I remember that not everything that is old is worn out and worthless. Jeremiah struggled to express this when he was told to call the nation of Israel to repentance. He said, "This is what the LORD says: 'Stand at the crossroads and look; ask for the ancient paths, ask where the good way is, and walk in it, and you will find rest for your souls.'" (Jeremiah 6:16a)

I know that it is a mistake to plan your life through your memories, but I wonder if there is a way that we can move into the changing times of today and bring with us the good of the old times without appearing irrelevant.

May the Lord help all the Grandmas and Grandpas to be examples of godliness, patience and love and to continue to be the faith-builders they were designed to be. May the Lord guard us all from bitterness and resistance to change so that we can still be useful to each new generation that needs to know God. May every one be an example of prayer and of loyalty to His Word. Times may change but God is still God!

█ **LEARN YOUR LESSONS WELL**

*"Take my yoke upon you and learn from me, for I am gentle and humble in heart, and you will find rest for your souls."*

~Matthew 11:29

If you would have seen him walking the hills of the countryside or shooting rocks at twigs that were his imaginary enemies you would never have recognized the potential within him. He was the youngest in the family; the baby, with all the special treatment that goes along with that special position. He was given some of the menial tasks of the household as a part of his responsibility, which included tending sheep. It was there with the sheep that David learned how to use his slingshot. On one occasion he took on a bear and another time he killed a lion. These were pretty fair accomplishments for any young man. They were experiences that would serve as lessons well learned when it came to facing giant obstacles in the future. It was obvious that he took his job seriously and that anyone or anything that came to disturb the peace of his little flock would know the wrath of this little boy. It sounds funny, but God gave him success.

No doubt, it was out in the pastures that he learned the value of music in calming the animal instincts, which became very useful to him later in life. It was there that he learned how to communicate with his Creator. He sang his praises to the Most High in poetry that became a part of the hymnal of the nation of Israel, which is remembered and sung to this day.

But the greatest lesson he learned and passed on to future generations was the example of the tenderness of his heart toward God. In his deepest trials, he sought the Lord with all his heart. In his greatest accomplishments, he sought to give the glory to his Lord, who won the victories for him. Even in his deepest moral defeat he sought the Lord in sincere, humble repentance. His lonely times, when he sometimes despaired for his life, were comforted by his loving, devoted relationship with his God.

David learned many of the most valuable lessons of his life while he was still a youth. It was his formative years that made this young man into a General and the King of the nation of Israel. The lessons could be placed in two categories:

1. *Learn how to deal with the difficult situations in your life* (trust God when it seems impossible to overcome the obstacles).

2. *Learn what it means to have a living, vital relationship with God* (absolutely nothing can take the place of knowing and serving God).

It all has to begin somewhere. For David it began many years before anyone recognized what was going on in his life. Perhaps that is where you are today. God knows you and has a very special plan for your life. Be encouraged! He loves you.

222

▌ **YOUR VERY BEST FRIEND**

*"A friend loves at all times, and a brother is born for adversity."*

~Proverbs 17:17

I am sure that you have heard about Him, but I know that you have never seen Him. He's been around for eons and you've had many dealings with Him throughout the years of your lifetime, but I'm sure that you have never shaken His hand. You may not always recognize His voice but I know that He has often spoken to you and constantly has your best interests at heart. He's very humble and rarely speaks about Himself because He has a very close relationship with Jesus and that, most often, fills His conversation. The Holy Spirit is a person who possesses all the characteristics of personality and individuality as well as being totally equal with God. He is God's gift to us. His ministry is to reach out to people who are broken, hurting and living wasted lives. His purpose is to rebuild, restore, recreate and give real value to living. He is not impressed with our earthly accomplishments because He has higher goals. He wants to make us look and act more like Jesus by His influence and His enabling power.

He is the One who makes us aware that we need God because we are sinners. He is the One who shows us that there is nothing we can do to change that on our own. He is the One who leads us to Jesus, who alone can forgive us of our sin. He makes His home in our lives so that He can work from within, with full understanding of our emotions, our intelligence and our will. He is the One who begins the lifestyle change by His presence and His counsel. He is the One whom we receive when we are filled with the Spirit. He adds blessings to our lives by enabling us with speaking in tongues and the gifts of the Spirit. Because He leads and guides, He is present to prompt us with the correct responses when temptation and trials come against us. He is the One who gives us Peace and Comfort in the midst of sorrow, loneliness and trying circumstances. He is Faithful. He is the One who makes the Word come to life and who reminds us of Jesus. He is present to lead us into Praise and Worship by His precious anointing. He inspires our hearts as we seek the Lord Jesus and press in to know Him better.

He was present when the world was created (Genesis 1:1-2). He was present on the Day of Pentecost when the Church was begun and approximately 120 were filled with the Spirit in a dramatic experience that drew more than 3000 souls to the knowledge of Jesus Christ as Saviour. He is still calling people around the world today into a personal relationship with Jesus.

▌ **THE END TIME MIRACLE MAN**

*"When these things begin to take place, stand up and lift up your heads, because your redemption is drawing near."*

~Luke 21:28

The prophecies of Daniel tell of a boastful man who will arise in the latter days as a person of great influence (Daniel 7). The book of Revelation introduces us to one who is called the antichrist. In both of these prophetic messages, God is giving us a preview of coming events. Jesus spoke of the signs of the end of the age in Matthew 24. The last book of the Bible deals specifically with the tragic end time events that will bring all worldly kingdoms to an end.

I believe we are living in the last days. It has nothing to do with the fears that accompanied the scare of Y2K, nor September 11, 2001. The fact that the Bible indicates, in great detail, that we are living in days that appear to be the fulfillment of the prophetic pronouncements should be enough to make us aware that the end is near. To some people, that's bad news. To those who love the Lord, that is an exciting announcement because Jesus is coming back again to catch us to our reward and to our heavenly dwelling.

But let me share with you one sobering thought. It is very possible that somewhere in the world today there is a person who has been born to have a great influence on worldwide affairs. He will be a person who will speak with great wisdom and authority and will persuade world leaders to bring peace to the world and especially to the troubled area of Israel and surrounding countries. It is possible that he will develop a monetary plan that will be recognized around the world that will bypass money and credit/debit cards for buying and selling. Perhaps it will be some form of invisible tattoo that will contain all your personal information, your financial access codes and a number that will entitle you to use this "new universal system." His demeanour in public will command respect and many will pledge their allegiance to him for the imaginative solutions he presents to the world's troubled situations. He will be the apparent fulfillment of all the characteristics that the world would want in a universal leader. You might even be impressed with his abilities and vote for him to be the worldwide leader. But he is the "antichrist." He's coming soon to your neighbourhood through television and video. Watch for him. You won't be disappointed. He will, deceitfully, be exciting and command your attention.

The bottom line is this: it is not what a person does that is important in God's sight. It is <u>who</u> a person is and his or her relationship with Jesus Christ that is absolutely important. Teach this to your children. They need to know this and be prepared for the greatest scam of deception that the world will ever see.

224

▌ **YOU ARE CALLED TO PREACH**

*"Preach the Word; be prepared in season and out of season; correct, rebuke and encourage—with great patience and careful instruction."*

~2 Timothy 4:2

I think that everyone is a preacher at some time in their life. I know my Mother was. She wasn't in the "ministry," but she had a clear story to tell and we heard it almost every day. The truth is that anyone who has had a message to give and needed to do it persuasively and clearly has been a preacher. It is also true, however, that we confer a special honour to the preaching of the Gospel message as an exceptional commission from the Lord. Preaching is God's method of teaching, exhorting, challenging and revealing His purposes to the world. It is His idea. It is very possible that some may wish for ways other than preaching to get the message across, but that is the way He has selected that it be done. The Apostle Paul reminds us that God has chosen "the foolishness of preaching" to save those that believe. As a matter of fact, he considered his own ministry as a special privilege that he was responsible to perform. He said, "...I have been *entrusted* with the task of preaching the gospel..." (Galatians 2:7, emphasis added).

On the other side of the pulpit, on many occasions, we cannot measure the amount of effort that is needed to pay attention to the preacher. Paul had to tell one of his congregations, "listen to me patiently" (Acts 26:3b). I'm sure that is the plea of most ministers as we struggle with the message that we need to share. Sometimes the words don't come easily but the message is heavily resting on our hearts.

There is another perplexing side to the preaching process. Every message is a mixture of what God wants to say and the personality of the speaker. That has always been a strange but accepted combination since the days of the early prophets when God's message was obviously touched by the messenger in his/her delivery.

The bottom line of every message that comes to us in the name of the Lord, whether it's from Mother or the Pastor, is that it should be heard, examined and absorbed with the understanding that God wishes to speak to us today, and preaching happens to be His method of delivery in the majority of cases. I advise the "examining" process because sometimes we throw out the message because of the messenger. But remember, if God can use a mule to get His purposes across, He can use any of us (Numbers 22:28). Maybe it has crossed your mind that some Churches have a mule for a preacher. (I had better not go there!) Even so, the message still needs to be *heard*.

Paul exhorts us to, "...devote yourself to the public reading of Scripture, to preaching and to teaching" (1 Timothy 4:13). It is all for our personal benefit.

**HOME SWEET HOME**

*"...I...have taught you publicly and from house to house."*

~Acts 20:20

The poet wrote, "Be it ever so humble, there's no place like home." It has also been said that, "a man's home is his palace." Without a doubt, many of the fondest memories we treasure are the memories of home and childhood.

Jesus did a lot of His ministry in the homes of His friends, both the merely curious and the fully interested. A home setting is a more relaxed and congenial atmosphere for having heart to heart conversations. That was Jesus' specialty. You can't feel threatened if you're settled into the comfort and security of your own home.

The early church used the principle of home meetings to advance the gospel into the communities of the first century. "Day after day, in the temple courts and from <u>house to house</u>, they never stopped teaching and proclaiming the good news that Jesus is the Christ" (Acts 5:42). It was the home meeting places that became the heartbeat of the Church. So much so that when Saul, the persecutor, tried to stop the spread of the gospel of Jesus he focused on the home meetings as the source of his aggravation. "Saul began to destroy the church. Going from house to house, he dragged off men and women and put them in prison" (Acts 8:3). He discovered that the real strength of the church and its growth was in the homes of the believers who would worship and pray together and encourage each other in their faith. The real life of the church was not in a large building but in the many smaller groupings of people who practiced their faith in their neighbourhood.

Wherever the Apostles travelled in those early years of the Church, they chose to meet in the market places and public arenas and then in the homes of the new believers. God blessed that pattern in extending His Kingdom here on earth. Although times have changed it is still important to continue with small group sharing and fellowship times.

There are a number of challenges in our very busy lifestyles that we must confront in order to bring this to pass:

1. It is important to make time to meet with others during the week for the building up and encouragement that each can bring to the other.

2. It is important to realize that we need advice, counsel and direction from the Word of God more than once a week.

3. It is easier to ask questions and discuss difficult situations in a small group than in a larger group.

4. It is important that we work on getting to know each other on a more personal level. This is possible in a smaller group.

5. God has promised that "where two or three come together in my name, there am I with them" (Matthew 18:20).

226

| ## THE INVISIBLE WORKER AGAINST THE SECRET POWER

*"For the secret power of lawlessness is already at work; but the one who holds it back will continue to do so till he is taken out of the way."*

~2 Thessalonians 2:7

I'm grateful for the work of the Holy Spirit! We may not be aware of all the things that He does each day in those who are a part of the body of Christ (Ephesians 1:13-14)—He is the one who works on the perfecting of the saints to conform us to the image of Jesus Christ. It is interesting that we do not see Him working, but we do see the evidences of what He does as the change is registered in the lives of believers.

The passage of scripture above also reminds us that He is the One who holds back the free movement of the power of lawlessness in the world today. We have known His faithful prompting in our hearts when temptation would cause us to fail. He is there to warn us that wrong choices displease the Lord and have a damaging result on our spiritual growth. He is always present to be our "guide into all truth" (John 16:13).

I wonder what this world would look like if He were not around? While the Church is still in the world, He remains to do His work. When the Church is taken out of the world at the coming of our Saviour, He, too, will be withdrawn. The world will be left without the inner prompting of the Holy Spirit and His unseen ministry in holding back the vigour of iniquity. We already see the power of lawlessness at work in our world and it causes us concern. But what will the people be able to do to combat evil influences without the assistance of the Holy Spirit?

Let's look at the positive side for a moment. We are still able to speak of the love of God to our generation. In spite of the violence that is going on in our world today, we have the liberty and the responsibility to share the grace of God with those around us. Until the Church of Jesus Christ is removed from this world, we need to be a reflection of that love in order to influence those who are unaware of this future event. Let's allow the Holy Spirit to be the Guide in our lives so that we may be a part of reaching out to those who do not possess the hope that we do. Remember, He is an absolute "Gentleman." He may be invisible, but He is doing an important job of reaching the lost through gentle means. Be aware...the Holy Spirit is at work and He is counting on us to be a part of God's program to care for those without Jesus Christ. The time is short.

227

**WORKING TOGETHER WITH GOD**

*"... So in Christ we who are many form one body,*
*and each member belongs to all the others."*

~Romans 12:5

Listen, the message is in the cows, Pardner. If they ain't gettin fat, there's gotta be a problem (Genesis 41:1-27). Ah nose, 'cause cows kin tich good lessuns to aller us too. It's a clear sign. God gives us lessuns through some very obvious signals like thet, thet we don't always unerstand. Some folks just cain't read signs thet well, so someone has to interprit for them. Joseph had to tell Faeroah the king of Egypt exackly what his dream meant. Maybe thet's a lesson on real life. Sometimes we need to trust other folks to tell us what's goin' on in ar own lives, too. Ah've learned thet many times thar viewpoint is different then mine, but thet others sometimes have a clearer pichure than Ah do. We could belabour the point thet we are intelgent critters and quite able to handel our prolems all by areselves, however, God has made us "inter-de-pendent." Thet's a big word thet means, "I needs you and you needs me so thet we kin be better prepared fer the future."

Yo'all bemember thet verse thet goes, "There is a way that seems right to a man, but in the end it leads to death" (Proverbs 16:25). Some may think it's wrong to ask fer someone elses 'pinion but ah think thet's bein' vury wise. Could you 'magine what would have heppened to Faeroah an Egypt if'n Faeroah would have jest considered his dream a bad nightmare and not consultated with Joseph?

God spiks to us in strange ways a time or two. We think thet He only talks to us through the Bible or through the Pastor or sum Prophet. Yo'all probably already no this, but God also spiks through circumstances, feelin's and 'motions; through our frens and spouses and who knows how many other ways. The impertent thang to aks is, are we listenin'? Ah thank it's possible fer all of us to become akwainted with the Holy Spirit in His messages to us through the speriences of our daily livin'. But we need to larn to be opin with our lives so thet we become transparent to our friends. We used to be proud of areselves in a past generation when we could hide our feelin's and our troubled thoughts behind the mask of our pride. But this secular generation has been teachin', fer some time now, thet yo'all just need to be yoself and yo'all'll feel a lot better fer it. The trouble is thet Christians feel they need to proteck their spirichal image so we'll jus' hide the signs of God's dealin's in our lives an no one will never know the diff. Don't fool yerself, you hear. From the outside, we read the signs, but we don't always unerstand the meanin. We need to git together on this so thet we can interpretate the signals and then my and your struggles will be resolved and our future'll be so much brighter. Will you all REACH OUT and TRUST someun this week? God cares more than words kin say.

**■  YOU HAVE A FINE WAY**

*"For the LORD God is a sun and shield; the LORD bestows favour and honor; no good thing does he withhold from those whose walk is blameless."*

~Psalm 84:1

There are some passages of scripture that jar me into the reality of practical counsel, both by the frankness of the truth as well as the expressions that are used. Here's one that caught my eye and made me chuckle at the directness and clarity of the colloquial English. The NIV challenges us to the process of self-examination: "You have a fine way of setting aside the commands of God in order to observe your own traditions!" (Mark 7:9). Isn't that the TRUTH?

A conference speaker who was challenged by someone in his congregation complaining that he was not deep enough in his preaching is reported to have said, "We already know more about the Word of God than we are prepared to obey." Does that hit home or what? Someone else would remind us that we need to return to basics. We are not here to scratch comfort into an itching intellect, but rather to challenge ourselves with the claims of the Gospel message and to follow up with obedience to the leading and guiding of the Holy Spirit. Remember, Jesus didn't save us to make us happy; He died to make us holy. So don't get confused. We need to examine ourselves and ask, , "WHO ARE WE PLEASING, ANYWAY?" Do we actually choose the parts of the Bible that make us feel good and neglect our duties and responsibilities because they sounds like "work" and that might lead us out of our comfort zones?

There are many statements in scripture that clearly state what Jesus wants in His servants. They should be a people committed to Him, dying to self, serving in love and, if necessary, suffering in peace and joy. After all, we should have our eyes fixed on a higher prize than anything this world could offer us. Whether it be people, pleasure, possessions, position or pension, God wants us to place everything after HIMSELF. Jesus said, "But seek <u>first</u> his kingdom and his righteousness, and all these things will be given to you as well" (Matthew 6:33, emphasis added).

We need to redefine our principles and our goals in the light of His claims on our lives and put them in line with what pleases the Lord. After all He has done for us, after all the promises of what He will do for us, and after all He is to us each day, we ought to be concerned with expressing our gratitude to Him through more than words. He is calling us to live for Him in a lifestyle that honours HIM, which means that we will respect and obey His direction in spite of our own personal feelings. He should be the King of our lives with absolute dictatorial authority to command as He pleases.

Let's learn to do things that bring Joy to *His* heart.

▌ **THE PLEDGE OF BLOOD**

*"In the same way, after supper he took the cup, saying,*
*'This cup is the new covenant in my blood;*
*do this, whenever you drink it, in remembrance of me."*

~1 Corinthians 11:25

One of the strongest teachings about "covenants" is found in the experiences of David and Jonathan. They had built up a friendship of mutual confidence and trust to the point that each was willing to lay down his life for the other. In spite of the fact that Jonathan's father, Saul, hated the young shepherd boy from Bethlehem, Jonathan pledged his loyalty to his friend through some very difficult circumstances. They often met to confirm their commitment to each other through the blood sacrifice that sealed a covenant.

It may be hard for us to understand the kind of relationship that they developed, but let's give it a try. When we read passages like 1 Samuel 18:3, 20:16 and 23:18, we begin to understand a little more about the depth of their dedication and devotion to each other. The pledge they mutually made entailed the sacrifice of a lamb. It involved the shedding of the blood and the sharing of a pledge of loyalty, and God was their witness. It was as though the blood of the covenant ceremony had become the glue to bind them together as one. Each time they repeated the act of dedication, they were reminded of the, "till death do us part." This was intended to demonstrate the seriousness of the words that they had spoken. Death was in their message of commitment to being faithful and loving to each other. That pledge drew them both into a confession of devotion and allegiance to protect each other and preserve their families through future generations.

Jonathan had to bridge a gap between the hatred of his father and his own love for his father's enemy, David. He walked a tight rope but faithfully maintained his commitment to his dear friend.

Jesus came into the world to fulfill the pledge of eternity. Not only does His precious blood speak of our future inheritance, but also of our present protection. We are bound to Him through His sacrifice on the cross. His precious blood shed serves as a binding element that holds us securely to Himself. The fact that He is the King of Kings and Lord of Lords puts us in the place of absolute provision because nothing "...shall separate us from the love of Christ" (Romans 8:35a).

When the enemy comes against us, the pledge of the Covenant of Calvary forms a barrier of defence that protects us from his accusations and his condemnation. Jesus is our Defender. We are "in Christ" and free to serve Him. Each Holy Communion service becomes a reminder of the pledge of His loyalty to be our Loving Friend.

▌ **JESUS, THE CENTRE**

*"But Jesus came and touched them. 'Get up,' he said, 'Don't be afraid.'*
*When they looked up, they saw no one except Jesus."*

~Matthew 17:7-8

Jesus is the Centre. He was the Centre of many a crowd, the Centre of attention in many home visits, the Central figure in meetings at the Temple or Synagogue, the Centre of the Father, Son and the Holy Spirit and the One who hung on the Cross in the Centre.

He was meant to be the Centre of our worship, the focus of our lifestyle and the goal of our eternal hope and reward. Jesus, the altogether lovely One (Song of Solomon 5:16), the desire of all nations (Haggai 2:7), the author and finisher of *our* faith (Hebrews 12:2), the One and Only who came from the Father, full of grace and truth (John 1:14), should be granted nothing less than the throne at the Centre of our hearts.

The attention of the angelic hosts is focused upon Him. The Apostles preached about Him, re-taught His teachings and verbally pointed to His return to earth. Multitudes through the years have surrendered themselves to Him and committed their lives to serving Him—even to the point of death. No other person in all of history has consistently been the centre of the interests of poets, artists, authors, philosophers, kings and rulers as Jesus.

Centuries of believers have honoured Him in the liturgy of worship services, in the retelling of the details of His life and ministry among the multitudes of witnesses of His earthly activities. Heavenly worshippers victoriously proclaim, "Worthy is the Lamb who was slain, to receive power and wealth and wisdom and strength and honor and glory and praise" (Revelation 5:12).

When all is said and done, sometime in the future, when we are together in the Palace of the King of Kings, we will acknowledge that Jesus is the only one who could bring salvation to this world. He alone can transform our lives from what we are today into what we will be in heaven. He deserves to be acknowledged and worshipped as the Lord over all of creation.

With excitement, the Apostle Paul reminds us that Jesus will be recognized in a public fashion: "Therefore God exalted him to the highest place and gave him the name that is above every name, that at the name of Jesus every knee should bow, in heaven and on earth and under the earth, and every tongue confess that Jesus Christ is Lord, to the glory of God the Father." (Philippians 2:9–11) Every eye will be focused upon Him as all other things that we value so highly fade from our view and He becomes the Centre of our attention. That day is not too far away.

▌ **WHERE IS GOD?**

*"If I go up to the heavens, you are there;*
*if I make my bed in the depths, you are there."*

~Psalm 139:8

Where is God when you need Him? Maybe you have never asked that question, but I have a few times in my life. If it hasn't been for my personal pain it's been for tragedies that visit folk that I know and love. I know that the authors of the Psalms had similar questions many times as they tried their best to serve God and keep on the victory side. If you'd like to try them out, I've got a few pat answers that I've used to temporarily resolve that query, but let me confess they aren't always satisfying. Here's one: "We'll understand it better, by and by." Or perhaps you'll like this one:. "God has his reasons."

Of course, those answers are true, but they sound too evasive to be of any help during trying times. When you're hurting, words just don't satisfy. Let me tell you something that you probably already know. When it appears that God is silent we need to apply two basic principles that I call the backward look and the forward look.

1. *The backward look* – is reviewing your past experiences with God. The history of how God has blessed and invested His love in our lives until now is based on the fact that He came to seek us out, to save us and fill us with His Holy Spirit. That is such a tremendous expression of love. The Psalmist said, "...and forget not all his benefits..." (Psalm 103:2). God has been good to us in the past and we need to remind ourselves of that. Anyone who has been serving the Lord will recollect the wonderful times in His presence and the blessings that He shares with us, deep within. He has been there before.

2. *The forward look* – is to review His promises. Whatever our situation right now, He is still God and He has declared that He will never leave us nor forsake us. He has promised that we will be more than "overcomers" and able to rise above the problems that surround us. He is committed to giving us the strength and the grace to come through every situation and to be better for each trial. He has pledged that He will come again soon to receive us to Himself where we will retire for eternity to His mansions.

Don't think it a strange thing when your faith is tested, and don't be embarrassed to confess that you need the Lord's help. It's when we "feel" like the heavens are made of brass and God isn't hearing us that we need to grip onto the anchor that "his compassions never fail...great is his faithfulness" (Lamentations 3:22-23). He always considers us as the most valuable of all of His creation and His affection for us is beyond measure. He will not fail you; even in His silence He is there and He is listening.

232

**THE CALL TO WORK THE HARVEST**

*"Swing the sickle, for the harvest is ripe. Come, trample the grapes, for the winepress is full and the vats overflow—so great is their wickedness!"*

~Joel 3:13

Every day is harvest time. Jesus said, "Do you not say, 'Four months more and then the harvest'? I tell you, open your eyes and look at the fields! They are ripe for harvest" (John 4:35). I know that Jesus is seeing more than we do. We are humanly trained to be seasonal, but He saw the souls of men perishing every day. As far as He is concerned, the only thing that was missing from His plan to reach out to the lost was the willingness of the labourers to enter the harvest fields. That has been the problem throughout the ages. It's not the lack of things to do but the lack of a sincere desire on our part to do the things that God wants the Church to do that has been the obstacle to the fulfillment of the Great Commission. Basically, it's the lack of labourers.

Let's look at a few things concerning the task of reaching the lost:

1. God has given clear instructions: "...go and make disciples of all nations..." (Matthew 28:19).

2. He has set a clear example: "For the Son of Man came to seek and to save what was lost" (Luke 19:10).

3. He has given us a simple message to share: "For God so loved the world that he gave his one and only Son, that whoever believes in him shall not perish but have eternal life" (John 3:16).

4. He has given us a new authority: "You will receive power when the Holy Spirit comes on you; and you will be my witnesses in Jerusalem, and in all Judea and Samaria, and to the ends of the earth." (Acts 1:8).

5. He is willing to give us special giftings to get the job done: "... eagerly desire the greater gifts" (1 Corinthians 12:31).

6. He has promised that He would go with us at all times: "And surely I am with you always, to the very end of the age" (Matthew 28:20b).

7. He has promised that if we lack wisdom we only need to ask Him: "If any of you lacks wisdom, he should ask God, who gives generously to all without finding fault, and it will be given to him" (James 1:5).

The harvest field is the world. The area that we see every day is where we ought to begin. It touches our families, our neighbours, the people we work and do business with, the people we like and the ones we don't like so much. Jesus saw the need and was willing to leave heaven to bring the message to our world.

What should we do?

- Let's pray for the lost of our world.

- Let's pray that the One in charge of the harvest would ensure that there are Labourers to do the task.

- Let's be prepared to go wherever He leads us.

- Let's be prepared to give to Missions that will support others who are presently involved in reaching the Lost.

233

**ONE WAY**

*"I am the gate; whoever enters through me shall be saved.*
*He will come in and go out, and find pasture."*

~John 10:9

There is only *one* door. It could be called a "Fire Escape" door, but it does serve higher purposes than that. It is the entranceway to the presence of our Heavenly Father and the fullness of the riches of His Wisdom and Love. Some have said that we are very narrow-minded when we announce that Jesus is the *only* way to get to heaven.

Like it or not this is the reality of the matter; and like it or not, we can not compromise that truth. If there had been other ways to get to Heaven to enjoy God's blessings Jesus would not have needed to come into the world. There is no other way! He even made a last minute check with His Father when He prayed in the Garden of Gethsemane, "My Father, if it is possible, may this cup be taken from me. Yet not as I will, but as you will" (Matthew 26:39b). Then He went through the whole terrible suffering process that led Him to die on a rugged cross outside the city of Jerusalem. He did it because there was no other way.

You had better believe that if there were a better way to bring freedom and forgiveness to men, the Father would have done it the other way. There was no other way. Calvary was no picnic. Jesus knew that. It was expensive, but the price was paid to open the way to the Father and the rewards of heaven through Jesus' death on the cross. The only way to settle the account was very costly in both pain and energy, emotionally and physically.

The plan was that Jesus, and not any other, would die on the cross in our place because He alone could atone for the transgressions of all of us. He was willing to pay the ultimate price for our waywardness, giving us the Liberty to come before the Father forgiven and cleansed from all the things that could keep us out of His presence. No one else in all of creation could do such a thing. Jesus alone could open the door for us to be able to enjoy the blessings of God who, then, receives us as His own sons and daughters.

When we celebrate the communion service it reminds us that Jesus gave Himself in sacrifice as our One and Only Saviour. His body was beaten, bruised and pierced for our transgressions. His blood was shed to wash away all our sins. His brow was pierced with thorns that we might have peace of heart and mind. He took upon Himself the terrible consequences of my sinful ways and in exchange He offers me His righteousness. The moment I asked Jesus to come into my life and to forgive me, a decree was sounded out in the realms of Heaven; "A sinner has been redeemed!"

There is an outstanding invitation to all to come to the Father through Jesus Christ His Son. You can do that right now! God loves you!

▌ **THE DAYS OF HARVEST**

*"You have enlarged the nation and increased their joy; they rejoice before you as people rejoice at the harvest, as men rejoice when dividing the plunder."*

~Isaiah 9:3 (emphasis added)

You may not be familiar with autumn harvest fields, unless, of course, you have come from the prairies. If you have never seen a field of standing grain moving with a warm, gentle breeze, you have missed a thing of beauty. An experienced farmer's eye can calculate, very closely, the quantity of bushels per hectare for the harvest as well as the quality of the grain for its real worth. But more than picture value, it is the evidence of the sowing of good seed, rain, sunshine and the waiting for an extended period of time that is finally showing results.

That's what Jesus expressed when He challenged His followers, "I tell you, open your eyes and look at the fields! They are ripe for harvest" (John 4:35b). Jesus saw the magnificence of the crowds about Him as would a good farmer who evaluates his crops at the end of his seasons of labour. He knew the worth of every wandering soul and considered it imperative that He get involved personally in the ingathering process to bring each one into the Father's presence. As far as Jesus was concerned, there was nothing of more importance than to assure that the grain in the fields was brought in ...NOW! "Open your eyes," He said (my interpretation is "Don't miss this!"). Everything else that we do in the world should be geared toward equipping us to obey the directions that Jesus gave to His disciples. "Go! ...preach the good news to all creation" (Mark 16:15). There is nothing more important to the Lord than the ingathering of men and women into His Church for the day when the final trumpet will sound. It's harvest time right now.

This is our Mission. We are all called to be labourers in the Master's fields of harvest. The work must begin at home where we live, work and do business. It should saturate our hearts so that we do not miss opportunities to express the wonder of God's love to our generation. It extends over the kilometres where, in cooperation with missionaries, we become a part of the team working on the harvest of lost souls who live far away from us. Someone needs to do the job! We ensure that the task of sharing the gospel will be accomplished as we prayerfully share our personal finances with those who are telling the good news. Jesus emphasized the fact that the time is short and that labourers are few. Yet, it is a matter of urgency. What are you doing in these days of Harvest? What should we be doing? That's a matter that we need to discuss with the Lord of the harvest. He has a plan. If we are prepared to listen and then obey, He will share that plan with us.

Be a Missions supporter at home and to other countries. It pays greater dividends than any other investment this world can offer.

▌ **ARE RULES FOR FOOLS?**

*"Don't you know that when you offer yourselves to someone to obey him as slaves, you are slaves to the one whom you obey...?"*

~Romans 6:16

Someone has said that "Rules are for fools." We say that with tongue in cheek when obedience to the rules is inconvenient. Someone else has said that, "Laws are made for those who want to obey." The lawless don't care about laws because they are not a part of their chosen lifestyle. Then there are some Christians who say, "We are not under the law anymore; we are under grace." Watch out! All of these are pretty dangerous ground to stand on. You see, God is a God of law and order. That is a part of His perfect nature and infinite wisdom. Everything we see in all of creation has to abide by His rules of authority. All things are subject to His Word. His controls keep planets, stars, moons and tides all under a very strict schedule. We become fools when we argue about that.

It follows, as well, that He has established certain guidelines and rules that are important for us to abide by if we ever hope to live a life that pleases God and has no regret. There are some who think that they can play God and set their own rules for their actions and lifestyles. There are always consequences that bring us back to reality. Sometimes we act like God is a "spoil-sport" who doesn't understand what a modern society is like and that He has arbitrarily laid down rules that ruin our pleasure.

Hear me clearly—He has given guidelines that are intended to protect us from experiences that would be harmful to us or that would injure our relationship with Himself. His rules establish boundaries that are intended to keep us in secure territory. They are designed as good advice that will protect us from the dangers that are around us. It's plain and simple. Remember that when we are tempted to do something that displeases the Lord, He will provide a way to escape the wrong decision so that we can still be open to the blessings of obedience. That kind of surrender is an expression of our trust and love in a God who has proven faithful through all generations. His protection over us is one of the reasons He has given us the Ten Commandments.

We are not saved by obeying the rules; rather, we show the world that we are different by obeying the rules. Of course, there is one who will cast doubt upon God's directives. Break the rules and you prove that you have another master who is not the Lord. His goal is to lead us to paths and places where we lose our joy and stumble into pits of despondency and despair. Whose rules do you want to choose to obey? Those of the enemy of our souls? Those of the world? Those of your own pleasure? Those of our peers? Let's re-examine our lifestyles and test whether what we do meets with the Lord's approval or not. It really does matter.

█ **REAL HEROES**

*"The lions may grow weak and hungry, but those who
seek the LORD lack no good thing."*

~Psalm 34:10

They say that heroes are those who make an extraordinary effort to save lives under difficult or dangerous circumstances. Generally a hero is one who responds to a situation spontaneously, without thinking of the consequences or in spite of the consequences. They usually don't see themselves as being exceptional people but just your average "Joe" who happened to be available at the right time.

There are a lot of heroes in the Bible. Bible stories often tell of the lives and exploits of individuals who victoriously contributed to the peace and prosperity of the people of God. Some accomplished extraordinary things during tremendous times of need. These are the true heroes of the faith. But there is a recurring key to their success—most of them were absolutely sold out to God and were plugged into the power of prayer. For example, there's Daniel who prayed three times a day. His three friends also knew the value of fasting and prayer. Jonah called out to God from the belly of the fish. Abraham walked and talked with God. David's psalms speak of an intimate relationship with God through all kinds of life experiences. The Prophets' messages, recorded throughout the Word of God, describe encounters with the Lord followed by empowered pronouncements that sometimes caused the hearers to tremble. Their key was prayer.

James writes, "The prayer of a righteous man is powerful and effective," and he quickly reminds us in the next verse that, "Elijah was a man just like us" (James 5:16-17). But when Elijah prayed, things happened. *Things happened!* You see, God has a resource of rewards that He freely gives to those who serve Him, who call upon Him and who continue to believe that God will intervene in the activities of men. We look back at this kind of hero and admire the results that happened because of that individual getting involved. What we often fail to see is the fact that before they prayed they were just ordinary people doing very ordinary things. They were just like us. But then they prayed, and they became our heroes today.

I've often wondered, "How many dormant, potential heroes sit in our churches, who have not discovered the power of prayer available to all believers?" You and I know that our generation is living at a time that requires ordinary people to get involved in prayer in order to make a difference in our families and in society. God has promised that He rewards those who earnestly seek Him (Hebrews 11:6). Be a hero!

237

▌ **THE HIDDEN THINGS**

*"A man ought to examine himself..."*

~1 Corinthians 11:28a

It is said that the strength of a tree is in the roots rather than in the branches. It's what we don't see that gives real stability and strength to the tree. Unfortunately we cannot gauge the steadfastness of a tree by looking at it or measuring the circumference of the trunk or the length of the branches. However, when the storms come and the high winds blow the evidence of the permanence of the tree will be seen. It's the test of the tough times that proves the strength of the tree.

God told Moses that he led the children of Israel through the wilderness, "...to humble you and to test you in order to know what was in your heart..." (Deuteronomy 8:2). The nation needed to learn that their strength was not in the numbers of people they had in their army, nor in the number of friends they could count on in time of need. Their strength was determined by their heart attitudes. They could never demonstrate their true strength by flexing their muscles. Both their courage and their strength could only be demonstrated through their faith and confidence in God.

I think it's interesting that God allowed the tests of the desert journey to show them what they had inside. As you know if you've read the book of Exodus, they needed a lot of work to bring them into the kind of shape that would give them permanence in their service for God. The doubting, the mumbling, the resistance to God's chosen leadership and their lusts were some of the issues that needed correction. It took them forty years to get that out of their system and in line with God's purposes in order to prepare them to receive the promises of God. The whole time, they were still an amazing group of people, but it was the stuff on the inside that made them weak.

Now, I know that I'm not off the track when I look at our world today and wonder, "How strong is the Body of Christ today?" I mean, we all need to look at the inside of our lives in the areas that no one else sees and do some personal examination and testing in order to prove our hearts. That's where we will discover the real strength of the Church.

This is not intended to point the finger at anyone. I extend an invitation to be honest with God and ourselves by working on the stuff that is not pleasing to God. Remember that it's "the little foxes that ruin the vineyards" (Song of Solomon 2:15). It is said that these little animals would use the vineyards as their place of security and dig holes for their dens, thus exposing the roots and destroying the plants that were their camouflage. It's the little things that get into our hearts that impose limitations on our spiritual growth and eventually destroy us. It's those things that most people don't know anything about, but deep down inside, we know that we need to deal with them through the grace of God.

▌ **THE GREAT CELEBRATION**

*"The Sovereign LORD will wipe away the tears from all faces;*
*he will remove the disgrace of his people from all the earth."*

~Isaiah 25:8

There's a great feast being prepared for the family of God. The place of the dinner is known but the exact date of when it will be served is yet to be announced. The Lord has given us ample signs to indicate that the day of that celebration is very close.

Just before He died on the cross Jesus said, "I tell you, I will not drink of this fruit of the vine from now on until that day when I drink it anew with you in my Father's kingdom" (Matthew 26:29). That statement comes to us from the shadow of the cross. But it was what was beyond the cross that brought joy to His heart. "Let us fix our eyes on Jesus, the author and perfecter of our faith, who for the joy set before him endured the cross..." (Hebrews 12:2). He understood that there was coming a day when, because of the cross, a multitude of people called "Overcomers" would be a part of a triumphant exodus from this world with His Father's house as their destination. It will be a parade of valiant men and women whose lives have been redeemed through Calvary that will be marching to their reward. The awaiting banquet called the Marriage Supper of the Lamb will feature Jesus and His Church in a time of great celebration that will include the faithful of all the ages. It's impossible to describe the excitement of that moment as together we will stand in the Presence of the King of Kings and Lord of Lords. What an experience that will be to leave this place and all we know of the physical world and enter into the realm of the Spirit in the Glory of God! I imagine that the scenes of beauty will be amazing beyond words. I envision that the sounds will be overwhelming as the praises of God's people rise without hindrance as we worship the Lord together. The heavenly host will join us at the Throne of God as we meet our Heavenly Father face to face for the first time.

Somewhere in these moments of delight, Jesus will welcome us to His table and fulfill His promise, "I will not drink of this fruit of the vine... until... I drink it anew with you in my Father's kingdom." We will share together in a "Holy Communion Service" of grateful remembrance as we rejoice in the fulfillment of the work of the cross. We will take another backward look to review the price that was paid to bring us into the Presence of our Heavenly Father. Perhaps it will be then that the Lord will wipe away all tears—some of shame, others of humble gratitude—for the understanding of the magnitude of His wonderful love.

We await that moment as we remember Him in Holy Communion services. Look up! Our redemption is near!

| **A WONDERFUL FRIEND**

*"And I will ask the Father, and he will give you another Counselor
to be with you forever."*

~John 14:16

We have often dreamed of what it must have been like to live in the times of Jesus and actually be a member of His itinerant congregation. Besides the many miracles that Jesus did, there was His ministry of the Word that was done in such a refreshing and fulfilling fashion. He could take a piece of heaven and apply it to the earthly situations of the needy. Yet, He was very down to earth and seemed to understand the pressures that were imposed on the people of His day.

He used illustrations from a mother's kitchen and from a father's construction site. He spoke of sheep, gardening and fish like He knew what He was talking about. He freely mixed with all kinds of people. He ate meals in the palaces of the wealthy and in the homes of common people. His mode of transportation was walking—the same as the average person in Israel. Wherever He went, He left a great impression on the people. Crowds thronged Him. He was so practical in all He did, yet He spoke with loving wisdom and simplicity. He had a way of making people feel like God was reaching out to them and that He, truly, was a heavenly Father.

Religion became a relationship rather than a set of rituals and ceremonies. He made knowing God a real pleasure instead of rigorous servitude. What a change!

Then He left the world. Needless to say, things didn't look that good after He was gone. But before He left He had promised that He would send another Comforter who would take His place. This person would be a constant faithful companion, encouraging and strengthening those who continued to put their trust in the Lord. He would come into the believers' lives as an indwelling Guest to help their thought lives and to be the Prompter of their hearts to know the will and purposes of God.

The Holy Spirit is the Comforter. He comes into our lives the moment we invite Jesus to forgive us of our sin. That is a true and wonderful experience for every believer.

But there is another experience that is important for everyone. We refer to it as the Baptism of the Holy Spirit. There is an enriching relationship that occurs when He confirms His presence in a supernatural way that we know as "speaking in tongues" (Acts 2:4, 1 Corinthians 14:4). He comes into our lives to make the scriptures come to life (John 16:3); to bring us a greater understanding of Who Jesus is; to give us power to witness (Acts 1:8); and to help us live clean and pure lives (John 16:8). He makes our worship alive and enjoyable. He comes to us just like the incarnate Jesus of past days.

What a rich blessing He is to us!

240

| **GOING IN THE WRONG DIRECTION**

*"I have other sheep that are not of this pen. I must bring them also. They too will listen to my voice, and there shall be one flock and one shepherd."*

~John 10:16

Before He left the Ivory Palaces of Heaven and the adoring throngs of angelic hosts, Jesus was prepared to lay down His life for the sins of mankind. There was a purpose for His coming to this world and it was no accident of timing. Nor was He taken by surprise that the very people He had created would turn against Him. That was the main issue of His coming.

The scriptures are faithful to tell us that sin came into the world by the deliberate choices that Adam and Eve made in the Garden of Eden. As a result, that same influence of indwelling sin, like a hidden gene in all humankind, was passed down to successive generations and compounded by the wrong choices of each of us. That is a part of every person, without exception.

Sin, like a plague, was loosed into the lives of every man, woman and child. Ultimately, we may not be blamed for the entrance of Sin into the world, but we must be to blame for doing nothing about it. It's the wrong choices that we make that send us in the wrong direction from God, and no one else is to blame but ourselves.

Jesus came to set things right. He came to deal with the destructive influences of sin in the hearts of men and to take care of the consequences that hang over the heads of all who have ever done things to offend God.

Jesus came into the world as a little baby, but, to the surprise of all of creation on earth and in hell, He never stopped being God. He lived like us and among us but He always possessed the purity, power and authority of the eternal God of creation. Because of that wonderful combination, He could take our place as a universal, representative man and deal with the eternal and universal issue of Sin. Because He was a man He *could* die for our sins. Because He was God He could die for *all men* of all time. No other created being could accomplish that. He became an "exchange" person for our sin so that we could have His righteousness.

Because He is LOVE, He was willing to step out of the realm of eternity into the time limits of creation and pay the absolute price to set everyone free from our sins. His goal was "to seek and to save that which was lost" (Luke 19:10). That is still His purpose. That is the reason we have a missions outreach program. Our praying, giving and going to those who are lost are continuing expressions of the purposes of God for the Church. If He was willing to lay down His life for sinners, we who represent Him and His love in our world today ought to be willing to make an investment in His plan to be the Saviour of all men.

**THE KINGDOM OF HEAVEN IS NEAR**

*"We are therefore Christ's ambassadors, as though God were making his appeal through us."*

~2 Corinthians 5:20a

I wonder how long God will wait before He sends judgment upon our generation. I know that He is very patient; "...not wanting anyone to perish, but everyone to come to repentance" (2 Peter 3:9). That doesn't mean that He approves of the lifestyles and actions of so many in the world today. He still hates sin; it still grieves His heart when people do not trust Him, and I expect He will not be silent forever. History proves that. It is said that a people who do not learn the lessons of history are bound to repeat the same. That's scary when you remember the flood, Sodom and Gomorrah, the judgments upon the early nations in Canaan and the succession of kings that ruled in Israel.

There is a principle of sowing and reaping. It has been true since the beginning of time. God's warnings about avoiding sin are intended to protect us from the consequences that sin brings. Paul wrote, "Do not be deceived: God cannot be mocked..." (Galatians 6:7). We must not hear God's admonitions and at the same time continue to do whatever we want as though we didn't care about His opinion. There will surely come a day of consequence. Yet, it is His greatest desire to set us free from the wages of sin. His patience, holding back the consequences of sin, gives us opportunity to repent and to return to Him.

Let me remind you that no one will ever love you as much as God does. That doesn't mean that we should continue the way we are.

Let me send out a prophetic call that you've read many times before, but is more real today than ever before: "Repent, for the kingdom of heaven is near" (Matthew 3:2).

I sincerely believe that God wants to pour His Spirit out upon the World as never before. He's about to return to take us home and I don't believe for one moment that we are leaving here with a whine and a whimper. We will rise as a triumphant army to report to our Commander in Chief, cleansed by the blood of the Lamb.

God is already stirring the embers of revival around the world. He is calling the Church to be alive in our worship, to hunger for His presence in our meetings and to serve Him in practical ways in the world today. We should all understand that our regular occupations and income resources are means to help us fulfill His call upon our lives. The main purpose of our living is to honour Him with all our hearts, not as unholy hermits, but rather, serving God each day of our lives "where the rubber hits the road." God still loves the lost. Somehow we need to be sensitive to the things that happen around us that grieve His heart and, at the same time, be loving and patient to those who need to see His love in us. We have not been appointed to be Judges but to be Ambassadors representing His Kingdom.

▮ **WORKING WITH MISSIONARIES**

*"Finally, brothers, pray for us that the message of the Lord may spread rapidly and be honored, just as it was with you."*

~2 Thessalonians 3:1

The Lord spoke to Paul one night in a vision and told him, "I have many people in this city" (Acts 18:10). Those were the very words that Paul needed to hear to encourage him to continue serving the Lord when things didn't appear to be going the right way. He had heard the call to minister specifically to the people of that region but he wasn't seeing the expected results. But God saw the whole process. It was a sowing time that would eventually bring a great harvest. He saw what Paul could not see. God saw many people in the city who, eventually, would respond to the ministry of the Word. Paul needed to believe that, although he did not see the results that he expected to see, God was doing some very good things behind the scenes. At the same time, the success of the Missions project still depended upon someone preaching and teaching the good news even though they didn't see immediate results.

That is still one of the difficult situations that missionaries face today. We all want to see dynamic things happening all the time as our Missions representatives labour on the front lines. But sowing the seed of the Word in the beginning can be discouraging unless we understand that God works in the lives of people who are given the Word. The results may take time, but God will not let His Word go to waste. It will accomplish its purpose.

To this we raise the challenge; just as Jonathan strengthened the hand of David in God (1 Samuel 23:16, KJV), so we must be the encouragers of those who are a very important part of our Missions Outreach team. It is a blessing to Missionaries when they know that…

1. There are people who care and are praying for their ministry. These people may never see the results of their intercession until they arrive into God's company, but their investment of time on the behalf of others does not go unnoticed in the presence of the Lord.

2. There are concerned Saints in our Church who back up their words with a financial expression of their commitment to reaching the lost. We're prepared to back the project that is so close to the heart of God.

3. If the Lord lays His hand upon our Children, Youth or Young Adults, we will be behind them to encourage them to move out in God and be obedient to do whatever He wants them to do. We give our Children to the Lord.

4. We will be faithful to seek every opportunity to speak to someone each day about the Lord. Not all the lost are overseas. There may be some in your home or in your neighbourhood that should be reached.

Let's share our blessings for Missions outreach the next time we're asked to give to Missions.

243

**STRONG TO SERVE**

*"But even if you should suffer for what is right, you are blessed. 'Do not fear what they fear; do not be frightened.'"*

~1 Peter 3:14

"Finally, be strong in the Lord..." (Ephesians 6:10). That is Paul's exhortation to one of the best Churches he ever pioneered. He was speaking as a caring Pastor who was aware that the world can be pretty intimidating from time to time. He could speak out of experience, though, because he confessed, "I came to you in weakness and fear, and with much trembling" (1 Corinthians 2:3). That's probably a pretty accurate picture of those in the Church who try to witness to the unsaved today. Can you see it? Telling others about Jesus sometimes has that kind of effect on some of us at first.

Paul comes back to challenge us with the need to be bold in spite of the threat of being made the brunt of some kind of criticism or persecution. It's a challenge that calls us to dig down deep into the resources we have in the Lord and not be wavering in our commitment to serving Him. As a matter of fact, that same passage carries us on to an understanding that we are in a war and that we need to be clothed with the "full armour of God." This is war! But it's a war to share love to those in need. We fight against an enemy who doesn't want that kind of message to get out.

Unfortunately, more souls have been lost in this conflict because of what we did not do than because of what the enemy could do. The truth is that we have a more powerful resource available to us than he has. The Lord is on our side and there is absolutely no foe that can be successful against Him. "The LORD is a warrior; the LORD is his name" (Exodus 15:3). God has also given us the Holy Spirit, who gives us strength, wisdom and the right words to speak at the opportune time. He still answers prayer and does for us far above anything that we could ask or think. Believe that and test it out.

You know that the common picture that the world has of the Church is of a foolish little mentally challenged weakling who can't adapt to a modern society. That is neither the Jesus I know, nor those people who were a part of the early Church; nor is it anywhere like some Christians we know who are bold to stand for what they believe because they're made of better stuff than the world.

Paul's exhortation "to be strong" is a challenge to do something brave and positive in your area of the world. I believe with all my heart that in spite of the lack of integrity and morality in our world today there are many people who are looking for those qualities and would be willing to follow a leader who would demonstrate those characteristics. So, "be strong!" Don't back down! Stand up and be counted! We're part of the winning team. Keep up the good work and believe for His blessings upon you.

▌ **THE MESSAGE OF MISSIONS**

*"Ask of me, and I will make the nations your inheritance,
the ends of the earth your possession."*

~Psalm 2:8

You've probably noticed that there are a lot of people in the world that you don't know. If you could multiply that by the number of problems that each of them has you would realize that we are living in a big unexplored world that is full of problems. I think it's fair to say that we know that we have a responsibility to reach and influence the world that we are familiar with, but what about the others that we do not know? Here are a couple of basic rules for all of us to follow:

1. Our first responsibility to share the story of Christ's love begins at home. That is, we need to practice our faith in our own household and with those that we are in contact with. Jesus gave this advice to one who wanted to follow Him. "...Go home to your family and tell them how much the Lord has done for you, and how he has had mercy on you" (Mark 5:19). The saying we sometimes use is very true: "Let charity begin at home." The story is told that a lady with five children came to the altar to dedicate herself to foreign missions during D.L. Moody's service. D.L. Moody pointed at her children and said, "There are the heathen. Go to them." One of Jesus last commands was to teach his disciples to witness at home, first. (Acts 1:8).

2. Then come the needs of others that we do not know. How can we reach them, for the gospel is meant to be shared with all people? Our first task is to do what Jesus told us to do: "Ask the Lord of the harvest, therefore, to send out workers into his harvest field" (Luke 10:2b). Before we do anything else, we need to be a people who pray about the lost and earnestly desire that they be found. The Holy Spirit knows them all by name and as we pray, He sends the workers.

3. We should give of our income to support those who are working in other parts of the world. We call them "Missionaries." They are actually God's servants, doing God's business in obedience to God's call and God's plan. We support God's idea because it is His heart's desire and we show our love to Him by being a part of His projects.

4. God may call you to be a part of a team that actually goes beyond the borders of our family, community and country. Be a willing servant. There is no better place to be than obediently in the centre of God's will.

**A MEMBER OF THE LOCAL CHURCH**

*"And the Lord added to their number daily those who were being saved."*

~Acts 2:47b

Membership in your local Church is your personal decision to accept the responsibilities of commitment to the policies and vision of the local assembly of believers. It is not a measurement of spirituality, nor is it designed to bring special benefit to the individual any more than joining the army makes you a better human being. The most important matter, though, is that we are born again as a part of the family of God and a member of the Church Universal. The membership roll of the Church of Jesus Christ is recorded in the "Lamb's Book of Life" and is not dependent upon our accomplishments or abilities.

However, being a member of a local Church does demonstrate the fact that those who are prepared to work together will make a public declaration of commitment before others. To the Church body, we acknowledge that God gives wonderful gifts to the Church in the lives of individuals. Each comes with special giftings and talents that make up the whole body. In the same way, every Church seems to have its own personality and makes its own contribution to the community. It is obvious that God deals with local congregations as a very important part of the whole CHURCH and that each congregation, whether big or small, is very important to Him.

The book of Revelation includes two chapters (2 & 3) that demonstrate the interest the Lord has in the details of individual churches in dealing with their specific problems and challenges. I believe that God has given special people to help through those particular situations. They are those we call "active members." They have chosen to belong to the local Church.

Membership is by request, not by legislation. Identifying yourself with the local Church means you are willing to help the Pastor and Congregation in the challenges they face and to develop the vision that the leadership sees. Most of all, it demonstrates the Unity of a common calling to serve the Lord Jesus Christ in the general program of the local assembly. We shouldn't ever take our membership lightly because of the seriousness of the tasks before us. Commitment to working along with others is the real mark of our commitment to the purpose of Jesus—to build His Church.

Becoming a member becomes a public declaration to accept the responsibility of being an active part of what God is doing in our area of influence.

**▍ BRING YOUR CHILDREN TO JESUS**

*"I tell you the truth, anyone who will not receive the kingdom of God
like a little child will never enter it."*

~Mark 10:15

Parents brought their children to Jesus so that He would touch them. The disciples thought that the kids were a bother to the Lord and they rebuked the parents for their thoughtless imposition on the time and energy of the Master. They took upon themselves the responsibility of sifting through the relevant and the irrelevant. After all, He was a very important and busy person and what could be more important to the whole world than to let Him alone to preach and teach?

The disciples' intentions seemed reasonable, but that was not Jesus' method of ministry. Jesus made it clear that of all the things He had to do at this time, the most important was to touch and bless the children. Forget the lengthy discourses. There's something about reaching out to the sincerity and innocence of children that brought great joy to the heart of the Lord. It was the little children who reminded the Lord about those who live in heaven. It seems that the disciples missed that until they were admonished to change their ways.

I'm sure there are moments when sincere, loving and caring parents sometimes wish they could send their children away. Some would have taken the view of the disciples. Let the parents take their children to the back of the Church. Anyone who has cared for those little ones for any length of time knows that they aren't always little angels. They are sometimes mischievous and sometimes overactive, but you can't forget they are little children and have not learned the kinds of things that grown-ups have learned. They are still innocent. It's for that simple reason that all parents ought to understand that the thing that is going to bring the greatest benefit to our kids is the touch of God upon their lives.

It is important that we watch for every opportunity to get our children to a place where they will be taught godly Christian values. We all know how little of that there is in our world today. Our great delight is that the Lord is pleased when parents are concerned enough to get their kids into that kind of atmosphere. The benefits are eternal. He can plant something, like a compass, deep in their hearts that will help to give them direction for the rest of their lives.

It is an interesting statistic that more than 80% of the people who have accepted the Lord as their personal Saviour did so before they reached the age of eighteen. I can almost guarantee that the soccer field or baseball diamond isn't the best place to make that kind of decision. That's why there are children's ministries programs in most Churches. Will you bring your children to Jesus for His touch?

247

| **GOD IS ALWAYS FAITHFUL**

*"I the LORD do not change."*

~Malachi 3:6a

You don't have to be a rocket scientist to know that the sun is always shining. Even though we don't see it at times because of the clouds and the darkness of the night, we know that the sun is continually doing what it's supposed to do. Sometimes it is clearly seen on the other side of the world while we are covered with darkness and we understand that that is the way things are. It is not a question of privilege or right, goodness or evil. It is the way God has designed the sun and the weather patterns of our world. All of nature exists because of God's plan of light and dark.

It's funny, though, that in life we think we should always have things the way we want in order to be comfortable and that everything should be bright and happy. We want to cancel all the dreary days as not important to the believer. It isn't always that way. The truth is that God has created us to enjoy Himself all the time because He never changes and He's always there whether the sun is shining or not. The truth is, when the sun isn't shining on us, the dark and trying hours that we sometimes encounter do serve us for very important and practical purposes. But, still, God is always there.

"For the Lord is good and his love endures forever; his faithfulness continues through all generations" (Psalm 100:5).

"Indeed, he who watches over Israel will neither slumber nor sleep" (Psalm 121:4).

Heroes of the faith through the centuries have believed that the victory is not in our feelings or emotions but in our trust in God. He is the rewarder of those who confidently rely on Him at all times.

"Weeping may remain for a night but rejoicing comes in the morning" (Psalm 30:5).

There is coming a day when the storm clouds will no longer hide the face of the One we have learned to love and trust. The weakness of our confidence and faith in God in trying hours will not hold back the joy that belongs to those who enter the presence of the King. It will be a great day of rejoicing as we are caught up to be with Him through the countless ages. Like the footprints in the sand, when things got rough, the single set of prints were the evidence that He was there all the time holding us closely to Himself.

We are never alone. He is a faithful friend.

**WORK IS HONOURABLE**

*"By the sweat of your brow you will eat your food until you return to the ground..."*

~Genesis 3:19a

To most people, Labour Day marks the end of summer and the beginning of another school term and the fall season, but it was officially designed as a special holiday to honour those who work. Some people believe that work was one of those curses extended upon all mankind that were caused by the sin of Adam in the Garden of Eden

I believe that work is one of the important purposes that God instituted as part of the normal duties and responsibilities of His majestic creation. He told Adam to "...fill the earth and subdue it..." (Genesis 1:28). To me, to "subdue" sounds like work. Everybody and everything needs something to do. Being occupied gives us a sense of importance and a reason for existing. I can only imagine that work was designed to be a pleasurable activity as Adam went about his duties and admired the handiwork of what God had so wonderfully put together. I'm sure there was a sense of importance as, under God's personal direction, he fulfilled the tasks that he was meant to do.

It was sin that made work a tedious monotony of effort-filled days. We get stuck in the rush and scratch of each day, eking out some kind of "living" in order to keep life and limb together. If our attitude could be changed so that we didn't view work as something we "have to do," but rather, as a way to demonstrate God's giftings wherever we are planted, we would watch for ways to serve the Lord. Every day can be a time of exploration and discovery as we see how God leads us in our commonplace occupations to fulfill His will.

Sure there is sweat, weariness and drudgery in some of the things that we do. To tell you the truth, that won't go away until Jesus comes back again. Those who know the Lord should understand that there is no free lunch. Work is not just a time-filler, it is an ethic. We demonstrate our personal integrity and understanding of our individual responsibility to our families and society by applying ourselves to being occupied until Jesus returns. Paul wrote to the Thessalonian Church; "we gave you this rule: 'If a man will not work, he shall not eat'" (2 Thessalonians 3:10). It appears that Paul's counsel was intended to reprove those who wouldn't consider looking for employment because they were happy to "just trust the Lord." This may sound pretty harsh, but I believe he was saying something like, "Don't come looking for food at the Church door if you are not prepared to get out and find employment." A good hard day at work is good medicine for the mind and the body, and Christians ought to see that as a sacred honour. We're not working just for the money, but as an opportunity to serve the Lord in the Mission field of the labour force. May God bless you with a real sense of joy for your efforts, a great paycheck with regular upward reviews, and many souls for your service.

█ **HEAVEN, SOME DAY**

*"He sent his servants to those who had been invited
to the banquet to tell them to come…"*

~Matthew 22:3a

I used to wonder why God didn't take us right up to heaven from the altar of repentance. If ever I was ready to enter heaven it was when His forgiveness was granted to me at the moment of my confession of my need of a Saviour. It was then His precious blood washed away all my sin and I became an adopted son with a promised inheritance in His eternal Kingdom by His heavenly decree. That is what His word declares. I was made to be a child of God, wilfully submitting to His Divine purposes and ready for the streets of gold and the palace of the King.

But I'm still here and this is not heaven. If those who are "saved" were taken away, who would there be to tell the story of His saving grace and His love for the lost? Who would be here to show the power of God and demonstrate what a changed life can be like? Who would God use to be His representatives to invade the kingdom of darkness and share a godly influence with those who have been blinded by the enemy? We have been chosen to do those tasks. The work at the altar of repentance simply made us candidates for higher service. We have been set free to serve the King of Kings in the same neighbourhood where we have been living. We should count it an honour to be able to demonstrate to the whole world the change that has been given to us through His love.

That leaves us right where we are. That also means that, although there has been a real change inside, everything else is the same on the outside. There are temptations and tests; people will still be people; the enemy will continue to distract us from God's purposes and we are working in a world whose morals are different than those of our Master. But God is our Resource. He has promised to be our Helper (Hebrews 13:6). He is available in every time of need. He has promised to never leave us nor forsake us (Joshua 1:5). He has assured us that every trial, test and temptation will have a way of escape; through the test or from the test (1 Corinthians 10:13).

He has not promised that we would be free of pressures and stresses. He has not promised that we won't feel the burdens of life from time to time. He knows our human frailties and the weaknesses of our natural resources, but He has made it clear that He knows those who are His—and we are His Children. He will care for us like His own sons and daughters. Every burdensome situation will become an opportunity to demonstrate His love and His life so that those without the Hope we possess will see the difference that God makes in our lives.

At the same time, we know that this world is not our home. We are pilgrims walking through each situation of life with a clear call of God to honour and serve Him There are rewards for faithfulness that the Father has reserved for us when we get "Home." Meanwhile, in each of the areas of our lives, let's shine for Jesus Be wise! Be careful! Keep trusting!

250

▌ **IT TAKES EFFORT**

*"Diligent hands will rule, but laziness ends in slave labour."*

~Proverbs 12:24

Maybe I'm a little crazy and out of the ordinary, but I like to be busy doing things. I know that I'm like you in that I enjoy my free time just to be able to take it easy, but physical labour was never a problem to me. As strange as it may seem, it is almost relaxing to be able to swing a hammer or dig with a shovel. When we talk about honouring the work ethic on Labour Day, perhaps it should be said that mothers understand the real meaning of "labour" better than anyone else.

Labour Day was designed as a special time to honour people who do manual work. It was the common worker who built this nation out of wilderness and forests into what it is today. The farms, mines, logging and development of industry began with people who dreamed that some invested effort could make this nation great. Good hard work is honourable and not to be deplored. Wise King Solomon put it nicely when he said: "All hard work brings a profit, but mere talk leads only to poverty" (Proverbs 14:23).

Work is the practical side of life where the rubber meets the road. It may be menial. It may be humbling. It may just be a means to get some money to buy some grub, but all hard work brings a profit.

Beware of the guy who tries to sell you on the program that the government has provided a way to live without working. That lifestyle may appeal to some but there are consequences to slothful habits that can destroy the innovative dreams of the people who want to make something of themselves. It sets a bad pattern for future generations who get snagged into believing that the government was designed to take care of its citizens. Paul wrote to the Thessalonian Church and said: "If a man will not work, he shall not eat" (2 Thessalonians 3:10b). The Word encourages us to apply effort to being useful and productive with our lives. It's true that we "do" work, but work "makes" us. To avoid it is to miss out on the lessons and development that good physical activity brings to us. There are thousands of people across Canada today that are out looking for "work" and would give their eye teeth to find something to do to build their self-esteem, give them some purpose in life and lift them from their personal depression.

Work was God's idea in the beginning. I don't know for sure all the tasks that Adam had to do in the Garden, but I do know that he was commissioned to "...fill the earth and subdue it..." (Genesis 1:28). "Subdue" sounds like work to me. I cannot envision Adam sitting under a Palm tree, sipping lemonade. It sounds "divine" but Adam was designed with a higher purpose in mind— to be an industrious representative of the Creator who had a plan for Adam to accomplish. In gentler terms than I could put it God's instructions were: "Get out there and make it happen!!"

▌ **HIS COMPASSIONS NEVER FAIL**

*"Know therefore that the LORD your God is God; he is the faithful God,*
*keeping his covenant of love to a thousand generations*
*of those who love him and keep his commands. "*

~Deuteronomy 7:9

You might have called him a crybaby if you had met him on the street. He is called the "weeping prophet." He had a very difficult ministry, but he was obedient to the Lord. Jeremiah knew that his nation was about to be judged severely for their neglect of the Lord's Day and their unwillingness to hear and obey the Word of God. His heart was so heavy it drove him to tears, but that wasn't enough to change anybody nor anything. Even so, in the midst of his grieving, praying and frustration, Jeremiah gives us a positive glimpse of God. "...his compassions never fail. They are new every morning; great is your faithfulness." (Lamentations 3:22b-23) He had found God to be like a faithful, compassionate Father who had reached out to a people who had often failed Him.

That truth was the source of blessing and inspiration for Jeremiah that sustained him when things got pretty rough. God will never fail! His mercy and compassion are as fresh as the morning sunrise. He will always make Himself available to the searching heart.

In spite of the things that caused Jeremiah such profound distress, there was a deep, settled confidence that God would work things out for the good. He faced some very strong persecution from the religious leadership but he was always secure in his own personal faith in God. He said, "It is good to wait quietly for the salvation of the LORD" (Lamentations 3:26).

You see, if you really believe that God cares and that He is in control of every situation, you learn to roll with the punches and continue to trust in the midst of disappointments. It's not a time to give up. It's a time to reach up. It's a time to demonstrate where your faith really is. We all moan and groan sometimes, because pain really hurts, whether it's from the outside or on the inside. But let me remind you that God knows. He has promised to never leave us nor forsake us. He told the Apostle Paul, "My grace is sufficient for you, for my power is made perfect in weakness" (2 Corinthians 12:9a). His compassion and grace are basic qualities of His Nature and He is with you all the time to show He cares.

The wonderful thing about every trial is that it will not last forever; but God's love will. There will come a time when we'll be able to experience and repeat the words of Jeremiah: "...come, let us tell in Zion what the LORD our God has done" (Jeremiah 51:10).

He has done marvellous things throughout our lifetime. We serve an Awesome God!

| **WORKING WITH GOD**

*"Alarmed, Jehoshaphat resolved to enquire of the LORD,*
*and he proclaimed a fast for all Judah."*

~2 Chronicles 20:3

There are many areas in our lives in which God works with us to accomplish His purposes. Where would we be without Him? Why God would want to call us into partnership with Himself is one of the mysteries of His Wisdom that we may not comprehend at this moment. The fact that He would entrust any of His workings into our care is almost overwhelming, yet it is His choice to allow us to play a part in the fulfillment of His divine plan.

That is why we are called to fast in these days. I believe that God is calling us to humbly seek His face through fasting and prayer, that He might be free to do a new thing in this generation. It was one of the prophets of the Old Testament who sounded out a call to God's people. "Declare a holy fast; call a sacred assembly. Summon all the elders and all who live in the land to the house of the LORD your God, and cry out to the LORD" (Joel 1:14).

Fasting is a discipline that takes a very common and sometimes urgent personal need and puts it second to seeking the Lord. The truth is that most of us think first about ourselves and our own comforts and God is relegated to the extra time that we have. Fasting puts God first.

Fasting puts an appropriate emphasis on spiritual matters. God made us spiritual beings in His image and we live inside of a physical body, but we often neglect the fact that the most important part of who we are is our spirit. Fasting redirects the values of our lives toward honouring the Lord through concerted prayer. Frankly, it is paying the price to be the kind of people that God wants us to be.

Fasting is a spiritual power-building exercise. Like muscle builders who pump iron, Jesus told His disciples that it was sometimes necessary to fast and pray in order to defeat the enemy. He said, "Howbeit this kind goeth not out but by prayer and fasting" (Matthew 17:24 KJV). What the disciples could not do in their own strength would only be accomplished when they committed themselves to prayer and fasting. The impossible becomes possible.

Fasting places us in a position of submission to the Heavenly Father through the act of humbling ourselves before Him. How He longs for a people who will humble themselves and pray!

I challenge you today to set aside time to seek the Lord earnestly for His blessings upon His Church. I am sure that if we do our part, God will do the rest. He seeks for that kind of close, cooperative relationship. You can do something about it today.

**LEADING TO FAITH IN CHRIST**

*"Train up a child in the way he should go,
and when he is old he will not turn from it."*

~Proverbs 22:6

It all began just outside the gate of the Garden of Eden. Adam became a Father. Because there was sin in the world, he could not have known the tremendous responsibility that had fallen upon his shoulders to raise his children to love, honour and serve God. He did give them a spiritual value system, for both of his boys were God worshipers. But as we know from the rest of the story, giving to God and worshipping God as we know best does not assure us of a perfect life. These are two very important principles that our kids should learn early in life. To put it in simple terms, we need to lead our kids to know Jesus Christ as Lord and Saviour.

Fathers, it's time that we recognized that the kids we bring into the world are not going to go to heaven because they are our kids. They aren't going to go to heaven because they go to Church with you. It is our responsibility to guide them in their faith to accept Jesus Christ. That is not always an easy task. We have some heavy competition out there.

Let me give you some suggestions about bringing kids up to serve the Lord:

1. Pray for your kids every day and as you think of them during the day. (YOU'VE GOT TO DO IT!)

2. Organize a time each day when you can PLAY and PRAY with your kids. It's important that they learn how much you value your relationship with them and with the Lord.

3. Be PATIENT with your children. As much as you may give them guidance with the spoken word, many of the things they learn they discover by trial and error. Be a gentle instructor, examining the lessons of their experiences with them.

4. The best gift you can give your children is to LOVE their Mother. Demonstrate affection in the privacy of your home. (A warm hug—often; a stolen kiss; a gentle pat...)

5. Next, and very importantly, if you love your children you need to learn how to discipline them. This is not to make them angry, but to clarify that there are consequences to disobedience and doing wrong and there are benefits for obedience and doing right.

6. Finally, our generation needs godly Fathers and Holy Spirit anointed wisdom.. Fathers need an up-to-date experience with the Lord in order to pass the same on to their Children.

Dads, let me call you today to a new commitment to being the kind of father that God wants you to be. Do yourself a favour and check up on yourself. If you need to do some correcting in your personal life, I can guarantee that it will pay tremendous benefits down the road.

254

❚ **REMEMBERING SEPTEMBER 11TH**

*"He rules forever by his power, his eyes watch the nations—let not the*
*rebellious rise up against him. Selah."*

~Psalm 66:7

It will be a while before the images of the catastrophe in New York leave our
minds. The pain of so many affected all of us as we stood shoulder to shoulder
with those who were hurting at that time. There were some who were maintaining
their hopes that there would be some positive results for their families as the
workers continued to dig through the rubble and twisted steel. Needless to say,
there were a lot of very angry people who were calling out for justice. As Billy
Graham said, "God understands our anger." Counsellors and clergymen around
the world were all looking for words that would take away the hurt and, truthfully,
it was very difficult to find something that would satisfy. As for the Christian, in
times like these we know that God is still on His throne; He is faithful and His
grace and comfort are extended to all that seek Him.

Most of us remain anxious to see what future developments will bring as the
winds of war swirl around the world.

Let me give you a few words of advice in the midst of all the happenings of
these days.

1. I believe that the devil knows that his time is short. More than anyone else
in all of creation, he is aware that Jesus is coming again. He will take advantage of
every weakness and spiritual laxity that we allow to invade the Church.

2. It has always been true that, "It is always darkest before the dawn!" God
has promised to be with us. His Beloved Church is in the world and He will not
stand idly by while suffering goes on. I believe it is time for Christians around the
world to claim a part of their inheritance as the Sons and Daughters of God, that
His power be released in salvation and signs and wonders. This is not the first
time that believers have been pushed to the edge in order to learn to rely afresh on
His power.

3. It is past due for the Church to take prayer seriously. We have ignored a
deeper walk with God for far too long. It is time to review our routines and put the
proper emphasis in the right places. We need to bare our hearts in sincere
repentance and humility as we draw near to Him. He has been waiting for seeking
hearts to make their way into His presence and we must not delay any longer.

4. Whatever our personal trials may be, we must be confident that our lives
are in His gracious hands and that He is able to make all things to work out for the
good as we trust in Him. I believe that it is for times just like these that Jesus said,
"Don't let your hearts be troubled. Trust in God; trust also in me" (John 14:1). We
may not see a resolution to all the battles that we face. That is not the issue. The
issue is that we maintain our confidence that God is in control.

255

SEPTEMBER 12 | **GRANDPARENTS DAY**

*"Do not move an ancient boundary stone set up by your forefathers."*

~Proverbs 22:28

I would like to dedicate our theme today to grandparents. Let's call it "Grandparents Day." Most of us had grandparents who blessed us with their cookies and stories. You may even be a grandparent.

They're the folk who, in one lifetime, have come through the greatest changes seen since the beginning of the world. Some still remember the horse and buggy days and the old Model A Fords that made such a change in our traveling habits. In one century, our mode of travel has moved from about 5 miles per hour to the rocket speeds of 20,000 miles per hour. It seems that life moves at that rate of speed every day.

One Grandfather was telling his little grandson about the chores that he used to do when he was a little boy. One of his tasks was to bring in the wood so his mother could make a fire in the stove. The little guy, with only an understanding of the electric stove, had a hard time figuring out why they wanted to put a fire in the oven.

It is said that one of the first three things to go in old age is your memory. (I forget what the other two are!) In a recent visit with a dear old Gramma, she informed me that she had something funny to tell me. In her own words, she said, "It's a funny thing that I have lost my memory but I have not lost my faith in God." We laughed together to think of such a thing. I guess it's because our physical frames will eventually wear down, but our inner man (our spirit) is growing stronger as we get closer to home. Paul wrote to the Corinthian Church with these words. "Though outwardly we are wasting away, yet inwardly we are being renewed day by day" (2 Corinthians. 4:16b).

Amid all the changes that have occurred throughout this last century, we are reminded that, "Jesus Christ is the same yesterday and today and forever" (Hebrews 13:8). The same gospel message that brought hope, joy, peace, deliverance and healing to so many generations is the same message that meets the needs of people today. Our experience with God doesn't grow stale and mouldy, as do so many other things in the world, because we serve a living Saviour. Changes are occurring all around us. We call it progress and growth. But more regular than the Old Faithful geyser is the truth that God loves and cares for you. No matter your age or your condition in life, He is a Faithful Friend. The Pioneers of the Faith, (our grandparents), are a tribute to the power of the Grace of God. They have gained some very valuable experiences that will be a blessing to us as we're sensitive to them. We wish all Grandparents a very Happy Grandparents day!

256

| **BAPTISM—OUR DEATH**

*"We were therefore buried with him through baptism into death*
*in order that, just as Christ was raised from the dead*
*through the glory of the Father, we too may live a new life."*

~Romans 6:4

If every person that was ever born were alive today, this world would be a very crowded place. There is finality to death that makes us aware that the old must pass away and make room for the new. It is true about the seeds in the ground as well as the temporariness and frailty of human life. But it is good, because we learn lessons from the experiences and knowledge of the old, which, like reliable foundations, serve as good platforms to go on from here.

That's what water baptism means to us, as well. The waters of baptism serve as emblems of the grave, where the "old man" and his "old ways" are buried and a new life, committed to Jesus Christ, arises. We should not forget the lessons from the old ways that remind us that a life without Jesus Christ really offers us no permanent good thing.

*We need to remember* that there are wages for our sinful ways that became collectibles the instant we disobeyed God. The scars and hurts that are the result of our rush and passion for pleasure and selfish goals are the evidence of a way that is not pleasing to God.

*We need to remember* that when we were without Christ, we were the targets of the enemy of our souls, who takes great pleasure in driving us farther away from a loving Heavenly Father.

*We need to remember* that the real cause of wars and arguments is the selfishness and pride of hearts that are not content with putting God first.

These are all terrible lessons to learn, but they are a good basis on which to build something new. I do not believe that it is God's will that we be haunted by the offences of the past. When they are left in Christ and we obediently follow the Lord in the waters of baptism we can rightfully say that we have learned that it pays to serve God and be submissive to Him

The very interesting fact is that, as we leave behind the past in sincere repentance demonstrated by the act of baptism, we choose to begin a new walk with Jesus Christ as Lord of our lives. He offers us his personal companionship and the friendly prompting and guidance of the Holy Spirit. He leads us into inheriting the rights and privileges of the sons and daughters of God. We are drawn into a new Hope that one day, because of the change of direction in our lives, we will be eternally with Him and share the abundance of what He has prepared for us in Heaven. It all begins with the Cross, but the waters of baptism are very important as a declaration to everyone that Jesus has done something new in our lives and we choose to leave behind all the old ways.

**LOVE DISCIPLINES**

*"Train a child in the way he should go,
and when he is old he will not turn from it."*

~Proverbs 22:6

We may be from an older variety of standards than what we see today, but welcome to the "Gen X" era. This is the result of a new generation that wants to set its own value system. That means that times have changed and we need to adapt to a new philosophy of life. I personally resist some of the changes that are common in the world today. Some of the "old fashioned" principles were designed to train us in matters of courtesy, faithfulness and trust from early childhood. The fact that "anything goes" has pushed me out of my comfort zone because I feel that I have been robbed of guidelines to respectful and healthy social interaction.

I'm from the old school that taught, by example and by action, the positive value of severe, loving discipline. To say that pain is the only way to learn a lesson would be absolutely ignorant. But to not learn the place of proper controlled Biblical discipline would be equally ignorant. The basic foundation of all discipline is Love. "Because the Lord disciplines [KJV–'scourgeth'] those he loves and he punishes everyone he accepts as a son" (Hebrews 12:6).

Now, I know that sounds bad if you are bad, but you need to understand the heart of the Father; He is not an indiscriminate, austere judge. There is always a great investment of gentle, loving, patience on His part before there is any other type of action. Let me be the first to admit that this discussion is a borderline conversation that some could interpret as advocating abusive behaviour according to the standards of our Social Services system. However, I know it is more important to listen to the advice of the Bible than the advice of the trends of society.

There is a very important life-principle here that especially affects our spirits. We need to learn to do what is right before God or there is a consequence that will be paid. If we fail to teach our children that principle by our lack of training or by discipline, then we've failed to make a very valuable investment in their lives. I believe it is offensive to the Lord to let our children do whatever they feel is right. That would be to totally disregard the importance of parenting. It is time that we got personally involved with the re-directing of the values of our generation.

Let's set a united pattern that all of us can follow:

1. Sit down with your kids and try to understand where they are at.

2. Let your children know your heart and your desires for their lives.

3. Lead your family to understand that what the Lord wants from us is very much different than what the world expects.

4. Give spiritual leadership to your family. (Pray together, read together, visit parks together, spend home time together, etc…)

5. Let your kids know that they are VERY important to you even though they make mistakes. (They are a gift from God.)

| **THE WORTH OF A CHILD**

*"Whoever welcomes one of these little children in my name welcomes me;
and whoever welcomes me does not welcome me but the one who sent me."*

~Mark 9:37

We have often sung the Sunday School chorus, "Jesus loves the little children, all the children of the world." It is important to notice the value that Jesus placed upon Children. He used Children as examples of the attitude that would be expected in those who would be a part of the Kingdom of heaven (Matthew 18:3). He saw the innocence, simplicity, faith and tenderness of heart in the little ones and He loved them. No wonder He would take time out of a busy schedule to welcome the children by taking them up in His arms and blessing them (Mark 10:16). They were not a bother to Him. It appears that He held each one like a Jeweller would hold a diamond. Like no one else, He knows the worth of each little child and the potential they have within them.

In our generation, some may become very influential leaders in our country or community. Some will become explorers of medical science or prominent social services directors. Some will commit themselves to serving the Lord in full-time public ministry as spiritual leaders. Children are the generation of the future and deserving of proper recognition.

Notice the emphasis of the scripture passage above. Jesus makes it clear that if we treat Children with kindness we are doing it for the Lord. Our attitude towards Children is somehow connected to our relationship with Jesus. We need to see the little ones as worthy of loving attention as He does. Obviously, the early years of childhood are the most impressionable period of their lives. These will be the years when personality and character will be influenced by the actions and words of the significant people in their lives.

Someone has said, "Children are like wet cement. Whatever falls on them makes an impression." Words, gently spoken, give understanding. Encouragement and approval build confidence. Kindness leads to courtesy, and example teaches moral values. We make a contribution to our own future when we apply these principles in our association with Children. What an opportunity that opens up to us to make a noteworthy input for the Lord in young lives. Watch for an occasion to make a positive impression on Children. That will be your homework for awhile.

Someone has said, "Be careful how you treat your children because they will be the ones who choose your Seniors Residence." Better than that, we want a world with proper spiritual values, and we can help to see that happen by caring for Children. Practice looking at Children through the teaching of Jesus and be a godly, loving example to them.

Winning values…let's pass them on.

259

**EXCUSES, EXCUSES!**

*"Therefore, my dear friends, as you have always obeyed—not only in my presence, but now much more in my absence—continue to work out your salvation with fear and trembling..."*

~Philippians 2:12

It's easy to make excuses and "pass the buck" when we get frustrated or feel that we are not satisfied with results. Someone else must be to blame! We don't often talk about our own inadequacies or failures. Those are things that we don't want people to see. It is a fact that none of us are perfect and that we all have areas in our lives that need either construction or renovations. This is part of the growing process of our lives.

It's the same in the spiritual world. We are growing and should continue to grow into maturity. (By the way, maturity is not an age thing. It is the development of character and personality and has nothing to do with the tally of years.) We should strive for excellence and perfection in all we do because we are called to serve the living God and represent Him in this world. Whatever we say and do will have some reflection on the God we serve. We want to be the best that we can be so that our witness will bring blessing to the Lord. Making excuses about our humanity and our inabilities does not work. Even the "one talent" man was expected to do his best with the little that he was given. The fact that he did not do what he should have done was evidence of his lack of trust and confidence in his Master.

In John chapter 5 we read the story of the healing of the man at the pool of Bethesda. He had been crippled for thirty-eight years and was lying beside the pool expecting to receive his healing. Jesus asked the question, "Do you want to get well?" Let me rephrase that:. "Do you want to get better?" or "Do you want to change your situation?" What would your response be? This man replied to Jesus' question with two distinct responses:

1. "I have no one to help me." That makes me ask the question, 'What do you think Jesus was there for?' He wants to help you to get better/be better/to change. Jesus cares about your situation, too, and you need to look to Him as the answer for your need.

2. "... someone goes down ahead of me." In my interpretation he is saying, "People are selfish. They get in the way. I'd be different if it wasn't for some people. I can't change because of those around me."

Perhaps he had some reason to say those things, but then, he was talking to the One who can by-pass all of the reasons why we have not grown into being the kind of people we or God wants us to be.

Here's the key to our growing in God—do what you can do and look to the Lord for the rest. He has promised to never leave you, and it is His purpose to lead you on into Christian maturity. Without excuses, be the person God wants you to be and trust Him.

**GRACEFUL ENDURANCE**

*"Teach me to do your will, for you are my God;
may your good Spirit lead me on level ground."*

~Psalm 143:10

There are a lot of people in the world who are working in situations they do not enjoy. If you asked them why they stay in their jobs they will probably tell you that they do it for the money. Of course, that is an important reason to work, since we need the income in order to survive—unless we're prepared to sleep in the park or under a bridge. But there is nothing like doing a job for the personal satisfaction we get at the end of the day. It's great to have the peace of heart and mind that we have made a difference and that we have pleasure in doing what we do best.

Jesus tells the story of three employees who were given tasks to do. The Master knew the abilities of each so that the delegated challenge that lay before them was proportionate to their personal potential. Now, if that doesn't sound like a God thing, then I'm not tuned in to hear His voice. I'm sure that the task that the Lord gives to each of us is as different as our personal abilities and personalities. It's very possible that there may not be anyone with the same kind of challenges as another. The Lord is the One who delegates duties and responsibilities to each of us with our expectation that when payday comes we will be rewarded.

Don't forget that the "Boss" has an expectation, too. He is expecting that we will do our best to accomplish the goal that He sets before us. But here's the end of the story; you know it well. Two employees gave their best effort and by using their talents were able to double their trust. That's all the Master asks for that we "do our best." There's was a commendation from the Master: "Well done, good and faithful servant!" Can you imagine the joy of these who were generously rewarded for their efforts? However, one, like too many of us, did nothing. Try as he might to rationalize his decision, he had no acceptable excuse to justify his negligence. To his surprise, there was no reward for doing nothing. Plain and simple... No reward! No Payday!

Now, I know that God can do whatever He wants, all by Himself. But I also know that He has promised to work with us; to be there as a resource for our strength and wisdom; to be our supply for whatever need we may have. I understand the principle that Jesus wanted to get across in His story was to emphasize that it's diligence and effort that will be rewarded. Applying effort is the working out of the faith and confidence that we have in a God who has a job to be done and has called us to be privileged to be a part of His program. That may sound like "work" or "works" but be assured, "Payday" is coming and our faithfulness will be recompensed far beyond our greatest imagination.

▌ **GOD'S COMMISSION**

*"Again Jesus said, "Peace be with you!*
*As the Father has sent me, I am sending you."*

~John 20:21

The Challenge of "the unreached" remains an unfinished task. The Great Commission is the Mission of the Church. "Therefore go and make disciples of all nations, baptizing them in the name of the Father and of the Son and of the Holy Spirit" (Matthew 28:19). Everything else should be secondary.

1. It is a program that began in the heart of God when He sent His Word and brought all created things into existence.

2. It continued as He spoke to the early generations with a revelation of Himself and His will.

3. Prophets, sent by God, carried the Word of the Lord under some very severe and austere circumstances because He wanted both His will and His nature to be known.

4. He sent His One and Only Son into the world to be the message of His love, that all might know that He cares and has always been seeking for the lost.

5. Finally, Jesus told His followers, "As the Father has sent me, I am sending you." (John 20:21b)

The moment we become believers in the Lord Jesus, we become His message to a lost world. Our influence should touch and affect the situations we live in every day. That includes our home and wherever we work and do business. It's the everyday "to do" and shopping list of every believer. That's the healthy process that each of us should follow as we serve the Lord. To continue to fulfill the Lord's purposes, our influence with the gospel message is to reach beyond ourselves into a world that needs to know His love. We become an extension of His plan when we pray and give to Missions. We send Missionaries to various parts of the World to share the gospel message with other peoples and nations. They represent the Lord and us with a passion to see the lost found and brought to the knowledge of Jesus Christ as Saviour.

a) Our GIVING helps to make the Missionary's ministry a lot easier because they shouldn't have to worry about who is going to pay the bill. That is the responsibility of everyone who knows the Lord as our Saviour. We may not see the benefit of our investment in Missions in our lifetime, but we know, beyond the shadow of a doubt, that God sees every penny that we give and He keeps the records for the day of Great rewards.

b) Our PRAYING helps to roll back the forces of darkness so that the missionaries can do their tasks with greater freedom. We want the servants of the Lord to be strong, healthy, wise and powerful in the Word. That is God's will too! We need to be encouraged that, "The prayer of a righteous man is powerful and effective" (James 5:16b).

| **SEE THE FUTURE WITH BLINDFOLDED EYES**

*"And if I go and prepare a place for you, I will come back and take you to be with me that you also may be where I am."*

~John 14:3

On December 31st, we tear off the last month of each year from our calendar. It will become history just as all of our yesterdays have. We will look back over the previous twelve months as part of the growing and maturing process that makes us all that we are today. Not all of those days have been sunny. Some have held some dark and stormy experiences that we wouldn't want to go through ever again. Let's remember the blessings and be confident that every experience does work together for good whether we enjoyed it or not. As we look into the future, we see with blindfolded eyes the path that we should take. We are facing unfamiliar territory in a world system that doesn't offer us a lot of hope apart from the promises of God. Ira Stanphill penned the words to a beautiful song that should express the faith of our days as we trust God. Hear them again:

"Many things about tomorrow,
I don't seem to understand.
But I know who holds tomorrow,
And I know who holds my hand."

One thing we do know for sure—we are getting closer to the fulfillment of some of the greatest promises of God that have ever been recorded in His Word. Jesus is coming back again. There are signs that have been left for us to study that help us realize the nearness of His return. God has not left us without fair warning that the end is near. This is not intended to be a prophecy of doom but rather an anticipation of great joy to all who love the Lord and long for His wonderful purposes to be accomplished.

Anyone who fears the second coming of Jesus does not understand the love of God. Again and again we are reminded that His return has love as the key emotion. The Bridegroom, Jesus, is coming for His Bride, you and me. Do you get the picture? As much as some of us have fallen in love with our Saviour, we could never compare what we feel for God to what God feels for us. How awesome that day will be when He takes us to His house and offers us His abundant blessings. That can only be described as, "No eye has seen, no ear has heard, no mind has conceived what God has prepared for those who love Him" (1 Corinthians 2:9).

It is a fact that we don't know the day nor the hour when this moment of triumph will be brought to pass, but we do know that for all those who have put their trust in Him there will come a day when history will be completed and eternity will begin

Jesus said, "Behold, I am coming soon! My reward is with me, and I will give to everyone according to what he has done" (Revelation 22:12).

263

█ **REVIVAL**

*"Will you not revive us again, that your people may rejoice in you?"*

~Psalm 85:6

We are believing for a revival. Most of us have never seen one but we have all heard about them. The Toronto Airport meetings and the Brownsville, Florida, meetings and a few other distant spots throughout the world are points where God has begun to do a new thing. There is no one who wants to see a revival among God's people more than the Lord Himself. It is His desire that His people learn to seek His face and trust Him more, and that the dramatic and the dynamic become a demonstration of His power in the world. We live in a generation where those kinds of things are not thought to be possible nor very important. Christians in many places have fallen asleep to the opportunities to see God demonstrate His power in our generation. Each of us, as children of God, ought to have a deeper appreciation for the things of God and be familiar with His promises.

The fervency of our faith is not the same as the faith of the early Church, and we know it. They were often willing to lay down their lives for the Gospel. They held on to all things lightly and shared freely with the family of God. They had servant hearts and were willing to go to the extreme in order to share an example of the Love of God. They were committed to one another in caring concern. They lived in constant anticipation of the Lord doing in their Church family what only God could do,. And God added His blessings to them because of their inter-dependence upon each other and their dependence upon God and His provisions.

Revival begins at the point of recognizing that we are not what we are supposed to be. It proceeds to the determination that we will do what we can to change things through sincere repentance, and follows through with the heartfelt search to touch the heart of God and be moulded by Him.

The prayer for revival focuses on the truth that we need new life. Our lifestyles and our weak expectations have brought shame upon the Church. The saying is "Confession is good for the soul." More than that, confession is imperative in order to bare our hearts humbly before Him.

We must not content ourselves with what we are presently, nor where our Church is spiritually. The fact that our world has a tremendous need of a visitation of God is beyond question. We can't blame the evangelist, pastor or Sunday School teacher for that lack of spiritual life. We need, individually, to be sincere about seeking God's will to be done on earth just as it is in heaven. It's then that the Holy Spirit will have the kind of material that makes a Revival happen.

Invite the Lord, today, to work in your life, your home and your Church. He is more willing to give than we are to receive.

SEPTEMBER 21 **CLEANSING POWER**

*"This cup is the new covenant in my blood, which is poured out for you."*

~Luke 22:20b

You may not feel comfortable being called a sinner, but that is the way the scriptures speak concerning all of mankind. "...for all have sinned and fall short of the glory of God" (Romans 3:23). That puts us all in the same position.

Some would argue that we should not be blamed for what Adam and Eve did in their rebellion against the will of God, but the connection to our humanity is very obvious. The old adage is, "Like father, like son." Never is that more true than when it is applied to our human nature. There is something wrong in all of us that needs to be changed; and yet, there is not a thing that we can humanly do about it. That's the reason why Jesus came and died on the cross of Calvary. What was impossible for us to accomplish, He was able to do. He came with the authority and power to release us all from the binding influence of wrong-doing. The Bible teaches that "the blood of Jesus, his Son, purifies us from all sin" (1 John 1:7b). The shedding of the blood of Jesus on the cross was sufficient to deal with all the sin of all men for all time.

The passage of scripture above speaks of "my blood, which is poured out..." Notice two things:

1. Jesus said it was "His blood." There is no other way to deal with this matter of sin that is a part of all mankind except through His blood.
2. His blood is "poured out." To me, that indicates quantity sufficient for all our transgressions. It is like a spiritual river that washes away all the things that impede a loving relationship with God.

But here is an important matter to remember: We need to believe and accept this Biblical principle in order to have it applied. It is not sufficient to give mental assent. Each of us needs to indicate a confession of need for forgiveness. "If we confess our sins, he is faithful and just and will forgive us our sins and purify us from all unrighteousness" (1 John 1:9).

We cannot alter the fact that we are sinners by inheritance, but we can do something about the matter of what we do with that sinful nature. If Jesus came and died to bring us forgiveness and a new inheritance, we should accept His provision. We cannot blame Adam and Eve for our lost state if we have the opportunity to have a change in our lives. The Lord has promised to accept us as His own Sons if we but believe in Him. "Yet to all who received him, to those who believed in his name, he gave the right to become children of God" (John 1:12).

▌ **IT'S NOT THE WRAPPER**

*"We have this treasure in jars of clay."*

~2 Corinthians 4:7a

I don't ever remember keeping the wrappers on my birthday or Christmas presents—not that they weren't pretty and heart warming. Through the years I've chucked out a lot of ribbons and bows and colourful paper that somebody took the time to put together to make a gift very special. Most people are very forgiving about that because it's what's IN the wrapping that is the important thing. The true value is on the inside. Funny, I received some after-shave lotion as a gift one time and the top had come loose, slightly. It wasn't hard to guess what was on the inside of that gift-wrap.

When the Apostle Paul wrote about "treasures in jars of clay," he was referring to the fact that God has placed something inside of us that is tremendously valuable. The problem is that people don't readily see what's on the inside because of the outside. The truth is that some people live their lives in such a way that no one could ever tell what's on the inside. Now, there's got to be some way that this treasure we hold in our hearts can be shown to the whole wide world.

I've discovered that, without taking off the trimmings, many times you can find out that what is on the inside of a gift if you apply pressure to the wrapping. (That's when no one is looking, of course.) You get a feel for what the "treasure" really is. Some folks need some extra pressure from time to time so that others can see what they are really made of. That's not the most comfortable way to show what's on the inside, but it is a very effective method that God often uses to let the world know that we have peace, patience and love within. These are ingredients that are absent from a lot of people's lives.

I've also discovered that you can learn what's inside the package if it leaks out. Is it possible that we could be so full of God and His blessings that we become "leaky" vessels that willingly allow others to detect what we hold as the most valuable treasure in the world? The best way for this to begin to happen is to get into the presence of God. Like Moses, who came down from the mountain top with a glowing face that removed all doubt that He had met with God, we should display some evidence to those around us that we have been changed on the inside. We have seen so much evil flaunted around us every day that it's time for the goodness of God to be leaked out into a world where only Jesus can satisfy.

If we are true to living the way the Lord wants us to, people will be wondering what makes us tick. It's then that we can let them know what is on the inside. It's not a guarded secret. There is no reason to wait for a day of special revelation in order to disclose what lies within us. Every day can be a birthday or a fresh Christmas where, with genuine excitement, the wonderful gift of God can be revealed. He is our wonderful treasure and He was meant to be shared with everyone.

| **JESUS PRAYED**

*"For where two or three come together in my name,*
*there am I with them."*

~Matthew 18:20

Jesus was a man of prayer. The accounts of scripture tell us that He often sought out the quiet times to get away from the hustle and bustle of His busy schedule and to wait in the presence of His Father. Even the disciples were aware of the prominence that prayer played in the life of their Master. One day, when Jesus returned from His special time of prayer, the disciples approached Him and said, "Lord, teach us to pray, just as John taught his disciples" (Luke 11:1b). That's when Jesus instructed His followers to pray what we now call "The Lord's Prayer." The disciples had probably noticed the difference that prayer made in the life of John the Baptist and in Jesus' ministry. They were prepared to do whatever was necessary to make the same difference in their lives and prayer seemed to be the key. There are a few times during His public ministry that His prayers were remembered and recorded. But when He was alone, did He pray out loud? Did He just think high and holy thoughts and His Father understood without a word being spoken? What kind of things did Jesus talk about that He would spend so much time in prayer? Why did He pray when He always was and always will be God and He could do whatever He wanted?

Obviously, there are a lot of lessons we can learn from the example of the Lord's prayer life.

Let me suggest a few things:

1. Jesus' times of prayer were clearly a lesson for all mankind that we need to set aside periods of our life to wait in the presence of our Creator. We demonstrate by that habit that we are absolutely dependent upon God. Jesus was seen to pray.

2. Jesus prayed in public and His words were remembered. There was the time He prayed by Lazarus' tomb (John 11), He prayed a lengthy prayer in John 17, and His prayer in the Garden of Gethsemane was remembered by His disciples even though they had fallen asleep. He was heard to pray.

3. Jesus taught some parables to teach specifically that men "should always pray and not give up" (Luke 18:1). He taught about the exercise of faith and persistence in prayer; to be humble and contrite and come as little children.

4. He offered license to ask the Father for anything in His name and the Father would do it. Clearly intended is the principle that those who are committed to serving the Lord would not pray for anything outside of His purpose. We have the privilege and honour to use His authority in that kind of prayer.

5. His example teaches that God hears public prayers and the kind that are done in secret. He hears open air prayers and prayers in the closet. He hears midnight prayers and daylight prayers. Jesus prayed often and we should, too!

267

▌ **NO SURPRISE**

> *"Why does this fellow talk like that? He's blaspheming!*
> *Who can forgive sins but God alone?"*
>
> ~Mark 2:7

It came as no surprise to the Father. Jesus, too, knew exactly what was going to happen and what was expected of Him. They worked together on the decision for Jesus to come into this world and to die on the cross for all the sins of mankind. That was the plan that was established even before the creation of the world and man. It is interesting that from the very first couple that found this world their living space, sin began a destructive infection in the creature that God made in His own image. Again, this was no surprise to God. But the Father was not prepared to leave the plague of sin to continue to grow without a remedy. The one who caused the invasion of sin to come into this world should have realized that the love of God would not permit such a thing to destroy what He had made.

For that reason, a plan was revealed from the Garden of Eden that would grant a sin covering and eventually a perfect cleansing to wash away all the stains of sin's effects. At first, it was the blood of an animal sacrificed upon an altar that served as a temporary release from the consequences of sin, but the sacrifice had to be repeated at least once a year. However, when Jesus came and died on the cross, the annual pilgrimage to the temple for the ablution of sin was terminated. His death on the cross effectively washed away all the stains of every confessed sin, and it was a sacrifice great enough to never have to be repeated. At Easter, we remember that Jesus died once for all our sins, for all mankind, for all time. That's the full expression of the love of God on our behalf.

You see, everyone needs to know the truth of this marvellous story of the grace of God. We all have sinned, and that is not even a question, but God has provided a way to have complete release from the condemnation and the consequences of sin.

Here is an important fact about His forgiveness: He only forgives those who ask Him, personally, for forgiveness. I mean, I can't grant forgiveness nor can any other man. That is a matter that each of us has to take up with God. But listen carefully; He is waiting with arms of love to welcome you to the place of forgiveness. It doesn't matter the magnitude or the agony of the sin. He is willing to grant His pardon and forever forget about it. He waits for you as He waited for me and many others. Make it a point today to talk to Him about your need. But let me add, there is more to a relationship than the matter of forgiveness. He also grants to us the privilege of becoming a part of His heavenly family. That's what the resurrection is all about. You see, Jesus conquered Death when He died. He rose again to prove that He has all power over even the most awesome enemy of our lives.

This is the hope that we possess; because He lives, we too, shall live. So when the last chapter of your earthly journey is written, Heaven is your sure reward because of Calvary.

**PRACTISING PRAYER**

*"Therefore let everyone who is godly pray to you*
*while you may be found."*

~Psalm 32:6a

There may not be a lot of good news in the world today but God is still on the throne. There's war, again, in Israel. They are still shooting it out in Iraq. A good friend of the family passed away after a lengthy battle with cancer. The wife of one of our Pastors passed away, quite suddenly. The economy isn't acting in a very pleasant manner. Women on the street have been targeted by a mass murderer who until now has been free to play his treacherous game. A man involved in the distribution of child pornography received a lecture and was set free to continue his "works of art." The diseases of cancer, aids, heart failure and mental anguish are affecting every one of our families in some measure. I know I haven't even touched on personal issues that I'm sure are heavy on your heart that you, too, would like to see resolved.

Let me assure you that if ever there was a time that God's people needed to reach out to Him, this is the time. Many of these matters are far beyond our control; after all we are just little cogs in the works of things that are way above our abilities. But listen to me carefully! God answers prayer. He has promised, "If my people, who are called by my name, shall humble themselves and pray and turn from their wicked ways, then I will hear from heaven and will forgive their sin and will heal their land" (2 Chronicles 7:14). God will hear.

It's time that Divine justice and righteousness are seen in the world. It's time that the headlines of the newspapers shared some good news to all people living in these depressed days. God cares! I don't understand why He waits for us to get involved in bringing the solution to the world, but that is His choice. He has worked that way throughout history. We need to make the decision to intercede for some of these tremendous matters. Perhaps the little that we do, seen alongside of the little that others are doing, will eventually become a torrent of prayer that will reach the heart of God. We need His help.

My concern is that we haven't personally felt the pain of others sufficiently to compel the need of prayer more seriously in every one of our lives. We have been relatively blessed under His protection in the midst of the turmoil. Thank God for the answers to prayers of the past. Thank God that He is still loving and caring and providing protection and daily supply for all our needs. Thank God for a wonderful church family that is faithful to honouring Him in worship and service. Thank God that He would count us worthy to be "workers together" with Him in reaching out to a lost world.

We can all become involved in prayer. There is no special time, nor place, nor posture that gives us more priority than right now, right here and just as we are. God is looking for a people who will seek His face. He has promised to draw near to us the moment we seek to draw near to Him. Let's purpose to get involved, right now!

269

**BAGGAGE CARRIERS**

*"Therefore, since we are surrounded by such a great cloud of witnesses, let us throw off everything that hinders and the sin that so easily entangles, and let us run with perseverance the race marked out for us."*

~Hebrews 12:1

Most of us carry some baggage from our past. It's the kind of stuff that we have difficulty letting go of and it just hangs around inside our thoughts and our hearts. To some it is a personal hurt through something said or done that we just can't get out of our minds. It hangs like the proverbial albatross around our necks. It infiltrates our nightmares and our moments of solitude. It could be as simple as coming out second best at the spelling bee in grade 4 or as heavy as the tougher issues that brought down a marriage. That happens to be the real world. I'm sure that almost everyone remembers some kind of experience they would like to undo in their past. I could guarantee that as long as we are human, there will be something that will challenge our patience and our "get-up-and-go." Not being a winner all the time is hard to take for some people and put-downs are never much fun at the best of times. It hurts when you know you are innocent; you've done your best and there's not a thing you can do about it.

Let's face it! Life isn't always kind. But God is! We have to learn to let go of the past. I'm still in the learning process of dealing with some of those kinds of issues that hang on to our lives for too long. But let me tell you one thing that we all need to learn—your future is far more important than your past. I know that to be the truth because Jesus came with a better plan. He said, "I have come that they may have life, and have it to the full." (John 10:10b) We need a focus adjustment that will bring us to the place where "what has been" is overcome with "what can be." The Lord has promised that He would grant us forgiveness for all the mistakes, hurts and failures of our history if we would only confess them to Him.

Even so, I have discovered <u>there are two</u> who will not let us drop the "baggage" of the past.

1. *One is called the "Accuser of the Brethren,"* and I want you to know that nothing good you ever do will please him nor stop him from blabbing about your hurts and weaknesses. We need to challenge him with the blood of Jesus because we have assurance that the blood cleanses us. It's a done deal. The past has been dealt with. Gone! Gone!

2. *The other one is the condemnation of our own hearts.* We need to deal with that matter just as much as with the enemy of our souls. We need to stand upon the Word of God and remember that because of what Jesus did on the Cross, the past is past—once and for all. We are designed to begin to experience new liberties of faith in God. Sometimes we are our own worst enemy. Be free, in the name of Jesus. We are living for the future, not the past, and God has good things reserved for us as we focus on pleasing Him. Forgive and be forgiven. God is love and cares very much for each of us. Trust Him for a new joy to fill your life. This is a new day!

▌ **SEE GOD!**

*"We did not follow cleverly invented stories when we told you
about the power and coming of our Lord Jesus Christ,
but we were eyewitnesses of his majesty."*

~2 Peter 1:16

He was born under a bright shining star, but destined to die on an old rugged cross. That's the short story of both sides of His life. It is that mysterious combination of being the Son of God wrapped up in a human frame, just like yours and mine, that is still so difficult for us to comprehend. Before He left heaven, He laid aside the brilliance and glory that He possessed as the Creator and Ruler of the universe. He came to earth and lived as naturally as any other individual man of His time. He grew weary on occasions; hungry on other occasions; He felt sorrow and grief like anyone else; He felt the pressures of His generation and looked to be a man beyond His years. Yet, He never stopped being God even though He willingly accepted the frailties that, by nature, are a part of our humanity. He was able to demonstrate the personality and will of God in practical human ways that we all should be able to understand. During the time that He lived on earth, we could see and hear glimpses of what the heart of God was like, uninterrupted by the beauty and majesty of His Royal position.

The recorded history in the gospels reminds us regularly that God cares for the people that He made, and the actions of this Man of Wonder taught us the reality of the care and concern of a loving Heavenly Father.

He was on a Mission to reveal God's love to a world of hurting, frustrated, depressed and rebellious people. This group was the focus of His ministry; not the self-righteous, nor even the "religious." He came to minister to the poor and needy; the sick and the helpless; and to those who had been rejected in society. He found them in the towns and cities as well as the countryside. He related to all kinds of people and all kinds of situations every place He went. He walked among "us" as God in the flesh.

Jesus came to be the Saviour, the Healer and the Prince of Peace for all mankind, and though He often was unrecognized for who He really was, He gave Himself in loving and caring service. He came to release those who were bound by the habits and lifestyles of sin that were destroying the true joy of life. The power of the darkness of the evil one had obviously left his mark on creation, but Jesus came to halt his invasion and to restore joy and peace to this world.

One of the purposes of His coming was to bring us life and that more abundantly. Because He is the same yesterday and today and forever, He can do it again in our time and for those we love. It is still Jesus who makes the difference in our lives, and, of course, in the whole world.

271

| **UNIQUELY YOU, UNIQUELY ME!**

*"But now, this is what the LORD says—he who created you, O Jacob,*
*he who formed you, O Israel: 'Fear not, for I have redeemed you;*
*I have summoned you by name; you are mine.'"*

~Isaiah 43:1

When the writers of the Bible talked about the Church they used two clear illustrations to describe the interaction of all believers.

- Peter describes us as a "building" composed of living stones built into a spiritual house to serve God as priests offering continual sacrifices to Him.

- Paul describes a "body" with a variety of members, each committing themselves to service in an inter-dependent fashion.

In both illustrations, the success of the building and the body depends upon the participation of each of the "stones," or members, in fulfilling the function which the Architect/Designer intended in His plan. Our problem is that we often compare ourselves to others around us instead of looking to the One who put us in our place with the kinds of talents and abilities that we each possess. There is a brief dialogue in the last chapter of John that describes Jesus' attitude toward such a reaction. Jesus is talking to Peter and they see John come ashore with the rest of the disciples. Peter asks, "Lord, what about him?" Jesus responded, "If I want him to remain alive until I return, what is that to you? You must follow me!" (John 21:20-22). My understanding is that Jesus is saying, "Looking at others is really none of your business. Your job is to follow me."

The call of God for each of our lives is unique. There is a uniqueness in the kind of giftings and abilities that God has given to each of us and we can't compare what we are called to do with what others are called to do. It's comparing apples to oranges. The real challenge is that we need to be obedient to use the talents that God has given us individually. We must be careful to not fall into the trap of the one-talent man in Jesus' story. He hid his talent because of one thing. —he was fearful. He was afraid that things wouldn't work out the way he wanted and the Master would be upset with him. He was afraid of failure. If he had known the Master a little bit better he would have found out that each gift is guaranteed to accomplish the purpose of the Master, if it is used the way it is supposed to. It's a guarantee of success; either now or in the near future.

A little closer to home is the fact that there are a multitude of talents in the chairs and pews of our churches that are collecting dust, growing moss and spoiling with time.

How can I get involved in doing what God wants me to do?

1. Pray that God will lay on your heart an area that you can be of service.

2. Be prepared to move out of your comfort zone and apply some effort in a new endeavour.

3. Talk to someone who is already involved to let them know your interest.

4. Seek advice from a mature believer.

You are needed in the service of the Master!

272

| **TOOLS FOR SERVING THE LORD**

*"Create in me a pure heart, O God, and renew a steadfast spirit within me."*

~Psalm 51:10

Damascus is a long journey from Jerusalem, but if you would have had a festering hatred for the things that God was doing, it probably wouldn't matter. At least that was the intention of Saul, the Pharisee, who hated anyone that mentioned the name of Jesus, the Christ. All of his religious learning and the traditions of his forefathers had made him blind to the arrival of God's wonderful gift to mankind in the form of His Only Begotten Son. He is an example that demonstrates that being religious is no way to find God unless the heart beats for the reality of a living experience with Him. Paul tattled on himself when he said, "Knowledge puffs up..." (1 Corinthians 8:1). This is one of those times when the principle is simple; it is not what you know that counts; it's Who you know.

Sometimes we are tempted to stop at our accumulation of head knowledge and not press in to the experience part of knowing God. You see, the devil is happy at having us all feel comfortable with a theology that knows the facts, but he trembles when we practice what we've learned in our secret places of prayer and devotion to God's word. Most "Christians" don't scare him one bit because they have never learned to use the principles they've acquired. So let's get back into the scary business of being the kind of people that God wants us to be.

Allow me to list a few very important matters.

1. "A broken and contrite heart you will not despise" (Psalm 51:17b). A humble approach to God does wonders for the soul. Work on cultivating tenderness towards God in yourself. It brings awesome rewards. (Loose yourself from anger, bitterness and doubt. These will only send you down the wrong road, with wrong attitudes.)

2. Let the Word of God talk to you regularly. That's God talk. Make a point of reading the Bible with the question on your heart, "What will God say to me today?"

3. Pray. Pray with a passion to meet with God. Memorized prayers serve their purpose, but God wants to meet with you on your territory, personalized by your voice and thoughts.

4. Seek the friendship/companionship of godly people. They will bless you and stretch you in your walk of faith. God has so designed us that we need fellowship, and the very best kinds of people we can find are in the family of God. As much as there are some really great people who don't know the Lord, we need to find times of associating with others in the body of Christ.

Let's get back on track and Go the way God wants us to Go!

▌ **WE'RE TRANSIENTS**

*"Let us not give up meeting together, as some are in the habit of doing,*
*but let us encourage one another—and all the more*
*as you see the Day approaching."*

~Hebrews 10:25

Heaven is our hope; our home. We are all transients here as we take this awesome journey to a wonderful destination. The trouble with most of us is that we get caught up with the day-to-day living with its struggles and distractions that we forget, "this is not where it's at." Now, that might not be very grammatical, and I hope you'll forgive me for being colloquial, but we do put too much emphasis on enjoying these passing pleasures to the point that we are forgetting to lay up treasures in heaven. I'm not against having fun. The Lord knows that there is not an awful lot of that in our average routine. However, there's more to life than meets the eye and brings pleasure to a weary body. The greatest, most important part of the purpose of our existence is to work on our relationship with our Father in heaven.

Someone has said that Sunday Church services today are substituted by activities for our own pleasure; to be free to do whatever we want. To some it is a ball or hockey game, or picnics and fishing or some other thing. That can become a substitute that replaces my time with God. The truth is we make a choice of being in God's house on the Lord's day or not. The question I ask is this: 'Why should God make heaven for those who would rather do something else than to meet with Him in His house?' Would you call that hitting below the belt? The truth is, if you compare our average lifestyle with what heaven and the activities there will be like, most people won't be happy up there because their whole time will be occupied with the Lord God Most High. That would be totally unfamiliar territory. We already have the option of being with those who will be with us throughout eternity and to be an encouragement to them as they journey with us until we reach the Father's house. Having friends and family of the same faith is a real blessing to all of us when we fellowship together. That is one of the reasons for the Lord's Day, as well.

As for me and my house, we have made it a point, through the years, that the Lord's Day is the Lord's Day and not My Day. He gives me six other days to do the things that are necessary for my life and family and He asks me to recognize and honour Him for one day a week. In case you think that my house is a cloistered monastery, I want you to know that I'm still hooting for my favourite hockey team, I still watch some television and we have more that a few laughs around the place, but we've learned a long time ago, "Seek first his kingdom and his righteousness, and all these things will be given to you as well" (Matthew 6:33).

# YOU HAVE TO LET GO

*"But my people would not listen to me: Israel would not submit to me. So I gave them over to their stubborn hearts to follow their own devices."*

~Psalm 81:11-12

Why didn't Jesus go after the "Rich Young Ruler" and persuade him to follow Him? The scriptures accurately recorded that, "Jesus looked at him and *loved* him"' (Mark 10:21a, emphasis added). There must have been something that the Lord could have done to change the young man's mind and bring him into his discipleship family. What would you have done? The issues were important. The young man asked Jesus, "What must I do to inherit eternal life?"' He was asking the right questions and obviously he had great potential if he would only commit himself, his talents and possessions to serving the Lord.

Why didn't the Father of the Prodigal Son follow his boy and try to persuade him from going the way he was heading? Why didn't he send armed guards to protect his son? After all, it appears he was quite a wealthy man.

What is it that possesses a person to walk away from the most important decision of a lifetime? What is it that would cause a person to leave his family and friends just to experience whether the grass is greener on the other side of the fence or not? What would you have done about that?

The truth is that sometimes we just have to let go. As much as we love them and desire only the best for them, some people have made up their minds and chosen to go where their heart draws them. Their ways are not always right, and sometimes there are very severe consequences to their choices, but we have to let go. It hurts us to see people make foolish/wrong choices, but imagine what God feels like when people choose ways that are not good.

With some, God is allowing them to learn some new lessons that will eventually make them into better believers and more committed to obeying the Lord. The fact that they are out of our sight does not mean they are out of God's care. But what, then, should we do? Let me suggest a few things:

1. We need to *pray* for them. God loves them far more than we ever could. We need to lift them to the Father and entrust them into His care.

2. We need to *reach out* to them when opportunity presents itself. God may use us as His method of bringing back the wayward one. We should not stop loving them just because they are not doing what is right.

3. We need to be *patient* and remember that God is in control. One of the mysteries of God's grace is that we can step out of God's will any time by our own choice and free will. God will not forget. He is watchful and caring.

4. We need to be *confident*. "And we know that in all things God works for the good of those who love him, who have been called according to his purpose" (Romans 8:28). Sometimes it hurts to let go, but some people need to discover for themselves that hard lessons are not easy to learn.

275

█ **GOING TO THE HOUSE OF THE LORD**

*"I rejoiced with those who said to me,*
*'Let us go to the house of the Lord.'"*

~Psalm 122:1

So sang the Psalmist, anticipating God's marvellous blessings as he presented himself to the Lord to listen to His Word and to worship at His holy temple. He had known many of the dark and hurting valley experiences of life. He understood what it was like to be accused of doing evil when he had only good intentions. He knew what it was like to be hounded by an enemy who wanted to harm him physically. He understood what loneliness was all about while on the battlefield, away from his caring family. These experiences were very real to him. I'm sure he even felt spiritual fatigue when anger and frustration filled his heart and it was difficult to pray.

But something happened inside of him when friends came to him to invite him to go to worship—his heart was lifted in rejoicing. It was there that he would meet with his God and humbly acknowledge his dependence upon Him. It was there that he would meet with the people who had meant the most to him. For a time, he could lay aside his disappointments and sorrows to lift his voice with the multitude in praise and adoration because God is faithful. The sights and sounds all spoke of the majesty of God and served as reminders of the Awesomeness of God. Indeed, "Great is the Lord and greatly to be praised" (Psalm 145:3). He would go away refreshed and renewed. What a joy to be in the presence of the Lord!

There is something about coming into the House of the Lord that deposits rich blessings upon us that we could not possibly gain anywhere else. We are called to Honour the name of the Lord and to serve Him as "one body" with a variety of gifts and abilities. It is there that we place ourselves into the hands of the Holy Spirit to be worked upon and enriched by the Word of God. It is there that we can identify with the coming together principles (1 Corinthians 14:26) of the "called out ones" whose loving care encourages the lonely heart. And it is there that our spiritual "batteries" can be recharged to face the activities and rigours of another week. "Let us come before Him with thanksgiving and extol Him with music and song" (Psalm 95:2). What strength there is in the unity and harmony of believers reaching out to God together in the congregation of the righteous!

"...let us rejoice and be glad in His salvation" (Isaiah 25:9b). "Sing to the Lord a new song, for He has done marvellous things..." (Psalm 98:1). "Great is the LORD and most worthy of praise..." (Psalm 145:3a). "I will be glad and rejoice in you; I will sing praise to your name, O Most High" (Psalm 9:2).

▌ **JESUS AND JOHN**

*"I am the voice of one calling in the desert,*
*'Make straight the way for the Lord.'"*

~John 1:23b


They passed like ships in the darkness. John's public ministry was clear and to the point. He didn't mince his words. He called people to repentance in preparation for the coming of the Lord. It appears obvious that, although he and Jesus were cousins, they were not personally acquainted until they met somewhere down by the river, out near nowhere. I'm sure that they knew <u>about</u> each other, but apart from this encounter, they each went their separate ways and carried on their distinct ministries.

Sometime after John's death, Jesus asked His disciples, "Who do people say the Son of Man is?" (Matthew 16:13b). Without hesitation, they replied, "Some say John the Baptist" (Luke 9:19). I know that there were a lot of people who had worse names for Jesus and accused Him of some pretty bad stuff. But those who heard Jesus teach and those who observed His miraculous works were sure that John the Baptist had risen from the dead and was alive with greater powers than ever before.

Look at Jesus and John with me:
1. They were both prophesied about in the Old Testament.
2. Their service to God was very different from the Temple services.
3. They both held a sense of contempt for the phoney lifestyle of the religious leaders.
4. They had neither homes nor personal possessions.
5. They ministered in the countryside and in desert places.
6. Their message was given without compromise (Matthew 3:7; 23:33)
7. They both had disciples.
8. They both depended upon prayer.
9. They were both filled with the Spirit.
10. They both died very tragic deaths by command of the leaders of the nation.

But it is the differences that are important to us, today. John was the voice of one crying in the wilderness; prepare the way of the Lord (Matthew 3:3). Jesus, on the other hand, is the Lord who came to be our Saviour.

"Simon Peter answered, 'You are the Christ, the Son of the living God'" (Matthew 16:16). Peter was persuaded that Jesus was the promised Messiah. The words and works that He did were a testimony to who H

e was. He was neither a duplicate John nor an imitation prophet. Jesus is the real thing.

▌ **HEAVEN'S MISSION**

*"'For I know the plans I have for you,' declares the LORD, 'plans to prosper you and not to harm you, plans to give you hope and a future.'"*

~Jeremiah 29:11

The journey of faith sometimes leads us through some very frustrating times. That's called the "testing of our faith" (James 1:3). Those are moments when the unexpected pops up and causes us to wonder what God is doing. I don't think that our "wondering" is wrong. Those times are intended to be a part of the process that will initiate a prayer conversation with the Lord. He allows some circumstances to happen in our walk of faith that will bring us closer to Himself. That is the place where we will find the peace and provision of God for every situation.

We need to learn to trust Him with all those mysterious details that are intended to work out for the good of those who love Him (Romans 8:28). Trusting Him is especially important when the trials or tests don't go away as quickly as we would like. Sometimes the greatest benefit that results from those frustrating times is not in seeing the situation change but in our attitudes and confidence in God staying strong. After all, the most important work that God does in our world today is not in "things," but rather, in our hearts and lives. Praying, trusting God and then adjusting to the circumstances are keys to a successful walk of faith. Don't despair; don't give up; don't lose hope; don't become bitter and angry.

It is still Jesus who makes the difference in our lives and, of course, in the whole world. There is no situation that is beyond His control even though it may be beyond our understanding. His word says, "As the heavens are higher than the earth, so are my ways higher than your ways and my thoughts than your thoughts" (Isaiah 55:9). He can take the deepest, darkest valleys of our lives and fill us with His peace and hope and help us learn lessons that can only be understood through trying times. He is the Great Creator of all things and now He is the Reclaimer of all things in His creation that have fallen out of His will. He demonstrated this by personally coming to the world and revealing the heart of the Father in such a wonderful way. When we come to Him, He is a faithful, loving Friend who understands our feelings, our hurts and pains and is able to do something about them. That's the result of the combination of His Divine nature dwelling in a body just like ours. That's why He invites us to come to Him with confidence and a heart full of assurance (Hebrews 10:22). He knows everything about us and He loves us with an everlasting love. He has better plans for us than we could ever comprehend at this moment. Wait on the Lord and trust that His ways will bring blessing. God is still in control and He has a wonderful plan for you.

▌ **JESUS IS COMING AGAIN**

*"Be on guard! Be alert! You do not know when that time will come."*

~Mark 13:33

Even before He left, He said that He would be coming back again. It must have sounded confusing to the disciples who hadn't yet caught the idea that He was going away. The fact that something very abnormally dramatic was about to happen had not sunk into their hearts. Something supernatural happening at some point in the future was many times more difficult to comprehend. ...until the cross! Then suddenly the possibility of His return, as He said He would, became more of a meaningful possibility. Then the timing became the issue.

"Lord, at this time are you going to restore the kingdom to Israel?" the disciples asked Jesus, just before His ascension (Acts 1:6). Jesus never gave them a date. He wanted to teach them, and us, that the date is not the important matter. It's the keeping ourselves in a ready attitude on a daily basis that is one of the greatest witnesses of the gospel to a lost world. The fact is that a lot of Christians live as though He will never come back again. We sit in comfortable and effortless cruise control and let the world "do it's thing." The world may not be aware that all things are coming to a conclusion, but we know that it is true based on Biblical prophecy.

Jesus is coming again. He said He would. His followers were prepared to lay down their lives in the belief that Jesus was coming back again, in power. Each of the writers of the New Testament Epistles makes reference to Jesus coming back again. The early Christians lived in expectation that He would come in their lifetime. That does not alter the fact that, although He did not come according to their expectations, He will fulfill His promise to return just like He said.

We need to read passages like Matthew 24 for some of the daily reminders that are going on around us in a magnitude never before seen on earth. The fact that the warnings are recorded should be enough to let us know that we ought to be busy in preparation for His return. It's time we took the admonitions of Jesus in Matthew 25 very seriously and begin to question, "What on earth are we doing for heaven's sake?" No, that's not a verse in the Bible but it does express a need for self-examination because the end of all things is at hand and soon we shall stand in His Divine presence to give account of ourselves before God. Some people are going to have a lot to answer for because of their neglect in responding to opportunities to serve God. Watch for the signs. He is coming back again. Let's be doing the very things that He wants us to do.

▌ **LOST**

*"The Lord is not slow in keeping his promise, as some understand slowness. He is patient with you, not wanting anyone to perish, but everyone to come to repentance."*

~2 Peter 3:9

It's not the one lost sheep that is intended to be the focus of the story in Luke 15:1-7. It is the principle that Jesus was making that is the important matter. Those that are lost need to be found. Anyone who has been literally lost at some time in their life will remember the confusion and frustration that they felt until some clue suddenly made them aware of their location. If you've never been lost, you've missed out on a very frightening but enlightening experience that would help you to understand the terror of those who can't find their way.

The strange thing about being lost is that you can be among crowds of people and still not know where you are unless someone around you is willing to give you clear instructions. But here's the real life tragedy—if someone doesn't find their way before life is over, there are some terrible, eternal consequences. Add to that the fact that there are so many that are heading down "the broad road" totally unaware that they are heading in the wrong direction and that an awful disaster awaits them at the end of their journey.

I suppose you could say, "Too bad for them. They made their choices." It's easy when we don't identify someone we know to just shrug our shoulders and silently continue on our way. There are some, though, who care enough to stop and give directions and make sure that the lost are pointed in the right path. Jesus said that, "(He) came to seek and to save what was lost" (Luke 19:10). To say that He cared is to put it mildly. He was consumed with a passion to reach the wayward and make sure that every lost person was given a solution to finding his or her way Home.

When we accept Jesus Christ as our Saviour, which to us is such a blessing, we should also be willing to accept the things that are a burden to His heart. To ask Him for our own salvation without any consideration of those around us that Jesus loves so much seems to be very self-centred. That can't be pleasing to God! It's like the story of the lepers who found a treasure of food, clothing and wealth while the people in the city were dying of starvation and mothers where eating their babies to survive. They "ate and drank" and hid some of the wealth for themselves. Then they said, "We're not doing right. This is a day of good news and we are keeping it to ourselves" (2 Kings 7:9a).

What then should we do? Let me briefly suggest a few things:
1. We need to *seriously pray* for those that are lost.
2. We need to be prepared to *talk* to the lost.
3. We need to be willing to *give* to those who are seeking the lost.
4. We need to prepare to *receive* the lost.

| **WALKING AND WORKING**

*"But thanks be to God, who always leads us in triumphal procession in Christ and through us spreads everywhere the fragrance of the knowledge of him."*

~2 Corinthians 2:14

For more than three years Jesus walked the paths that coursed across the countryside of Israel as He traveled from community to community to share the message of His Father's great love. His hands reached out to all kinds of needs. They were placed upon little children and lepers. He laid his hands upon the dead and raised them to new life. He touched the blind, the deaf, the lame, and the mute and gave them back the freedom to be all they were designed to be. All through His earthly ministry He walked and reached out to the hurting, suffering over-burdened of His world.

The day came when those feet and hands were nailed to a cross. The same hands and feet that had brought miraculous relief to so many were now pinned to a stationary cross planted on the outskirts of Jerusalem.

The true battle was not in what His hands could do. The war was in the spirit realm where demon powers had launched their attacks against God's creation for too long. The Bible tells us that although His body was crucified, He descended into the headquarters of demon authority and tore away the keys of death and hell (Revelation 1:18). His powerful voice preached deliverance in the chambers of the departed saints. They heard the news that God's plan of redemption, announced from the days of the Garden of Eden, was fulfilled as planned. (1 Peter 3:19).

Crucifying and burying Him was no way to stop the absolute power of the King of Kings. His earthly authority may have been questioned by His critics and unjust judges, but there was no way they could hinder the Master from completing the task that He was given to do. Crucifying His body set His Spirit free to work, unrestricted by time and space, to accomplish His Father's purposes in the greater sense. There is no question that the healing of our bodies is part of the wonderful plan of Salvation, but it was the war in the heavenlies that finally put a stop to the overwhelming power of our enemy. Wounded Himself, Jesus stomped on the devil's claim to wisdom and power. The devil is a defeated foe. He must flee from the presence of the most humble saint who lifts his or her voice in a simple prayer to the Father in Jesus' name.

It must be torture for the devil, who has always tried to take the place of God, to find himself helpless and weaponless before those who are made of the dust of the earth. Jesus has won an awesome victory for us. "Thanks be unto God, which always causeth us to triumph in Christ" (2 Corinthians 2:14 KJV). Jesus demonstrated that victory both through His life and through His death. We are more than conquerors through Jesus Christ.

281

▍ **ATTITUDE OF GRATITUDE**

*"Let us rejoice and be glad and give him glory! For the wedding of the Lamb has come, and his bride has made herself ready."*

~Revelation 19:7

Gratitude should be a permanent feature in the faith of people who have seen the hand of God move in their lives. We live more miracles in our time than in any other generation until now. God is at work all around the world and doing marvellous things. It is true that there are a lot of tragedies that make the news, but there is so much that God is doing that goes unrecognized. I'm sure that He has done many things for you, just as He has done for me.

Thanksgiving reminds me of the triumphal entry of Jesus into Jerusalem. For timeless eternity past, the angels of heaven had given full expression to the adoration of the One who sits on the throne. But at this time, the angels were not allowed to give free reign to their praises but confined to their invisible position, and could only observe the reaction of God's creation. Could the crowd on that first Palm Sunday have had ears to hear the invisible, I'm sure they would have heard the hosts saying, "It's about time!" There was singing and dancing, laughter and great rejoicing. The crowds did for Jesus, that day, what was usually reserved for the heroes returning from conquering battles. Palm branches and coats were laid on the dusty trails for Jesus to ride over on His borrowed little donkey.

What a day! I'm sure there were many people present who had been touched by the Master's hand who took this opportunity to express their gratitude. Many had heard the wisdom and felt the heart of His messages. For those few moments, on Palm Sunday, Jesus received the recognition He deserved.

But you know the end of the story. It didn't last. In just a matter of days, the gratitude and sounds of rejoicing wore off and the crowds turned into an angry mob. How soon we forget! It was all for a purpose, but it's a shame that those who had received such wonderful things from the Lord could have continued to live in the victory of their experience.

Let's purpose to be a joyful people, living with a vibrant attitude of gratitude because the next noteworthy events on God's calendar are for a great move of His presence and then the trumpet call that will summon us homeward. It's all going to be over soon. We shall be caught up into the glorious presence of our wonderful Lord. The hosts of heaven will observe the expressions of praise and adoration from the multitudes redeemed by the blood of the Lamb. What a time of rejoicing that will be! All the battles that caused us so much concern will be remembered no more. We'll hear the stories of God's goodness repeated again and again as we visit with the Saints in glory. We have so much to thank the Lord for, even from our personal memories of the past, and only a wonderful anticipation for what we will share in the future. God is so good!

▌ **THANKFUL FOR HIS BLESSINGS**

*"Give thanks to the LORD, for He is good;. his love endures forever."*

~1 Chronicles 16:34

Who can count the abundance of blessings that the Lord has given to us out of the storehouse of His love and good pleasure? He is an Awesome God and His kindness is beyond measure. The Psalmist David expresses it like this: "Many, O LORD my God, are the wonders you have done. The things you planned for us no one can recount to you; were I to speak and tell of them, they would be too many to declare" (Psalm 40:5).

It would be impossible to list all of God's wonderful blessings, both His deeds and His promises but the Psalmist shares a few in Psalm 103:.

1. He forgives all your sins. (You name it to Him and He forgives.)

2. He heals all your diseases. (His power is sufficient for all our sicknesses.)

3. He provides a blessed alternative to the pit. (Heaven is the home of the righteous.)

4. He crowns us with love and compassion. (He is in love with you and daily protects, provides and blesses you.)

5. He has a way of satisfying our desires with good things. (Maybe He doesn't always give us what we want; but good things just the same.)

6. He has a way of restoring youthful strength to weary, perplexed and pressured lives. When we learn to cast all our care upon Him, we find that it is true, He cares for us (1 Peter 5:7).

Every Believer has his or her own story to tell of the wonderful miracles and answers to prayer that the Lord has supplied. It is true that life is not always rosy and comfortable, but our joy and the peace we possess does not depend upon our circumstances. This is because we know, beyond the shadow of doubt, that there is so much more reserved in heaven for us when it's all over down here. After all He has done for us on the cross of Calvary, could we ever question the interest of His wonderful plan for timeless eternity? Listen to the Word of God; "He who did not spare his own Son, but gave him up for us all—how will he not also, along with him, graciously give us all things?" (Romans 8:32).

For that reason, do not become discouraged when the pressure is on. "Lift up your head. Your redemption is drawing near" (Luke 21:28).

Especially on Thanksgiving Day, let's be obedient to Paul's exhortation. "In everything give thanks..." (1 Thessalonians 5:18 NKJV) Remember, everything means *"every* thing."

283

▌ **GRATITUDE**

*"Give thanks in all circumstances,*
*for this is God's will for you in Christ Jesus."*

~1 Thessalonians 5:18

The Lord has been working on building a people with an attitude of gratitude. We haven't always responded to His benefits with thankfulness. The story of the children of Israel leaving the slavery of Egypt in such a miraculous fashion and following the leading of the Pillar of Fire by night and the cloud of smoke by day is always so dramatically interesting. The fact that their daily provisions were supplied, like clockwork, each morning was a clear witness of the care of their Heavenly benefactor. Add to that the dynamics of Mount Sinai, as God spoke to Moses to reveal His purposes for His people, and the evidence of Divine protection against the marauding enemies of the land, the nation of Israel had so many up-to-date witnesses of the blessings through the kindness of God. But the people were complainers. They murmured against the leadership and against God. They became enraged because they couldn't have a menu to select from to satisfy their own desires. Complain, complain, complain, complain.

But God was patient. God is patient!

We have evidences that God is faithful and caring for us each day. We need to learn from the Old Testament experiences that we need to be a people who appreciate the things that God does for us.

The Psalmist says: "Praise the Lord .... and forget not all his benefits" (Psalm 103:2).

- He forgives our sins.
- He heals all our diseases.
- He redeems our life and crowns us with love and compassion
- He satisfies our desires with good things.
- He renews us each day.

We may not always like the wrapper that contains His purposes but the fact remains true that God can bring Joy out of Sorrow; Peace out of Pain and Supply out of Need. Add to that the wonderful sense of His presence as we enjoy a personal relationship with Him. Consider the abundance of material blessings that we take for granted. Look at how the major part of the world exists. Truly we are a very blessed people. An attitude of gratitude should not be difficult. Let's be thankful and express our appreciation to Him in joyful worship. We serve an Awesome God.

If we're not thankful, we just may have to go around the desert a little while longer. So let's rejoice, for our God is good.

**Being Grateful Could Save Your Life**

*"Therefore, since we are receiving a kingdom that cannot be shaken, let us be thankful, and so worship God acceptably with reverence and awe."*

~Hebrews 12:28

He was wealthy and had all the comforts that his riches could buy, but he was a cranky and bitter man. He thought only of himself, and his personal possessions were his treasures. His own wife described him as being a wicked man and that his name should explain all that you needed to know about him. His name is Nabal, which means 'the Fool,' and according to his wife, he lived up to that kind of reputation (1 Samuel 25:25).

The story comes at a time when David is living in the wilderness with his rag-tag army, fleeing from the anger and jealousy of King Saul. But this was no waste of time for David. He began to train his followers in matters of order, discipline and combat strategies. As a regular exercise, they watched for wandering looters from the nations and tribes who hated the nation of Israel and he dealt with them severely. Many times, they had come to the rescue of Nabal's shepherds. David and his men were like a wall of protection to keep the shepherds from the harm and danger of the blood-thirsty thieves and the workers appreciated that security.

But Nabal didn't. He couldn't care two hoots about David and his problems. He was careless, thankless and heartless. He was an absolute ingrate. It was his wife who saved his life by her intercession and offering. When David was hungry Nabal would not give him even a loaf of bread. However, his wife was grateful for the watchful care that David and his men had demonstrated to her property and to her family. I think it's fair to say that being thankful could have saved Nabal's life from an untimely death. It appears that he had a stroke or heart failure and became as a stone and died (1 Samuel 25:37).

Gratitude is an exercise of the heart. Deny that and there are some very serious consequences. Some of the happiest people on earth are those who are thankful for everything. Whether we're poor or rich; from Timbuktu or right here in Canada, being thankful is a way to demonstrate a healthy heart. That's why Paul would advise us to, "give thanks in all circumstances, for this is God's will for you in Christ Jesus" (1 Thessalonians. 5:18).

God has been so good to us. He has provided a way to have our sins forgiven. He has promised us many wonderful things because we are a part of His heavenly family. He is available as our Healer, Provider and Protector. He guides, gives wisdom, helps us in our weaknesses and He is always available as our friend.

Let us rejoice and give thanks today and be blessed in doing so. Someone has said, "Thanksgiving is good; Thanks*living* is better."

▌ **Be Thankful**

> *"Devote yourselves to prayer, being watchful and thankful."*
>
> ~Colossians 4:2

There are lots of things in this world that I just do not appreciate. Things like broccoli, pain, sickness, bad weather on a day off, temptation and people being late for appointments.. All that stuff makes me feel uncomfortable and sometimes moves me to anger. But then, I am reminded by the gentle voice of the Holy Spirit that I am to "... *give* thanks *in all circumstances*" (1 Thessalonians 5:18, emphasis added).

I may think that I have good reason to not approve of the "circumstances" that cause me discomfort or distress, but I must realize, too, that there is a bigger and better plan that is in effect and that God does not miss out on any of the most minute of details. As one who trusts in the purposes of an Awesome God, I need to apply some very basic principles that He outlines along side of this little challenge to be grateful; each of these principles are intended to be timeless. Listen:

*1. Be joyful always.* Come on, now, let's see some smiles. I've seen some Christians that look like they just climbed out of a lemon tree, whose faces are as long as a mules and who've lost the excitement of facing new challenges in life. Get a hold of yourself! For the Christian, our choice is to rejoice and, as Paul says, "again I say rejoice!" Smiles given receive smiles in return.

*2. Pray continually.* You mean to tell me that I am not spiritual enough already? I didn't say that, but come to think of it, we all need the spiritual exercise now more than ever before. This is not to be a once for all experience but rather a day by day, moment by moment relationship with God. It doesn't require a change in posture or place. Anywhere and anytime are all parts of God's schedule.

*3.* Then comes the exhortation to give thanks in *all circumstances*. That's the reminder of this day.

These three exhortations are tied together with this fact..."this is God's will for you in Christ Jesus." My own translation would be, "This is the way God wants it." That kind of puts the onus on me to swallow my feelings, to stop defending "my rights" and to learn that God is bigger than all my emotions and situations. He is able to help me through all circumstances to be a happy, peaceful and grateful person.

Now if all "us Christians" would practice these things, what a wonderful world we would be living in. It comes down to a simple expression of confidence. We need to believe that God loves us and that every experience that comes our way is either an opportunity to see God's provision or a lesson for us to learn some valuable truth.

Lord, teach us to be thankful!

▌ **LEARNING TO PRAY**

*"...Lord, teach us to pray, just as John taught his disciples.*
*He said to them, When you pray, say ..."*

~Luke 11:1-2

Prayer was always an important part of Jesus' life. It was His lifeline to a wonderful relationship with His Father. The disciples appreciated His example as well as that of John the Baptist who taught his disciples to pray. They realized that one of their greatest needs in the development of their spiritual lives was to do what these two "men" were doing so effectively. I'm sure that the disciples had been to the Temple many times before and had watched the 'professional prayers' doing their thing, but the way Jesus and John prayed was so different. Their prayers were not only satisfying their need to know God but also were followed by results. There must be some lessons to be learned. Who better to teach the secrets of prayer than the "Prayer Master"?

Allow me to share a few things about Jesus' pattern for prayer:

1. Jesus did not begin His instruction with the word "if." The fact of the matter is we *must* pray. This should become a normal component of our daily Christian life. The biggest problem with modern prayers is that they are not prayed. Jesus lays the emphasis upon the fact that praying ought to be a part of our daily agendas. He said, "When you pray," not "if you pray."

2. Jesus, in contrast to the priests and the Pharisees, taught that the approach to God should be with the same confidence that a little child has when he comes to his father. Our approach to our Heavenly Father is to be without fear, with a simple faith, with respect and with love. That basic principle blew the minds of the religious leaders who for centuries drew near to God only out of duty and with fear; going through the process. Jesus wanted to make it clear that God really cares for us as His own children in relationship style as opposed to regulations and structure.

3. The approach to God was not intended to be "high-fallooten", but rather, in terms of a daily conversation expressing praise and petition to God without drama nor memorized religious terminology. I think we will be surprised at how God appreciates the simplicity of the average "six-pack Joe" who comes to God to pray with simple and humble faith.

Let's pray! And let's do it often each day, to make Him the centre of our lives.

**REPENTANCE AND RESTITUTION**

*"A man ought to examine himself before he eats of the bread and drinks of the cup."*

~1 Corinthians 11:28

Jesus had a wonderful way of teaching principles to people that made them sit up and think. He wasn't stuck in the old clichés of the religious leaders of His time. Some that came to hear and criticize Him were amazed at the clarity and authority of His message. The leaders were sometimes embarrassed by Him, but the common people gladly heard Him. Those leaders had to acknowledge, "Look how the whole world has gone after Him!" (John 12:19b).

On one occasion, Jesus attacked the reasoning of the Jewish leaders who underestimated the value of the individual before God. They had insisted that if you offend someone, all you have to do is give a gift to God and your wicked actions will be forgiven. Knowing the heart of Jesus, I'm sure that His concern was toward what was being done to fix up the human side of the problem; after all, "hurt people, hurt people." To Jesus, it was a matter that could not be passed off as easily as that. He so candidly said to the Pharisees, "You have a fine way of setting aside the commands of God in order to observe your own traditions!" (Mark 7:9). In other words, "What you're doing is not the way God wants things to be done." This put pressure on the "comfort zones" of the religious leaders and it didn't make them happy.

You see, Jesus was dealing with professional hypocrites who were firstly interested in people looking to them for spiritual advice and then secondly, referring to what God said about the important issues of life according to their interpretation. Before we get too uppity about it, though, I guess I need to ask us this question. Does it really matter to anyone today what God thinks about our morals and our lifestyles? You will hear all kinds of opinions about homosexuality, abortion, respecting the Lord's day and using the Lord's name as a swear word in daily conversation. There is nothing wrong with hearing the philosophies and ideas of others, but the standard that really matters is, "What does God say about all this?" This is a principle that we cannot escape.

I think that it is especially important for Christians to examine our stand on some of these issues and repent and change our ways. After all, we are to be examples of the Kingdom of God, not of the kingdom of this world. We need to understand that God has a higher role for us to follow than the one that is accepted in society or even in our personal desires. What would Jesus do? Don't get stuck in the hardheaded stubbornness of the Pharisees, who were not prepared to submit their traditions to the eye of God's Word.

**TAKE A LOOK INSIDE**

*"What goes into a man's mouth does not make him 'unclean,' but what comes out of his mouth, that is what makes him 'unclean'."*

~Matthew 15:11

One of my rose bushes has been holding on to a bud for the last two months. It hasn't opened up because of the cold and the rain, but it is hanging on "for better times." I love flowers of all kinds, but they all fade away in their season. I've taken pictures of plants to treasure their beauty, knowing well that what I see right now will eventually go the way of all the other flowers and fall to the ground. I've noticed that even the beauty of youth goes through a transformation that changes the gentle blush to the mature look, and then the wrinkles appear. This is the reason for makeup, perfume and lotions. We want to hold on to the strong, the beautiful and the glamorous as long as we can. We know there is coming a time when the roses will fade, the glamour will be lost and life will go on in a different way.

Peter wrote of having an unfading beauty on the inner self. (1 Peter 3:4). Unfading beauty! We wish that the secret of the mysterious fountain of youth would do that to our bodies while Peter is reminding us that the important "stuff" is on the inside. We pay a lot of attention to the outside but have not taken a lot of care for the inside.

I love watching the children open their gifts on birthdays and Christmas. They don't care about the wrappings! They aren't gentle or orderly. As far as they are concerned "let's get to the good stuff" that is covered with the unnecessary paper. It's what's inside that counts. That's a Bible story, too. It's what's on the inside that makes our living so important. As a matter of fact the book of Proverbs reminds us, "Above all else, guard your heart, for it is the wellspring of life" (4:23). Anything that is worth something in our lives has its source in our hearts. Our values, our reactions, our attitudes, our self-worth and who we really are comes from the spring in our hearts. These are the really important things in life and somehow we need to beautify ourselves in these areas.

Let me suggest a spiritual beautician's formula to making ourselves attractive on the inner self:

1. Prayer—the more time we spend with the Master, the more we become like Him. It's His nature in us that will bring us a lasting benefit.

2. Put out of your heart and mind anything that would be negative and bitter. We need to learn to grow on the sweet, pure and loving matters in order to flavour our lives in healthy ways.

3. Choose your friends. Those that have a negative affect should not have a chance to rob us of much of our energy and time. Find friends that are upbeat and joyfully positive.

4. Exercise your mind by reading items that will help you to grow spiritually and will challenge your heart for a deeper walk with the Lord.

**IN HONOUR OF OUR SENIORS**

*"Everyone has heard about your obedience, so I am full of joy over you."*

~Romans 16:19a

Peter was not supposed to be considered "the foundation of the Church" as some might think. He was one of the first leaders and there is no question that his ministry and influence was very important in establishing the Church in the first century. It's often the beginnings that set an example for us to follow. For when we lose sight of the intended focus of those who have gone before us, we also lose the primary purpose that the original was designed for. Like a plant that must not forget that it grows out of an unseen root, there are some "former" things that must not change because they are basic to healthy development and growth. From the same illustration, the plant is entirely distinct from the root because it was designed to fulfill a different purpose although still a part of the whole. However, there is a flow of life that comes through the root and into the plant that demonstrates that anything that is going to be on "the top" must come through the bottom. The latter comes from the former.

That's why it is important to remember that there are others who were a part of the Church long before we came on the scene. They laid a good, enduring foundation that we have inherited from their sacrificial dedication. We may not see all that these first-comers have done, but this one thing is sure, the pioneers, founders and builders of our Churches have laboured with love to provide what we enjoy today. They willingly gave their energies, time and tithes through difficult years (and sometimes through persecution) in order to establish the facilities and the recognition that we enjoy today. Some, literally, stood on street corners in open-air meetings to sound out the message of the love of God.

Others drove buses and their own cars to round up the kids from the neighbourhood and bring them into the Church Sunday School and Kid's Club. The parents of these children eventually followed them and here we are today— vibrant places of spiritual influence that continue to send out a message of hope to a lost generation. The roots were faithful to do "what they could" and we reap the benefits. Faithfulness is not a commodity on the market today, but we see the evidences of a past generation and we are the recipients of a wonderful treasure. The rewards of their faithfulness have fallen into our lap.

We are grateful for the Seniors who continue to give godly examples to us. I'm glad that there hasn't been any wavering in their commitment to serve God. Our Seniors are worthy of special recognition. We appreciate their labours of love through the years of their committed service. We extend a heartfelt expression of gratitude to them.

**AT THE COST OF HIS FIRSTBORN**

*"And in him you too are being built together to become a dwelling in which God lives by his Spirit."*

~Ephesians 2:22

When the walls of Jericho fell in the days of Joshua, a prophetic proclamation was made that anyone who ever tried to rebuild another city in the same place would do so at great personal cost. In the words of Joshua, "At the cost of his firstborn son will he lay its foundations..." (Joshua 6:26) During the reign of King Ahab, a man by the name of Hiel began to rebuild Jericho, and true to the prophetic message, all of this man's children died during the construction of the city walls. (1 Kings 16:34).

Prophetic messages often use the principle of a *"double application."* For example, Isaiah 7:14 is the announcement, firstly, of the birth of our Saviour Jesus who came to be God with us. Secondly, to Isaiah this was God's way of telling him that he and his wife would have a child and that before the child would know to choose between the right and wrong, there would be a judgment on the land.

This message of Joshua to Jericho also has a *"second application."* Let's hear the message again. "At the cost of his firstborn son will he lay its foundations..."

God's intentions to choose a people for himself out of all of creation is known as the building of the Church. Peter calls those same people "living stones" who are to be built into a spiritual house. (1 Peter 2:5). That "spiritual house" is being built today as the gospel is preached to nations around the world. Its construction began at great personal cost to God the Father, who gave His One and only Son in the laying of the foundation. Before He entered into the project of building His Church He already knew the end cost. And it's the cost that lets us know the value that God had in mind before the undertaking of this very special plan began. He is building for eternity and each one of us is a part of His plan. The price that was necessary to commence the project was the death of His Son on the cross of Calvary.

Although the original prophecy of Joshua's day was totally negative, the double application has totally positive benefits for all of us. When Jesus died on the cross, He made it possible for everyone to be included in the miracle of God's developing plan. The whole idea was God's, and it meant that Jesus would "die in my place so that I could move into His place." Every one of us can say the same thing. It was necessary for Jesus to lay down His life or there would be no foundation for the Church. It's because He did lay down His life that He is the foundation for Christian homes, Christian lifestyles and the basis of our Faith. There is no other way. It is Jesus or nothing. There are no other options. Our Heavenly Father knew all of this before the earth was formed and yet He willingly allowed His Son to come to earth to die so that a firm foundation could be laid for us.

291

| **TOUCHING GOD**

*"This day I defy the ranks of Israel! Give me a man
and let us fight each other."*

~1 Samuel 17:10

King David was a marvellous mixture of talent and passion. It all seemed to come together most clearly when he heard the challenge of Goliath. Something "tweaked" in David's heart. Perhaps it was the memories of his hand-to-paw combat with both a lion and a bear. He said, "The LORD who delivered me from the paw of the lion and the paw of the bear will deliver me from the hand of this Philistine" (1 Samuel 17:37). David was not afraid of a good fight even though it carried some heavy odds.

It was his faith in God that was the key to it all. If God would not have been with him, he would have been nothing more than another little boy in the neighbourhood. But God was in this matter. He knew that God was the one asset he possessed that the enemy could not overcome, and the proof was not in the pudding. It was in the face-to-face encounter with someone who was a lot bigger than himself. He learned that if he gave what he had, God would do the rest. That describes the heart of David. He wanted God's will, God's way, in God's time. He was prepared to offer his little self if God would use him. He loved what God would do in a life that was sold out to Him. He loved the fact that when God was honoured, he would be blessed, and David revelled in the face of impossibility.

But it wasn't just on the battlefield that David expressed such passion. There were quiet moments of worship where his longing for more of God broke into songs that we read and sing today. "Oh God, you are my God, earnestly will I seek you; my soul thirsts for you,. my body longs for you, in a dry and weary land where there is no water" (Psalm 63:1). He was a great warrior who possessed a passion for the heart of God. Like a magnet to iron he was drawn to seek more and more of God. Marked as one of the greatest warriors in Israel, it is sometimes difficult to picture him so tender and hungry in spirit for the presence of God.

He was sidetracked, occasionally, by things that were displeasing to God, but the cry of his repentant heart always displayed the sensitivity of a humble, childlike yearning to be restored to the place that would please his heavenly Father. The evidence of his passion for God is more of a lesson in life than all the victories won on the bloody battlefields. What makes a person important in life? What could be the greatest contribution that we could make to the next generation? Let me assure you that if we could leave behind a legacy of touching God and of experiences in His presence, our children would value that more than wealth or education. The curse of our time is that we focus more on the battle for bread and bacon and the comfort and security of things than we do on getting closer to God. Some of those battles are important, but there is absolutely nothing that can take the place of what God can do in our lives when we seek Him.

█ **SOME AREN'T LEAVING WITH US**

*"Therefore keep watch, because you do not know the day or the hour."*

~Matthew 25:13

One day, our hope will become reality. We live in the expectation of the fulfillment of the promise Jesus made when He said, "I will come again and receive you unto myself" (John 14:3 KJV). He **is** coming back again to receive us to Himself. That will be a day of relief from pain and suffering, from the pressures of our world and from the conflict of temptation. We'll be ushered into the eternal presence of the King of Kings to inherit the pleasures of His eternal love.

But not everyone we know will be there. Jesus said, "All the nations will be gathered before him, and he will separate the people one from another as the shepherd separates the sheep from the goats...Then the King will say to those on his right, 'Come, you who are blessed by my Father; take your inheritance, the kingdom prepared for you since the creation of the world'" (Matthew 25:32, 34). I like the basic principle of that passage. There is a special place already created for those who trust in Jesus.

But there is another side to the whole story. The other "separated ones" don't have the kind of hope that we have. They live with us, work with us, shop where we shop but they are not going where we are going.

*Listen to me carefully!* **They are not going where we are going.** Jesus warns, "...on that night two people will be in one bed, one shall be taken and the other left" (Luke 17:34). That's the separation of husband and wife. He also said, "Two men will be in the field; one will be taken and the other left. Two women will be grinding with a hand mill; one will be taken and the other left." (Matthew 24:40-41). People at the work place will be separated as one goes to be with the Lord and the other is left behind.

Both sincere "love" and "Missions" have got to begin at home. It is possible that our own loved ones will not know the great blessing of going to be with the Lord. They will be left behind. Their destination is not the same as ours. That must be an agony, for those who love the Lord, to think that the possibility exists that those who are closest to us will miss the coming of the Lord and not make it to heaven.

Let me suggest a few things concerning this matter:

1. Let's get serious. This is a situation of urgency.

2. Let's pray, like never before, that God will send the Holy Spirit to work on their hearts and use us to reach our loved ones.

3. Let's be bold. The subject of eternity needs to be raised before a generation that is caught up in seeking for pleasures and living well for today.

4. Let's live so that there will be no question of our loyalty to our Lord. Our spouses and our kids need to know that we believe that Jesus is coming again.

▌ **CROSS-BEARING SERVANTS**

*"Let us fix our eyes on Jesus, the author and perfecter of our faith,*
*who for the joy set before him endured the cross, scorning its shame,*
*and sat down at the right hand of the throne of God."*

~Hebrews 12:2

He was speaking about the cross, but the emphasis was on service and commitment. He said, "If anyone would come after me, he must deny himself and take up his cross and follow me" (Matthew 16:24).

He raises some very critical issues about those who would be His followers. One of those matters was to teach that there may be a very serious price to pay for being one of His disciples, but we prefer the other side of the coin. We are all happy to acknowledge that our sins have been forgiven because Jesus went to the cross, but we are not so happy when He asks us to be willing to give ourselves in sacrifice. Most of us are content to follow "a long way off" in places that are more comfortable in our society than being near the cross. Perhaps the worldly influences and the comforts we enjoy have made us grow soft in our willingness to stand up for the truth and carry the cross; to lay our lives on the line for His sake.

It is a lot simpler, and more comforting, to let others do the work and make the sacrifices. We are willing to pay Evangelists and Pastors to do the cross-bearing while we, together, reap the benefits of being where God is working. There is a payday coming. Guess who gets the wages for faithfulness? Those who have been found faithful. The truth is that we need an Old Fashioned Pentecostal experience to revive us once again. I don't mean the kind of revival that makes us feel happy with the warm fuzzies all over. I mean the kind of revival that gives power and boldness to do the work that has been set for us to do; like speaking to people about the Gospel claims; like praying for the sick and needy; like believing for extraordinary things to happen when we pray.

There are great opportunities available for all of us, each day, but we've got to be serious about doing what Jesus wants us to do without regard for what others may or may not be doing. It's Cross-Bearers that will make the difference in the Kingdom of God. They're people who know their God and are sensitive to the leading of the Spirit who is searching for the lost in the world today. They are people who are willing to overcome timidity and fear to speak up when the opportunity arises to speak of the love of God and the gift of His One and only Son. Cross Bearers are gutsy. They don't mind being ridiculed and mocked on occasion. They remain faithful because they know Someone who carried the cross for them. He went all the way to Calvary and counted it all joy. So let's be ready to give ourselves to serve Him.

294

**▌ RETURNING TO EARLY CHURCH PRINCIPLES**

*"But you will receive power when the Holy Spirit comes on you;*
*and you will be my witnesses in Jerusalem,*
*and in all Judea and Samaria, and to the ends of the earth."*

~Acts 1:8

The Day of Pentecost was the birth of the Church. Many nations were in Jerusalem on that day and many quickly became a part of the move of God over all the earth. The Spirit of God began calling men and women to a personal relationship with Jesus Christ. It was no longer just the Jews, but now it was all men everywhere who were welcome to become a part of what God was doing.

As the Word went out through those who had experienced this Wonderful visitation of the Spirit, the hearts of many were deeply touched and God worked signs and wonders in their midst. The Christians were bold in their faith and shared their influence wherever they went. They lived with the constant expectation that when they prayed, God would answer. Add to that basic principle that they had seen the Lord ascend into heaven but believed that He was going to return again at any moment.

They shared their faith because they really believed that the lost needed to be found before the Lord came back. They realized that they were called to be involved in the matter that was closest to the heart of God, reaching the lost. What a blessing to be able to work with God in such a powerful project as that of sharing the good news that, "God so loved the world."

The interesting thing about the whole story of the history of the Church of Jesus Christ is the fact that we have the same privileges as the Early Church in that we, too, can share the same message with others. The Day of Pentecost introduced a new Divine involvement to the whole project. The Holy Spirit would come and dwell inside of the believers to empower them to share the message. Simple words spoken would be endued with Power to bring conviction and demand decision. The Holy Spirit came to help us live like Jesus lived. He came to remind us of things that Jesus said. He came to be a new source of comfort and strength on a daily basis as we wait upon Him. We may learn to hear His gentle promptings to do the things that please the Father and reach out to a very needy world.

The early Church received the Holy Spirit and told the story of God's love. Within a generation, almost the entire world surrounding Israel had heard the message. The critics of the Church and the believers said, "These men who have caused trouble all over the world have now come here" (Acts 17:6b).

There are some in your area of influence who need to hear what you have to say. Please, do not be embarrassed about sharing your experience with the Lord Jesus Christ. Let's set our goals on reaching those around us.

▌ **TRUTH OR CONSEQUENCES**

*"Test me, O LORD, and try me, examine my heart and my mind."*

~Psalm 26:2

We teach children that if they play with matches they'll get burned. If they play with electricity they'll get a good shock. If they don't look both ways when they cross the street they may be hurt, and they need to know that stop signs are there for a purpose.

The counsel of parents is designed to protect children from harm and danger because there are consequences to wrong actions and choices. Only a fool would argue that the parents lay down these rules just to spoil the fun of our kids. Those who are uninformed about these kinds of rules will probably learn their lessons by hard experience. Someone has said that "experience is a bad teacher because it gives the test before it gives the lesson." I heard a man say that the reason his son failed his class was because he had a poor teacher. As much as that may be possible, we need to acknowledge that the learning process is ultimately hearing right and doing right by our own choice. Obedience to following the rules established by parents is the beginning of learning the best way to keep out of trouble and danger. There are consequences to those who think they know better. Many's the time, during my years of ministry, that I've heard young people say, "If only I had listened to my Mom and Dad!"

That's what the Ten Commandments are all about. God has no intentions of spoiling the joy of our lives. He wants to protect us from the very serious dangers that result from breaking those rules. Obedience is the key. Like a true, caring Father, His advice is to give us guidelines to successful living; not only here and now but also then and there.

One of the most wonderful blessings we receive when we accept Jesus Christ as our Saviour is the gift of the Holy Spirit who moves into our lives (John 14:17). He represents the wisdom and counsel of God and He comes to prompt us from within (John 14:26). He is like a vocal unwritten law who will gently speak to us if we are not doing the right things (John 16:13). He is there as an Envoy of heaven to keep us on the right track and out of harm and danger. He can become the gentle "Nagger" in the halls of our heart and mind if we are disobedient. He will not let us go until we make matters right. Even that is a blessing.

You see, He wants to live in a clean house where even the garbage cans are cleaned out regularly. The key, of course, is that we need to listen to Him and obey His promptings, because there are consequences to offending Him and disobeying His guidelines. This is not intended to be an epistle of accusation but rather a gentle prodding to examine ourselves and do what we know is right before the Lord. We should recognize our privileges as the Children of a loving Heavenly Father who only wants the best for us.

Let's fix our eyes on Jesus and do what He wants us to do.

| ## A MEMBER OF A LOCAL CHURCH

*"They all joined together constantly in prayer, along with the women and Mary the mother of Jesus, and with his brothers."*

~Acts 1:14

The Church of Jesus Christ is Universal. All around the world, those who confess Jesus Christ is Lord are a part of that Church. The Church is made up of individual congregations in the local community.

Why should I become a member of a local Church?

1. I want to let everyone know that I am in agreement with the teaching and direction of this Congregation and that I am willing to give my support to see God's will done in the local Church.

2. As a God-given privilege I want to be a part of the decision-making process that is given to the members of this Congregation at their annual meeting and special business meetings that may determine the direction of the Church programs and outreach.

3. If possible, I want to be able to express my confidence in the leadership of the Church by the nominating and voting process that is offered to the membership.

4. I want to make it known that I am willing to participate in some of the Committees and activities of this Congregation as my talents and abilities will allow. I believe that the Church is the visible expression of the body of Jesus Christ and I want to offer myself to be a part of what He wants to do with my giftings and talents.

5. I believe that it is important to choose to place myself under the leadership, teaching and example of those that God has placed in authority in the Local Church.

6. I believe that it is God's will that I commit myself to fulfilling His purposes for the Universal Church in the setting of the Local Assembly of believers which is our Church.

7. I wish to affirm that my commitment to being a member will be demonstrated in other practical ways with my tithes, gifts and offerings for the support of the purposes and the Mission of this Church.

8. I want to be a visible part of caring and ministering to the people in the Church and to be able to say that I do it for the Lord and His Church, which is our local Assembly.

9. I believe that being a member, by choice, is a witness to the world that I have a loyalty to what God is doing in this world and I wish to demonstrate that by being a part of the Local Assembly.

10. I wish to publicly acknowledge that I am joining heart and hands with others of like faith and commitment to honour the Lord through the Ministries of the Local Church.

| **A MAN WITH A BAD ATTITUDE**

*"Glory in his holy name; let the hearts of those who seek the LORD rejoice."*

~Psalm 105:3

He was the first baby to be born into this world. As far as his mother was concerned he was "the man." If you talk about the rights of the first born, this was "the man." We don't know a lot about him apart from the fact that he was a gardener by profession and that he was the first person to make the choice to offer a thank offering to the Lord. In the record, it's the first time we find mention of giving back to God a part of the benefits of living in His world.

But there was something missing in the process. Abel followed his brother's example and brought an offering as well. I know that some have said that Abel's offering was accepted because he offered a lamb while Cain's offering was rejected because he gave of the fruit of the soil. One surrendered a life while the other gave plant life. I won't make this a point of argument, but I believe that the Lord was looking at the life and attitude of the giver more than at what was laid on the altar. The Word says, "The Lord looked with favour on Abel and his offering" (Genesis 4:4b). God looked at the man, first. Jesus conveyed the same idea when He said, "If you are offering your gift at the altar and there remember that your brother has something against you, leave your gift there in front of the altar. First go and be reconciled to your brother; then come and offer your gift." (Matthew 5:23-24) The gift/offering was important; but more important was the attitude or condition of the heart. Cain showed what was on the inside because, "He was very angry" following the worship service. God was so concerned about his attitude that He came down and spoke to Cain personally about the matter.

There is no question that giving is an important part of our worship service to the Lord. But more important is thanksgiving; that is, the sincere expression of gratitude that comes from the heart. That's what no one else can see but what God is looking for. The gospels tell the story of Jesus observing as many gave their offerings at the temple and it was reported that some put in "much." Then a widow lady came along and humbly threw in 2 mites (two brass coins worth about a 1/5th of a cent). Jesus saw it all and drew the attention of his disciples to the fact that the woman put in more than all the others. He saw her heart. She put in all that she had (Luke 21:4).

You see, the amount isn't the important thing. Someone has said, "The heart of the matter is the matter of the heart." That's what thanksgiving and worship are all about. We can say all kinds of words and do all kinds of things, but God looks at the motives, attitude and condition of the heart, and that is the key to His acceptance or rejection of the gifts we bring. I've never heard of God discarding the gifts; He just won't receive them until the heart is right. When that is all fixed up, we can return to the altar to a personal encounter with the living God.

▌ **GETTING CLEANED UP**

*"Wash away all my iniquity and cleanse me from my sin."*

~Psalm 51:2

There's a complete aisle of shelves filled with cleaning agents at the store where we shop. The containers come in all kinds of shapes, sizes and colours. You can buy them in bar shapes, in boxes of powder or in liquid form. The soaps come in a variety of fragrances from roses to ammonia. There are specialty cleansers for spots and stains; for different types of materials; for paint and grease and for getting out the things that shouldn't be there. You can choose from generic products or your favourite brand names. It seems there's no end to the choices.

But there's no detergent on the shelves that can take away the stain and blemish of sin. It's been a serious problem since the Garden of Eden. People have been looking for an answer to that difficulty through the generations. Some have tried alcohol, but that only hides the stain for a little while and then it re-appears. It's the same with drugs and that kind of stuff. Some have tried to change their lifestyle to rid themselves of their past, but that was like a vacation from reality and soon all the problems returned because not even that can wash away the guilt of sin. Some people try to live their lives by ignoring the promptings within, but that's one of the reasons that our world is in such a mess today. In case you think that I'm selectively picking on a group of individuals, I want you to know that we all have to deal with the same problem and get serious about it. "If we claim to be without sin, we deceive ourselves and the truth is not in us" (1 John 1:8).

Here's the deal. There is only one thing that will ever get us out of the guilt and the bad feelings that our sin has created. The Bible says, "...the blood of Jesus...purifies us from all sin" (1 John 1:7). When Jesus died on the cross, He provided a way that we could be made clean and restored to a right relationship with God. There's no other way in all of creation that can deal with that problem. Although He died almost 2000 years ago, the moment I decide to believe and trust that His sacrifice was sufficient for the stains of all mankind until the end of time, I automatically receive the kind of cleansing that makes me a brand new creation. I can experience true freedom from guilt and the despair that always accompanies it. I can come before the Lord as a child comes to his father. I become the recipient of an eternal inheritance because, by faith, I'm washed in the blood of the Lamb and all my sins are buried where they will never be remembered again.

It sounds so simple that it's difficult to believe. That's what the love of God has provided for every man, woman and child. The simplicity of the process makes it available to all.

▐ **THE CAPTAIN IS IN THE BOAT**

*"He performs wonders that cannot be fathomed,*
*miracles that cannot be counted."*

~Job 5:9

It was during one of those "furious squalls" that sometimes swept across the sea of Galilee that the experienced fishermen seriously feared for their lives. They awakened Jesus from His slumber. He stood up at the back of the bouncing boat, looked the wind in the face and said, "Quiet! Be still!" Immediately, the wind stopped and there was a great calm. The story in Mark tells us that His disciples were terrified to think that their friend had such power. You would have believed that it was a wake up call for the disciples to realize that Jesus was not just a good teacher; he was not a mysterious magician who knew some pretty good tricks. The passenger in their boat was the Captain of all of creation. He had authority to re-create the damage in human bodies that sin had inflicted upon humanity through the centuries. He could command healing and forgiveness for those who came to Him. He was unique. His words were not the memorized speeches and prayers of others. His were words fresh from the heart of God and launched into the hearts of those that the Father had loved from before the foundation of the world.

In a matter of moments they would see His power over a super-strong man, possessed by evil spirits, who lived among the tombs of Gadara. He had obviously caused many problems in the neighbourhood. People had tried to chain him into inactivity, but time and again he had broken loose and returned to his angry ways. Jesus spoke freedom into his captive heart and set him loose from the demonic tormentors who had used him to destroy and cause fear to those who came near his stomping grounds. Peace suddenly filled his heart. And what a change! Can you imagine him returning "home" that night for the first time in a long time? That was a story that needed to be told to his family and friends. Jesus set him free!

Jesus has a way of changing the unchangeable. Someone has said that he is able to unscrew the inscrutable. There are powers beyond our control that the Master can command into obedience and order. We see many of these kinds of situations in our world and also in the lives of believers today. Jesus wants us to possess a quietness in the midst of the storms of life. He wants us to have Peace when the pressures seem to overwhelm us. He has the authority to make the changes that are necessary. It may surprise us to see how willing and able He is to respond to the things that trouble our lives. We need to remind ourselves that there is no situation that is beyond the control of the Creator of the universe, the Lover of our souls. Let's learn to come to Him with confidence when the need arises. Meanwhile, rest assured, He is in the boat with you, and although the way does get quite bumpy at times, He has the power to speak into every one of our lives and makes a difference. We're not going under. We're going to the other side. Trust Him! He's in control.

300

▌ **MY SINS ARE GONE!**

*"I write to you, dear children, because your sins
have been forgiven on account of his name."*

~1 John 2:12

He's forgotten everything. It wasn't amnesia. It was a choice. He just declared that He would never remember my sins ever again. I confessed them to Him and He cast them into the sea of His forgetfulness (Micah 7:19) and, if I understand the interpretation of scripture, He doesn't know where they are today. As far as He is concerned they never existed. The matter of the degree of sin in the past is not important because He takes all our confessed sins and deals with them in the same manner. We could list them as individual transgressions that displease God and call them all by name. However, He has only one name for them all. Sin!

Now I can come to Him with a forgiven, clean heart freed from condemnation because that's what Calvary does for each of us. Jesus died on the cross to cancel out the debt that I owed to God because of my transgressions. I am declared righteous through the Son. That is not a privilege that I can say was of my own making. It's God's gracious gift to me because I simply believed that Jesus died in my place and paid the price for my sin and, at the same time, made a way that I could stand before my heavenly Father in Himself as an heir of God and joint-heir with Jesus Christ.

Just as God's memory is far, far better than mine, His "forgettory" is, too. But here's a problem. As far as God is concerned, all confessed sins are gone, but the enemy of our souls, the one called "the accuser of the brethren," tries to resurrect the memory of things of the past. He is the one who plants condemnation and guilt. He tries to tear down the peace we possess and the joy of our relationship with the Father. He reminds us of our past; the past that God has forgotten and will not hold against us. Many struggle with the battle of living in God's forgiveness when the memories of our failures are often brought before us. Let's make the enemy understand that we know "the blood of Jesus, His Son, purifies us from all [every] sin" (1 John 1:7b). That's a fact that does not change with our feelings. It is a principle that every believer needs to exercise on a regular basis so that the enemy will not be able to rob us of our joy. *Our sins are forgiven*!

We will not accept any of the condemnation the old enemy tries to put back on us. When Jesus died on the cross He set us all free. That is the reason He could promise, "I have come that they may have life, and have it to the full" (John 10:10b). Living with a bag full of burdens as baggage from the past is not the way to enjoy life. We've been designed for better things, so don't let the enemy rob you of your gift of new life in Jesus. That's His promise to us for today and infinitely greater for our future when we finally stand in the Father's presence to enjoy His holiness to the full.

301

▌ **DID YOU UNDERSTAND THE LESSON?**

*"A student is not above his teacher, nor a servant above his master."*

~Matthew 10:24

He hung the used towel near the open window where the gentle evening breeze would dry it. He put on His cloak and returned to the place at the table reserved for Him. There were many nervous glances from the embarrassed disciples in the silence of the upper room. "'Do you understand what I have done for you?' he asked them" (John 13:12). He was their Teacher. He was their Master, yet He was the one who took up the towel and stooped to wash their feet. Did they understand?

The Apostle Paul was not in the picture when all this happened but he captured the full message of Jesus' teaching. Jesus, Paul said, "made himself nothing, taking the very nature of a servant..." (Philippians 2:7). The message is "being a servant." There are none so important that they can't become servants, and there are none that are too insignificant that they can't become servants. We must become like our Master and learn the valuable lessons that serving others is being like Jesus. Pity the person who believes that there are tasks that are too degrading for the hands of God's children.

You may have heard of Father Damien who dedicated his life and ministry to the service of lepers on the Island of Molokai in Hawaii. He had seen the ravages of that dreaded infection and had noticed that no one had taken the time nor expressed concern for the personal and spiritual needs of those who had that disease. He cared. He became a servant to do what he could to help those rejects of society, with the full intent of leading each one of them to know the Lord as their Saviour. After years of service, he felt that he was not accepted by the lepers, and that his message had fallen on deaf ears. He decided that it was time to leave the Island and pick up a new ministry somewhere else. As he waited for the boat to pick him up he noticed some white spots on his hand that he had not seen before. He soon discovered that he, too, had been infected with leprosy. He returned to his pulpit, but now the Church was full of people who wanted to hear the message from a man who was willing to be like them in order to tell the story of the love of God. Father Damien died at 49 years of age, but his message reached a generation of neglected lepers who would have finished their lives as the cast-offs of humanity. He understood the message that Jesus gave to His disciples that day many centuries before.

Becoming a servant can be a life-changing process. First of all, it should change our perspective of what God sees as being very important in our world today. Then it should change our attitude towards others around us because there is no higher calling than to be like our Master in service of the needs of those God loves. Then we need to understand that the enemy would prompt us to think that we should be served because we are important too. But we're not going to let that happen, are we?

302

▌ **SEEING IN THE DARKNESS**

*"Even though I walk through the valley of the shadow of death, I will fear no evil, for you are with me; your rod and your staff, they comfort me."*

~Psalm 23:4

It seemed like a normal routine until the lights went out. Our host had put us in a small bedroom and we were tired after our day's activities of doing what people usually do on holidays. To our amazement the ceiling came alive in the dark with a surprising glow of crescent moon and dozens of stars. The room had been decorated with invisible stars that only became observable when the lights were off. What was there all the time only came into view in the darkness. When we were prepared to surrender to the darkness we realized that there were hidden blessings that could only be released when the lights went out.

God does that often. There are hidden gems of beauty and blessing that become ours only when we go through the dark valleys. It's then that He comes near in new ways to comfort and strengthen when we least expect it. No wonder He says, "My grace is sufficient for you" (2 Corinthians 12:9). And again, "Surely I am with you always, to the very end of the age" (Matthew 28:20). There is a simple principle that we should learn early in our Christian walk. We are encouraged to "carry each other's burden" because that ought to be the concern of every believer who sees another facing issues that are difficult to understand. (Galatians 6:2). This is a reflection of the compassion that Jesus showed to so many when He ministered among the hurting and the weary of His generation. We need lots of that kind of love in our world, today.

But just a couple of verses farther along in Galatians 6:5 the message focuses on us as individuals who ought to learn to trust God in the darkness. The Word says, "each one should carry his own load." In brief, the mature, who have come to understand and trust in a living God who never fails, should show our confidence and faith by believing each dark and gloomy path is a new opportunity to see what God can do. It's not a time to throw up our hands and lament our poor condition. It's not a time to doubt whether the love of God is still there when we feel so down and alone. Those are moments when we need to lift up our eyes and look for the gems that God wants to reveal to us that are only visible when we cannot see our way. Sure, those can still be painful times, and we wouldn't let them come to us naturally by our own choice. But God knows what we need and He will not lead us into experiences that would cause us to fall. No matter what degree of discomfort we may experience, He is there. He knows and understands.

It is reported that someone asked Billy Graham's daughter, "Where was God on September 11th at the World Trade Centre?" Her response was, "He was there…and He was crying." There is no question that God understands the stresses and struggles that come to each of us and His compassion will never leave us alone. It's in those kinds of moments that we need to trust and not be afraid because He is still able to "work all things for the good of those who love Him."

303

▌ **GOD KNOWS**

*"But he knows the way that I take; when he has tested me,*
*I will come forth as gold."*

~Job 23:10

They brought out the gold and silver instruments and vessels that were used in the Temple worship in Jerusalem and filled the goblets with their wine to toast the anniversary of their conquest of the holy city. It was then that a hand appeared and began to write on the plaster of the wall. The message was difficult to understand but Daniel was able to give them the interpretation. It was a simple but clear communication of the impending judgment of God. God knew what He was about to do. Israel had gone through their testing time and God was about to make a change to restore His people back to their nation. Israel had been led into captivity many years before because of their unfaithfulness to the covenant of God. Now God was beginning to prepare for the restoration of the kingdom of His chosen ones. A new page of history was about to begin. God would return His people to their homeland, to the land of promise, and give them another opportunity to serve Him.

Let me tell you a couple of things that relate to this story and to the practical moments of our lives:

1. God is mindful of the misuse of His vessels. Don't think that any who ignore His guidelines will be able to avoid the eyes of God as He views what we do with the things that are designed for His service. How we use the things of God is important to Him and He will not stand idle forever. His patience has been demonstrated throughout history, but it should never be mistaken as indifference. Because He cares, His love and mercy will give us opportunity to return to Him and submit to His plan.

2. God is faithful to His promises. He can move the nations of the world to fulfill His plans. There is nothing in the world that can hinder His plan and purposes. This is very significant to the daily routine of our lives. He is always ready to hear the cry of His people when we seek His face with all our hearts. He loves with an everlasting love and is committed by His faithfulness to follow through on His promises. Find one and claim it.

3. God longs for the worship of His people. The re-building of the Temple was one of the first projects that the returning captives focused upon when they arrived back "home." There is nothing that brings more joy to the heart of God than a people who know the value of worship and practice it. Worship is still an important feature of our gatherings as a body of believers. But worship is a lifestyle, not just a "Sunday, goin' to meetin" activity. He is worthy of the praises of His people—all the time. Come "home" to worship.

**WALKING IN DARK PLACES**

*"Surely God is my salvation; I will trust and not be afraid. The LORD, the LORD, is my strength and my song; he has become my salvation."*

~Isaiah 12:2

There is an agony in waiting while Faith does its work. You've been there many times in your life, as well have many saints throughout history, that place where you express your confidence in God and believe that He's going to do something, but Mr. Doubt throws arguments at you and the inner struggle begins. It feels like a battle while the inner voices grind away at each other. I know that God understands the turmoil that goes on inside the Believer in these situations. It may appear that He is not very caring at the time, but His promise is to reward those who stand strong in their trust. "In this you greatly rejoice, though now for a little while you may have had to suffer grief in all kinds of trials. These have come so that your faith—of greater worth than gold, which perishes even though refined by fire—may be proved genuine and may result in praise, glory and honour when Jesus Christ is revealed" (1 Peter 1:6-7). There is a purpose in these kinds of experiences.

I haven't met the person, yet, who likes trials. To tell you the truth, I am very grateful when the trials are over because there is a reward at the end. How we deal with the matters that cause us discomfort and concern is very important. It's interesting that when God sees the conflicts that are going on in the Believer He uses such phrases as, "Be still and know that I am God..." (Psalm 46:10); "...do not worry..." (Matthew 6:25, 31, 34) and "Cast all your anxiety on him..." (1 Peter 5:7). These are not expressions of exasperation; they are invitations to continue our trust in Him in spite of the situations. As much as we struggle with the process, He wants us to learn to possess peace in our hearts when we go through trials. That is the mark of a person of strong faith.

Do you remember the experience of Job? He was a righteous man of integrity and beloved of God. When everyone else despaired for his condition, he maintained his confidence that God was still right in what He did. He demonstrated his inner personal struggles when he questioned the value of his life and even cursed the day that he was born. His faith and confidence did not remove his pain. He continued to suffer, but his unwillingness to blame God eventually brought a great personal reward and he was able to bring a blessing to his "friends."

Let me set the record straight! Trials may be an attack of the enemy or they may come as a result of some bad choices that we have made. But they will always come to us as tools that we can use to demonstrate our faith in God. It is possible that our struggles will be viewed by unbelievers and our reaction will be the determining factor of whether they will decide to serve the Lord or not. "Finally, my brothers, rejoice in the Lord! It is no trouble for me to write the same things to you again..." (Philippians 3:1).

305

**THE MAIN THING**

*"But seek first his kingdom and his righteousness,
and all these things will be given to you as well."*

~Matthew 6:33

In many countries around the world, November 1st has been established as a day to remember loved ones who have passed away. It was begun as a special remembrance day when family members would go to the gravesites and lay flowers and reminisce of past loving and enjoyable experiences. During the Middle ages, the Roman Church set aside the night before as an evening of prayer for the departed and it became known as holy evening or hallowed evening. From there it became known as Hallowe'en.

I do not know how the ghosts, pumpkins and goblins became a part of the special occasion, but it is interesting how the main purpose of so many spiritual celebrations has been manipulated to distract from the main focus that they were designed for. Christmas and Easter have been accepted as times for great festivities and family gatherings, but the emphasis is now on snowmen, bunnies, candies, all kinds of food and decorations. Sundays, as well, were sacred times and respected, even in the secular world, but have been turned into, "my day off" and God is left out of the picture once again. The world has a way of taking the edge off of the things that are important to God. But "we are not unaware of his schemes" (2 Corinthians 2:11). The enemy of our souls has always worked at making the important things seem unimportant and replaced them with things that appear to be so good. That's why we need to be on guard. Somehow we need to see the things we do through spiritual eyes and know the purposes of God instead of doing "whatever" out of habit.

Someone has said, "The main thing in life is to keep the main thing as the main thing." Now, I'm not just talking about the special days we call holidays or holy days, but I refer as well to all the choices of life.

I've discovered that it's easy to be "busy," but it's not so easy to determine the difference between what is important and whatever is designed to look important but just occupies our time. We may have lost sight of the values of the Christian faith that other generations have esteemed so highly, but let's find out what God wants to do now and sincerely desire to do His will. It may take us out of the comfort zone that we treasure so highly and put us into some uncomfortable new experiences.

The sum of the whole matter is that we need to determine where our energies are being spent and whether or not they are being used to honour the Lord and bless others. We need to clean out the cobwebs of distraction and get back to the main thing. The whole aim of our life is to keep the Lord and His purposes clear before our eyes. Time is short! Let's examine where the emphasis of our energy is going, know His will and do it.

**THE PROMISE IN THE SKY**

*"It's like a man going away: He leaves his house*
*and puts his servants in charge, each with his assigned task,*
*and tells the one at the door to keep watch."*

~Mark 13:34

There wasn't a pot of gold, but the beauty of the rainbow was to remain as a sign of the grace of God in fulfilling His promises. Noah had lived through the biggest storm the world had ever seen. The evidence of the floodwaters still filled the horizons when he brought his family and all the specially chosen of creation out of the ark. This was a brand new world washed clean of all the evidence of the wickedness of man.

Noah and his family had an opportunity to begin again. He was a righteous man and had found favour in the eyes of the Lord. God knew the hearts of each member of His creation. He was mindful of the things that were done in secret as well as the things that were flaunted in public and there came a time when "enough was enough." I know that the mercy of the Lord endures forever, but when the time of repentance is passed and there is no turning back to God, He releases His protection and the action of the consequences of sin begins. Because He knows every heart, He also knows if someone will make the decision to return to God. If they have purposed to continue in things that are contrary to His will, He will allow the "wages of sin" to come into effect.

We still have rainbows to remind us of God's faithfulness. Some are in the sky and others are seen in the fulfillment of His written Word. We know that there are warning signs as well. We look up with hope for the completion of His plan for His Church.

At the same time, we need to be prayerful for those who deliberately turn their back on the Lord and ignore the warnings of a very patient and loving God. That's one of the matters that cause me concern. "Just as it was in the days of Noah, so also will it be in the days of the Son of Man" (Luke 17:26). I know that the Mercy of God still gives us room to come under His protection, and I also know that there are many in the world who are totally unaware that God still loves them, no matter what they do. However, God knows each heart. Could we be living in the last days before the judgment of sin falls once again upon a sinful world? The law of consequence still applies.

When we humble ourselves and pray, God will hear from heaven and forgive and heal. He will not rain His judgment upon mankind indiscriminately. If there are righteous people praying and interceding, there will still be hope. Every Christian must hold on to the promises of God and work to share the message of the love of God to a wayward generation. The end of all things is at hand. This may be the generation that will see one of the most dramatic expressions of the justice of God poured out upon the world. Believers? They will be caught up out of harm's way and then, "look out!"

307

▌ SEE THE VOICE

*"He must become greater; I must become less. The one who comes from above is above all; the one who is from the earth belongs to the earth, and speaks as one from the earth. The one who comes from heaven is above all."*

~John 3:30-31

These are John's words. What a guy! Most of his life is uncharted history. One day he began to tell other people what was burning deep in his heart. It was a hard message, but God-given. His call to repentance moved the hearts of people to hear the truth. He spoke with clarity and authority in rebuking the sins of his generation. He quickly became loved, despised, honoured, feared, sought out and hated. His message was undiluted, direct and often confrontational. He feared no one. He ministered to the whole strata of society without prejudice. He told it like it was. He had time for neither the hypocritical attitudes of the temple courts nor the luxurious fancies of the Palace. He was a man sent from God with a very special mission. It was time.

It was time to clear the deck; to make room for the "Lamb of God." It was time to call a nation back to God. If you saw him in a crowd, he was the one with the index finger raised to make his point. He was anointed before birth for this moment in the history of man and he did his job well. He was not drawn to the pleasures of the world, its laughter, lusts, wealth and popularity. He caught a glimpse of the eternal and was willing, at great cost to himself, to sacrifice his own life, without compromise, so that the Lamb of God could come to deal with the sins of mankind.

This was serious business and John played his part well. It had been a long time since someone spoke publicly about the claims of God upon His creation. The voice of the Prophets had not been heard for more than 400 years until John stepped out of the wilderness and the silence of God was broken by the thunder of the voice of this man.

His was a voice to be reckoned with and his boldness made it hard to resist. He was a man of integrity and purpose; a man who sensed the urgency of his hour and was not prepared to back down in sharing what burned in his soul. There was a cost to such a lifestyle. Though accepted and honoured by many, he died in the royal dungeon as payout for the lustful dance of a beautiful young woman.

After all he did for the Kingdom of God it seems little reward to end it all this way. You see, we measure most things by the kinds of benefits we receive here and now. He lived his life in deprivation, under some very austere conditions and circumstances. He was able to look beyond himself to the One who would come after him and humbly acknowledge his need to decrease that the Lord be seen above all else.

I have a feeling that if John had to do it all over again he wouldn't do anything differently. What a guy!

▌ **THE MORAL COMPASS**

*"Your word is a lamp to my feet and a light for my path."*

~Psalm 119:105

It seems a part of human nature that we look for the easiest way to do things. That is the success story of the fast food distributors. It's easier to buy a quick lunch than to take the time to make a sandwich with wholesome stuffings and a piece of fruit. You had better believe that students of commerce have discovered that flaw in our human nature.

Deep down you know that not everything that is fast and easy is good. Sometimes time and effort are necessary investments for the more enduring and healthy things of life. "Now," you'll say, "you're sounding like my Mother." Well, let me tell you the truth; I'm actually trying to sound like the Apostle Paul, who said, "Do your best to present yourself to God as one approved, a workman who does not need to be ashamed and who correctly handles the word of truth" (2 Timothy 2:15). I'm sure that most of us are embarrassed when someone asks us how much we read and study the word of God. It's easier to sit in front of the TV or busy ourselves with some kind of handcraft than to open the scriptures and read the message that is intended to equip us and make us better believers. The prophet Amos saw a day when there would be a famine across the land. Not a famine for lack of bread and water and the essentials of the physical life, but a famine of the Word of God. (Amos 8:11). Obviously, the reference applies to a generation just like ours. We get after our kids for stuffing themselves with "junk food" and yet, spiritually speaking, we do the same thing by not putting ourselves up to a daily diet of the Word. Many years ago, we used to have Bible reading before our first class at school. In case you haven't heard, it's not happening any more.

If you want to know why it is so easy for kids to go wrong, let me explain. "There's a famine of the Word." Our kids aren't getting the moral teachings of scripture. They're not hearing that anger, brutality, abuse/self abuse, disrespect for authority, matters of sex and other serious issues all have very dangerous consequences. That's not their fault. We have got to get the principles of God's Word into their hearts, and one hour in a Bible class on Sunday is just not going to do it. Every one of us, as parents, needs to get the Word into the lives of our kids on a regular basis. If we don't have family devotions, or at minimum a reading of a devotional book at the level of our children that is used every day, we are not giving our kids an adequate spiritual diet to help them when the time comes for the important decisions on the real issues of life. Please listen to me carefully! The spiritual heritage of the next generation is at stake. We've got to take this matter seriously and make time for and invest energy in directing our kids to what God is saying to the world today. There is no better time to begin a new program than right now. Visit your Christian bookstore for ideas on devotional aids.

| **THERE ARE SHADOWS IN THE VALLEY**

*"Even though I walk through the valley of the shadow of death, I will fear no evil, for you are with me; your rod and staff, they comfort me."*

~Psalm 23:4

I'm the motor behind the shopping cart. My main responsibility is to weave between the boxes and the people as we meander down the aisles between the stacks of groceries.

It was one of those days when I was faithfully doing my duty and we had arrived at the bakery area. I stood by the pastry table while my wife made a selection nearby. At first our eyes did not meet, but I watched an elderly man checking out the pies. He lifted one after the other and carefully examined them. Finally, with a real sense of victory he said, "This one is mine." To make sure that I heard him, he repeated, "This one is mine. Do you want to know why?" I knew I was going to hear his reason whether I wanted to or not. "If you notice, this one is smaller than all the rest and it's only $2.50. You know it's hard to buy for yourself, alone, after so many years of married life."

I saw that his eyes had suddenly filled with tears and I caught the meaning of his words. I soon discovered that his wife had passed away just a couple of weeks before and now all the children were gone and he was left by himself. The motor on the shopping cart came to a quick stop. I was beside a man who had not found satisfying comfort in these past weeks. Suddenly, this stranger became my friend. We spoke of the joys of a happy lengthy marriage with three healthy and prosperous children. He had retired a long time ago and was committed to being with his life-long companion even after the stroke, six weeks ago, that laid his wife in the hospital and then to a special bed at home.

Walking through the valley of the shadow of death is not fun. But, for the person who believes in the Lord, there is a wonderful resource for peace and comfort. After we've asked the "Why me God?" questions, we can get on to the fact that death is an awful reality that everyone must face but that it does hold a bright side to it.

For example, I would never wish that my Mother and Father would return to this world when I know that they are in the Everlasting Presence of the Lord who loves them much more than words could say. He has prepared for them a place of beauty beyond description where neither sickness, pain nor sorrow will ever touch them again. They are free in a greater sense than ever before and, praise God, one day we will meet again.

What a day that will be! No more tears in the market place and no more sorrow in the heart. What a wonderful hope we possess!

Our shopping trip took a little longer than we had planned, but I came out feeling blessed, because years ago I had received a real bargain through Jesus and I had shared that with my new friend.

310

▌ **Go!**

*"I tell you, open your eyes and look at the fields! They are ripe for harvest."*

~John 4:35b

It's funny that when we talk about giving, our thoughts often run to thoughts of finances; how much do I have in my wallet or in my bank account, or how much is the Pastor going to ask us for today? I acknowledge that money is a very important matter for the ministry of the Gospel, but I want to talk about a different kind of giving today.

In part it concerns a bit of giving of ourselves. That obviously is always a necessity for getting the message out to others. Most of us believe that the Great Commission of "Going into all the world" is a message for others who are more qualified concerning the "going" process. We are happy to confess that we are followers of Jesus, some at a greater distance than others, but there are not many who would profess that they are leaders for Jesus. That kind of commitment takes us out to where Jesus would go if He were here once again and that requires dedication and recognition that we are the holders of the most wonderful story that should ever be told. That's where I would like to focus our talk today about giving. It's the passing on of a wonderful message of the love of God. That message tells the world that God has not forgotten us and that He wants to welcome all to come into an awesome relationship with Himself.

When we see the world in the terrible circumstances that we see, we should realize that there isn't a lot of good news out there. But we know that our sins can be forgiven; that Jesus has promised to be with us through every situation and that heaven is our eternal home. We can talk so freely about many other things that may be of interest to the world, but it's the message of the Good News that needs to be broadcast around the world today.

Let me remind you there is a place of peace; there is a place of hope. In the Church, we share in wonderful fellowship with others who believe that Jesus Christ is alive and that He cares for us. Pass the word along. Speak blessing to your neighbours and the people you work with. Let your conversation reveal what you really believe down in your heart. Let your mouth speak it out! Don't be shy! We need to choose to give a vocal expression of our faith. Let me remind you that every time you speak about the Lord and the things that He has said or done you are planting seed under the direction of the Holy Spirit. You become an instrument under Divine care. The words that you share will go into the hearts and minds of the hearers and are guaranteed to accomplish the purpose for which they are sent. "So is my word that goes out from my mouth: It will not return to me empty, but will accomplish what I desire and achieve the purpose for which I sent it" (Isaiah 55:11). Now, that's the kind of giving that's a fail-safe investment. The process involves sharing the greatest treasure the world will ever see and the promise is that it will bring you eternal dividends.

311

| **REFRESHING TIMES**

> *"And Saul's son Jonathan went to David at Horesh*
> *and helped him find strength in God."*
>
> ~1 Samuel 23:16 (emphasis added)

We are living in awesome times. Supposedly, we have more "helps" to make life simpler and to allow us more time for ourselves and our families because of the advances of modern technology. We have fast foods, cell phones, computers, catalogue ordering systems, calculators, airplanes, cars and the list goes on. But truthfully, who has more time to enjoy life now than before? You've heard the saying, "We're in a rat race and the rats are winning."

I'm not sure that we do more things now than we used to, but where does all the spare time go? We are living in a world of pressure and stresses that other generations did not know. People expect more to happen and happen more quickly than ever before, yet the idea of rest times and more time for relaxation just doesn't seem to be happening. Road rage is a scourge of the roadways. Some, in a hurry, have blown a fuse in anger at the doddling of other drivers. When will we experience the calm times that we thought would come to us because of the expansion of technology?

We all get caught up in the same pursuits of life, but let me advise you that we need the times of refreshing that only the Lord can give. Even Paul, back in the olden days, expressed this need when he wrote to Philemon. He said, "...refresh my heart in Christ." (Philemon verse 20) That sounds like he was feeling overwhelmed with the pressures he was under and he needed someone to care enough to help him find that place of rest.

We need to be careful that we don't run down our spiritual systems by being stuck in the influences of the world. There has to be a shut-down period for all of us when our focus is readjusted and we relax to catch our breath. This is one of the reasons the Father designed the Sabbath. He rested on the seventh day as an example and we ought to take one day out of the week and do the same. But let me remind you that the New Testament calls that special day "the Lord's day." It's not my day. It's the Lord's day and it is intended to be a day of refreshing, rest and blessing. In effect, it belongs to the Lord, but He wants me to share it with Him. We need the kind of refreshing that not only brings rest to the body but uplifts the spirit as well. That can only happen when we take time or make time to read, pray, fellowship and honour the Lord. The summer season comes to us when the warmth of the sunshine and the longer days tempt us to let go of everything. Let's plan to spend some time in the sunshine and the Word; at the beach and in Church; in the garden and in prayer. These are always good combinations to restore us physically and spiritually.

"He restores my soul." Psalm 23:3a

▎ **HE GAVE HIMSELF**

*"[Jesus] gave himself for our sins to rescue us from the present evil age,*
*according to the will of our God and Father."*

~Galatians 1:4

The highest, most valuable gift that anyone could ever give was what Jesus shared on Calvary. He gave Himself! A number of young men thought they were doing something similar when they flew the planes into the public places of New York and Washington on September 11th. Based on hatred, they gave themselves with selfish, misguided motives. I find it hard to imagine that anyone could hate to that extent. In the process they took many unwilling, innocent lives with them, leaving scars of pain on so many others around the world. The effects of their efforts brought destruction on more than the famous buildings of two American cities. The suffering of broken dreams and destroyed families will not go away quickly. In the words of one observer, "A little bit of all of us died that day!" Absolutely no one benefits from this atrocious crime against humanity.

Jesus' way was different. His motive was love for others. His sacrifice was to deliver people from the consequences of sin. What He did was provide a way to lift people from pain, despair, guilt and condemnation and to give all of us a better life. The price that was paid was charged completely to His personal account. No one else was involved in paying the price. He was alone. He broke through the kingdom of darkness and the powers and authorities that had exercised spiritual bondage over the hearts of mankind. Jesus, alone, and in the kind of love that knows no bounds, provided a way that all who come to Him in simple trust would find that a loving God has been reaching out to all of us. He gave Himself, "…a ransom for many" (Matthew 20:28b).

The benefits are many:

1. We have access to our Heavenly Father. Prayer becomes a channel of communication to express our need of God's assistance with our personal problems and a process to strengthen our confidence in Him.

2. We have peace in our hearts because our sins are forgiven. Jesus paid the price that would have been the consequences of our bad choices.

3. We have an inheritance that will never fade, eternal in the heavens. As sure as Jesus died, arose from the grave and ascended to the Father, so shall we rise to be with Him in the future.

4. The barriers of division, whether colour, culture or language have been broken down. We are on universally equal ground as brothers and sisters in a very large family of faith. We are made one in Jesus Christ. And the list could go on.

There was nothing selfish in what Jesus did on the cross of Calvary. When we remember his death during each communion service, we should express our gratitude for that kind of surrender that flows from the love of God.

313

▌ # CLEANSING LEPERS AND ME

*"But Jesus came and touched them. 'Get up,' he said. 'Don't be afraid.'"*

~Matthew 17:7

He was a leper. He knew, as did generations of lepers before him, that there was a special "protocol" that people like him had to follow. There were laws, rules and regulations that placed him and his disease at a disadvantaged position. Lepers were expelled from their homes and their families. They were obligated to cover their faces and sound out an ominous warning, "Unclean! Unclean!" lest any one approach them and be contaminated with their disease. Many regarded them with fear and some with disgust. Some supposed that these people were caught under the judgment of God for sins they had committed. Those who did have compassion on them could leave gifts of food and clothing for them but only at a distance. Communication was limited to shouts and charade actions. Contact, by lepers, with those who were healthy was totally forbidden. These "unclean" lived in the shelters of caves and some in the open tombs in the graveyard. Their dreams, hopes and desires for family, business and personal enjoyment could never be fulfilled. Theirs was a hopeless existence in exile with a sentence of an early death. Yet, to these, the pleasure of death always seemed so long in coming. What was there to live for?

Then Jesus came. The leper saw the crowd in the distance and a glimmer of hope began to glow in the depths of his soul. Ignoring "the rules" and the displeasure of the multitude, he came and bowed before the Master. "Lord, if you are willing, you can make me clean." Jesus replied, "I am willing." To the great surprise of all who observed, *He touched him* and said, "Be clean!" The storyteller expresses simply: "Immediately he was cured" (Matthew 8:2-3).

It was the Master's touch that changed the direction of that man's life. Jesus did in a moment what no other person could ever do. The exiled dreams, hopes and desires were released to find fulfillment in the possibilities of a brand new day because of the "something new" that flowed into his life.

Jesus still does that kind of thing in lives today. Too many live on the border of life but have not come to know the fullness of God's promises. Theirs is a bleak existence with little hope of change unless the Master comes by and does His thing in their lives. I could never possibly express the love of Jesus in His willingness to touch the lives of everyone who comes to Him. I know that the longing to draw men and women out of the tragedies of life has always been the desire of the heart of God. He wants to make a difference in me and you and all those around us. To not be satisfied with anything less than the fullness of His plan for our lives becomes a personal decision we all must make. There is no other solution, no other person, no other way than coming to Him to be touched by His gracious hand. Let Him touch you, too, as He has so many others!

314

**THE STANDARD OF FREEDOM**

*"Then you will know the truth and the truth will set you free."*

~John 8:32

Who really knows what "Freedom" is? I know that our Canadian forces have fought in a number of wars throughout the young history of our nation to defend it. They went into the fields of conflict to protect Democracy and the freedoms of peoples in various parts of the world.

I've discovered, however, that we don't always understand what this matter of freedom is all about. We once thought that freedom was decided by the majority decision of electors, but then we were introduced to such things as the protection of the rights of the minority. I understand that some minority rights need to be protected, but I wonder when the decisions of the minority groups should determine what the majority must do or accept as normal. Is that freedom? I believe that true freedom must have an unchanging standard of reference and that rules and regulations that forbid certain activities must be a part of the process of freedom.

I know that I am not free to drive down the highway anyway that I want. The police protect us when people think they can speed, drive over the lines or neglect to stop at red lights. I know that I am not free to take your possessions. —that's called stealing, and there's a consequence for that. I don't believe that people should have the freedom to teach my kids things that I do not agree with. That's stealing my authority and right as a parent, and there ought to be a law against it. I don't believe that anyone has the right to change the meaning of marriage to mean anything other than what has been the historical significance since the beginning of time. Call it something else, but don't compare it to what a husband and wife have. Don't even try to tell me that it's the same thing and don't try to sell that package to my kids.

Our nation is called "The Dominion of Canada." That title was taken from God's Word, "He shall have ***dominion*** also from sea to sea, and from the river unto the ends of the earth" (Psalm 72:8 KJV, emphasis added). Obviously, the Fathers of Confederation understood the significance of using that passage of scripture as the foundation of our nation. Their dream/desire was to see the freedoms of our nation based upon the authority of God. There is a lot of latitude in interpreting the rules and regulations of His commandments based upon His grace and mercy as long as the principle is guarded. But complete disobedience to what He has established as right and wrong is not one of the freedoms that we should consider. Besides disobeying His purpose and plan for humanity, there is a consequence as a result of not following "the rules."

Will we continue to be a vibrant, healthy nation if we rebel against the standard that God has established? You and I are the ones who will help to determine the direction that this generation will take. What will you leave as your heritage for your children? It's time to learn that true freedom is a gift of God and is related to fulfilling God's will every day.

**315**

▌ **REMEMBERING THE FALLEN**

*"Others were tortured and refused to be released,*
*so that they might gain a better resurrection."*

~Hebrews 11:35b

Once a year we remember the sacrifice of many who, through two World Wars, the Korean conflict and other wars, were willing to lay down their lives for the defence of freedom and democracy. On that day it is also an opportunity to give special recognition to the many throughout Church history who were willing to lay down their lives for the sake of the gospel. Jesus told his disciples that he was sending them out, "...as sheep among wolves" (Matthew 10:16). He told them that they should be willing to carry their crosses and follow Him. There is no doubt that He knew that although the message of God's love for the lost sinners of the world was the most wonderful, good news ever told, that many would hate the believers to the point of persecution. Unfortunately, history relates the stories of the deaths of many of those who have traveled around the world at great personal sacrifice to tell the story of Jesus and His love. Every one of the disciples of Jesus, except John, was put to death in terrible ways.

We have been told that there have been more people put to death for their faith in this last century than in all of the preceding years to 1900. Statistics report that more than 150,000 Christians are killed every year for their faith.

We live in a land of freedom where we can worship the Lord whenever we want and however we want with total liberty. But we often forget that in other parts of the world, Christians today meet in hiding places and in constant fear of harassment and fear of death. Yet, in these places, the message of the saving grace of Jesus Christ is being shared with humble believers. Brave men and women risk their lives to teach the Bible and to preach the good news. They have responded to the call of God to be willing to lay down their lives in order to reach the lost. Their lives are not as important as the message they preach and live. Their example is Jesus, who came into the world to lay down his life for the lost. "They are not ashamed of the gospel of Christ."

Recently, in the Sudan, an Australian missionary and his two young sons were brutally slain. In Sri Lanka and Indonesia churches are burned and pastors fear for their lives. The leading violators of religious freedoms in the world are: China, Afghanistan, Burma, Iran, Iraq, Serbia and the Sudan.

In spite of the persecutions, the Church is continuing to grow, often at the cost of the leaders who give themselves unreservedly to spreading the gospel message. Let's be prayerful to support the Believers in these countries that God would bless His people and give them signs and wonder to follow their ministries.

NOVEMBER 12 | **DO ALL YOU CAN, PLUS FAITH**

*"If you can?" said Jesus, "Everything is possible for him who believes."*

~Mark 9:23

The story of what a very sick lady had done had reached the ears of the people on the other side of the Sea of Galilee. That's one of the stories that is told in Mark 5 that concerns the faith and effort of a lady who worked her way through the crowd with the intention of just touching the hem of Christ's garment. She had spent all that she had looking for remedies from many doctors but was no better for her efforts. Through the word picture we can imagine her, sick and very poor, but with a hope that Jesus could bring the solution to her problem. She pressed through the crowd until she was close enough to reach out and touch Him. Perhaps out of concern that her efforts for healing had failed so often before, she purposed to not bother the Master but to just reach out and *touch the hem of His garment* with faith. "I will be healed," she thought (Mark 5:28).

She had tried all the other remedies and options that human intelligence and science could offer. Now she was prepared to risk a step of faith. I imagine her with arms and fingertips extended as she passed her last obstacle and touched the hem of His robes. She was healed instantly of her blood disorder. Jesus noted, instantly, that faith was in action through someone in the crowd. Among the multitude of people jostling for a position for a better look at the Master there was one who had exercised exceptional faith.

1. It was the kind of faith that had been persistent enough to get past all the obstacles.

2. It was a faith that was humble, to stoop to touch the fringe of Jesus' garments.

3. It was a faith that worked "one-on-One" with the needy and the Master.

4. It was a faith that confidently believed, "I will be healed."

Jesus called attention to the simplicity of the faith of this dear lady who had done something that day that no one else in the congregation had done, and she received the reward of faith. She also demonstrated another characteristic of faith.

5. It was a faith that was thankful. She bowed, reverently, at His feet and confessed what she had done.

What this woman did and the results of her faith were soon broadcast around the area. On the other side of the Sea of Galilee word arrived that Jesus was to make a visit to their cities. They brought the sick on mats to where He would pass by and "begged him to let them *touch even the edge of His cloak*, and *all* who touched him were healed" (Mark 6:56b, emphasis added).

Let me tell you that faith in action has a way of multiplying blessing. Out of all the crowds that will be attending Church this Sunday, it only takes one person to believe who can be instrumental in leading many others to believe that Jesus can make a difference in all our lives. Let that be my faith! Let it be your faith!

317

▌ **WALKING THROUGH THE SHADOW**

*"Be joyful in hope, patient in affliction, faithful in prayer."*

~Romans 12:12

Paul wrote, "For to me, to live is Christ and to die is gain" (Philippians 1:21). Most people in the world don't look at the end of the road with that kind of attitude. Paul was clear on his priorities. His life was to be lived in such a way that everything that he did would somehow bring praise to the Lord. I imagine he purposed, each morning, that his words and actions would show the very nature of Christ. I know from personal experience that self-discipline must be used to guard the thoughts, the lips and the actions from doing things that could be misinterpreted and care must be used to make the right choices. That was Paul's goal. When you read about his journeys and the trials that he went through you understand that there sometimes is a high price to pay if you are prepared to avoid compromising the message of faith in Jesus Christ. After all, that's the message that the world needs and that Jesus commissioned every one of us to proclaim. Everything else became a secondary matter in Paul's life. In the words of another great man of God, "He must become greater; I must become less" (John 3:30). That strikes a blow at our self-importance. It's got to be all about Jesus or it really isn't of any permanent value.

I notice that the Apostle Paul realized that his earthly life would eventually come to an end. After serving Jesus all the days of his life, he could look forward to whatever lay beyond his death. He called it *gain*! You could never say, "The Apostle Paul *lost* his life in the defence of the gospel." He viewed death as an added benefit to serving the Lord. You can sense the joy of that kind of faith when he says, "I desire to depart and be with Christ, which is better by far" (Philippians 1:23b). He wasn't in a hurry for that appointment because he recognized that the Lord sometimes has special things for us to accomplish before that date of departure. As long as that task remained unfinished, Paul had a job to do. But that didn't take away the anticipation of the moment when he would join the Lord on the other side of the gates of death.

Now, I know there are a lot of folk who don't desire that exodus from this life, and many still fear the dark shadows of the valley of death, but I want to assure you that once you purpose to make Jesus the priority of your actions and your thoughts you'll find that there is a very special peace that He gives to those who put their trust in Him. We treasure the fact that there is life beyond life and that it is a life without the pain and problems, the sorrows and sickness, the failures, frustrations and frailties that we experience today. Our hope is sure— because Jesus rose again from the grave we, too, shall rise to be with Him in a freedom that is hard to imagine. "No eye has seen, no ear has heard, no mind has conceived what God has prepared for those who love Him" (1 Corinthians 2:9).

I believe, for some reading this article, that moment is very near.

318

**|** **ACCORDING TO HIS CALENDAR**

*"Teach me to do your will, for you are my God;*
*may your good Spirit lead me on level ground."*

~Psalm 143:10

The summer of each year is officially over near the middle of September. The seasons continue to come and go right on schedule as planned more than 6000 year ago. How's that for keeping an agenda? That just reminds me that God is never late in the things that He does. I have to confess, He doesn't always work according to my calendar, and I can't explain why not, but History and scripture teach me that His ways are not our ways. The Psalmist did say: "My times are in your hands..." (Psalm 31:15a) Just as sure as God has performed His plan for creation through the thousands and millions of years, He is just as faithful to develop what He wishes in each of our lives. You can count on it!

However, as much as that speaks of God's committed faithfulness, He has prepared His plan to give room for our free will. How often through the centuries has that been a snag in allowing God to move through humanity the way He wants? I can definitely say that God is going to have His way, anyway, so I should work along with Him; not because I'm forced to, but because His ways are the best ways and I should stop any kind of resistance that would delay the inevitable. Knowing that what He does is based on His loving nature should be incentive enough for me to learn that surrendering to Him is really no loss to me.

It's a strange thing, but we often believe that God always does things in a dramatic and dynamic way, and therefore, that is evidence that God hasn't done anything in most of us. However, that is far from the truth. I believe that God works in the routine, the mundane and the common times of our lives as well as in the exciting times. Our problem is that we don't always recognize how interested He is in the details that make up the smallest moments of our lives. "Our times are in His hands."

Peter writes: "For the eyes of the Lord are on the righteous and his ears are attentive to their prayer..." (1 Peter 3:12a). Is there any better way to express how God is observant and interested in what happens in the daily experiences of our existence? He is with you and me, all the time!

One more thing—we all know that He has promised to come back again to take us to be with Himself. We don't know the date of that appointment, but as sure as God has kept to His schedules of the past, I am confident that He has His heart fixed on that date. There are times when we soooooo passionately long for His return to terminate the sorrows that are a part of humanity. How much more must He be longing for that moment to arrive when we will be caught up to be with Him forever?

While we have today, let our prayer be, "Lord what do You want me to do?"

**OBEDIENCE IN BAPTISM**

*"Let it be so now; it is proper for us to do this to fulfill all righteousness."*

~Matthew 3:15a

The old Prophet spoke with authority as he declared, "To obey is better than sacrifice, and to heed better than the fat of rams" (1 Samuel 15:22b). What could be more important to God than any sacrifice we make? God says that obeying what He has already commanded is more important than any other gift or praise that we could give Him. As much as we may express our worship and praise with clarity and fluency, the matter that pleases God most is that when all is said and done, more is done (in obedience) than said.

The first basic principle of training in the military service is to get the new recruits to obey, immediately, the commands of the officers. This is true of every member of a great team in sports; each member of the team must do what he or she has been trained to do. The process requires doing the same thing over and over until it becomes a natural reaction. The process often requires that a person's ability is stretched to its limits. In that arena you will often hear, "Sacrifice your body; sacrifice your body!" The lesson is that you've got to surrender complete obedience to what your coach says.

That brings me to remember that our Heavenly Coach has a training plan for each of us in order to be successful in the "Game of Life." We must learn the importance of reading the rule book, the Bible. We must apply ourselves diligently in the matter of Prayer as we seek to learn to hear and understand His voice and His commands. Then we must apply ourselves with all our hearts to obeying His commands. One of Jesus' last commands to His disciples was, "Go make disciples of all nations, baptizing them in the name of the Father and of the Son and of the Holy Spirit" (Matthew 18:19). The main direction He gave us was "GO." No benchwarmers. No hesitant members. Obedient to His last command. —that's obedience.

Peter, on the day the Church was begun, preached a sermon that caused conviction in the hearts of many. The question the people asked was, "Brothers what shall we do?" Peter replied, "Repent and be baptized" …" (Acts 2:37-38).

The significance is clear. It is the Lord's will that everyone who comes to know Jesus Christ as Lord and Saviour should be obedient to follow the Lord's command and be baptized. You may already have discovered that every act of obedience to the purpose and plan of the Lord brings a blessing to us. The Lord wants us to learn that many of the steps of faith that we take require an outward expression that is visible to the world. It is most important that the spiritual experience precede the outward confession of our faith by way of the waters of baptism. That is, we do the act of sincere repentance and then follow His command to be baptized. Again, it's obedience to His command.

320

**OPEN LINES**

*"My tongue will tell of your righteous acts all day long..."*

~Psalm 71:24a

Modern technology has propelled us into a brand new world. Who could have imagined how communication would change over the last 100 years from the first wireless conversations to what almost everyone carries in their pockets or purses today for personal use? There are all kinds of messages that are invisibly zooming past us every moment of out lives. There are TV images, radio voices by way of AM and FM, walky-talkies, microwaves, telephone conversations, prayer, fibre optics, infra-red signals, radar, lazer beams and who knows what else. Every one of these has become imperative to our modern lifestyles as invisible messages slip by us continually each day.

You probably noticed that I snuck prayer into the middle of the list. Most people don't realize that it is one of the most important forms of communication that the world has ever known. It has nothing to do with electronics, but for your interest, it has been the form that God honours since the beginning of creation. In spite of the simplicity of His prayer program, His system has never been tested to the maximum. There is no monthly payment plan and you don't have to invest in any "high-falooten" technical stuff in order to become a part of His company. Communication with God begins in the name of Jesus and ends, generally, with an "amen," although I know there are a lot of people who often forget the formalities and just tell God whatever is on their mind. He is open to that kind of call as well. You see, you pay a lot of money to call long distance, and the more secretive you want your call to be the more expensive it is. But with God, you can let Him know your most confidential, hidden secrets and He gets the message right away, unscrambled from obtrusive emotions and clear as a bell.

There is no question that He takes pleasure in keeping His lines wide open for your call. Night and day, He's prepared to respond to the urgent requests and cares that cause all of us concern. It would do us all very much benefit to open a line of communication with Him more often, just to let Him know that we appreciate His kind attention to us and that things are going O.K. You might like to let Him know, while you're at it, that He is Wonderful and that you are grateful for the health and strength that He gives you each day, and that His plan to save you out of the darkness of sin through the kindness of His grace is the most fabulous gift you've ever received.

Then again, while you're at it, you might like to let Him know that you are available to accept and obey His commands for the schedule of your day because He has a lot to do with what the results of our lives will be. Somewhere along the conversation, we could slip in some words of love and adoration because, after all, He is the Lover of our souls and He is blessed by those kinds of expressions.

▌ **THE BEST GIFT**

> *"...God gave them the same gift as he gave us,*
> *who believed in the Lord Jesus Christ..."*

~Acts 11:17

They're singing carols in the malls again. It's that time of the year when a lot of people are bargain hunting for the special gifts for their loved ones. There is always excitement in the air, in spite of the extra stresses that crowds give to all of us, because we look forward to being together with family and friends and the special things that happen at Christmas. I guess there are probably still some "grinches" in the world who struggle with the "giving" aspect of the season. Maybe it's not the spirit of the "grinch" as much as the resistance to the offensive commercialism that goes on in the name of Christmas. It is a fact that many businesses stand or fall according to the amount of sales that go over the counter during the next few weeks. Christmas has become "big business." You have probably noticed that before the end of October stores already begin to advertise the importance of getting your Christmas shopping done early. Then there's the count down of the shopping days 'til Christmas that reminds us daily of the nearness of December 25th. Forgive me if I come across sounding like "old Scrooge," but I do get concerned that somehow, through the years, we've lost the true significance of the Christmas season. A lot of intruders, from Frosty to Santa, have made us digress from the purpose of the celebrations that we are intended to enjoy.

It seems, in these last few seasons, that a new Christmas character is born each year to promote a fresh commercial interest that will attract the attention of our children, but even so, "Jesus is still the real reason of the season." This is supposed to be a time to remember that God gave His One and Only Son who came as a Baby, born in a manger in the city of Bethlehem. It is Jesus who came to heal the sick, not Santa. It is Jesus who came to bring peace to the anxious, not Frosty. It is Jesus who came to speak pardon to the sinner, not Rudolph. It is Jesus who came to grant hope to the hopeless and be the Saviour of the whole world. The kind of gift that the Father gave keeps on giving from year to year and never at any cost to us.

It was Jesus who said, "It is more blessed to give than to receive" (Acts 20:35b). He not only said those words, He actually provided an example by living His life in practical service to meet the needs of all people. The Good News is that He still makes Himself available to any who will call upon Him through simple prayer. As Christians, we know the real significance of this season. It is a time to rejoice and be glad, and with great joy we can let it be known that we have received the most awesome gift that anyone could ever receive. If you have not yet received Him into your life, you could not possibly understand what a joy it is to know Him as your personal Saviour. Don't let this Christmas pass you by without receiving Jesus into your life. He will make an eternal difference in you!

█ **IMPORTANT TO GOD**

*"For God so loved..."*

~John 3:16a

Our God is the Creator of all things. He makes them beautiful and with great purposes in mind. Our universe attests to that. He is Visionary, for out of the nothingness of pre-time, He designed our universe. The details are minute and delicate. Distances are unbelievable and objects, such as planets and moons, are immense.

Yet, of all that has been made by His Word and Powerful Hand, the thing that He loves most is the finite creature called MAN. He set all of creation into its orderly path and spoke His Word to maintain it in its proper orb and let it go, but He chooses to visit with man. He speaks to us in more endearing terms than most gardeners speak to their plants. He watches with Fatherly love over each moment of our existence. We are the objects of Divine attention. Nothing under heaven is more important to Him than you and me.

But let me remind us, together, that there are others who as yet have not committed their lives to Him. They bear the guilt and condemnation of Sin. Their lives are being wasted in the service of self and the pursuit of pleasures. He loves them as much as He loves you and me. Someone needs to speak, on His behalf, to each of these. They need to be told that God is not an enemy to be feared but a friend to be loved; that He is ready to forgive our sins and grant us special privileges in His presence; that NOW is only preparation time for the future. We are all important in His plan. The gift of His only Begotten Son is absolute proof. He came to pay the penalty of our sins. "He who did not spare his own Son, but gave him up for us all—how will he not also, along with him, graciously give us all things?" (Romans 8:32).

## QUESTIONS HARD TO ANSWER

How high is up? Why is it that if you keep going north that you eventually will go south, but if you keep going west you never go east? Inquisitive kids invent these kinds of questions. Then there are the "deep theological ones" like, Can God make a stone so big that He can't throw it? and When the Bible says, "In the beginning God..." what year was that?

Isn't it great that you don't have to know all the answers to survive in life? It is wonderful that God does bless us with enough assurances to give us peace that He has all of the mysterious unknown under His control. Why do Christians suffer? Why do serious accidents happen to those who trust the Lord? Why do catastrophes hit upon the believers just like on the unbelievers? Why does God allow the innocent to suffer in wars and revolutions? I don't profess to know all the answers, but I've learned that God is a good God—all the time. We have all learned that as we go through difficulties we are sometimes almost overwhelmed. But after a time, we can look back and laugh at what actually occurred. Like the warp and woof of a tapestry, different coloured threads become a beautiful design. The Master Weaver does the same with our lives as He weaves all kinds of experiences, trials and tests into a beautiful reflection of Himself. Let's learn to have confidence in His love for us. Don't become bitter or a complainer. He will make it all clear to us some time down the road of life. TRUST HIM! !

**PLEASE AND THANK YOU**

*"Give thanks in all circumstances."*

~1 Thessalonians 5:18a

It's one of the first lessons that parents teach their children. "You must say thank you!" But then, some people never learn that important lesson. Jesus told the story of ten lepers who came to Him for healing. He instructed them to go and show themselves to the priests for their examination. As they made their way to the city, they suddenly realized that they were healed. Well, you could imagine the joy of being a living, walking miracle. Suddenly, by Divine decree, their whole future was changed. What would you do with your life if you were raised from a deathbed to stand in perfect health and you knew who was responsible for the change? You know the story. One out of the ten came back to thank the Lord. To him, it was very important to give an expression of humble gratitude before he did anything else with his life.

This fresh beginning commenced with THANKFULNESS. The others were not in the crowd that day. They may have thought that they had better things to do than be at a religious meeting. It is interesting to note that Jesus was aware of their absence and drew the attention of the congregation to that fact. When you read the story, do you get the feeling that Jesus was sorrowful that they didn't all return? It's a story that has been passed down through the centuries. Did their mothers not teach them to say PLEASE and THANK YOU? Then again, gratitude is a choice we all make on a regular basis. "In everything give thanks." The Lord has done so many good things for us as routine for our lives. His Protection, Provision, Presence and His People are all wonderful gifts to us. We express our thankfulness and gratitude in a special way on Thanksgiving Day.

At each Holy Communion service we remember, with gratitude, that Jesus died on the cross for each of us. It was the fulfillment of a plan designed in the Wisdom and Love of God from long before the world was made. His provisions are many. Jesus' death:

- satisfied the justice of God in that the wages of Sin had been paid through the sacrifice of His life.

- conquered the powers of darkness and evil that had taken undeserved authority and control over the hearts of all sinners.

- provided peace for all those who trust in Him.

- made us subjects worthy to be adopted into the family of God.

- provided us an access to the Heavenly Father's presence. We are invited to come with "boldness and confidence" to Him.

- seals our eternal destiny with an inheritance in heaven that will never fade.

- places us in Himself, His Church, of which every believer becomes a part. We are welcomed to become involved in what He wants to do in the world today.

- prepared room in the hearts of all believers to personally receive the gift of the Holy Spirit, who comes to be a Guide, Teacher, Comforter and resource of Power.

The price for all of these benefits was Jesus' death on the cross on our behalf.

█ **CHANGE HIS MIND?**

*"Ascribe to the LORD the glory due his name;*
*bring an offering and come into His courts."*

~Psalm 96:8

Do you think that you can make God change His mind? Some people believe that this is the purpose of prayer—to make God do what we want Him to do. If you had to arm wrestle with God, guess who would win! Prayer is designed with two purposes, and neither of them are intended to demonstrate our powers of persuasion.

*Firstly*, God wants us to pray because it is His desire that we meet with Him and spend time in His presence in an endearing relationship. His intent is to allow us to experience His personal affection and to demonstrate His willingness to bless us for spending the time with Him. We forget that we were designed for this kind of contact with the Lord. Of all the things that have been created there is nothing that is more valuable to God than each of us, individually. He is ever waiting for us to express our dependence upon Him and our commitment to loving and honouring Him. At the same time, I am confident that we bring joy to His heart when we learn to catch ourselves, in the rush and bustle of each day, to spend time in prayer in fellowship with Him. He is blessed, which ought to be the main reason for praying. Too often we measure the success of our prayers by the visible results. But just being with Him ought to be reward enough even if we don't hear Him speaking back to us.

*Secondly*, there are things that He wants to do in our world today that He will not do unless we are willing to become a part of His plan. He holds in reserve all the power of His ability until we come into agreement with Him to see His purposes fulfilled. He does that by His own choice. The truth is, God is calling the shots, not me or you. It is also true that He wants to effect changes in our world. That is why He will lay burdens upon our hearts, or lead us into situations that blatantly show us that things must change in order to conform to His will. The fact that He gives us an opportunity to become those "agents" of change is a great honour, but I think it's also true that there are many things left undone in our world because of our unwillingness to spend the time in His presence. Somehow, we need to get a grasp of the fact that God is Supreme and in absolute control over every detail of our world all the time. We can't change His mind for the simple reason that His will is to make all things "work for the good of those who love him..." (Romans 8:28).

More than anything else, He wants us to know that He loves us with an everlasting love, through all circumstances, and will not turn any away when we come to Him.

▌ **Make Him Pay**

*"For Christ died for sins once for all, the righteous for the unrighteous,*
*to bring you to God. He was put to death in the body*
*but made alive by the Spirit."*

~1 Peter 3:18

It is a fact that every criminal will have to give account, someday, for the crimes that he has committed, whether it's simply a parking ticket or multiple murders. We expect those kinds of principles of justice, which are important for the proper functioning or a healthy society, to work for our benefit all the time. Our problem is that sometimes the officers of the law don't have enough clues to capture the offenders. Then there are other times when the offender is very influential or a smooth-talker and he or she is able to persuade the judge to drop the case. In both situations, the law-breaker goes free and gets away from paying the penalty for his crime and justice is not served because of the failure of our system.

However, there is a flawless court in eternity that is not only fully aware of the crimes and offences that are made against society and God, but also has the power to unerringly prosecute every offender without exception. No one escapes that Day of Judgment.

I've learned a few lessons from the "handbook" of the Judge. First of all, the wisest thing that anyone who has offended God can do is to turn himself or herself in. There are very severe consequences for anyone who has to appear before Him without a prior confession because His justice is swift and sure on that Day. (Hebrews 9:27). However, He has provided a way that the matter can be settled today; right now, out of court. You see, God sent His one and only Son into the world to stand in the place of each one who asks for forgiveness. (John 3:16). Jesus not only hears our plea but He also takes upon Himself the complete punishment for every crime/sin that the guilty person confesses to Him. (1 John 1:9). He becomes our substitute and He willingly submits to paying the absolute consequences for the actions we have committed that are offensive to God (Romans 5:8). Justice is satisfied because the penalty is paid in full upon Jesus. The price is paid through the pain and loneliness that He endured. The agony was very real and the benefits for us are very great.

We may not grasp all that is involved in the transaction that brings us deliverance from condemnation and the Day of Judgment for those who do not receive Jesus' forgiveness. We are made free of fear and guilt because He took our place in judgment. There is no cost to us for the process. It is a wonderful gift of God's love, extended to everyone who believes. The Father welcomes us into a loving family relationship with Himself because the obstacles that require His judgments are removed and completely eradicated. That was the reason that Jesus came to die on the cross. He paid the absolute penalty for sin.

**THE OLD RUGGED CROSS**

*"If someone asks him, 'What are these wounds on your body?'*
*he will answer, 'The wounds I was given at the house of my friends.'"*

~Zechariah 13:6

It's too bad that the cross has become such a beautiful symbol in the Church. We have lost sight of the awful consequences that the original cross was intended to convey. It was a tool of execution. To those who stood to be judged by a Roman court it was a fearsome thought that sentence could be passed for one to be nailed to the cross as the penalty of their crime. It was generally a public open execution where crowds could observe the shame, agony and suffering of the criminal. It was designed to be a deterrent, as well as a sentence of death. It provided a slow death of lingering suffering and pain and gave the cruel soldiers an opportunity to play agonizing games with their prey.

It would be very difficult for us to fully understand the degree of suffering that was inflicted on the prisoners. So severe was the prolonged agony that this means of execution has been eradicated from a civilized society. But what amazes me is that Jesus knew, well before He came to live in our world, that He had an appointment with the nails and a cross on a hill outside of the city of Jerusalem, and yet He willingly came. There were no surprises to Him. I understand, from the human perspective, why Jesus dreaded the cross and why His prayer in the Garden of Gethsemane was so intense. Just hours before the Garden experience He said to His disciples, "Now my heart is troubled, and what shall I say? 'Father, save me from this hour'? No, it was for this very reason I came to this hour" (John 12:27).

It was obvious throughout His ministry that He was in charge of every situation and had a way of taking control under difficult circumstances; but to die on a cross, He needed to surrender His authority to the fury of an angry mob and the cruel hands of the Roman soldiers. That was the decision that He had already made well before He came into the world. He affirmed that decision when He told His disciples, "...I lay down my life...No one takes it from me, but I lay it down of my own accord" (John 10:17a-18b).

Now, I don't know about you, but I do everything possible to avoid pain. I don't like shame, either. There are very few circumstances that would cause me to consider enduring painful situations for the benefit of others. But Jesus, knowing that His suffering and death would open an opportunity for ALL men everywhere to find forgiveness of sins and an opportunity to become heir to the promises of God, was willing to lay His life down. Without His willingness to go to the Cross, we would have no hope of pleasing the Father. The writer of the book of Hebrews caught the feelings of the heart of Jesus when he said, "...who for the joy that was set before him endured the cross, scorning its shame..." (Hebrews 12:2b). His joy was to provide hope for each of us by dying on a cross in our place.

327

| **DUTIES AND BENEFITS OF LOVE**

*"But the greatest of these is love."*

~1 Corinthians 13:13b

We all know by now that true love is not an emotion. It's a decision. We all enjoy the sparks in our hearts when we are "in love," but that is not the true proof of love. Love has been the theme of poets and authors through the centuries, and every one of them has had difficulty in putting words together to describe what love is. It probably would take pages to describe what love is all about. Even so, allow me a little bit of liberty to tell you some things that you may already know.

Love is more than words and feelings. Its expression is in action and waiting. Its best demonstration is in the doing and in the patient waiting. It is putting others first. It is not proving yourself right all the time. It is serving, submitting, in honour preferring one another and sometimes enduring for the sake of another.

Love is quick to forgive and to let go of hurts. Love does not hold bitterness or provoke to anger. Love is careful to guard the words that are spoken so that verbal injury will be avoided. Love prepares the truth to be soft and gentle in the face of weakness and failure. Love seeks to bless instead of looking for a method of retaliation. Love does not remind others of the errors of the past. Love delights in the hope that another opportunity will bring victory to one who has failed many times before—perhaps as much as seventy times seven. Love may be abused and taken advantage of, but will continue as "love" no matter the situation.

Love seeks the best in others and freely expresses appreciation for successes and victories won. Love is giving with no thought of return. It is freely sharing time, energy, finances, hopes and dreams. Love does not use people for personal enjoyment or advancement. Love seeks the best for the rest and is willing to sacrifice to see that come to pass. Love is watchful protection of the weak and frail and a guardian of the right.

Love seeks to do what is right before God and man. Love stands firm against foolish decisions. Love draws lines of discipline that will bring correction and a re-evaluation of personal choices. Love will not serve foolish appetites and desires.

Love will be prompt to lift up and bless the discouraged and the forsaken. Love will accompany the frustrated, the lonely and the heartbroken and bring comfort to the sorrowing. Love believes that God is able to make good to come out of the most impossible of situations and that He is able to change the heart of the most vile. Love believes that forgiving the offences of others is God's loving plan for all mankind. Love will not gossip about others' weaknesses but cover up the flaws of those who stumble. Love embraces all who come within reach and shares the joys of the victorious. Love seeks to minister to others at any cost at all times. Love is willing to go the second mile, turn the other cheek, surrender one's coat to the needy and accept abuse for Jesus' sake. Love is of God for "God is love."

▌ **BE WISE**

*"Wisdom is supreme; therefore get wisdom.*
*Though it cost all you have, get understanding."*

~Proverbs 4:7

Godly counsel is a valuable treasure that God has given to the Church. It comes in various forms.

1. There are mature believers that God has blessed with Wisdom and a devotion to seeing God's will performed in all our lives. If you ever require assistance, God has granted a wonderful encyclopaedia of resources in His Church that are available to minister to us in our time of need.

2. There is the Pastoral staff whose desire is to be a blessing to God's people and to guard and protect them from the snares that the enemy would use to damage or retard their spiritual growth.

3. How could we ever put a price on the input that the Spirit of God administers every day in His prompting and gentle correction and reproof?

4. But the most available and consistent tool of advice comes from the Word of God. Almost everyone has this Guidebook that helps in times of choices, opportunities and temptations.

God does care about the day-to-day routines that each of us go through right where we live. He is mindful, too, of the tactics of the enemy, who works at destroying our love relationship with God as well as preparing the consequences that are sure to affect our lives because of wrong decisions. God made a special promise that we all need to exercise at some point in our lives: "If any of you lacks wisdom, he should ask God, who gives generously to all without finding fault, and it will be given him" (James 1:5).

Let me remind us, together, that we can avoid the consequences of wrong choices by listening to good advice. We might reason that we have other solutions that disagree with the wisdom of other sources, but there is nothing in the world that will bring us through the storms of life like trusting in God's direction. The Apostle Paul was about to be tossed overboard with the whole crew and cargo of a ship when he made this simple statement, "Men, you should have taken my advice not to sail from Crete; then you would have spared yourselves this damage and loss" (Acts 27:21b). He may not have understood much about the weather or what a sailor does at sea, but He knew God and that was his source of guidance. There are a lot of people who have suffered "shipwreck" and serious hurts because of sincere but bad choices. I believe that God has designed us in such a way to have confidence in each other. We are like the body that depends on other joints and ligaments next to us in order to fulfill the purpose of our being.

Take heed! God does have a special plan for each of us, but independence is not one of His giftings. We are in this together. Loving each other must carry with it the fact that we will trust each other and communicate matters of concern together for the wisdom that God supplies. Be wise!

| **THANKFUL FOR HIS PURPOSES**

*"I will give you thanks in the great assembly;*
*among throngs of people I will praise you."*

~Psalm 35:18

An attitude of gratitude is the first step toward enjoying life. We have often heard the admonition that we should learn to be content whatever the circumstance. (Philippians 4:11). That clearly means that we may not get everything that we want but it does convey the healthy view of being grateful for whatever happens in life. Most of our discomfort in life comes back to the fact that we don't always get what we expect or that, sometimes, we get what we were not expecting.

Can I remind you that God is the One who is in control of all the details that come to play on our lives? He is a loving God. He is a Caring Friend. It is His wish that good things would come to us. "...no good thing does He withhold from those whose walk is blameless" (Psalm 84:11b). Yet, it is strange how some of the things that are meant to do us good come wrapped in disappointments and hurtful situations. If we could see the end of the journey as He sees it we would be more appreciative of the kinds of things that God allows to come our way. When you don't feel happy about a circumstance, remember that He has promised to be with us through every moment of our lives. You are not alone.

Paul, whose experiences were not always greatly appreciated, learned to give thanks for the thorn in his flesh that caused him much discomfort. You see, the difference between us as Believers and the person who does not yet know the Lord is that we believe God does have a perfect plan for our lives. That should be a great encouragement to us. It is a firm promise that will see us through every situation in life. So, "Give thanks in all circumstances for this is God's will for you in Christ Jesus" (1 Thessalonians 5:18).

"All" is a small word but it is extensive in meaning. There are no exceptions to that "rule." All is everything. Whatever the experience, we need to believe that there is a lesson to learn, or a new part of our character that needs to be developed that we had not recognized before. It is possible that through the rough times we will meet the Lord in a brand new way that the road of pleasure and comfort may not have revealed. Learning to guard our peace and to be joyful in those kinds of situations are lessons well learned. "Rejoice in the Lord always. I will say it again: Rejoice!" (Philippians 4:4). The world needs to see us as people of patience and peace because our faith in a loving God will not allow us to become anything less than appreciative for the work that He is doing in our hearts.

At the same time, we have so much to be thankful for in the blessings that the Lord shares with us each day. We are a very blessed people and we will not forget all His benefits. (Psalm 103:2). We are grateful for the things He has done and for the promises of things yet to come. Whatever experience we have with Him we know that it is covered in His precious love because He has honoured us with His friendship and His wonderful gifts.

| **MASTER OF THE VINEYARD**

*"If you love me, you will obey what I command."*

~John 14:15

There is no way that you are going to win all the lost. The task is too big and God knows that. You see, He's the Master of the vineyard and He's aware of the magnitude of the task that lies before us. The truth is, we are catching up on the neglect of past generation who did not do what the Church is supposed to do. Let that be a warning to all of us. We don't want to pass any more responsibility than is necessary on to the next generation.

Here's the key to getting the job done in the time that is allotted to us. —we each do what we can. God has given each of us an area of opportunity to reach the lost, and they are everywhere. We meet some of the lost at the breakfast table, at the place of our employment, where we do our shopping, on the highways and on public transportation. It's strange that we think that the Mission Field is on some other continent on the other side of the world where the lost speak another language and eat "funny stuff." The truth is, they can be members of our own family or members of our neighbourhood.

Jesus was concerned about the lack of vision that His generation had for the needs of lost humanity. He described two serious flaws in the reasoning of those that follow Him:

1. "Do you not say, 'Four months more and then the harvest?'" The attitude of His followers was simply, "There's lots of time before the matter is urgent." Jesus was reminding His disciples that the timing of reaching the lost is "right now." Any delay is to lose an opportunity. What we don't do today will be postponed to our children's generation because the task must be done. If it's a matter of timing, now is the best time.

2. Jesus said, "They are ripe for harvest." We may feel that the world/individuals we know are not quite ready for the message of God's love, but Jesus was saying, "They are ready!" We may have difficulty facing our responsibility, but that does not take away from the urgency that Jesus wants to impress upon every one of us.

Let me make a few suggestions:

Firstly, we need to be people of *prayer* who are moved with the same kind of compassion that Jesus demonstrated when He saw the multitudes burdened and frustrated. God help us to be concerned that people are not things. They are eternal souls that need a Saviour who cares for every detail of the humdrum routine of all of our lives.

Secondly, we need to *put feet and hands, thoughts and words to the message* of what God has already done in each of our lives. He can do the same for anyone else who calls upon the name of the Lord.

Thirdly, we need to learn the importance of giving to the causes of Evangelism and Missions. Finances are never wasted when they are given to the Lord. This is one of the important tools that God uses to extend His Kingdom on earth.

**|  MADE TO BE LIKE HIM**

*"And we, who with unveiled faces all reflect the Lord's glory,*
*are being transformed into his likeness with ever-increasing glory,*
*which comes from the Lord, who is the Spirit."*

~2 Corinthians 3:18

Christians are different than those who do not believe that Jesus Christ is their Saviour. When we commit ourselves to the Lord there is a deliberate action that occurs. The Bible teaches that the moment we invite Jesus Christ to come into our lives and to forgive us of our sins, the Holy Spirit comes into us and takes up residence. "Don't you know that you yourselves are God's temple and that God's Spirit dwells in you?" (1 Corinthians 3:16).

He comes into our lives as an absolute Gentleman with a specific purpose of teaching, leading, guiding, inspiring and empowering us so that we can live the Christian life in a way that is pleasing to God. He is faithful to let us know when we do things that are displeasing to God. But He's not there to accuse; He's there to help us through our frailties and failures to restore us to a position that will please the Father. He's definitely there for our benefit. You see, as much as God loves us "just as we are," He has no intentions of leaving us this way. We look too much like humanity and not enough like Jesus. That does not alter the fact that God's immense love reaches out to us "just as we are."

The truth is that we are not able to make all the changes alone that make us become more like Jesus. We need Divine intervention and that's why the Holy Spirit has come into our lives. God was willing to give us all the help that His love could offer in order to make us fit for heaven. It's important to realize that the Holy Spirit will work with us but He's not prepared to do all the work by Himself. He depends on us to "work together" with Him in making the important changes in our lives. He does His part by prompting us with a still small voice that no one else can hear. It's His way of giving directions from the inside and avoiding embarrassment to us. Learning how to listen in order to understand and then to obey is a process that may take some time, but is necessary if we intend to do things right.

The problem with most of us is that we do so many things to muffle His gentle voice and, either wilfully or unintentionally, we postpone the progress of His will. I believe that the Holy Spirit has been actively involved in our lives in more ways than we would give Him credit. What would our world be like if every believer was truly led by the Spirit of God? This is not yet reality, but God is still faithful and continues to work in every one of our lives in a very patient and gentle manner. He's not going to give up on this project of working His grace in us until the day the trumpet call is sounded and saints from all over the world are caught up to be with the Lord in the air.

Until then, let's be open to the leading of the Lord so that a Christ-likeness may be seen through us to a world that doesn't know the Saviour.

▌ **WAS IT WORTH IT?**

*"For the LORD will not reject his people;
he will never forsake his inheritance."*

~Psalm 94:14

The story is told that during the Second World War a number of young men were on patrol when they were suddenly caught in an ambush. The soldiers dived for cover but one of them was hit and lay seriously wounded on the ground out of reach of the rest of his platoon. He groaned in pain and called for someone to come and help him. After some time, one of his friends decided to make a try to rescue him, against the counsel of the rest of the soldiers who huddled together in sheltered security. He made a quick dash to the side of his wounded friend and began to drag him to the safety of their hiding place.

All was quiet for those few moments until they reached the edge of their temporary foxhole and another shot cracked the air and the young rescuer fell to the ground, mortally wounded.

When the war was over, the rescued soldier decided to try to meet the parents of the young man who had saved his life. He called and made an appointment for a certain day and time. He arrived at the door in dirty clothes and obviously in a drunken, slobbering stupor. He was invited into the beautiful living room and sat himself in a posh sofa across from the mother and father of his hero. His conversation was full of curses and blasphemies. He spoke in gross terms and vulgarities that would make any bar crowd blush. It was painful for the parents to maintain their composure as hosts to this man. When he finally said his farewells, the heartbroken mother, sobbing, turned to her husband and said, "Can you believe that our son would die for him?"

We often attempt to measure whether or not the goals we reach are worth the efforts we make. Things that we treasure as matters of great value are worth the investment of greater effort. Things that are not so important don't get the same interest. You can measure how much people value the projects they are involved in by the energy and enthusiasm they exert to see their goals reached. When all is said and done, it's the One who has a true perspective who will assess whether what we did or did not do is of any eternal value. It is a good idea to seek His advice and His guidance so that what we do will receive the reward of a faithful servant.

On the other hand, it is interesting to see how much interest the Lord had in rescuing us and preparing a permanent place for us to dwell. "For the Son of Man came to seek and to save what was lost" (Luke 19:10). I'm sure that the angels in heaven stand amazed that the Son of God would be willing to lay down His life to redeem the wayward sons of men. God was willing to give His best—His treasured and only begotten Son. That is a great perspective on the value that He has placed on each of our lives. One day, we'll go to the Father's house and personally offer our gratitude to Him for sending His Wonderful Son who saved our lives.

| **WORKING PATIENTLY**

*"But the seed on good soil stands for those with a noble and good heart, who hear the word, retain it, and by persevering produce a good crop."*

~Luke 8:15

Most people know that the biggest personal characteristic that a fisherman needs to possess is patience; drop your line and wait and wait. One of the greatest personal characteristics of a farmer is patience; sow your seed and wait and wait. Winning people to the Lord isn't that much different. The biggest part of convincing a person that Jesus is a wonderful Saviour is planting the thought and allowing the Holy Spirit to do the rest. Perhaps our missionary vision and soul winning process needs a revision. That is, although we are in a hurry to see people come to Christ, we need to learn that saving souls is not our business. Witnessing is.

You do know the difference, don't you? You see, there's a lot of pressure put on Believers to feel that getting people into heaven is our main job, while in fact that is the work of the Holy Spirit. Our part of being workers together with God is that we live our lives, speak about our joy in serving Jesus and do our deeds in such a fashion that people will recognize that we have a very wonderful experience in God. If people don't see the difference in our lives, then we are in big trouble. That would be the time to get back onto our knees and get charged up afresh in order to feel the urgency that God feels concerning winning souls.

We need to learn to practice patience. Dropping a line and sowing seed may just be the beginning of a great ingathering at some future time, and that is all the Lord asks us to do. Take courage! Be brave! Be bold to tell your story and to demonstrate that your God is Awesome. There are so many people with personal problems that are looking for the answers that we hold. We need to share the wonderful treasures of a life in Jesus Christ, and then be patient. God can do some wonderful things in people's lives if we will only do our part by sowing the seed at the appropriate time. Sometimes we feel like we have to keep on insisting until the unbeliever surrenders to the Lord. We need to learn that there does come a time when we have to let go and let God do what needs to be done in their hearts. That's where we need to be prayerfully, perseveringly patient.

Each Missionary Sunday we are reminded that we are a part of a wonderful team that is reaching out to a lost generation in various parts of the world. Everyone needs to know that God loves him or her. Only by uniting our efforts will that be possible. Although some may not surrender their lives to Him the message still needs to be told. The team is made up of the some who go and the some who give that others may go. At the same time, we all can pray. This is the purpose of Jesus' coming to this world and the matter that is closest to His heart. God bless you as you do your part.

▌ **PRECIOUS BLOOD**

*"Without the shedding of blood there is no forgiveness."*

~Hebrews 9:22b

Before He was born in Bethlehem the goal He set for His life was the cross of Calvary. That's the reason that Jesus came into the world. The plan was to deal with the sins of men. That required a perfect Lamb to pay the absolute price for all sinners. The ceremonies of the Law of the Old Testament were all designed with the purpose of painting illustrations of Jesus through the acts of sacrifices where the blood of animals and birds were poured out in order to provide an approach to God. Under that Law it was not possible to come to God with empty hands. That law was important to teach that coming to God had a price; but that the real price for permanent access to Him was humanly impossible. Even the design of the place of worship, with the heavy veil of separation where the High Priest alone could enter once a year, demonstrated the separation that sin had created. It is a serious matter, this drawing near to God. Many of the rules and regulations that were prescribed in the Law were designed to demonstrate that our sin had created barriers of division that made it difficult to come to God. That was what our sin justly deserved, because we chose to be separated from the Most High God by our disobedience.

**But God...**

...sent Jesus Christ to be the perfect Sacrificial Lamb who, by the shedding of His precious blood, satisfied every demand of justice that held us in condemnation. His death on the cross was sufficient to provide a permanent covering for all of our sin, that is, every person's sin for all time. At His death, on the cross, the heavy veil of separation in the temple between the holy place and the most holy place was torn in two. It was as though God was saying, "We don't need this anymore! Let's open the door into my presence." The way to have access to the Father was opened because Jesus died on the cross for us.

We now can approach Him by faith in the precious blood of Jesus and with the confidence that He hears us and welcomes us into His presence. The barriers have been removed and a new relationship has been extended to us. Jesus has taught us that our God is like a Heavenly Father and we are His sons and daughters. What a pleasure it is to know that we do not have to go through any ceremonies or rituals to come to Him. He has provided access to Himself through His Only Begotten Son. Jesus covered the cost. We are encouraged to come to Him with boldness and confidence because He opened the way.

335

**THE MEASUREMENT OF LOVE**

*"If you love me, you will obey what I command."*

~John 14:15

How do you measure love? If you ask the hymn writer to describe the love of God, he would tell you that:

*"The love of God is greater far, than any tongue could ever tell.*
*It goes beyond the highest star and reaches to the lowest hell.*
*Could we with ink the oceans fill and were the skies of parchment made;*
*Were every stalk on earth a quill and every man a scribe by trade.*
*To write the love of God above, would drain the ocean dry,*
*Nor could the scroll contain the whole though stretched from sky to sky."*

('The Love of God' – Frederick M. Lehman )

You can't measure love in pounds and ounces or grams and kilograms. You can't determine its bounds by feet and yards or centimetres and metres. You can't paint its portrait in bright and vivid colours or put it in a container to save for a rainy day. Thus, according to scientific methods of discovery, love does not exist.

Don't tell that to young lovers; or to the old grandparents who've survived years of married life; or the folk in-between who have found committed and faithful friendship and companionship.

How, then, do you measure love? You can describe it as emotion, pleasure, peace, commitment, sacrifice and many other words.

It seems to me that we ought to measure love by what we do and what we are willing to do without. We ought to measure it by what we give and what we are willing to give up.

1. At least that's the way we measure the love of God. "For God so *loved* the world that He *gave* His one and only Son" (John 3:16). *That's love measured by giving.*

2. Then Jesus also said, "If you love me, you will obey what I command" (John 14:15). *That's love measured by obedience.*

3. Then Jesus also said, "Greater love has no one than this, that he lay down his life for his friends" (John 15:13). *That's love measured in willingness to give up* one of our greatest privileges in order to benefit someone else.

Too often, we want to calculate the measure of love by how much pleasure we enjoy or by things that make us happy. We are all mixed up in the values that are important. Now, I know that it will not make a lot of people excited, but the fact remains that true love costs us something. Anything less than that standard is cheap emotion. **How do we show true love?**

❙ **SEEING WHAT GOD SEES**

*"I tell you, open your eyes and look at the fields!"*

~John 4:35b

Jesus said this to His followers who had just finished some business in town and were now busy filling their stomachs. That sounds like the routine of the average person today. I've seen them on the buses, freeways and in restaurants. They're not out-of-the-ordinary people; just average citizens. The truth is, our waking moments are taken up with a lot of stuff that, too soon, fills up a 24-hour day. Jesus' advice was, "Take time to see the real needs of people," or at least that's my interpretation of that verse. There are other things that we should be doing in order to please the Father. We need to consider the state of those without Christ who are hopelessly lost but are busily making a life for themselves with no consideration of their greatest need. It's interesting that Jesus does not place the responsibility upon the lost to find their way themselves. He challenges His followers, *"You,* open up your eyes!"

Jesus looked at the multitudes with compassion. He went to them and they found Him. There never was a question about Jesus' concern. He knew they were lost and they needed a Saviour. That's the reason why He left heaven's comfort and glory to come to this world. He came to seek and to save the lost. That was the decision of the Wisdom of God. The lost must be found, at any cost. And what a cost!

But the job is not completed. The lost still must be found. The truth is, they can be found everywhere but we need to open our eyes to see the opportunities of bringing the lost back to life. Jesus said, "Peace be with you! As the Father has sent me, I am sending you" (John 20:21). I suppose if you could choose a certain passage of the Bible that was just yours, you might not choose this one. The fact that we have been chosen and commissioned to do the same kind of stuff that Jesus did is absolutely astounding. That God would consider that we could be trusted with the same kind of work that Jesus did is also amazing. Until the task of reaching all the lost with the message of God's love is completed, we all have a job to do.

Let me suggest some things that we must "see" in order to complete the project that is so close to the heart of God.

1. Pray for the lost. (some of them are in our own families, our neighbours, and around the world in the field endeavours of missions). Pray by name and location in a specific way.

2. Watch for opportunities to share compassion and concern with those around you. (no words spoken yet).

3. Let your life be an example of your faith. Be patient, loving, honest and pure.

4. Give verbal expression to the questions that people ask about what makes you tick. (Why are you like you are?)

We who have come to know Jesus need to be on the frontlines of life giving clear demonstration to those around us.

▌ **THE SURPRISE OF A LIFETIME**

*"...in a flash, in the twinkling of an eye, at the last trumpet.*
*For the trumpet will sound, the dead will be raised imperishable,*
*and we will be changed."*

~1 Corinthians 15:52

We had just ordered our lunch in a crowded restaurant where people were no farther than three feet away. I saw it coming. My friend, across the table, wound up for a sneeze. It was going to be a belly shaker. I was ready, but I was sure that no one else was prepared for what happened next. It wasn't a little "achoo," it was a great roar that shook our table and resounded through the whole restaurant. A little boy in a high-chair across the aisle from us jumped and his head spun around, like an owl's, startled by the sound. For a split second everything in the room came to a sudden silence as eyes swivelled toward us. We all laughed; some for the humour of it, and <u>one</u> because of embarrassment.

*Don't be caught by surprise!* The Bible says, "For the Lord himself will come down from heaven, with a loud command, with the voice of the archangel and with the trumpet call of God..." (1 Thessalonians 4:16). I know that will be an exciting day. It is difficult to explain the emotions and feelings of all that will hear that call. For the Believer, it will be a moment of tremendous exhilaration as an instant transformation lifts our earthly bodies into the presence of the King of Kings to enter into eternity and the abundance of blessing that the Lord has reserved for that very special moment. For others it will be a time of sorrow because of the loss of loved ones and the realization of the loss of a great opportunity to be caught up with Jesus. To all who remain here on earth, there will be a recognition of a dramatic change in the activities of the world as a great leader takes control and begins to operate his powerful program to destroy all remembrance of God in the world. The time will be called "The Tribulation the Great One." The Old Testament refers to it as, "How awful that day will be! None will be like it. It will be a time of trouble for Jacob..." (Jeremiah 30:7). Uninhibited evil will take the place of truth and righteousness. Terrible persecution will fall on any who speak of the Lord and who challenge the works and authority of the anti-christ.

*Don't be caught by surprise!* The Bible gives enough information to let us know of His soon return. To those who are prepared, the transition will be a joyful experience as, finally, all the sicknesses, aches and pains, problems and frustrations, sorrow and sadness, hurts and misunderstandings will drop away, never to return again. Our loved ones who have "passed away" will be a part of the great celebration of life. The promise of Jesus that He would go to prepare a place for us will be fulfilled. We shall move into the inheritance of the love of God as we share the beauty of "His house" for the rest of timeless eternity. What a day that will be! The signs are all around us. It's time to live in the expectation that Jesus could return today.

**THEY ARE EVERYWHERE**

*"For the Son of Man came to seek and to save what was lost."*

~Luke 19:10

The lost are lost! That's not profound, at all. The Bible makes it clear that our generation, as well as so many others before, have no hope of peace with God and hope for the future unless the message of Jesus' love and forgiveness is shared and received. There are many problems involved in this situation as we look at the world around us. Let me tell you a few of them.

1. *The lost don't even know they are lost.* Well, some have come to the end of their tether and realize their hopelessness, but they don't have any solution to change their condition. Some have tried drugs and alcohol. Others have tried to busy themselves with activities and pleasures so they don't have to think about it. Some belong to clubs or societies to do good deeds, but that's not the answer. Some have discovered that money and many friends just do not satisfy the ache and longing of their hearts. There's a pain out there that bandages and medicines will not relieve. Each presumes that everyone is the same as they are, since we all have problems. Unless someone tells them that there is a solution to their condition with a provision for the "forever future" they will continue to live lost. That brings me to the next problem.

2. *What if no one is willing to tell the lost* that there is someone who loves them and has been searching for them for a long time? The lost will never be able to find their way without someone showing them how to find that new direction. That was the reason for the commission that Jesus gave to His disciples. "Go," was His command. Simply put, that is an expression of His concern for the lost and was intended to be the constraining impulse for every believer. We are all called to be witnesses who in basic terms tell what the Lord has done for each of us. Let me tell you, personally, that if you know some theology, forget it for witnessing purposes! Let your friendship and concern become the main instruments to convey the story of what Jesus did inside your life. This generation needs to see the practical side of your faith and not just the religious theories that have become "ho-hum" pat answers that don't bring encouragement to the souls of men.

3. *Keep your faith up to date.* Grow in God yourself. Read His Word and spend time in prayer. A real, living experience with the Lord is the best "bait" to attract the lost. The Word says, "Let your light so shine before men..." (Matthew 5:16). If the fire has gone out or has grown dim, that's not a very attractive experience for anyone who is "in the dark" to consider when they think about faith in God. We all need to understand the seriousness of the situation of the lost and hear the heartbeat of the Master who came to give His life to redeem them.

| **LEST THE STONES CRY OUT**

*"Let everything that has breath praise the LORD. Praise the LORD."*

~Psalm 150:6

I'm glad that the Word does tell me that the words will be fulfilled someday when, "...every knee should bow, in heaven and on earth and under the earth, and every tongue confess that Jesus Christ is Lord, to the glory of God the Father" (Philippians 2:10-11).

It's very unfortunate that "how we worship" has become such an issue throughout history. If you recall, the very first murder recorded in history was committed following a worship service. History will remind us that many have died for similar reasons, and so-called religious leaders have often been to blame. The Psalmist sends out a clarion call to everyone who has breath to rise in worship of the Creator and Lord of our lives. You may be aware that there are many different ways to worship the Lord. Some of the methods we don't do, but others we practice so freely. I need to recognize that God sees each of us as individuals and often the expressions of the heart will be according to our personality and character.

I heard a song leader say, on one occasion, "If you haven't worked up a sweat, you haven't worshipped." He then proceeded to work up a sweat. I'm pretty confident that those who lacked "sweat" were just as precious in God's sight and that the worship from the heart was sincere and acceptable to God. I know that God can read our minds and that He knows our thoughts from afar off. However, I do note that almost all the scriptures that speak of praising the Lord carry some expression of physical action. Clapping the hands, raising the hands, speaking, singing, shouting with a loud voice, falling down, kneeling, jumping and leaping, etc. are all scriptural forms of praising and acknowledging our gratitude and God's faithfulness.

I don't think that worship should be debatable. I think we need to do it and to give as much expression to our praise as we possibly can. Let the scriptural rule guide us so that we do not offend our brother by selfish and ridiculous actions. The Word teaches concerning the function of the "Gifts"—and I believe all expressions of service for God—"...everything should be done in a fitting and orderly way" (1 Corinthians 14:40). Let common sense rule because the Holy Spirit is a God of order and harmony and would not want anything to distract from the purpose of our Worship. Let Jesus be lifted up! Let His glory be recognized! Let God's people be a reflection of Who God is! Elegance should not always be an issue, but let the world recognize that our interests are not to show ourselves but to praise the One who loves us and who died for us.

Let me repeat what I have already said, we shouldn't have to discuss how to praise we should praise the Lord. Jesus said, "...if they keep quiet the stones will cry out" (Luke 19:4). I may not have a great voice, but I think I am able to give better expression of worship than the stones. Let's worship with all our hearts!

340

# HOW ABOUT YOUR HEART?

*"What goes into a man's mouth does not make him 'unclean,' but what comes out of his mouth, that is what makes him 'unclean.'"*

~Matthew 15:11

I have to take my car in this week for the air-care testing. They will run it through a number of tests to see if the exhaust will meet their standards for clean air. I don't understand all that they do once the hose is connected to the exhaust pipe because I have to step out of the car and remain in a small room until they are through putting my "baby" through whatever they do. I've noticed that they don't care, at all, what the outside of my car looks like. The truth is it needs springs, new shocks and struts, the paint has been worn off in some places and there's a small dent in the left rear fender. The windshield washer sends a spray over the top to the car behind me, but a little bit of the washer fluid does what it's supposed to do, so that's alright with me. Some may call my car an old wreck, but it still serves it's purpose in getting me to and from work and around to the chores that are necessary for the ministry. I would never take it on a long trip because I'm not so sure that it would make it there and back. However, when the proficient inspectors check out my car they are only interested in what comes out of the car and not what it looks like. They sincerely believe that what comes out tells them how efficient the inside is working. You see, we often judge people by the outward appearance because we believe that first impressions will determine where we go with our relationship with them. We can be fooled by a beautiful "bod" and make our assessments of an individual based on how well they are groomed and dressed.

However, I do know Someone who looks first on the inside, because that is where the important issues of life come from, and then deals with the outside. As a matter of fact, He told a great man of God, "The LORD does not look at the things a man looks at. Man looks at the outward appearance, but the LORD looks at the heart" (1 Samuel 16:7b). It is not my intention to take over His job and attempt to assess the real condition of those around me. I think it is important to know that I, personally, face daily checks from the Lord. He is interested in keeping my life sane, healthy and growing on the inside, in the heart, so that whatever this vessel does will show the good stuff of a life of faith and confidence in God. Some believe that the real "engine" of life is located above the shoulders. If I understand God's Word, the real "engine" of the believer is located just a little below the shoulders. God does use our intellect as well as other talents and the abilities He gives us, but the primary source of spiritual direction comes from the heart.

So—how is your heart? Have you failed any tests lately? Do you know that the Chief Inspector has a "call-back" process that will put us through the test again?

341

▌ **GOING HOME**

*"O LORD, you are my God; I will exalt you and praise your name,*
*for in perfect faithfulness you have done marvellous things,*
*things planned long ago."*

~Isaiah 25:1

It's all going to be over before too long. That's not intended to be a prophecy of doom and gloom because it's going to be a very exciting event. We have been given some pretty clear clues as to what the future holds when it's all over here. Those who read their Bible should be getting ready for the wonderful change that is about to happen. Perhaps it's hard for us to imagine what kinds of transformations will occur when what we know, today, is all changed. We may not understand all the details of what awaits us; that's because we have a limited capacity to comprehend the magnitude of God's love. It's His desire to reward the faithful and to transform us from the weaknesses and frailties of the human body, as we know it today, into something glorious and beautiful beyond our greatest dreams. "...No eye has seen, no ear has heard, no mind has conceived what God has prepared for those who love him" (1 Corinthians 2:9). That sounds like a challenge of comprehension to me.

Dream your biggest dreams; imagine your greatest ideas of the beauty, glory and majesty of what could be; all of that is still far inferior to what God has prepared for those who put their trust in Him. To top it all off, we'll see the Lord in all His splendour as the Creator and Ruler of the entire universe. We will understand why the angels worship together and cry, "Holy, holy, holy is the Lord God Almighty."

We may admire His creation from our present perspective as we appreciate the mountain scenes and golden sunsets, because God has done a wonderful job in making this place for our earthly habitation. But it was all designed for temporary purposes. What He's making in heaven for us is going to last for timeless eternity and will always represent the ingenuity, grace and beauty of a God who gives Himself in love. I don't believe we will ever be bored, as each moment of our existence will reveal the unsearchable riches of His inventive mind. Add to that the fact that His main purpose of creation was to build a relationship with each of us. What an awesome place heaven will be.

Let me remind you, heaven and the full rewards that are offered do not come to us automatically. They come by choice; your choice. Choose to accept Christ as your Lord and Saviour and you can be assured that you will be a part of God's "eternal" program. To refuse to make that choice is also a choice you can make. However, that choice will be to not enter the place of God's eternal presence with all His rich rewards, and what a tragedy that would be.

Make your choice today. Jesus said, "I am going there to prepare a place for you. And if I go and prepare a place for you, I will come back and take you to be with me that you also may be where I am" (John 14:2b-3).

342

| # GETTING IN SHAPE

*"Be on your guard; stand firm in the faith; be men of courage; be strong."*

~1 Corinthians 16:13

Fitness is fashionable these days. One of the rising business ventures that is reaching out to our generation, focusing on young adults and young marrieds, is the fitness gym. Pictures of how we ought to appear in public, and especially in swimwear, show images of fatless, muscular, trim and happy people who have made it through the gruelling paces of civilian drill sergeants. Diet programs are part of the rage to keep in shape. They offer "GREAT" deals that promise success in weight reduction to help you reach your goals. I know, for sure, that I will never look like the guys I've seen jogging on treadmills on TV commercials, but they would have me believe that this is the product that would change my life like it changed theirs. "Give me a break!" Now, honestly, I believe that we need to exercise personal discipline in our lives as good stewards of God's creation. My body may not be glamorous, but it is one of the means that God uses to reach out to the lost and I need to do my best to be a good representative of His presence.

God's word does speak to these kinds of issues. Paul wrote to Timothy and said, "Physical training is of some value…" (1 Timothy 4:8) . But the verse just before speaks in a similar fashion but upon a different issue. Hear his advice: "…train yourself to be godly" (2:7).

I'm not sure that we apply the same kind of energy in our spiritual life that seems to be demanded of our physical being. It may be that we have no photographs of what a godly person looks like so we don't have an image to challenge our energy. Obviously, the word "train" expresses a need to apply discipline in order to form good habits that will help us to be godly. There are certain exercises that help us to grow up in God and to become sensitive to spiritual matters. The problem is that there are no scales or measuring tapes that can help us to know if we are reaching certain goals. However, I believe that when we apply ourselves seriously to knowing God we will notice the change in our own lives. We need to determine that we will not just be lazy, content, out-of-shape believers but will be striving to be stronger in our faith and more faithful in our service for godly purposes. There is a training recipe for developing ourselves into being the kind of people that God wants us to be, but it requires decision and discipline.

You have probably heard these keys to spiritual success many times before, but let me remind us:

1. Above all, let's begin to pray earnestly, and more. Let's worship with more energy and spend time in the presence of God more devotedly.

2. Let's spend time reading His word and hearing His message.

3. Let's encourage one another as we serve God together

4. Let's not neglect the coming together opportunities each week.

5. Let's learn that God's promise is "give and you will receive."

| # COMPLETELY OBEDIENT

*"They overcame him by the blood of the Lamb*
*and by the word of their testimony..."*

~Revelation 12:11

The Bible tells many stories of heroes whose trust in God and actions of faith have been an inspiration through the centuries. Their stories are told and retold through the early Bible lessons of childhood until the very mention of their names brings to mind the vivid details of their accomplishments. They faced giants, walked through fire, slept with lions, called down fire from heaven, faced overwhelming odds, sang with loud voices before the battle and were fed by ravens in the wilderness. Each of them is deserving of the recognition of their confidence in a Mighty God. However, I'm sure that after we make a list of the names we know that the true list is far from complete. There were many more whose names are not recorded but whose confidence in God was just as real as the famous ones we recognize.

The writer of the book of Hebrews reminds us of "others," "some" and "still others" (Hebrews 11:35-36). In the book of Revelation there is a notable group of un-named people who are recognized for special acts of bravery and commitment to trust God through all circumstances: "...they did not love their lives so much as to shrink from death" (Revelation 12:11).

Obviously these are not cowards who run from the battle. They are not people of selfish ambition or interested in self-preservation. These are people who would not compromise their faith under any circumstance. They are true martyrs who lived their lives completely surrendered to God. History tells some of their stories. They faced trials and persecutions that would make most brave men tremble. When it came time to make a choice to deny Jesus and live or to continue to honour and serve the Lord and die, to them there was no choice. Jesus was their absolute Lord and they would sooner give up their lives than to deny the One who gave Himself to die on an old rugged cross.

We have been told that there have been more martyrs in the last century than in the previous nineteen centuries put together. We live in such freedom and liberty that we forget there are other parts of the world where to name the name of Jesus is to face the sure sentence of death. Just as on Remembrance Day we honoured those who gave their lives for our freedoms, we should acknowledge the faithfulness of the "unknown soldiers of the faith" of past generations. As a Church we are blessed. We inherit the freedoms and liberties of worship that have cost others their lives.

Let's not forget—there are saints around the world who count it all joy to suffer for Christ. They are not fools. They have purposed in their hearts that no matter what influences come against them, turning their back on Jesus is not a part of their lifestyle. Maybe we need to have our "comfort zones" shaken a little to show us what we are made of.

▌ **GOD / MAN**

*"But when the time had fully come, God sent his Son,*
*born of a woman, born under the law, to redeem those under law,*
*that we might receive the full rights of sons."*

~Galatians 4:4-5

The Prophets of the Old Testament spoke of the coming of a special person to be known as the Messiah more than 700 years before Jesus was born. (Isaiah 7:14). That was centuries before the angels appeared to Mary and Joseph in the small town of Nazareth and later, to the shepherds in the fields of Bethlehem. Then the special star appeared in the east and shone brilliantly over the stable behind the Inn in Bethlehem that guided the "Wise Men" to the manger where the baby lay. There was excitement in many parts of Israel in those days. Groups of people heard and saw the marvellous activities that suddenly brought some anticipation to the depressed hearts of a new "thing" that was going on in the nation. It was Simeon and then Anna, in the Temple, who without explanation would proclaim the fulfillment of the Promise of God that was wrapped up in the baby's blanket held in Mary's arms. The long-awaited Saviour/Deliverer had arrived on the world scene into the home of a humble carpenter. He would be the One who would bring Peace into the world and into the hearts of Believers. He would be the Conquering Liberator who would bring freedom from the oppressions of the Prince of Invaders who had subjugated mankind since the days in Eden. He would become the King of Kings and Lord of Lords (Isaiah 9:6-7) to rule the world in righteousness. His was to be the responsibility to restore a right relationship between God and man. His works would replace the heart of stone under the Old Testament Law to a heart with feelings and spiritual sensitivity under a time of Grace.

The world was unaware that the manger Boy would be all these things in His time. Many had expectations that He would be born in the palace of Jerusalem into a royal family of privilege. Preconceived ideas saw Him as a Champion on a white mule, leading great armies of deliverance. Who could have understood that God's ways were so different from the concepts of those of the theological spiritual leaders of the day? Their imaginations dreamed of a ruler, greater than Solomon who would develop a new "Golden Age" for the nation.

The way He came left the people "looking for another." Jesus purposed to come in a humble fashion, to taste the lowliness of mankind and to lift them up to understand how important they were to God. At the same time, the "Carpenter's son" taught the teachers. His superior authority put fear into the hearts of the Rulers of the Temple and of the Land. He could span the whole spectrum of mankind and be their equal. That's what truly indicates His interest in all of us.

During the Christmas season we celebrate His coming and the love He showed to all of us. He is still the King of Kings though we see Him in the manger scene. He is still the Lord of Lords in spite of the fact that He had no palace or worldly wealth.

**345**

▌ # ELIJAH HAS COME

*"A voice of one calling in the desert,
'Prepare the way for the Lord, make straight paths for him.'"*

~Matthew 3:3b

They had learned their Bible lessons well. They believed that the foretold Messiah had come and was now standing before them. But they felt that they had missed one of the important details that had been a part of their early scripture training to indicate the coming of the Messiah. "Why then do the teachers of the law say that Elijah must come first?" (Matthew 17:10). They were thinking of the prophecy from the last book of the Old Testament. "See, I will send you the prophet Elijah before that great and dreadful day of the LORD comes" (Malachi 4:5). Their question was simply, "How is it that you came before Elijah?" Jesus responds, "I tell you, Elijah has already come, and they did not recognize him." Then the disciples understood that he was talking to them about John the Baptist. (Matthew 17:12-13).

It is unlikely that John the Baptist and Jesus spent much time together. When Jesus went to the Jordan River, John did not recognize that Jesus was the Lord until he saw the Spirit of God coming down upon Him. Yet Jesus knew that John was His forerunner; that John had a special calling to point people back to repentance and to serve God. John was the first voice of Divine authority to bring an end to the long 400 years of silence. He became the messenger to announce the arrival of the Saviour of the world.

John stood alone in His ministry. The religious leaders were stuck in their formalities and were fearful of the political authorities of their time, but not John. He preached like he had a fire in his bones. His tabernacle was the open air in desert places. He was not concerned with the styles of the day or the formalities of the Temple. He didn't provide candles, images, pews or altars. There was no assurance of shelter from either the sun nor rain at his gathering places. He didn't offer a system of pick-up and drop-off to assure that his congregation was there on time. He had no sponsoring society to cover his costs. His diet was an indication of the simplicity of his lifestyle. Yet multitudes came from great distances to hear the passion of his message and the courage of his convictions. This was a man sent from God. He told it like it was. He was bold. His message was clear. He was aware of those who would become his adversaries but he didn't soften his message one bit when he saw them in the crowds.. I imagine him preaching with a bony index finger raised for emphasis and a powerful voice that thundered with conviction. This was a man who lived for God. He was prepared to lay his life on the line for the proclamation of the truth and the announcement of the coming of the King of Israel. He died as a young man around thirty years of age.

Jesus called him the greatest of the prophets. Clearly, the Spirit that indwelt Elijah was also resting upon this man. He was called to serve at any cost and he proved faithful.

▌ **ENJOYING THE GIFT**

*"You have made known to me the path of life; you will fill me with joy in your presence, with eternal pleasures at your right hand."*

~Psalm 16:11

We all like to receive gifts. I am sure you realize that the greatest gift that was ever given was the One the Father gave in His Only Son. There is no question that there is absolutely nothing that can compare in value and endurance to that wonderful heavenly present. But there is another thing that comes along with that gift that adds worth to the thoughts of the Father for our good. Through His Son, we have access into the Presence of a living, loving God. Prayer is the gift that goes on fulfilling His High purpose of bringing humanity into a committed relationship with Himself. You see, Jesus made it clear that when He left this world He would not leave us alone. Listen carefully—in our loneliness, we are never alone. The Holy Spirit has a way of bringing the living presence of the Lord so very real to our hearts and minds through concerted prayer. When we open our hearts, through prayer, we invite the Lord to come near to us; and He does! If you ever wanted to know the Lord in a deeper and more personal way, the method is through prayer.

Let me tell you a couple of other things about this wonderful gift of prayer:.

1. Prayer can become a love language where pray-ers express their adoration and praise to a very Special Friend for the many blessings that He shares each day. Like a conversation between two very close friends, prayer can be the channel where we express our innermost concerns and emotions because we know that our Friend will be faithfully listening. It's under that kind of circumstance that we know He will guard all confidences and listen to the real needs of our heart. No one else could offer us that kind of personal interest and security.

2. Prayer becomes a lifeline for communication with the One who can change every circumstance. We all face difficult situations from time to time that seem beyond our ability to resolve. But God can do anything! I am sure there are more miracles that occur each day than we could ever dream of because God hears the cry of a heart that reaches out to Him for His intervention. He is the supplier of all our needs.

3. Prayer is an equipping process that strengthens the heart and mind of the believer as he faces the attacks of the enemy. There is a special, personal, spiritual enduement that God gives to those who "wait on Him" that no other exercise could offer. It's an enrichment of faith to be able to tackle the onslaught of the personal conflicts that come to us. God cares about every detail of our lives and has promised that we will be more than conquerors as we put our trust in Him.

We need to be people of prayer because we are called to be people of faith. The Word reminds us to "Pray continually" (1 Thessalonians 5:17).

█ **THE END OF THE SILENCE**

*"Simeon took Him in his arms and praised God..."*

*"There was also a prophetess, Anna..."*

~Luke 2:28, 36

There was a long period of Divine silence in the recorded history of the Jewish nation and the Temple worship. Approximately 400 years went by, during which the nation of Israel fought its enemies and suffered terrible humiliation at the hands of the occupying forces of Greece and Rome. There was no prophetic voice spoken to the nation during that period of time. It was a period of spiritual dryness and famine. When you consider the faithfulness of God in the history of Israel you have to believe that those dark hours were important to show the people the shallowness of life without God. Could you imagine the demands that repetitiously going through frigid formalities must have laid upon people? There can't be anything more disconcerting than to go through the formalities of religion without having a personal experience with God. It is true that there is something comfortable about being familiar with the ceremonies and rituals each time of worship, but there does come a time when none of that satisfies any longer.

That moment arrived as some of the Senior citizens began to spend more time at the altars in soul-searching penitence to call on God for the "Consolation of Israel." It was not an emotion they were seeking; He was a person. Both Anna and Simeon felt the urgency of prayer on behalf of God's people.

I don't know if my assessment is accurate, but I wonder why it took so long for someone to realize that the Nation needed a visitation from God and that someone should rise to the challenge and begin a personal campaign to the Throne room of God in prayer. God heard in heaven and, as far as Simeon was concerned, the coming of Jesus was a direct answer to the prayer and longing of his heart (Luke 2:29).

We delight today in the fact that Jesus came into the world as a baby born in a manger, to be the Saviour of the world. Let me remind you that it may not be His intention to take away all of your problems, but without question He is available to be with you and give wisdom, strength and whatever else is necessary to help you be an overcomer through the trials and tests that come to all of us. He does not want you to be alone in the dark hours of life ever again. He came into the world to be the light of the world. The Old Testament prophet foretold that, "The people walking in darkness have seen a great light" (Isaiah 9:2a). John said, "In him was life and that life was the light of men" (John 1:2).

Jesus has come. He is the Saviour of the World and He's prepared to enter into your life to make the difference in you. Don't wait! Don't hesitate! Invite Him to share His wonderful loving Presence with you today.

| # THE PROMISED ONE

*"But when the time had fully come, God sent his Son,*
*born of a woman, born under law…"*

~Galatians 4:4

He came to a world that anticipated His arrival, but still His coming was relatively unnoticed. Prophets foretold His advent and announced the place where He would be born. The Spirit of God moved upon the hearts of some of the elderly in preparation for His arrival at the same time the world was walking through its darkest hours of history and people cried out for relief to a God who had been faithful in the past. But is spite of this, the One foretold, the expected One, arrived unexpectedly. How could that be?

Let's see!

1. There was the Shepherd crowd, who represent the poorer people of this world. They were the first to receive the message. They came to rejoice at the sight of the Miracle birth.

2. Then we are told that Eastern Wise Men followed a star to find the baby in the manger. They were obviously wealthy leaders who represented the more affluent side of life. They came to worship from afar because they knew that this was God's doing.

3. The next important figure in the Christmas story is the bitter, jealous King Herod who was taken up with His own selfish ends. He did not care for the people and viewed any Divine visit as an imposition upon his schedule, his authority and his freedom to be the man he wanted to be. He did not want to have anything to do with knowing God and His purposes. No man, no god, should interfere with his plans. He made the decree that all children under the age of two years should be eliminated because one of them could undermine his position as Ruler of the Jews. Can you imagine that, afterwards, in that region there would be no babies, no children under two years of age? For two years there would be no Grades One or Two in the school system.

4. There was one more important group that decided that they didn't want to get involved. The Shepherds told their story to many. The report was, "and all who heard it were amazed at what the Shepherds said to them" (Luke 2:18). But there was no recorded report of any action taken by the people who heard that amazing and wonderful story. The same star that the Wise Men saw from the east was shining on the people of the region, and yet no one took the initiative to investigate the reason for such an amazing sight. Many were totally ignorant of the arrival of the baby in a manger; or else they made the decision to admire the star and ignore the fact that it was designed to give direction to the place where they could find the Saviour.

It's an interesting thing; wherever Jesus is spoken about, you'll find that some people will rejoice, some will worship, some will get angry and some will just ignore Him although they see the evidences of who He is all around them.

This is a season to make some choices. As for me, I want to worship Him.

**GIVEN, THE UNEXPECTED**

*"Let's go to Bethlehem and see this thing that has happened,
which the Lord has told us about."*

~Luke 2:15b

Right after Mary received the announcement that she was going to be the mother of the Messiah, she went to visit her beloved cousin, Elizabeth, to share the awesome news with her. For a young lady, thought to be in her early teen years, all these happenings must have felt like a dream bordering on a nightmare. I can only imagine the questions that must have raced through her youthful mind as she weighed the impossibility of the situation and "what will people think?" When Mary greeted Elizabeth, the baby in Elizabeth's womb leaped inside of her. (Mothers would understand this better than anyone else.) John the Baptist, yet unborn, had to respond to the arrival of the mother of the One who would bring Salvation to the world.

John would not live to see the fulfillment of the work that God was about to do through Jesus, but even before he was born, John could express his great joy at the coming of the Saviour. Together with her cousin, Mary remembered, with great delight, that the people of Israel had been waiting and praying for the arrival of their Saviour for centuries. "The desired of all nations" (Haggai 2:7), was to be the promised Deliverer who would free Israel from their enemies. Most people believed that he would be born in the palace of the king or appear on the scene as a triumphant warrior, victorious from the battlefield.

But Mary had a different version of the story. Her experience was not born out of the academia, the dreams of religious leaders or from the surmising of Jewish philosophers. By way of an angelic messenger she had received the word straight from the Throne room of God. She was to be the virgin mother and Jesus was to be born, through miraculous circumstances, by way of Bethlehem into the home of a carpenter from the insignificant northern town of Nazareth. This was no wealthy, renowned, or royal family, and this was not the palatial estate of a king. What was happening was totally unexpected. There were clues throughout the prophecies of the great sages of history that were intended to prepare the people for His arrival, but the whole matter caught a generation completely off guard. Mary posed the question, "How will this be?" The angel's reply was simple. "Nothing is impossible with God" (Luke 1:37).

There couldn't possibly have been a more giant step than the one that Jesus took to leave the splendour of heaven, with the adoration of the hosts of angels, to be born in a feed trough. God was about to do something that would be the talk of the nations for eternity. The Lord of heaven became a baby to become the Man who would take away the sin of the world.

▌ **THE GIFT, A SAVIOUR**

*"Here is a trustworthy saying that deserves full acceptance: Christ Jesus came into the world to save sinners—of whom I am the worst."*

~1 Timothy 1:15

Long before the world was made and everything that was created was brought into existence, a plan was formulated in the heart of God. That plan included the creation of creatures who would be designed with a capacity to resemble their Creator. And so, after the world and all other things were created, man was formed in the hand and by the breath of God. Man was given wisdom and authority to represent God here on earth and everything that was made on the earth was to be subject to him. He was the boss by God's appointment.

Because every man was given the ability to choose, it was necessary that God step back to allow the exercise of that free will. Of course, God was concerned that the right things be done but, at the same time, man had to make his own decisions. He was not made as a mechanical robot that responds to programmed commands, nor was he like the animals that respond to trained habits. Man was to be different. He would have to reason and make choices that he decided would be the right thing to do.

We know "the rest of the story." God already knew what man was going to do and part of His plan was to send His Son from heaven to earth to demonstrate the purpose that God had in mind when He designed man. Jesus became the full expression of the will and purpose of God living in a human body, just like yours and mine. Born in a manger in Bethlehem, He ate, slept, walked, talked, and worked in the same world that we all live in, but He did nothing that would be an offence to God. In the words of Pilate's wife, "Don't have anything to do with that *innocent man...*" (Matthew 27:19b, emphasis added). There was no fault found in him.

We may say that no one is perfect, but of course, the exception is Jesus. When all is said and done, Jesus is the perfect example of all of God's expectations for man from the beginning of creation. We have all failed to live up to His standard. If God's plan was to succeed He would have to devise a way to give all of mankind an opportunity for a new start. That's what Christmas is all about. Jesus is not just an example but also the purchase price for all the failures we have ever lived. God gave His Son to become the substitute for every one of us. He took upon Himself all the things that we have done that have marred the image and likeness of the Creator. In exchange, He gives us the perfection of who He is. The key to the whole transaction is that we believe that this is true and personally invite Jesus Christ into our hearts.

Now that is what Christmas is all about. It's an opportunity for a new beginning; Jesus is the answer and wise men still seek Him.

| # CHRISTMAS IS AN EXPRESSION OF GOD'S LOVE

*"But when the kindness and love of God our Savior appeared, He saved us, not because of righteous things we had done, but because of His mercy."*

~Titus 3:4-5a

Love has always been the bottom line of God's dealings with us. Whatever else is said and done in our experiences and circumstances, God always adds His, "I love you." It's an unchanging principle.

Problems and trials don't necessarily go away because of that abiding principle. But the fact that I am loved by the Creator of all things, who has promised to never leave me nor forsake me, gives me confidence and courage to keep on trusting because He has loving purposes for my life.

This time of the year has become the most celebrated and busy time on the average person's agenda. Besides all the added hours of shopping and purchasing gifts, there are more parties and festivities happening in December than during the rest of the year combined. Even so, as you're probably aware, this time of the year is when more people commit suicide than at any other period of the calendar. What a paradox!

But let me remind us that the true sentiment of the season is not in doing something to bring a false happiness through inebriated joy but rather, it is accepting the gift of God through a personal relationship with Jesus Christ. That's what Christmas is all about. His love is not a one-time act celebrated in December, but rather an enduring commitment to care and provide something very special throughout time and eternity. His Son's coming to earth was but the beginning of a new opportunity to return to God and establish a life of true value. That is reason to celebrate.

The real purpose of our festivities is to acknowledge that we believe that Jesus came as God's gift to mankind and with deep gratitude we have accepted the loving expression of God who gave us His Son. We do appreciate and celebrate the fact that Jesus came into the world for two particular reasons:

1. He came to demonstrate the love of the Father, and

2. He came to deal with our problems because of sin.

What a wonderful love! What an answer to the real needs of all mankind!

Let me ask you to pledge yourself afresh this month to trusting Him more than ever before. He did come to make a difference in our lives. Inviting Him to be a part of the celebrations of the season is a giant step toward strengthening that loving relationship with the Lord. Let's be careful so that this time of the year doesn't become burdensome and tedious. We do have something to rejoice about as we remember the coming of the Saviour of the world, born in a manger in Bethlehem.

| **THE GREATEST LIFE CHANGER**

*"The Word became flesh and made his dwelling among us."*

~John 1:14

"For God so loved the world that he gave his one and only Son..." (John 3:16a). The greatest Being who ever existed loved with the greatest love ever known so that He could give the greatest gift that anyone could receive in His One and Only Son.

Jesus knew that when He left heaven He would need to accept the limitations that every one of us lives with each day. He had known no limitations on anything before He came to earth at Bethlehem. He was free to go anywhere He wished to go and free to do whatever He wanted to do, yet He never knew weariness. In the Heavenlies His audience of angelic beings proclaimed His worthiness in constant and sincere devotion.

The Creator of all things laid those special privileges aside and became like the creature that He had made. He became subject to our limitations and tasted life as we live it. He grew weary, knew hunger, felt the pain of false accusations and couldn't be in all places at the same time. His home, no longer the ivory palaces of glory, but now the confines of a poor carpenter's dwelling and often under a borrowed tree in an orchard just outside of town. The streets were no longer paved with gold as He had been accustomed to, but now His feet would be dirtied by the dust on the paths and sometimes made uncomfortable by a painful pebble in His sandals. Often His audience held self-righteous, religious pirates who sought to scuttle His teaching and preaching by their scepticism, criticism and unbelief.

Life, as we know it, was a great change for Him. But then, none of this was a surprise to Him. He knew that it had to be this way. He had willingly chosen to be like us—to face temptations, trials and tests like us and then to be the Saviour of mankind. Like us in His mortal frame but always like God in His Spirit. It was necessary that He be the champion of every fallen man to take on the god of this world in a battle to release us from his bondage. He could taste death because He was a man. He could rise from the dead again because He is God. He could submit to the satanically inspired torture and pain that would lead to His death and take back all the power and authority that the enemy ever claimed as his own.

The Father's gift has unending value. He goes on giving and goes on living that we might enjoy His love each day and eventually throughout eternity. I don't know of any gift like that in the shopping mall, do you?

353

▌ **TRY FOLLOWING A STAR**

*"Where is the one who has been born King of the Jews?*
*We saw his star in the east and have come to worship him."*

~Matthew 2:2

Have you ever followed a star? Sailors who have crossed the oceans used to use the celestial bodies as their guides and could calculate their location on the dark waters by the position of the stars. (Today, man-made stars mark their position electronically with pin-point accuracy.)

The Wise Men who came from the east on their ships of the desert followed the starry trail from their homelands to the bedside of the baby born in a manger, in Bethlehem. They came to pay reverence and to worship the One who was to be the King of Israel.

I'm sure we don't fully understand the difficulties that they faced to complete their journey across rivers, mountains and deserts, "camping" out each night. They gave up the comforts of their homes and their personal interests to explore the significance of the Star. From their far away lands they arrived to be a part of the miracle story that has touched our hearts through the generations, that the Father's gift of Love came to be the Saviour of all mankind.

The saying, "Wise men still seek Him," reminds us that we all can be a part of the miracle story of the birth of Jesus. The star that guides us to Him may not be the one in the sky but in the message that is repeated at this time of the year. We wonder how something as obvious as the Star of Bethlehem was not understood as being God's direction to finding His Son. How many had looked into the heavens at the brightness of the midnight sky and didn't realize that it was a sign that Jesus had been born?

Are Santa, Rudolph and Frosty inventions designed to cloud our spiritual understanding of the true story of Christmas? How many today are missing the message of the Season because they are caught up in their own plans and programs in spite of the fact that there would be no Christmas if there was no Saviour? Then what is the purpose of God's gift to us if we are not willing to receive Him? Obviously, God is willing to extend His love towards us whether we are willing to accept Him or not.

The original Christmas day was designed with you in mind. It's a day to commemorate the arrival of God's heavenly gift to mankind. At some time in everyone's life, we each need to have a personal experience with Jesus Christ. During these days we celebrate, in drama and in song, the fact that we have heard the message and have received Him into our lives. Whether we see a star or hear the message sounded out from speakers in Churches and Malls, it is a time for us to welcome the Saviour into our lives. If you have never done that before, consider doing that right now and with us celebrate the "Real Reason of the Season."

354

**WORSHIPPING THE GIFT**

*"Go and make a careful search for the child. As soon as you find him,
report to me, so that I too may go and worship him."*

~Matthew 2:8b

It wasn't the star that drew the weary Shepherds to make their midnight journey to Bethlehem. It was the message of the Angels with their joyful announcement of the birth of the Saviour. It wasn't the Angels that drew the Wise Men from their comforts in the East through deserts and across rivers to the manger in Bethlehem. It was the star that shone brightly in the Western sky that beckoned them to seek out the one who would be born the King of Israel. There were special messengers that prepared a reception for the arrival of the King of Kings. Then, I wonder, why were there so few that were interested enough to make the effort to seek out the Saviour after such heavenly demonstrations?

But then, is it possible that we have heard the message again and again and have not responded? Could it be that God has even done miraculous things to catch our attention, but, for one reason or another, we have not understood or have deliberately put off a personal encounter with Jesus Christ?

What a shame! What a wasted opportunity! Did the Inn Keeper live with regrets that he did not "make" room for Jesus? He must have heard about Him in the later years of His ministry. Was the stable turned into an old-fashioned tourist trap as added income for the one who blew the opportunity to have the baby born in his house instead of the manger? Why didn't Herod follow the Wise Men and render homage to the King of Kings? He missed the opportunity of a lifetime to join the Eastern Strangers who followed the star to where the Baby lay.

Listen carefully. There are lots of voices that call for our attention in celebration during these days, but there are none so important as the ones that call us to humble worship of the Lord Jesus. At this time of the year, we have many reminders that Jesus came into this world through a miraculous process to bring "Peace on earth, good will to all men." He is the Gift of God's wonderful love to our world. Jesus came of His own accord to become a physical demonstration of the Father. He still seeks for the hearts of men and women who will acknowledge that He is their Saviour. Someone has said, "Wise men still seek Him."

At Christmas, we celebrate His coming. Don't miss the opportunity to lift your voices and hearts in praise. He is a wonderful Saviour!

355

▌ **MIRACLES OF CHRISTMAS**

*"Mary treasured up all these things and pondered them in her heart."*

~Luke 2:19

If you don't believe in Miracles, then you shouldn't celebrate Christmas. As far as miracles go on a scale of 1 to 10, the Christmas story is an "11." All that was involved in bringing to birth the little baby that was laid in a manger in a barn in the city of Bethlehem is far beyond our ability to comprehend. It's a marvellous story of the Love of God reaching out to a dark world and sharing His very presence with us.

Let me list some of the details and some questions:

- there were the Angelic conversations with Mary and then with Joseph

- there was the mysterious conception; that a virgin would become a mother.

- before John the Baptist was born he leaped in his mother's womb for joy when Mary came to visit

- How did Elizabeth know that Mary was going to be the mother of the Lord?

- When Zechariah's son was to be born how did he know that his son would be the forerunner announcing the arrival of the Saviour of the world, who was Mary's son?

- Prophecies foretold that the Saviour would be born in Bethlehem, but Joseph and Mary lived in Nazareth, over 120 kilometres to the North. How could they arrange to get a pregnant mother from that far away to the prophetic place of birth?

- What really persuaded the Shepherds to leave their flocks to the perils of the darkness of night to seek a newborn child in the crowded city of Bethlehem? Who would think to look for a newborn baby boy in a barn?

- Who were these guys from the east that followed "a star?" How did the star lead them from some far eastern country to the correct address, pin-pointing the place where the Mother and Child were resting? From where did these travelers get their information, so precisely?

- Why did Joseph call this baby Jesus?' (which means 'Jehovah is Salvation')

- How did two old timers, Anna and Simeon, know that Jesus was the promised Deliverer?

But what amazes me most of all are:

- How does God fit into the body of a little baby boy?

- And why would the Father send His One and Only Son to this world?

It's all a marvellous mass of miracles that demonstrates the kindness of God. And the story is still being told and sung after nearly 2000 years!! It has to be a God thing!

▌ **REASON TO CELEBRATE**

*"We saw His star in the east and have come to worship him."*

~Matthew 2:2b

There's a song in the air, but some of the excitement of this season has been created for purely commercial reasons. To some businesses, it's the season to make the big bucks because people are willing to part with their money easily in kind expressions of love during these days. But behind all the tinsel and hype the real reason for the season is still alive and well.

We rejoice, with the heavenly angels, that the Father in heaven would be willing to grant us the Gift of His own dear Son. What a wonderful present He is to all mankind. Though generations have come and gone since His arrival, each Christmas season reminds us that He is still available to those who seek Him.

We bow low, with the humble shepherds, who were the first visitors to see the baby born in the barn and acknowledge the presence of God come to earth as a babe in a manger. Apart from the family, they were the first to be made aware of the arrival of the Divine visitor through the Angelic praises that shattered their calm, watchful midnight hours.

We give, as did the Wise Men from the east, our worship and pledges of loyalty to the One who always was and always will be "The King of Kings and Lord of Lords." He alone is worthy of our adoration, praise and gifts of worship. We return with our gifts of love as we celebrate His coming.

We are encouraged by the prophecies of Zechariah, John the Baptist's father, who joyfully proclaimed the fulfillment of Old Testament announcements concerning the arrival of the Messiah, born into the household of David. God's Word is true and will continue to be fulfilled.

We admire the faith of old Simeon and Anna who cuddled the baby Jesus in their arms, the answer to their hearts' desires and intercessions. Rest could now overtake these warriors of prayer at the fulfillment of their greatest dreams. Their hope was rewarded as will ours be at the return of the Son of God.

We tremble to realize that just as Herod feared and despised the arrival of Someone as wonderful as Jesus, our world, blind to the gift of God, would sooner choose to think of Santa, Frosty and Rudolph and reject the Gift of God to this world. How easy it can be to be caught in the rush of activity that is all around us and neglect to acknowledge the real purpose of the season.

Let's keep our focus during these wonderful days. We sincerely celebrate Jesus coming into our world to be our Saviour.

Our hopes reach beyond the Christmas festivities into the anticipation of His return. May He find His Church watching and waiting in preparedness for His Divine appointment.

**357**

█ **HE ALWAYS GIVES HIS BEST**

*"He who did not spare his own Son, but gave him up for us all—how will he not also, along with him, graciously give us all things?"*

~Romans 8:32

I can imagine that if you are like me and are going to give something away, you probably wouldn't choose your very best. When I went to school I didn't mind sharing a sandwich with my buddy, but the dessert (cookies, cake or pie) was all mine. You'd have to fight to get that from me. Whenever we've given clothes to the "Thrift Store," it's usually been pretty good stuff, but not the best. The best I keep in the closet where it is kept dry and in relatively good shape. I have a way of reasoning my actions, if you're interested. I say, "Well, if God allowed me to have it, I should keep it for myself and take good care of it." I'm sure you'd agree with me on that one, right? Well, let me tell you about One who gave His very best, and He does that all the time.

But first, let me take you back many centuries in time. God told His people that at a certain time they were to take a perfect little lamb from their flock. There were to be no spots on its coat, no disfigurement in its body—even the way it bleated was to be perfect. The lamb was to be the best that could be found. It was to be brought into the home and live with the family for four days so that it could be checked out completely to see if there was any fault in the way it walked, ran, jumped, slept, cried, ate, etc. Only if the owner was completely satisfied that this was a perfect little lamb could it be offered to God as a sacrifice for himself and his family.

That's what God did. He chose His best, His one and only Son, and sent Him to earth where He was observed for three and a half years of public ministry. He was tested to the limit to see if there was any flaw in His character, but in the words of one who judged Him, "I find no fault in Him" (John 19:4 KJV). His most severe critics tried to create ways to belittle Him or to catch Him in a compromising situation, but they failed. He lived under circumstances and in situations very similar to ours, yet He never committed a sin. He always did what pleased His Father.

So the Father gave Him for you and me at Calvary. Not second-hand stuff, but the pure and holy; the best that the Father had, He gave to be our Saviour. Jesus was willing to become the Father's gift so that by His death on the cross He would take away all my weaknesses and failures (SIN), and I could have His righteousness and be welcomed into His Father's house because I'm made perfect through His Son.

**THE GREATEST WONDER OF THE WORLD**

*"For God so loved the world that he gave his one and only Son, that whoever believes in him shall not perish but have eternal life."*

~John 3:16

There are said to be "Seven Wonders of the World" that are recognized by historians and archaeologists as being phenomenal monuments of beauty and majesty. However, I would like to add to the list, the Eighth Greatest Wonder of the World that really should be acknowledged as the first and most impressive of all.

I'm speaking of the Wonder of the Amazing Grace that is found in the gift of God through His Son, Jesus. Many of the other "Wonders" have been worn away by the winds and rains of time, as do all the things that man creates. Our works, as beautiful as we possibly can devise, will eventually turn to rust and dust. But God's Grace shines brilliantly through the millennia and never tarnishes or ever shows signs of wear.

God has always reached out to mankind to lift us above our weaknesses and frailties. He abides faithful even when we deny Him. I heard Dennis Vancooten say, "God loves you and there's nothing you can do about it." That's a summary of the Greatest Wonder of the World.

It's at this season of the year that we focus our attention on the coming of Jesus as a Baby to the Manger—not to earthly palaces or kingdoms of man's making. He arrived to an earthly existence just like everybody else. He was born of a humble, young mother, whose youthful dreams were interrupted by His coming. He was significantly insignificant. No one else could have discerned that this baby was any different than the many others brought into the world that day. But this child was God's gift. He came as a gift to an unwed mother; to a confused betrothed groom; to bewildered parents and family who, together, felt the sting of shame through all these strange happenings. He came as a gift to a universe that possessed little hope at a very dark time in the history of mankind.

Few understood that He came as the "Son of David" to be the Saviour of the world. Simeon believed it. Anna understood it. The Shepherds explored the announcement to know the truth. The "Wise Men from the East" discerned it. Herod feared that it could be true. And the rest of us slept through it all just like every other night.

This is the Greatest Wonder of the World, that the Grace of God would be shared with a world that had chosen to walk away from the Creator. This is the season to rejoice, to reconcile and renew our commitment to honour the Lord for His wonderful love for us. It is the season to remember that He came to seek and to save that which was lost. That means every one of us.

DECEMBER 25 ▌ **CHRISTMAS**

*"Do not be afraid. I bring you good news of great joy that will be
for all the people. Today in the town of David a Saviour
has been born to you; he is Christ the Lord."*

~Luke 2:10-11

We should always enjoy attending our Church Christmas Celebrations. It is always a very busy but joyful time of the year as we prepare for the holidays and the "Reason of the Season." In the midst of the festivities, the hustle and the bustle, we try to make it a time for family and friends to relax and enjoy each other. After the holidays, we will do the usual complaining that we've eaten too much and put on too much weight,. but we wouldn't trade the pleasure of being together with the laughter, the chatter, the sharing of gifts and being blessed in return.

We really have a lot to be thankful for. The fact that Jesus came into the world to make a difference is the reason we enjoy what we are celebrating during these days. Add to that the truth that our Country was initially built upon principles that are taught in the Bible and by the instructions and lifestyle of Jesus. We do have many reasons for being grateful that Jesus arrived as a Baby in a manger. I believe one of the reasons that our Country has been designated, "the most desirable nation in the world to live in" is because of our connection to the godly principles that have come to us through Jesus. Without Him as the centre of our merriment, we are no better than the heathen who believe they are directed in their lives by the position of the stars in the sky or bones on the dusty floor.

We celebrate the message, repeated each year, that Christ came into the world to save us from our sins and to share His wonderful blessings with us. What a joy to know that we join a host of Christians around the world who proclaim anew the arrival of the Saviour of men. We repeat the scenes of the Angel's messages to Mary, Joseph and the Shepherds. We watch as our "Wise Men" duplicate the worshipping of the "Wise Men of old." Through drama and song we remind ourselves of the wonderful story of God's love in the giving of His Son.

Think about it! We have a song to sing that even angels cannot fully comprehend. We have received pardon from our sin and a privileged title of inheritance as God's children because He came. That's the gift of our Heavenly Father. His Own dear Son. You just can't beat that.

Joy to the World!

| # THE MIRACLE—GOD WITH US

*"The Word became flesh and made His dwelling among us."*

~John 1:14a

Talk about miracles! Greater than healing the sick and raising the dead; more dynamic than calming a stormy sea and pulling money out of the fish's mouth; more dramatic than walking on water or passing through closed doors was the fact that God, who controls the vastness of the universe, became an infant. He laid aside the Glory of His essence and the immensity of who He is to dwell in the wiggling form of a newborn baby. He willingly became confined to the limitations of the human body and suddenly subject to the effects of time and the expenditure of energy. He became aware of weariness, hunger, loneliness and the feelings of pain and sorrow. This is God. Emmanuel...God with us.

That's the amazing story of Christmas and the greatest miracle of them all. The wonderful thing about it all is that it is true.

That God should take such a giant step from the realm of His Majesty to this world and to our lives as Creator to created is the story of His marvellous, eternal love reaching into a lost and darkened world. He could have sent a flaming angel to tell the story of His love. He could have created clouds to write across the sky the description of His interest in our earthly affairs. There wasn't anyone else who could clearly describe the story of God's love with the passion of concern for fallen man that God felt, so He chose to come Himself. He bypassed all other means and methods because, of all of creation, there never ever was anything that He was more interested in than you and me. He personally came to share His heart and reveal the purposes of the Father. No other messenger could do what Jesus had planned and came to do. His coming was only the beginning of a journey that would patiently touch the lives of so many and come to the painful experience at Calvary. After all, "He came...to give His life a ransom for many" (Matthew 20:28).

As much as our celebrations of the season are intended to be joyful, behind the excitement of His arrival to earth was the fact that He knew that His life would have a tragic yet victorious end.

This is the Greatest Miracle of all. It's amazing because it's all God's idea and could only be accomplished by Him. What a wonderful story is the one we celebrate at this time of the year!

**THE MIRACLE OF HIS BIRTH**

*"Where is the one who has been born King of the Jews?*
*We saw His star in the east and have come to worship Him."*

~Matthew 2:2

Who has not stood under the awesome canopy of a clear summer night's sky to look for a falling star? You've probably seen the Big and the Little Dipper somewhere out there among the sparkling diamonds of God's handiwork. You've got to be amazed at the immensity and beauty of it all. If you know a little about what Astronomers tell us of the magnitude of the distance between each of those shiny dots you've got to be impressed with God's creation. And yet, our God is far bigger and more beautiful than all of that. "The heavens declare the glory of God; the skies proclaim the work of his hand" (Psalm 19:1).

It was that same sky that attracted the attention of Wise Men so long ago. The stars spoke to them in a guiding language that apparently only they could understand. Their interpretation, obviously inspired by the Spirit of God, told them of a King that would be born. Somehow, they followed the footprints of that special star that led them to the King's palace in Jerusalem, then to the Word of God and the voice of the Old Testament prophet who told them where they could find the One to be born King of the Jews. They arrived at their destination in Bethlehem to find satisfaction in the fulfillment of their expectations. A baby had been born in a humble feeding trough and they knew Him to be Christ the King.

What a story! We remember, with great joy, the details of the encounter, and pass on the history to our children in living drama as actors relive each scene. We already know the various chapters of the story from the perspective of the sweet young mother, the sensitive and trusting father-to-be, the stunned Shepherds, the eager and adoring Wise Men and the ancient expectations of Simeon and Anna. Yet, each year, we are awed anew at the magnificence of God's wonderful love in sending His precious Son to live among us.

To me, that's the greatest miracle of all. That God, who is bigger than all things that He has made, would stoop to live in a human frame, among people of feeble abilities, bound by so many limitations, tasting of all the same things that make up my life and yours. It's awesome. It's amazing. Don't ever surrender the joy of the season to the hollow tinsel of the commerce and humanism of our day. Keep the excitement alive. Pass on the fact that you don't just celebrate a season, you celebrate the Person who came to make a difference in our lives. May His sweet and precious presence be extra special to you and yours during these days.

| **YEAR-END**

*"My times are in your hands... "*

~Psalm 31:15a

Another year is drawing to a conclusion and with gratitude we give thanks to the Lord for His blessings. He is good. A number of things come to mind at this time that cause us to make some extra special decisions.

Generally folks review, through *the backward look*, what has transpired over the past twelve months and take inventory over the results. Some find that it wasn't all good but, then, it wasn't all bad. The truth is that we've learned a lot of lessons through the experiences and have benefited from each adventure, both the up times and the down times. We measure our accomplishments and weigh our successes and our failures. Some of our investments may not be measured by the standard of what the world calls success, but they remain as unseen seed, planted to bear fruit in the future. Some will pause and with fresh commitment will pledge to work more fervently toward a change in habits, routines and relationships in order to better our efforts to do what God wants us to do. That's the backward look.

*Then there's the forward look.* In a matter of days we will have a brand new start to a brand new year. No one has ever lived those fresh days before. They are special gifts to us. For those who trust in the Lord, that's a great blessing because we know that He has reserved some very precious promises concerning our future. One that has often brought blessing to us is shared in Matthew 28:20, "I am with you always." Never forgotten or forsaken. He's always available to be the strength of our lives and to help us in times of testing and trial. We can dream and desire for the very best times of our lives and strive to attain the greatest joys of our existence as a hope in the unseen of our tomorrows. The truth is, we don't know what the future holds, but we know who holds the future and we can trust Him.

*Then there's the look forward of anticipation—the upward look.* This may be the year that Jesus returns to earth to receive to Himself those He loves. This has been a message preached and expected through the centuries. Prophets, Angels and the Lord Himself have all foretold that Jesus is coming back again. Although we don't know the day or the hour, one day there will be a great surprise as we are caught up to be with the Lord in the air to forever live with Him. What a time of rejoicing that will be!! The Spirit of God is preparing the Church for that wonderful moment and His cry is "Even so, Come Lord Jesus!"

▌ **TIMES MAY CHANGE**

*"What is your life? You are a mist that appears
for a little while and then vanishes."*

~James 4:14

The time of the end is at hand. We all know that, because we've checked our calendars and it's true; this year will soon be history. We've all had a part in composing another piece of history through our many activities this past year. Some will say, "Where has the time gone?" Others will gladly lay this past year and the pains and problems to rest as part of life that doesn't always have a reason in the here and now. To each of us, this one thing remains true through every experience in life, "We serve an awesome God and He is faithful!"

There is something in that statement that reminds me that there are some "unchangeables" in life that only add to the good that is a part of our Faith. We can be assured that our circumstances will change—perhaps not as quickly as we may desire, but He never changes and He still answers prayer. That, of course, offers us hope for tomorrow, for although we bid farewell to another fragment of history, our future is bright with the assurance that in our unknown tomorrows He will never leave us nor forsake us. We have His promises as our guarantee and His Word will never fail.

One of the important facts that yet awaits fulfillment in our lives is His pledge to return to receive us to Himself. What impressive thoughts that brings to mind! We shall all be changed, in a moment, in the twinkling of an eye; we shall be like Him for we will see Him as He is. We'll be transformed and robed in the Glory of the Sons of God. The scriptures say that God Himself will wipe away all tears. The tears of pain and sorrow; the tears of remorse and regret; the tears of the pressures of life; the tears caused by the injuries of others. All of these situations will fade in the glory of the beauty of His Divine presence. Suddenly, all of the experiences that caused us so much concern will lose their wrenching strength, as together we are captivated by the magnificence of heaven along with the multitudes of the redeemed. Each of the saints through the ages will tell of their experiences with God.

What joy there will be as we view the eminence of Jesus, our loving Lord, who gave Himself for us! What emotions will be stirred by His awesome presence! What ecstasy will flood our hearts as we are ushered into our inheritance and the loving rewards prepared by our Heavenly Father!

This may be the year that will bring our pilgrim excursion to a conclusion. I'm looking forward to my personal walk with God. It could happen any day.

█ **SIGNS AT THE END OF ANOTHER YEAR**

*"Even so, when you see all these things, you know that it is near,
right at the door."*

~Matthew 24:33

It's all coming to an end, anyway. We live each day as though there is an unlimited amount of time that we can draw from. The fact that my hair has turned grey (what's left of it), that other things are not what they used to be, and that this week we move another year farther along in history should remind us that a great big change is coming.

I would like to announce that Jesus Christ is coming soon. Now, that may not be brand new news to you, but let it be a reminder that things will not continue as they are. There will be a loud noise in the heavens like the sound of the voice of an archangel and the trumpet call of God will summon us into the Divine presence of our Wonderful Saviour. Now that's worth celebrating. It could happen before this evening comes to the midnight hour. It could be tomorrow or the next day, but the fact remains, Jesus is coming soon.

It's interesting to hear the world talk about this subject as never before. There is a sense of expectancy as we draw near to the end of another year. Hollywood has issued their versions of how things could happen, but it's time that we settled on what the Word of God has to say about it:

"As it was in the days of Noah, so it will be at the coming of the Son of Man" (Matthew 24:37). Check it out!! We now wear different kinds of clothing, but the attitudes of men are the same. Sin abounds and righteousness is ridiculed.

The signs that Jesus spoke about in Matthew 24 are as fresh to us as the daily newspaper. Jesus has given us enough warning of His returning that we ought not to be taken by surprise. Things will not continue as they are for long.

As we come to the conclusion of another year, it can serve as a fresh marker for a fresh commitment to invite the Lord to make a difference in our lives in the coming days.

Everyone enjoys the feeling that a brand new year offers. It's like a new package of time has been placed within our grasp and we receive it as a special gift from God. Soon there won't be any more time left. It will all be used up. But while it is today, let's open our hearts to the Lord and surrender all the rooms and partitions of our lives to Him. The King is Coming and He's looking for a Church that is without spot or wrinkle. Let's take this opportunity to draw near to Him and be renewed in His presence.

**NEW YEARS**

*"See, I have placed before you an open door..."*

~Revelation 3:8

An open door, that's what this New Year is all about. It sometimes appears that the door opens up to a foggy darkness and we can't discern what lies ahead. That's all right. The fact that the Lord promises us that He will be with us "through it all," should be sufficient for us to trust in Him. Most of us wish that we could see farther ahead than the "right now," but that knowledge is reserved for God alone. The future is God's business. We need to remember that He does all things well and that He does take personal interest in those who are willing to follow Him. He said, "If the LORD delights in a man's way, he makes his steps firm" (Psalm 37:23).

Let me assure you of a number of things as together we enter this New Year:

1. God loves us and has a wonderful plan for our lives. Now that doesn't mean that you're not going to have a few lumps and potholes along the way. Nor does that exclude you from the "valley of the shadow," but it definitely means that He will never leave you alone. He's too much in love with you to not express His concern for every detail that goes into the making of your life. He does care.

2. He has designed us to be vessels of His glory. He has chosen you because you are who you are. He has given you talents and abilities that no one else possesses. There are tasks that He has directed for you to undertake. The Holy Spirit will give you the right kind of gifts, power and anointing that each situation will demand. When He gives us a job to do He also gives us the tools to do that job. But we need to seek Him and trust Him.

3. He has given us hundreds of promises that should bring great joy to our hearts. You see, His promises are like keys that open up the problems that our world faces. Sometimes we need to take those keys and in prayer loose His authority on the difficulties around us. As someone has said, "More things are wrought by prayer than this world dreams of." We need to learn to stand fast against discouragement and depression by speaking out His promises that wash away every bit of defeat. We are Children of the King.

A New Year reminds us that we need to rededicate ourselves to being the kind of people that He wants us to be. Sometimes that means letting go of our own will and plans in order to hear what He has to say to us; but trusting Him is absolutely essential.

# BIBLE INDEX

CPSIA information can be obtained
at www.ICGtesting.com
Printed in the USA
LVOW08s0352180217

524701LV00001B/16/P